The Penal Crisis
and the
Clapham Omnibus

QUESTIONS AND ANSWERS IN RESTORATIVE JUSTICE

Putting justice into words

Also by **David J Cornwell** on Restorative Justice

Doing Justice Better:
The Politics of Restorative Justice

'This book identifies the organizational stresses and strains, the target-setting, the policy "blips" and all the problems of trying to bring radical change to our criminal justice system': **Sir Charles Pollard QPM**

'Provides true food for thought in well argued fashion': *The Justices' Clerk*

'Should be heeded by politicians and practitioners alike. Whether either have the courage to take this way of thinking remains to be seen': *Internet Law Book Reviews*

Aug 2007 | P/back | ISBN 978-1-904380-344

Criminal Punishment and Restorative Justice:
Past, Present and Future Perspectives

'Provide[s] an optimistic road map for the future of criminal justice':
International Criminal Justice Review

'Lively and accessible... a valuable and relevant text for practitioners, academics and students': *Vista*

Feb 2006 | P/back | ISBN 978-1-904380-20-7

Free previews at WatersidePress.co.uk

℘ WATERSIDE PRESS

The Penal Crisis

and the

Clapham Omnibus

QUESTIONS AND ANSWERS IN RESTORATIVE JUSTICE

David J Cornwell

With a Foreword by **Heather Strang**

The Penal Crisis and the Clapham Omnibus

QUESTIONS AND ANSWERS IN RESTORATIVE JUSTICE

David J Cornwell

Published 2009 by
Waterside Press
Sherfield Gables
Sherfield on Loddon
Hook
Hampshire
United Kingdom RG27 0JG

Telephone 0845 2300 733
E-mail enquiries@watersidepress.co.uk
Online catalogue www.WatersidePress.co.uk

ISBN 9781904380474 (Paperback)

Copyright © 2009 This work is the copyright of David J Cornwell. All intellectual property and associated rights are hereby asserted and reserved by the author in full compliance with UK, European and international law. No part of this book may be copied, reproduced, stored in a retrieval system or transmitted in any form or by any means, including in hard copy or via the internet, without the prior written permission of the publishers to whom all such rights have been assigned. The Foreword is the copyright of Heather Strang © 2009 subject to the same terms and conditions.

Cataloguing-In-Publication Data A catalogue record for this pocketbook can be obtained from the British Library.

Cover design © 2009 Waterside Press. Based on an idea by Letty Cornwell.

North American distributor International Specialised Book Services (ISBS), 920 NE 58th Ave, Suite 300, Portland, Oregon, 97213-3786, USA
Tel: 1 800 944 6190 Fax 1 503 280 8832 orders@isbs.com www.isbs.com

Printed by The Good News Press in the UK

e-book The Penal Crisis and the Clapham Omnibus: Questions and Answers in Restorative Justice is available as an e-book and also for subscribers at myilibrary.com (e-book ISBN 9781906534776)

Contents

Foreword *viii*

Preface *xi*

Acknowledgements *xiii*

Introduction *xv*
    Determinants of Criminal Justice Policy *xv*
    The Structure of this Book *xx*
    Part One Overview – Issues of Principle *xxi*
    Part Two Overview – Rethinking Prisons *xxii*
    Part Three Overview - More Effective Community Sanctions *xxiii*
    Some Preliminary Observations *xxv*

Dedication *xxvii*

About the author *xxviii*

1. Why Are So Many Criminal Justice Systems Presently In Crisis? *29*
    The legacy of the 'Nothing Works' era *29*
    How do penal systems get into crisis? *33*
    The parallel effects on community corrections *36*
    Public attitudes towards crime and offenders *38*

2. What is Restorative Justice, and What Does it Offer? *41*
    Different justice or better justice? *41*
    A chance to think differently about justice *43*
    A new approach to guilt and harm *44*
    Inclusive justice *45*
    Community involvement in justice *48*
    A re-assessment of causes and effects of crime *50*

3. Does Restorative Justice 'Do Away' With Retribution? *52*
    Legally punitive responses to crime *53*
    Retributive justice 'undressed' *54*
    Restorative penology: a 'neo-rehabilitative' approach? *57*
    Is restorative penology anti-retributive? *59*

4. Would Wider Use of Restorative Justice Increase Public Risk? *63*
  Crime and public risk *64*
  Truths, myths and public attitudes *67*
  Restorative justice and public risk *69*
  Balancing the custody: community equation *72*

5. Could Restorative Justice Give Victims of Crime a Better Deal? *76*
  Great expectations: meagre outcomes *76*
  What do victims require from criminal justice? *78*
  Can restorative practices improve justice delivery? *81*
  A stakeholder approach to victim vindication *83*

6. Why Are Prisons as Presently Operated So Ineffective? *88*
  Management of prisons: order, amenity and service *89*
  Prisons, ideology and reality *93*
  The root causes of prison ineffectiveness *95*
  The need for a new custodial vision *97*

7. Does Restorative Justice Propose Less Use of Prisons? *100*
  Re-setting the prison population parameters *100*
  Building towards reduction: a restorative approach *104*
  The morality of prison reduction *108*
  Less prisoners and better prisons *110*

8. Can Prisons Rehabilitate Offenders Effectively? *112*
  What is penal rehabilitation? *112*
  Prisons and rehabilitation *115*
  Do the facts of custodial life rule out rehabilitation? *118*
  If not rehabilitation, then what? *120*

9. Reparative and Restorative Prison Regimes: Pipedream or Paradigm? *124*
  The importance of voluntarism *125*
  Responsibility and participation *127*
  Self-analysis and reparative action *129*
  Social reintegration *132*

10. How Can Prisons Become More 'Community Friendly'? *136*
  Balancing risks: taking a broader view *137*
  The custody: community equation *138*
  Creating a different custodial image *141*
  Changing the traditional custodial culture *143*

Encouraging community stakeholders *146*

11. What Should Be the Real Purposes of Community Corrections? *149*
Conceiving a change of penal direction *150*
Implications of penal system change for community corrections *155*
Community corrections with a new purpose *158*
Towards a structure for social reintegration *161*

12. Could Restorative Justice Transform the Community Corrections System? *164*
Community justice since the 1960s *164*
Back to basics: the need to limit 'managerialism' *165*
Envisaging a different concept of community justice *169*
Re-focussing community corrections *173*

13. Can Non-Custodial Sanctions Have Significant Community Benefit? *178*
How can public confidence in community sanctions be improved? *178*
Delivering effectiveness in non-custodial sanctions *183*
Communities as beneficiaries of corrections *186*
Creating space for community involvement *189*

14. Who Should Operate and Supervise Community Sanctions? *195*
Creating unity and preserving professional identity *195*
Making community sanctions visible *199*
Holism and realism in community sanctions *201*
Conceiving simplicity and effectiveness in community justice delivery *204*

15. Epilogue: The Case for Unified Restorative Corrections *210*
Corrections in context *211*
Reviewing the structure of justice *213*
Problems of enhancing operational justice *216*
Unification or bust? *220*

Bibliography *224*

Glossary of Some Key Terms Used in this Book *240*

Index *245*

Foreword

Restorative justice has made astonishing strides over the past two decades. In this volume and the preceding two in his trilogy, David Cornwell has tracked that history and eloquently explained the appeal of this different way of looking at justice.

Restorative justice has much to commend it in an intuitive sense: many caught up in the Criminal Justice System, whether as victim or offender, feel that conventional justice is far removed from the circumstances that brought them into it and is at best only marginally relevant to their lives. The experience of restorative justice can be truly life-changing for all the reasons that conventional justice so rarely is: it is often an extraordinarily emotionally powerful occasion where the people most affected by a crime can speak freely and for themselves about what happened, what the consequences were and what needs to happen to repair the harm caused.

This emotional power may be the 'engine' that drives the success of the intervention for the participants. Victims who have felt this often say that they have been able to recover from the harm caused by the offence they suffered and to put the offence behind them. Offenders who have been deeply affected by their encounter with their victims often say that for the first time they understand the harm they have caused and that they want to change the way they behave. Even onlookers to these meetings can be so struck by what they observe that they want to do whatever they can to encourage the wider use of RJ in the mainstream justice system.

I count myself among those who have been enormously affected by what I have seen in RJ conferences. I am not surprised that the power of these events, even when experienced indirectly, can make people believe that here at last is a 'silver bullet', a way to cut through the accretions of centuries in the court-based system and return justice to those who ought to own it – the people most affected by the crime. But after observing hundreds of these events in person, after talking to hundreds of victims and reviewing thousands of criminal records of offenders who have participated in RJ, I know that we can't tell the effects by looking and feeling – systematic evidence is what is needed to assess the value of this radical innovation.

It is precisely because the RJ process can be so dramatic in its impact that we need hard evidence about what is really going on. The impact that *can* happen may seduce us into believing that it *always* happens: that offenders will invariably see the error of their ways and reform their behaviour from this moment on and that the harm to victims will be miraculously repaired. But the reality, even though RJ sometimes achieves that, is that it will not always. Two questions need answering: when is RJ more effective than conventional justice in reducing offending behaviour and giving victims the satisfaction they seek; and in what kinds of cases is it most effective?

Over the past decade or more, research that my colleagues and I have conducted in both Australia and the United Kingdom has aimed to answer these questions. A series of experiments under the auspices of the Jerry Lee Program of Randomised Controlled Trials in RJ has tested RJ both as a diversion from conventional court-based justice and as an addition to it. It has compared the outcomes of cases that had been randomly assigned either to conventional justice or *diverted* to RJ (in the Reintegrative Shaming Experiments in Canberra); in another series of tests in the United Kingdom it compared cases assigned to conventional justice only with those that received RJ *in addition* to conventional justice. These experiments reported on both juveniles and adults, on extremely serious offences, including robbery and serious assault, and not so serious offences, and on different points in the justice system - before prosecution, prior to sentencing or post-conviction. In all cases victims and offenders met face-to-face in the presence of a trained facilitator, usually a police officer; in the post-conviction experiments the facilitator was either a prison officer or a probation officer.

The results of this programme of research are intriguing. When we compare the attitudes and feelings of victims who went to RJ conferences with those who did not, the results are clear. The great majority of victims who participated in all these tests in both countries said that they were glad they met their offender and that the meeting helped significantly in repairing the harm they had suffered. Many of them said that they felt far less angry, fearful and anxious after the conference than they had done beforehand. Compared with similar victims who had not experienced RJ they were far less vengeful in their feelings towards their offenders. And victims of serious crime who had met their offenders recorded significantly lower levels of post-traumatic stress than did similar victims who had not done so, a finding that potentially has important cost-benefit implications for RJ.

Reports of these and similar victim benefits are remarkably consistent with other studies around the world and are now widely accepted. The consequences of RJ for offenders are more variable and the results of our research present a more complicated picture than they do for victims. However, we can predict that except in rare circumstances it is unlikely to cause *more* repeat offending than conventional justice and can often reduce repeat offending.

When we parse out for which kinds of offences and offenders RJ may be most effective there are already some signs about where policymakers may best allocate scarce criminal justice resources. This evidence suggests that RJ may in fact be more effective with adult offenders than juvenile offenders. It is possible that meeting your victim may require a level of emotional maturity that many young people have not attained. Adults, on the other hand, may be tiring of their criminal careers; for them there are strong indications that RJ offers a pathway out of crime that the conventional justice system fails to provide. It may also be more effective with serious crime than trivial offending, perhaps because of the greater emotional power involved in these conferences.

There remains much we don't know about RJ. This is of course the case with all criminal justice interventions, and without doubt we know more about RJ than we do about any number of other responses to crime. There are many applications of RJ that are still in their infancy and remain untested but which we have every reason to expect would be successful. But we must not oversell RJ: to promise more than any single intervention can deliver harms the prospects of it being taken seriously. We should proceed on the basis of trial and error, rigorously testing RJ in different settings and building on the knowledge we gain.

Corrections are one such potentially powerful application of RJ and David Cornwell in this volume proposes a coherent and imaginative strategy for the implementation of a restorative penology

Research carried out in prisons and probation in the United Kingdom by my colleagues and I over the past several years has already shown that RJ can be successfully implemented in custodial settings and as part of community sanctions. RJ undoubtedly has a part to play in easing the current prison crisis by reducing the imprisonment rates of people who do not need to be confined for reasons of public safety. It may improve the effectiveness of rehabilitative programmes available in prisons. It also has good potential for easing the transition for prisoners being released from custody and assisting with their reintegration into their community of care.

This important book offers ideas and strategies for implementing RJ in ways that can be carefully tested and presented to a weary public alarmed daily by the claims of the mass media but who, as research has repeatedly shown, remain open to policies that are not retributive but that are demonstrated to make a difference. Passengers on the Clapham Omnibus have here a road map for change that can make the kind of difference so desperately needed.

Heather Strang
Director, Centre for Restorative Justice
Australian National University

May 2009

Preface

Having completed the work on two previous volumes *Criminal Punishment and Restorative Justice* (2006) and *Doing Justice Better* (2007), there remained a feeling that the potential of restorative justice to change contemporary penology continues to go largely unacknowledged because its message is altogether too challenging in a world in which so many penal systems are in or close to crisis. The focus of politicians and penal policy makers on these crises is almost myopic in its search for 'quick fixes', for means of shoring up penal systems that threaten to overspill into chaos, rather than to recognise that these crises recur because short term 'patching up' expedients are no longer a viable option in response to widespread over-use of imprisonment. There are, realistically, only two options: reduce your way out, or build your way out of trouble. At their root, criminal justice policies have two foundations:

- the inherited and traditionally accepted wisdom about what makes punishment work; and
- the politically precarious balance that has to be struck between measures to reduce crime and measures to reduce the causes of crime.

Thus if belief in the effectiveness of retributive punishment is strong, and that increasing the intensity of its imposition will deter crime, then the causes of crime can, on the face of it, safely be ignored. Retributive punishment becomes an inevitable *consequence* of crime since if crime persists, more and more punishment becomes necessary for crime reduction. Hence, the 'build your way out of trouble' option.

But what if this belief is mistaken, uncritical or uncertain? Suppose that we cannot determine with any confidence the extent to which increasing punishment deters crime, how much then should we punish, and more importantly, what is the compulsion to do so? Moreover, if the causes of crime remain unconsidered or ignored, how 'just' is the justice that is administered through retributive punishment? Better, perhaps, to use imprisonment less.

The manner in which we define crime seems to have some importance. Our 'Anglo-Saxon attitudes', to use Lewis Carroll's analogy[1], inform us that crime is primarily a violation of the state and its laws. But is this a sufficient explanation, given the harm that crime causes not immediately to the law, but to victims and

---

1. Lewis Carroll was the pen name adopted by the Reverend Charles Lutwidge Dodgson (1832-98), a mathematics don at Oxford University who wrote *Alice's Adventures in Wonderland* (1865) and *Through the Looking-Glass* (1872), both satirical works ostensibly of fiction for children. The quotation is from *Chapter 7* of the latter work.

communities? If we were to define crime differently as a violation of people and relationships there might, by implication, arise a need to ensure that 'wrongs are put right' rather than to punish as the first and dominant priority or reaction.

If we allow our prisons to fill to the point of overflowing, these places become scarcely more than criminal warehouses that can do little if anything to change attitudes or behaviours other, perhaps, than for the worse. If we are concerned only to punish then this may be an acceptable way in which to behave, however pointless it may seem. If, however, we wish to reduce rates of reoffending, and suspect that prisons are actually an expensive way of making bad people worse, then reason might dictate that *less* use should be made of prisons when to do so is possible and desirable.

In contemporary Britain at least, public and political confidence in community corrections seems to be at an all-time low level, and, according to the strident utterances of the powerfully persuasive mass media, public fear of crime is high. Yet in an era in which overall levels of crime are reducing and the actual risk of becoming a victim of crime is less than half of what it was in the mid-1990s, how does this 'fear' and increased use of imprisonment make sense? Can community sanctions be made more credible, purposeful and beneficial to communities? If so, might this encourage lesser use of prisons?

Primarily retributive punishment makes no demands on offenders either to accept guilt for the harm caused, analyse and change their behaviour, or make apology and reparation to victims. Restorative justice, by way of contrast, absolutely insists that these actions become central to the idea of the social reintegration of offenders and the vindication of victims. Which of these is the preferable agenda in the interests of victims, communities and offenders themselves? Moreover, if as part of the reparative process offenders can learn new skills and abilities to increase their potential for employment, does this not amount to an initiative to deal with many of the causes of crime?

All of these and a host of other questions have emerged from the former volumes within which the limitations of space precluded more than a sketching of solutions. This final volume of the trilogy represents an attempt to indicate the means by which better justice could be delivered, and how these means might be implemented in practice.

In *Criminal Punishment and Restorative Justice* the central theme was the need to re-appraise conceptual aspects of punishment philosophy in a manner that would allow restorative justice principles to provide the basis of a new and more humane system of justice delivery. This process of philosophical re-alignment was necessary in order to open up the possibility of moving restorative justice out of the margins and into the mainstream of criminological discourse.

In *Doing Justice Better* emphasis was placed on explaining the challenge of restorative justice in terms of the need for a new and appropriate contemporary penology that would give victims of crime due consideration, resolve some of the conceptual obstacles that stand in the way of viewing justice differently, and provide the platform for change that is so urgently needed within many penal systems at the present time. Above all, however, that particular work was designed to highlight the political dimensions of justice in many present day democracies that become shrouded in inconsistency and uncertainty due to the need of politicians and their advisers to retain electoral credibility. In the same volume, the need for and the means of making more constructive use of prisons and expanded use of community sanctions were identified, but considerations of space once again militated against explanations other than of an outline nature.

This work represents an attempt to provide more comprehensive explanations, and its chapters are structured to reflect, in as practical a sense as possible, the ways in which a restorative and reparative penology might be given operational effect. This stated, however, it would be arrogant to assume that the reader is familiar with the preceding volumes and the arguments set forward within them. To this extent, therefore, there is an element of repetition in certain areas of discussion, but this has been reduced to the absolute minimum consistent with what I trust will be deemed to be clarity of explanation.

I hope that this book will be found useful by practitioners working within the many different areas of criminal justice delivery, by academics and students within the law and social science disciplines, by penal reform groups, and also by politicians and their policy advisers. And because it deals predominantly with explanations of a practical nature, my hope is also that this account will attract a wider general readership within the media and the informed public since it seeks to set the record straight on a number of issues that are widely misrepresented or misunderstood, not only within Britain but within many other democracies facing similar penal system challenges.

It is a book that one might even dare to imagine being discussed by some of the passengers on the Clapham Omnibus!

Acknowledgements

This book is the third in a trilogy that has been compiled during the years 2005 to 2008. The two volumes that precede it, *Criminal Punishment and Restorative Justice* (2006) and *Doing Justice Better* (2007), owed so much to the contributions, support and encouragement of a host of colleagues and criminal justice professionals from all over the world too numerous to mention individually here. Many have provided material, comment, suggestions and discussion via e-mail that has, at times, been almost overwhelming. I am deeply grateful to them for their generosity and enthusiasm: restorative justice has a truly impressive network of proponents, and yet still faces an uphill struggle to have its important message heard and acknowledged for what it seriously proposes – better justice.

A number of 'lay' people who have read the earlier volumes have commented with, I believe, some justification, that explanations of restorative justice tend to be clear about what it proposes in principle, but seem not always as clear about how its prescriptions can be given operational effect within penal systems that are in, or close to crisis. How a restorative penology could be put into practice, and why, are now possibly more important to explain than its desirability that is already well established in the literature. I hope that these comments have been taken to heart within this volume, and I have been grateful for the prompting to attempt to do so.

Dr. Heather Strang's contribution to contemporary criminology in restorative justice and, in particular, to victimology, is both massive and also well known throughout the world. Her agreement to provide a Foreword for this volume is greatly valued, and I am truly delighted that she has been able to find the time from such a hectic schedule of international commitments to set the scene for this work. Heather's most recent (2007) contribution with Lawrence Sherman, *Restorative Justice: The Evidence*,[2] will be seen by many to be the most rigorous assessment yet completed of the potential of restorative justice to fulfil its expectations. Without commitment such as that which Heather and others have shown, restorative justice would continue to battle against the odds.

To Bryan Gibson and the editorial staff at Waterside Press I can only express continued admiration and thanks for their support and encouragement. Their patient and helpful suggestions for adjustment and amendment to the manuscripts of all three volumes in this trilogy have been timely and perceptive, and always gratefully received.

Finally, I would also like to thank most warmly all those who have undertaken and published reviews of the previous volumes, and in particular Warren Brookbanks at the University of Auckland in the New Zealand Law Journal, L. F. Lowenstein of Internet Book Reviews, Eric Assur of Prison Fellowship International, John Blad at Erasmus University, Rotterdam, in *Tijdschrift Voor Strafrecht*, and Heather Strang for Waterside Press. Their contributions and recommendations have been greatly appreciated.

David J Cornwell
Kersoe, Worcestershire, United Kingdom
May 2009

---

2. L. Sherman and H. Strang, *Restorative Justice: The Evidence* (2007), London: The Smith Institute in collaboration with the Esmée Fairbairn Foundation.

Introduction

This book is the third in a trilogy of commentaries on restorative justice. The two preceding works, *Criminal Punishment and Restorative Justice: Past, Present and Future Perspectives*[3] and *Doing Justice Better: The Politics of Restorative Justice*[4] left a number of important questions about restorative justice merely sketched, but for reasons of space, with the necessary discussion somewhat curtailed or not fully developed. This book picks up on a range of these matters and develops the discussion around each of them to an extent that I trust may provide the reader with a more comprehensive analysis of the issues involved.

Restorative justice remains an exciting and challenging impetus for change in contemporary penology: one that in many modern democracies is not only long overdue, but which is also urgently needed to take penal systems out of the crises that currently engulf them. It is also much more than an 'alternative' paradigm devised to take criminal justice in a different direction: it represents a considered and humane means of overcoming many of the conceptual, structural and operational issues that conspire to make delivery of effective justice so difficult in many contemporary societies.

Whatever the constraints of space in work of this nature, the reader is entitled to explanations that extend beyond the predominantly conceptual, and indicate how (and why) initiatives can be translated into practice. And particularly within the field of criminal justice, measures of reform need to be accompanied by a 'what works' approach that draws upon experience rather than the more esoteric explanations so frequently advanced as discursive argument rather than fact-related intuition. Experience in corrections is frequently hard earned within a professional environment that has to be constantly reviewed and re-evaluated. Sadly, as David Garland (2001) has indicated, those who fashion penal policies have, over recent years, paid too little regard to the advice available to them from criminal justice practitioners.

DETERMINANTS OF CRIMINAL JUSTICE POLICY

In *Figure 1:1* overleaf are shown what might be described as the principal determinants of criminal justice policy within most democracies. To the reader with a background in the social sciences the composition of the diagram will be largely familiar territory, indicating as it does the manner in which each of the determinants or 'influences' within the boxes has impact to a greater or lesser extent upon the manner in which criminal justice policies become shaped and formalised. To

---

3. Cornwell (2006).
4. Cornwell (2007).

xvi *The Penal Crisis and the Clapham Omnibus*

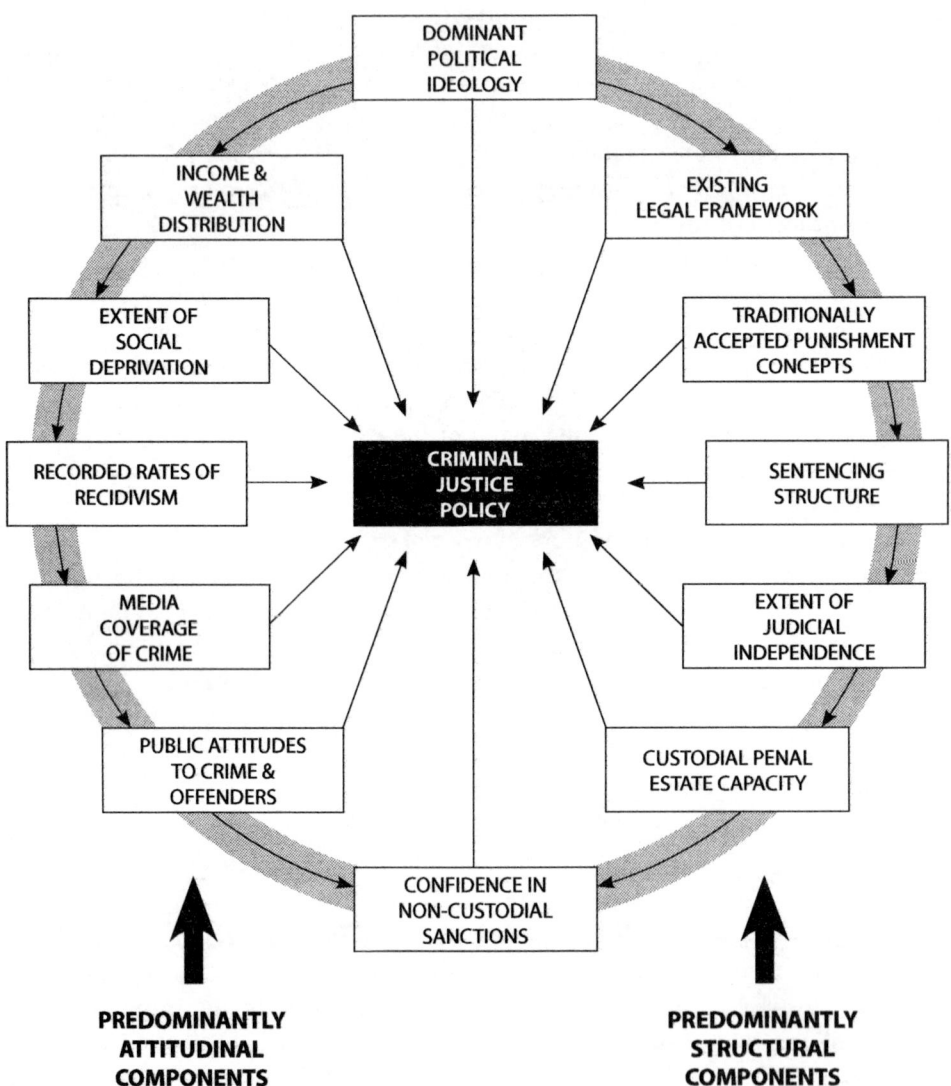

Figure 1:1: Principal Determinants of Criminal Justice Policy

a marked extent the nature of these policies will be consistent with, and indeed dictated by the political 'complexion' of the ruling governmental party(ies), and reflective of both its ideology in relation to crime control and its attitudes towards crime and criminal offenders.

This much stated, however, I would like to suggest that there are other important 'cause and effect' relationships that significantly affect the formulation of criminal justice policies which may not be quite so apparent. For instance, the dominant political ideology will most often determine the way in which income and wealth are distributed, and thus the extent to which differences between the wealthy and the poor are marked and relative deprivation becomes manifest. Moreover, as we shall note later, the poor and socially deprived are disproportionately represented in offender populations, and also tend to offend more repetitively than those who are materially better off. Persistent and serious offending attract media attention and coverage which in turn influences public attitudes towards crime and offenders, and also affects public confidence in crime control and social risk. Where the risk of becoming a victim of crime is perceived by the public (rightly or mistakenly) as high, then confidence in community-based sanctions becomes threatened. This cluster of relationships is described here as predominantly the 'attitudinal' components of criminal justice policy.

The dominant political ideology also determines the legislative and operational framework in which justice will be administered following traditionally accepted punishment justifications and within some or another form of sentencing structure. The extent to which the judiciary exercises independence of the executive within government will dictate the degree of conformity it will demonstrate with the sentencing structure, and also the extent to which custodial punishment will be used in preference to community-based sanctions. In addition, the attitudes of sentencing officials towards the use of custody will ultimately influence the size of the prison population and thus both the necessary extent of the custodial estate and the use of non-custodial alternatives where such are available. These considerations are described here as the 'structural' components of criminal justice policy.

As the chapters of this book unfold, we shall see that these relationships become far less clearly defined and apparently straightforward than this brief explanation might suggest. The critical relationship for the purposes of this account is that between the use of, and preference for, punishment involving imprisonment as opposed to sanctions within the community. More than this, however, we shall explore the extent to which adoption of a different penology based on restorative rather than on predominantly retributive justice might enable better and more effective justice to be administered than is widely the case at present in so many countries of our contemporary world.

But why this urgent search for 'better' justice? The answer, at least insofar as

England and Wales is concerned, lies in the simple fact that the penal system is almost in a state of meltdown caused by overuse of imprisonment and an apparent lack of confidence in community corrections. Similar situations exist in other countries of the world and for much the same reasons, and the general trend over the past five years internationally is one of increase. (ICPS, 2006a; Home Office, 2002a)[5]. Although the USA has the highest rate of imprisonment worldwide at 714 *per* hundred thousand of its population, followed by Russia and Belarus both at 532, the rates for major 'Western style' nations are of interest:

New Zealand	168 per 100k
England and Wales	148
Spain	145
Scotland	139
Portugal	128
The Netherlands	128
Australia	117
Canada	116
Austria	105

By way of contrast, Germany (96), Austria, Belgium and France (all 85), Sweden (75), and Finland and Denmark (71) all maintain much lower, even though slowly rising penal populations. The singular exception is the Republic of South Africa which, at 413 *per* 100K, has the highest imprisonment rate of any major 'Commonwealth' country.

The important question that has to be answered is that of why England, Wales and Scotland find it necessary to imprison citizens at twice the rate considered necessary by Finland and Denmark when, as we shall see later, there is considerable 'evidence-led' research that suggests that use of imprisonment does not reduce rates of reoffending, and that short prison sentences (of twelve months or less) may actually encourage it. Worse, perhaps, is the fact that overcrowded prisons tend to increase levels of institutional violence and disorder (e.g. Ellis, 1984; Fleisher, 1989; Adams, 1992), and deliver impoverished regimes that cannot have significant impact on offending behaviour.

Returning briefly to the diagram at *Figure 1:1* it will be noted that among the

---

5. The World Prison Population List edited by Roy Walmsley was formerly compiled by the Home Office Research, Development and Statistics Directorate (e.g. Home Office, 2002a), but is now compiled by the International Centre for Prison Studies (ICPS) at King's College, London. (ICPS, 2006a). The latest available data are published in the Seventh (2007) edition of the list.

'attitudinal' components that affect criminal justice policy formulation are those concerning the effect of media influence on public attitudes to crime and offenders, and the implications that this influence has for confidence in non-custodial sanctions. The United Kingdom, like many other developed nations, lives in a world of almost instant visual information communication, and has a tabloid press media that is entirely independent of government. Thus when media attitudes 'harden' towards crime and offenders, public opinion, conditioned to believe what is communicated, tends to 'harden' also. This leaves politicians and policy makers in a situation in which, to retain credibility, they have to be sensitive to the shifting moods of public opinion – however accurately this opinion is informed or otherwise.

It is, of course, not exceptional for the dominant political faction and its ideology to 'use' the media as a means of shaping public opinion in the direction in which its policies are oriented, and this is routinely attempted through 'on' and 'off the record' press releases, and even through 'leaks' of government documents and intentions in order to gauge the response of public opinion. In this particular respect it is of interest to note that in 2003 the New Labour government of the then Prime Minister Tony Blair expressed a marked interest in restorative justice, and released a number of documents purporting to pledge better support for crime victims and the implementation of restorative practices 'at the heart of criminal justice' (Home Office, 2003a and b; and 2005a, b and c). For reasons undisclosed to this time, this initiative was swiftly abandoned in favour of the more draconian legislation for custody 'plus', 'minus' and 'intermittent custody' introduced within the Criminal Justice Act 2003.[6]

There is also no doubt that the British media (both visual and printed) has an obsession with crime, and in particular with sexual offending. Scrutiny of television schedules shows very clearly that programmes dealing with crime investigation and reality crime are an almost daily occurrence[7], and this may to some extent contribute subconsciously to the fact that the public fear of becoming a victim of crime is widely over-estimated (Home Office, 2008)[8]. This is an important part of the contemporary backdrop against which this work is written.

---

6. As yet still unimplemented.
7. And in particular, programmes of origin in the USA such as CSI: Miami, Law and Order: Criminal Intent, FBI Files, and those of British origin such as The Bill, Real Crime, NCIS, Crimewatch and the like.
8. The Home Office (2008) document Crime in England and Wales 2006/07 Report, S. Nicholas, C. Kershaw and A. Walker (eds), is published in London by the Home Office Research, Development and Statistics Directorate. It provides a combined commentary on the findings of the annual British Crime Survey and data collated in Offences Recorded by the Police. The Report indicates that the statistical risk of becoming a victim of crime has fallen from 40% in 1995 to 24% in 2007, and that sexual crime decreased by 7% in 2006/7 from 2005/6 levels. Despite these statistics, public fear of crime has apparently increased, but the reasons for this are not attributed.

THE STRUCTURE OF THIS BOOK

The title selected for this volume, *The Penal Crisis and the Clapham Omnibus: Questions and Answers in Restorative Justice*, represents a deliberate attempt to bring together and discuss issues that critically affect the development of restorative justice as a mainstream penology for the future. Each of the three Parts of this book consists of five chapters, the titles of which take the form of questions that are central to an understanding of the present penal crisis in England and Wales, its development and effects, and the way in which a restorative penology might assist in resolving the difficulties engulfing the penal system.

Part One addresses issues of principle within contemporary British criminal justice that have to be resolved and accepted if restorative justice is to gain wider acceptance and mainstream credibility. *Part Two* is concerned with the prison system, its problems and the reasons for its present ineffectiveness, and the relationship that should exist between custodial and community justice in a reparative and restorative approach to criminal justice. In *Part Three* the focus of attention becomes the operation of more effective community sanctions within the context of a unified National Correctional Services that would ultimately replace the ill-starred National Offender Management Service (NOMS) established in 2003, but already scheduled either for demolition or at the least radical 'overhaul'. In the final chapter, *Chapter 15*, a case is made for the unification of the existing Prison and Probation Services while still preserving the professional identity and expertise of both, but within a national structure and accountability.

The reader thus far may now ask what is the relevance of the Clapham Omnibus? It is that within the long tradition of writing about the British legal and penal systems, recurring reference is made to that elusive and imaginary member of the public who is a regular passenger in this public vehicle within which the natural conversations of journeying people turn to matters of daily news, politics, issues of national importance such as crime and policing, and the like. The earliest reference that I have been able to trace in relation to the 'passengers in the Clapham Omnibus' is found in the historically influential Maccabean Lecture delivered by Lord Justice Devlin in 1957 under the title *Morals and the Criminal Law* (later published as one of a collection of essays in a volume entitled *The Enforcement of Morals* by that renowned judge in London in 1965).[9] Within the essay, the following quotation occurs:

> English law has evolved and regularly uses a standard which does not depend on the counting of heads. It is that of the reasonable man. He is not to be confused with the rational man. He

---

9. Here see: P. Devlin (LJ) (1965), The Enforcement of Morals, London: Oxford University Press, pp. 12-20, and also L. Blom-Cooper and G. Drewry (eds.) (1976), Law and Morality: A Reader, London: Gerald Duckworth & Co. Ltd., p.22.

is not expected to reason about anything and his judgement may be largely a matter of feeling. It is the viewpoint of the man in the street – or to use an archaism familiar to all lawyers – the man in the Clapham Omnibus. He might also be called the right-minded man. For my purpose I should like to call him the man in the jury box, for the moral judgement of society must be something about which any twelve men or women drawn at random might, after discussion be expected to be unanimous. (Devlin, 1965, quoted in Blom-Cooper and Drewry, 1976: 23).

This, then, is why the passenger in the Clapham Omnibus is so central to the discourse within this book. He or she is a figment of the collective imagination, but yet a repository of the received wisdom concerning the effectiveness or otherwise of criminal justice. With his or her support or tolerance the case for implementing a restorative penology could be compelling on governments of a 'hawkish' disposition towards crime control, on governments that use criminal punishment for the pursuit of social policy objectives other than justice, and on governments that purport to espouse restorative justice in principle and in practice, but then 'back-track' when the media reaction is such as to accuse them of being 'soft on crime'.

PART ONE OVERVIEW – ISSUES OF PRINCIPLE

In *Part One* and *Chapters 1* to *5* we shall examine a number of important issues of principle that affect the delivery of justice. These include questions (in *Chapter 1*) about why so many penal systems throughout the world seem presently to be in a state of crisis or close to it, how these crises arise, their effects on community corrections, and upon public attitudes towards crime and offenders. In particular, attention will be drawn to the significant impact upon criminology that resulted from the 'nothing works' era of the 1970s, and the manner in which this legacy not only opened the door to the 'justice model' of corrections, but also effectively closed the door to the rehabilitative ethic within criminal punishment. In *Chapter 2* we shall consider what it is about restorative justice that might help to alleviate crisis situations, whether it promises different or better justice, or rather, perhaps, an opportunity to view justice in a different context. In the same chapter we also examine the new approach that restorative justice provides in relation to guilt and harm, its inclusive nature and the implications of this for involving communities more widely in justice delivery, bearing in mind the causes and effects of crime.

In *Chapter 3* we shall discuss legal responses to crime through sanctions, and also question whether restorative justice is essentially 'anti-retributive', or whether, by way of contrast, it amounts to some form of 'neo-rehabilitative' prescription in a 'what works' era that has struggled to resolve the 'nothing works' legacy of the 1970s. In the following *Chapter 4* it is necessary to consider the question of whether a restorative penology, if adopted, would increase public risk. In the same chapter, some of the truths and myths concerning public attitudes towards offenders are discussed with a view to arriving at a better balance between the use of imprisonment and community penalties.

In the final chapter of *Part One* the focus of attention becomes the question of whether a restorative and reparative penology would better meet the legitimate needs of crime victims. We shall see, in *Chapter 5* how the British government 'backtracked' on its promise made in 2003 to place restorative justice 'at the heart of criminal justice policies', and then produced entirely contrary legislation, within the Criminal Justice Act published in the same year. In the final part of the same chapter the merits of a 'quadripartite' approach to criminal justice are discussed within the context of a restorative penology that might better meet the legitimate needs of all the stakeholders within the justice process.

PART TWO OVERVIEW – RETHINKING PRISONS

The five chapters that comprise *Part Two* of this book are devoted to 'rethinking' the social role and purpose of prisons and ways of making these institutions work more effectively. In *Chapter 6* the nature of prison management becomes the initial matter of discussion, and its bearing on prison ideology and reality is considered in some detail. This analysis leads somewhat inevitably to discussion of the causes of prisons becoming ineffective, the effects of prison crowding, and, in consequence, the need for a new 'custodial vision'. The debate in this chapter propels us to consider in *Chapter 7* whether restorative justice would propose lesser use of imprisonment, the ways in which the prison population in England and Wales might be reduced to more manageable proportions, and the essential aspects of the morality of pursuing such a course. In the final portion of this chapter we examine the ideal of less prisoners and better prisons as a means of achieving the ultimate goal of reducing offending and reoffending.

In *Chapter 8* the thorny issue of whether, in present circumstances, prisons can realistically be expected to rehabilitate offenders becomes the central feature of consideration. This obliges some discussion of what rehabilitation actually means, whether what is attempted in the name of rehabilitation is feasible in an institutional setting, or rather, whether the nature of prison life is inconsistent with such an ambition. Finally within this same chapter we examine some recent innovations in the field of offending behaviour analysis and the implications of these for reducing recidivism.

Chapter 9 is devoted to some explanation of the ways in which adoption of a restorative and reparative penology might enable a change to the nature of prison regimes, and the manner in which this might be achieved in practice. In particular, issues of voluntarism, individual responsibility and participation are discussed alongside the need for self-analysis and reparative action with a view to promoting the eventual social reintegration of ex-prisoners within the community. These issues lead logically to a further assessment in *Chapter 10* of the ways in which prisons might be made more 'community friendly' without undue risk, and in the interests of creating an altogether different custodial image. This would undoubtedly require a change in the 'culture' of prisons as we presently see them operate, and encouragement of an increased participation in prisons by community stakeholders. Such a transition might, it is suggested, ultimately benefit not only offenders and victims of crime, but also local communities and at the same time enhance the wider professionalism of correctional staff. Importantly, however, it is necessary to create a 'bridge' between custodial and non-custodial corrections, and as we shall see in *Part Three*, this has to be achieved by expanded use of 'conditional release' from reparative custody and greater use of community sanctions.

PART THREE OVERVIEW - MORE EFFECTIVE COMMUNITY SANCTIONS

Part Three of this work is the logical counterpart to *Part Two* and switches the focus of attention from custodial to non-custodial justice. It is predicated on the proposition that if decreased (and different) use is to be made of imprisonment in the interests of delivering better justice, then community sanctions have to be expanded, made simpler and more demanding, and create public confidence in their effectiveness. *Part Three* like the two parts that preceded it comprises five chapters, the first of which, *Chapter 11*, questions quite appropriately what the real purpose of community corrections should be. As in the case of custodial punishment previously discussed, in order to make progress it becomes necessary to envisage a change of ethos and direction in community corrections, and the implications of attempting this task are analysed in some detail.

In many respects, *Chapter 11* is the pivotal chapter of this book since it describes how the transition from custody to conditional release for offenders sentenced to reparative custody might be managed within what is described as a 'bifurcated' model of criminal justice. This is undoubtedly a contentious area of debate in penology, and would involve a radical re-appraisal of the relationship between the 'restorative' and 'traditional' models of criminal justice, both of which would have to be accommodated alongside each other for reasons that are discussed within this chapter. The implications of such a change of emphasis are profound, but also very challenging and exciting, and these implications are explored with a view to creating community corrections with an entirely new purpose and operational motivation.

Chapter 12 provides an important extension of the discussion in the preceding chapter by examining the ways in which a restorative penology would have to overcome the legacy of community justice as it has declined in an operational sense since the 1960s and the 'nothing works' era. We also examine in this chapter the increasing development of a 'managerialist' culture and approach to justice administration in Britain and elsewhere over the past two decades that has to be limited, and indeed ideally reversed, if true progress in corrections is to be made. If this could be achieved, the door would be opened to the development of community corrections with a new purpose, and a different but in many respects preferable structure for the social reintegration of offenders within communities.

In the final analysis, public and political confidence in community sanctions has to be recovered if substantial progress is to be made in contemporary corrections. This means, in effect, that the passenger in the Clapham Omnibus has to be convinced that use of prisons can be constructive beyond mere incarceration, and that community sanctions have 'penal bite'. This brings into consideration the question of how non-custodial corrections can be of significant community benefit while improving public confidence and creating opportunities for the involvement of communities themselves. These are the issues discussed in *Chapter 13*, and accompanied by suggestions about how the entire framework of correctional services might be re-structured to deliver these challenging objectives.

In *Chapter 14* it becomes appropriate to examine how community sanctions can best be operated and supervised, bearing in mind the historical divide within the penal system of England and Wales between the ethos of the Prison and Probation Services. The main focus is placed upon the creation of a credible and unified National Correctional Service that would preserve and maximise the professional expertise within both the Prison and Probation Services while at the same time providing a 'seamless' transition from custody to community sanctions for offenders sentenced to reparative custody. In addition, the need – previously identified – to make community sanctions visible and effective becomes an issue of major importance within the discussion, as does also the suggested necessity to ensure that offenders working within communities on amenity projects are evidently supervised on a consistent basis. Success in reducing recidivism suggests the need for a holistic and realistic approach to the design and operation of community sanctions, combined with simplicity and effectiveness in the delivery of the entire non-custodial justice process if public confidence is to be maintained.

The final chapter of this work (*Chapter 15*) draws together the main strands of the discussion that emerge from preceding chapters in a manner that suggests a new context and concept of 'corrections' for the future. It emphasises the clear need to modify the 'traditional' retributive approach heavily invested with its punitive ideology, and transform this into an agenda for corrections that is oriented towards 'setting right' the harm caused by criminal offending to victims, communities and offenders themselves. To some extent this extends the argument for 'holism' described earlier, and also for ceasing to maintain the belief that proportionality within criminal punishment is a credible or even an achievable driving component of deliverable justice. To some extent this means that the entire structure of justice stands in need of review if operational justice is to achieve greater effectiveness.

The closing section of this *Epilogue* chapter carries the sub-title *Unification or Bust?* This is indicative of the need to convince both politicians and the Clapham Omnibus passenger that effective corrections can be delivered in a manner consistent with reduced reliance on custodial punishment and enhanced use of community sanctions providing that a National Correctional Service adopts a unified approach to justice delivery. This means accepting the need for change, adopting a new approach and correctional philosophy, and making justice a vehicle for restoration rather than primarily of retribution. This is, essentially, the challenge of a restorative penology. It is a challenge that can be met with vision and a determination to deliver better justice. It is also a challenge that can be ignored, but only at considerable and avoidable social cost in the future.

SOME PRELIMINARY OBSERVATIONS

This book confronts many of the contemporary myths about penal crises, the morality of a predominantly retributive approach to dealing with criminal offenders, the widespread and continuing neglect of victims of crime, and the ideology that is 'tough on crime' without being 'tough on the causes of crime'. It asks the thoughtful reader to re-assess rather than accept as given the need for criminal justice to cause such extensive collateral damage while achieving such relatively meagre results in reducing reoffending by those whom it punishes with such dedication.

To be effective and acknowledged, however, a restorative penology must be as convincing in a practical as in a theoretical and philosophical sense. It must set forward proposals for change that are capable of implementation while at the same time reducing rather than exacerbating the feelings of crisis and frustration within penal systems as these operate at the present time. As will become evident, some of the suggestions for change within this work are 'structural' in nature, dealing with the custodial estate and its utilisation, and would require an extent of legislative action. Others are of a 'procedural' form, requiring a different approach to the relationship between prisons, offenders, and the communities that immediately surround them. Yet other proposed innovations involve the more challenging issue of 'attitudinal' change towards sentencing and the professional ethos within both custodial and non-custodial correctional services. The latter might, in the final analysis, prove to be the most intractable in terms of their ultimate acceptance and implementation.

This book displays evident differences from those in the trilogy that have preceded it. Its chapters are more numerous and relatively short, and deliberately so, since each deals with a specific question that is central to the establishment of a reparative and restorative penology within the contemporary correctional 'climate' that exists within many 'Western style' democracies. Though it is written predominantly from the viewpoint of the Criminal Justice System of England and Wales with its present critical difficulties, readers from many different jurisdictions will identify issues that have some considerable resonance for their own national situations. Indeed, since over-use of imprisonment is the root cause of most contemporary penal crises, the present situation in England and Wales should hover like a spectre over many nations headed in broadly the same criminological direction.

When all is said and done, however, politicians will continue to pursue criminal justice policies that attract public support as a matter of expediency and of electoral necessity. It is, nonetheless, voters who place politicians in positions of authority and who, through the taxes imposed on them, pay for the outcomes of these policies. When such policies also incur excessive cost, the public are entirely justified in demanding that these be changed. This book explains, quite straightforwardly, how this might be achieved, and with benefit to all the parties to criminal justice.

Finally by way of introduction, it is necessary to sound a note of caution. The terminology within which sentencing and operational penal practices in England and Wales are expressed have undergone almost continuous and significant change over the past two decades in particular. For instance, universally well known terms such as 'probation' and 'community service' orders have been redesignated several times, and other forms of sentence have been extensively renamed and the prison release procedures modified and given new or changing terminology.

In an attempt to clarify the situation a *Glossary of Some Key Terms Used in this Book* has been included (at the end of the book before the *Bibliography*) together with their origins in criminal justice legislation and brief explanatory notes. It is hoped that this may assist the reader who is confused by, or unfamiliar with these changes, though within the final part of this work when dealing with 'Community Sanctions', reference has, where appropriate, been retained to the 'traditional' nomenclature. It is also a fact that terms such as 'probation' are recognised and resonate internationally and seem more appropriate than their newer counterparts when discussing matters as they may apply across national borders.

Dedication

This book is dedicated to the memory of

Charles Theodore Erickson

1943-2002

A true friend and mentor, a robust pioneer of enlightened correctional practice; and an ever-delightful and sorely missed companion on the journey of life.

About the author

David J Cornwell is a writer, criminologist and former prison governor with extensive experience of operational practice and consultancy within both the state and privately managed sectors of prison administration, having worked in both UK and foreign penal establishments and correctional systems. His many career involvements include leading the Negotiating Team during the iconic events of the Strangeways Prison Riot of 1990 when he was tasked with persuading prisoners to surrender to the authorities.

His final post in HM Prison Service was that of Head of Security Audit in the Standards Audit Unit in the wake of the notorious escapes from Whitemoor and Parkhurst Dispersal Prisons in 1994/95. This post provided the unique experience of auditing security and control procedures in more than 90 prisons in England and Wales between 1996-97. It was followed between 1998-2003 by that as Operations Adviser to Group 4 (and later GSL and now Group 4/Securitas) during the design, building, commissioning and initial operation of the 3,000 bed Mangaung Correctional Centre at Bloemfontain in the Free State Province of the Republic of South Africa. He remains, in semi-retirement, an active consultant criminologist.

This volume completes a trilogy of books by David J Cornwell along with the acclaimed works: *Criminal Punishment and Restorative Justice: Past, Present and Future Perspectives* (with a Foreword by Tony Cameron) (2006); and *Doing Justice Better: The Politics of Restorative Justice* (with a Foreword by Mark S Umbreit) (2007).

CHAPTER 1

Why Are So Many Criminal Justice Systems Presently In Crisis?

Anyone who is inquisitive enough to access the internet to view international prison statistics will hardly fail to be amazed to discover that in many countries of the world today prisons are full to the point of overflowing. Whether this situation is measured in terms of numbers of persons imprisoned *per* hundred thousand of the general population, or in relation to the level of occupancy of prison estates expressed as percentages, the picture remains much the same.[1] The first question that then arises is: Why is this so commonplace? The second question that follows almost inevitably becomes: If keeping people in prisons is so expensive, then why do so many countries use penal custody so extensively?

The answers to these questions lie in the simple fact that in most modern democracies we have become almost obsessive about using prisons as little more than warehouses to prevent offenders from presenting a risk to the public, regardless of the fact that to do so is a very costly way of 'buying public protection', and that large numbers of them will re-offend within a short time of being released.[2] Prisons used as warehouses can do little to change the attitudes to offending, personal characteristics or circumstances of offenders, or give them the educational or practical skills to encourage law-abiding lives: such places merely 'contain' offenders for the period of time specified by the courts that sentence them.

THE LEGACY OF THE 'NOTHING WORKS' ERA

There was a time, way back in the middle years of the last century, when it was widely believed by academics and prison officials alike that provision of 'treatment and training' in prisons would change the behaviour patterns of offenders to the extent that many of them would not re-offend when released. This belief failed to work out in practice to the extent that disenchantment with the idea of 'rehabilitation' became widespread, and the 'Nothing Works' scenario became the accepted way of

---

1. See, for example, the statistics for world prison populations produced annually by the International Centre for Prison Studies available online from: http://news.bbc.co.uk/1/shared/spl/hi/uk/06/prisons/html/nn2.stm.
2. In the United Kingdom in 2006/7 it is estimated that between 60 and 70% of all prisoners released from custody re-offend within 24 months, though there are significant differences in patterns of reoffending between juvenile and adult offenders. See, for example, J. Cunliffe and A. Shepherd (2007), *Reoffending of Adults: Results From the 2004 Cohort*, London: Home Office Research, Development and Statistics Directorate.

viewing the reality of prison custody.[3] The outcome of this situation was critical in two important respects: first, for the way that prisons subsequently became used overwhelmingly for isolation and 'punishment'; and secondly, that the extent of the punishment was not only considered to be 'deserved', but also focused entirely on applying retribution to the offender for the assessed seriousness of the offence(s) committed.

To many members of the wider public as observers of criminal justice in action, there may not seem too much to be concerned about in this changed state of affairs. After all, criminals commit offences and so deserve to be punished: that much, in the view of many law-abiding people, is all there is to be said about it. But there are some major problems that arise when such a limited view is taken of criminal offending. It may be useful at this stage to point out where this leads, and why such a narrow approach to crime and punishment has had such a disastrous effect during the closing years of the last century and the early years of this one.

As belief in the idea of rehabilitation faded during the late 1970s, it became necessary to find an alternative means of justifying the process of criminal punishment that would fit in with the increasing mood of political and public frustration over continually rising rates of crime – and in particular offences against people and property. In other words, if punishment involving the idea of rehabilitation did not work, then how should offenders be dealt with? What happened during the late 1970s and early 1980s in an attempt to resolve this question was to have a lasting effect on our criminal justice system into this millennium.

As a result of large-scale studies completed in the USA[4] and also to a lesser extent in Britain, there emerged what came to be known as the 'just deserts' model of punishment which proposed a system of sentencing that attempted to make the severity of sanctions strictly proportionate to the seriousness of crimes – however that might be measured. This concept was taken up enthusiastically by the increasingly influential 'law and order' lobby within both the political and criminal justice systems in North America and Europe (including Britain), since it enabled a 'tough

---

3. The 'Nothing Works' perception about rehabilitation in prisons is (largely mistakenly) attributed to Robert Martinson who, in 1974, published a paper entitled 'What Works? – Questions and Answers About Prison Reform' in *The Public Interest*, Volume 35, pp.22-54. This argument was assumed to indicate that no programmes of a rehabilitative nature actually worked in reducing reoffending in the USA. In fact, Martinson's argument was widely misinterpreted, and what he actually concluded was that there was no conclusive evidence to show that any particular type of programme was any more effective than another in reducing reoffending. This became clear in a book released in the following year describing the results of an extensive research study in which he had collaborated. See: D. Lipton, R. Martinson and J. Wilks (1975), *Effectiveness of Treatment Evaluation Studies*, New York: Praeger Publications.
4. The most influential of these studies were compiled by the American Friends Service Committee (1972) with the title *Struggle for Justice*, New York: Hill & Wang, and the Committee for the Study of Incarceration under the authorship of Andrew von Hirsch (1976), *Doing Justice*, New York: Hill & Wang. For an excellent account of this development see Barbara Hudson (1987), *Justice Through Punishment*, Basingstoke, UK: Macmillan at pp. 37- 58.

on crime' approach to be adopted in combination with considerably increased penalties for serious offending.

Criminologists have described this important development during the 1980s and onwards as the era of the so-called 'justice model' of punishment which was to have a massive impact on the size of prison populations almost everywhere during the 1990s and into the present decade. It is interesting to note that in England and Wales in 1990 the average daily prison population stood at around 46,000, and that by 1998 this figure had increased to more than 65,000. In February 2009 it had reached 82,586, and is expected to rise even further within the immediate future unless the situation can be reversed.[5] If present trends are maintained, it is estimated that by 2013 the prison population will have risen to a level possibly as high as 106,500.

In Britain at present it is estimated that the cost of keeping an offender in prison is of the order of £40,000 a year. New prisons are vastly expensive to build and operate, and a continued rise in the prison population will require that many more prisons would be needed just to house the additional numbers adequately. This is little short of a nightmare scenario from which there is no escape unless a deliberate decision is made to do justice differently, and do so quickly. We are not the only country facing a similar future in terms of criminal justice delivery, but our citizens are entitled to expect that we do not waste scarce resources unnecessarily just because we have become locked in a 'punitive time warp'.

It is, however, the scenario that we in Britain and many other countries of the world today have inherited as a direct result of the 'Nothing Works' debate of almost half a century ago. In many ways it is as un-sustainable as the situation relating to carbon emissions because unless something is done to reverse its effects our lives are in danger of becoming chaotic. The argument is not just about cost alone, although that is also un-sustainable as a drain on national resources: but perhaps even more importantly, it is also about the unjust type of society that we are likely to become unless this punitive roller-coaster can be brought under some form of sensible control.

---

5. The Home Office assessment of the likely rise in the prison population of England and Wales up to 2313 is published in a Statistical Bulletin 11 of 2006. See: N. da Silva, P. Cowell, T. Chow and P. Worthington (2006), *Prison Population Projections 2006 – 2013, England and Wales*, London: Home Office Research, Development and Statistics Directorate.

'TRADITIONAL' CRIMINAL JUSTICE IN CRISIS

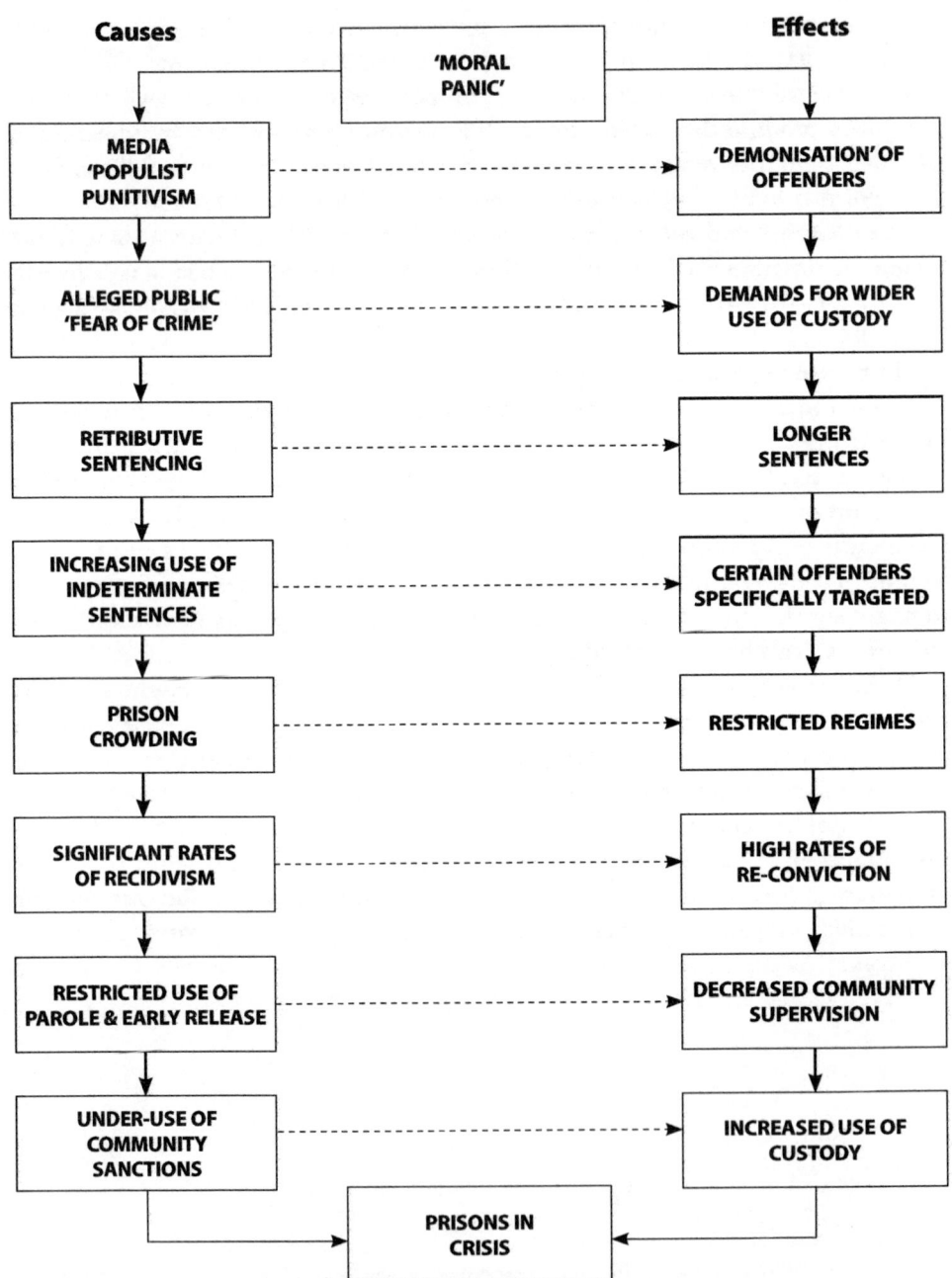

Figure 1:1: Traditional Criminal Justice in Crisis: Causes and Effects

HOW DO PENAL SYSTEMS GET INTO CRISIS?

Most, though by no means all crises within penal systems result from over-use of prison custody as a means of punishing offenders. This is frequently the result of some form of 'moral panic' or reaction to sustained media pressure on governments suggesting public alarm and fear of crime. The pressure is usually for 'tougher sentencing' of specific offences, and this results in what might be described as the 'demonisation' of certain types of offender. In *Figure 1.1*, the main causes and effects of penal crises are presented in the form of a diagram that indicates how these crises deepen, and also how the outcome is invariably evident in 'political panic'.

Prisons, by their very nature, are potentially unstable places that house large numbers of difficult and in some cases dangerous people against their will, and for lengthy periods of time. Jails filled to, or above, their reasonable operational capacity quickly become accidents waiting to happen. Too many prisoners means that space becomes crowded, the daily routine becomes difficult to operate, and the pressure of numbers on available resources for work, recreation, education, visitation and the like exceeds what is available for use.

Inability to provide and maintain active and purposeful prison regimes means that inmates spend far longer than normal locked in cells, and they become bored, resentful, and difficult to control. This, in turn, makes the task of correctional staff stressful and uncertain, since it is they who bear the effects of the disgruntled and often disruptive behaviour of disaffected inmates on a daily basis. Over-crowded prisons make reasonable discipline hard to enforce, and security liable to lapses of supervision and operational thoroughness. Ultimately, this places both inmates and staff at physical risk since the stronger and more predatory prisoners inevitably prey on the weaker, and the likelihood of violence increases.

Over-use of imprisonment by sentencing officials also means that many offenders who do not present a significant level of public risk, and whose offences are not extremely serious, end up in custody when this is not strictly necessary. Stringent restrictions on the use of parole release result in offenders spending longer in custody than is appropriate. Extensive use of indeterminate sentences has broadly the same effect, as does the use of extended sentences and discriminatory provisions for specific groups of offenders.[6] But this is not where the story really begins, for reasons that need brief explanation.

In Britain, as in so many present-day democracies that over-use imprisonment, it is a relatively small proportion of the total population that persistently commits

---

6. In the UK in particular over recent years, sexual offenders have been the subject of draconian severity in sentencing including the widespread use of discretionary life sentences. For a clear and unambiguous account of this development see: A. Matravers and G.V. Hughes (2003), 'Unprincipled Sentencing: The Policy Approach to Dangerous Sex Offenders', in M. Tonry (ed), *Confronting Crime: Crime Control Policy Under New Labour*, Cullompton, Devon, UK: Willan Publishing, pp.156-181.

criminal offences and creates not only a level of public risk, but also a wider fear of crime within society. Estimates vary, but in 2001 the Home Office published a report under the title *Criminal Justice: The Way Ahead* in which it was suggested that in England and Wales around 100,000 offenders were believed to commit almost half of the total volume of recorded crime, and that of these, some 20,000 were in prison at any one time.[7] If this proportion of the offending population has remained relatively similar since that time, and the present average daily prison population exceeds 82,500, then very large numbers of non-persistent offenders are present in our prisons.

It is, of course, the case that a considerable number of non-persistent offenders commit serious offences that justify their imprisonment, but it is also clear that many offenders also end up in prison as a result of committing much less serious crime. To make matters worse, a significant proportion of these people are sent to prison for short periods of time in what are, frequently, quite appalling and overcrowded conditions. In February 2009, of a total prison population of 82,568, some 10.7% (8,859) were serving sentences of up to 12 months, half of which time would be served in custody.[8] Of this same group, 6,149 were sentenced to periods of six months or less in prison.

To say the least of it, the situation outlined here is quite remarkable since in its own White Paper *Justice for All* published in 2002, the UK Home Office noted that available research evidence clearly indicated that sentences of twelve months or less were not only 'usually ineffective' (p.92), but also 'increase the chances of reoffending' (p.102).[9]

Almost a decade ago now, Michael Cavadino and James Dignan, two highly respected criminologists and commentators on the criminal justice system, wrote a most perceptive and authoritative account of what they described as the penal 'crisis' in Britain in the 1990s. (Cavadino and Dignan, 1997: 8-31). Their analysis of the situation at that time, and particularly in the wake of the extensive UK prison disturbances of April 1990, carried distinct echoes of similar accounts written another decade earlier (for example, Evans, 1980; Thomas and Pooley, 1980; Fitzgerald and Sim, 1982; Fleisher, 1989), but it was in many respects even more incisive. Within their analysis, Cavadino and Dignan identified a number of factors that are clearly contributory to crises in prison systems:

---

7. Home Office, (2001a), *Criminal Justice: The Way Ahead*, CM 5074, London: The Stationery Office, pp.6-7.
8. On 28 February 2009, the prison population of England and Wales was 82,568 with a rate of occupancy of available accommodation of 113%. Of this population, 69,614 were sentenced prisoners of which 6,149 were serving sentences of six months or less, and 2,710 sentences of between six and 12 months. Source: Ministry of Justice (2009), *Population in Custody Monthly Tables, May 2007, England and Wales*, London: National Offender Management Service, Table 1.
9. Home Office (2002c), *Justice for All*, CM 5563, London: HMSO.

- the high prison population (or 'numbers' crisis);
- overcrowding of prisons;
- understaffing;
- bad prison conditions (for both inmates and prison staff);
- staff unrest;
- poor security;
- the 'toxic mix' of long sentenced[10] and mentally disturbed prisoners;
- riots and other breakdowns of control over prisoners.

(Cavadino and Dignan, 1997: 10).

What is interesting about this 'list' of crisis-provoking factors is the inter-relatedness of the issues that are identified, all of which are well-known to correctional practitioners and criminologists, but not all of which need to be present simultaneously for a crisis to develop and deepen.

As we have noted earlier, the presence of excessive numbers of inmates in prisons leads inevitably to overcrowding of premises and the space within them, and thus to poor conditions of daily life, regimes, and boredom. Prisons may be adequately staffed, but staff will feel vulnerable if numbers are excessive and inmates, through boredom and inactivity or lack of purposeful activity, become restive and disruptive. The pressure of numbers can (though need not inevitably) lead to lapses in security, and these in turn provide opportunity for disturbances and breakdowns in control. Prisoners serving lengthy sentences particularly dislike disruptions to regimes, and any uncertainty about standards or quality of delivery of the routine aspects of prison life (food, recreation, visits, mail, shopping, etc.) that make life in prison 'liveable'.

It is a well-recorded fact[11] that a significant proportion of people in prisons display one or another form of mental illness, some of which can be acute and cause those who suffer from them to be abnormally disruptive, aggressive, and dangerous to themselves and others – both inmates and staff. Once again estimates vary, but there is some consensus among psychiatric professionals that about 70% of prisoners suffer from two or more symptoms of mental illness, compared with 5% within the general population. The presence of mentally ill inmates in over-crowded prisons (and even prisons at normal levels of occupancy) *is* avoidable, but this means that special hospitals of a secure nature have to be provided, staffed profession-

---

10. Prisoners serving long sentences include those serving life sentences of an indeterminate (or indefinite) duration and those serving fixed term sentences of five years or longer subject to release under parole procedures.
11. See, for example, the accounts of Maden et al. (1996), Fryers et al. (1998) and Singleton et al. (1998). Also BBC News 24 (2004), *Numbers Pressure Causes Prison Suicides*, http://news.bbc.co.uk/i/hi/uk/3157873.stm of 4 May.

ally, and deliver appropriate forms of treatment. The main point for this discussion is, however, that sizeable numbers of mentally disturbed persons within prisons bring with them management, physical well-being and security risks that are very considerable.

Many experienced observers of prisons would insist that the ingredients of potential penal crises are ever-present and naturally recurring, but this is far from necessarily the case. Prison overcrowding is avoidable, and is ultimately a matter of political choice and decision. Higher than normal rates of mental illness among prison inmates may be to some extent anticipated, but the presence of severely disturbed persons in grossly disproportionate numbers need not be tolerated. That such people carry with them high risks of suicide and disruptiveness is evidence in itself that prisons can easily become unstable and potentially dangerous places.

THE PARALLEL EFFECTS ON COMMUNITY CORRECTIONS

Over-use of prison custody has predictable effects on the non-custodial sector of sanctions within the community not only in practical operational terms, but also in relation to public confidence and political credibility. These effects become most marked when attitudes to offending demonstrated within the mass media and by politicians are overly punitive, sensationalist, and predominantly retributive.

The extensive prison riots and disorder in Manchester and elsewhere in April 1990 became a worldwide media circus of unique proportion, and the scale of the destruction so vividly displayed on television and in the international press was both unprecedented and alarming.[12] The extent and duration of the Manchester riot, the longest in recorded prison history, undoubtedly led to a hardening of political and public attitudes towards prisons and prisoners that was to extend throughout the 1990s and beyond. The glare of the mass media attention in which the rioting inmates basked with relative impunity from capture afforded their leaders an almost 'Robin Hood-like' status, yet the orgy of destruction, arson, looting and defiance of authority over twenty-five days was incredible to witness.

In the aftermath of the rioting and the official inquiry into its causes and effects (Woolf and Tumim, 1991), a major programme of prison reform and refurbishment was set in place to improve prison conditions and security, and reduce overcrowding and multiple cell occupancy. In the same year, the government published

---

12. The author was present throughout the period of the riot at HMP Strangeways in Manchester from 1 to 25 April 1990 as the leader of the Negotiation Team tasked to persuade rioting prisoners to surrender themselves to the lawful authorities. For an account of this mission see D. J. Cornwell and D. Boag (1991), 'The Multi-Perpetrator Dimension in Prison Siege Negotiation: Psycho-Strategic Considerations', *Proceedings of the Prison Service Psychology Conference*, London: Home Office, HM Prison Service, (October), pp.104-125.

a White Paper under the title *Custody, Care and Justice*[13] that reflected its acceptance of the main findings of the Woolf Report and identified key priorities for the reform of prison conditions in England and Wales. The White Paper did not, however, specifically endorse the recommendation within the Woolf Report in relation to the establishment of community prisons that were intended to enable prisoners to serve their sentences close to their communities of origin, and thus retain closer links with families and friends. And though the White Paper had much to say about the need for closer relationships between prisons and the Probation Service, it was in its prescriptions for dealing with mentally disordered offenders that the most important potential development for progress was described:

> Prison is not a suitable place for people suffering from serious mental disturbance. Whenever possible, such offenders should be diverted to the health or social services when they first come into contact with the criminal justice system. Where it is unavoidable that those requiring in-patient treatment are committed to prison, then they should be transferred to suitable health service facilities as soon as possible. (Home Office, 1991: 101).

Neither the recommendation for community prisons nor the initiative to reduce mental illness in prisons was followed up in any substantive action by government during the period following the publication of the White Paper. Indeed, much of the caring aspects of the document quickly drifted into the realm of abandoned pipe dreams and missed opportunities, leaving a residual emphasis on custody and justice which both emerged as the cornerstones of the political agenda for criminal justice during the mid-1990s.

By the autumn of 1993 the retreat from the progressive and enlightened Woolf Report was evidently in full flow. The (then) Home Secretary Michael Howard informed the Conservative Party conference in the October of that year: 'Let us be clear. Prison works. It ensures that we are protected from murderers, muggers and rapists – and it makes many who are tempted to commit crime think twice." In the same speech he added that he would not flinch from measures that would increase the size of the prison population, and, as we have seen earlier, it certainly did increase dramatically and has continued to do so ever since.

The problem that this raises is that in Britain, as in many other countries, we have become accustomed to an absurdly high prison population because the general public has been persuaded to believe (even though mistakenly) that 'prison works' on the basis of incapacitation and social protection.[14] This has led through an equally

---

13. The full title of the White Paper was: Home Office (1991), *Custody, Care and Justice: The Way Ahead for the Prison Service in England and Wales*, Cm 1647, London: HMSO.
14. Persuaded in the sense that the mass media have maintained, through sensationalism of crime – and in particular sexual crime – continuous pressure on politicians for ever more extensive use of imprisonment and longer custodial sentences. Politicians of both major parties (Conservative and Labour) have responded with 'tough on crime' criminal justice policies and measures which have been implemented by the judiciary. For an excellent account of this development, see Michael Tonry's (2003) edited volume

defective logic to a parallel assumption which might be termed: '*only* prison works' because what is required is not just and appropriate punishment but incarceration for public protection. And by extension of the same argument, because community sanctions do not afford community protection (and were never intended to do so), these cannot be effective because public risk cannot be eliminated.

The perceptive reader will immediately recognise that this is an entirely circular argument, but it has proved to be a very persuasive one in the public mind, particularly over the past ten years or so. The truth is that prison only works in buying short-term public protection (at considerable cost), and greater use of community sanctions need not necessarily increase public risk significantly. Prison does *not* work in reducing reoffending: in fact it is approximately sixty *per cent* ineffective in doing so at present. Furthermore, social protection should be only a by-product of criminal punishment, and not its central purpose within civilised societies. We shall return to this discussion in the remaining chapters of Part One.

It seems to be the case that as, over time, societies become more affluent, the gap between the richest and the poorest becomes ever wider and two important developments tend to take place. The first of these is that crime becomes more serious, and the second is that those who are relatively well off become much more punitive towards those who commit crime. One of the reasons why crime, and especially violent crime, becomes more serious is that within high surveillance societies the chances of evading detection and arrest are much less favourable to the criminal. This is one of the main reasons for the marked decrease in the offence of burglary since the mid-1990s in Britain.[15] It also explains, at least in part, why major drug trafficking for which the penalty on conviction is invariably a very long prison sentence, and the potential for financial gain is extremely high, is accompanied by so much firearm-related violence.

PUBLIC ATTITUDES TOWARDS CRIME AND OFFENDERS

The reasons why affluent societies develop punitive attitudes towards criminal offenders are more complex. The most obvious illustrative explanation is to be found in the offences relating to vehicle crime (which has also decreased significantly over

---

Confronting Crime: Crime Control Policy Under New Labour, Devon, UK: Willan Publishing. Another important contribution to this debate can be found in Anthony Bottoms, Sue Rex and Gwen Robinson (eds), (2004), *Alternatives to Prison: Options for an Insecure Society*, Devon, UK: Willan Publishing, at Chapter 1, pp. 1-27.

15. The British Crime Survey (BCS) 2006 illustrates this situation very clearly at Table 9.5. In 1997, a total of 1,621 thousand burglaries was recorded (of which it is estimated that some 61% were reported to the police). In 2002/3 this figure had decreased to 969 thousand, and in 2004/5 (the last years for which BCS statistics are available) it had fallen again to 756 thousand – the lowest level since 1981. Source: Office for National Statistics, (2006), *Social Trends*, London: HMSO / Palgrave Macmillan, p.132-3.

the past decade by almost 50 *per cent*)[16], but which has a high profile and capacity to arouse hostility within areas in which car ownership is perceived as an important aspect of mobility and social status. It seems to be evident that in spite of widespread CCTV surveillance and ever more sophisticated locking and alarm systems, car theft and vandalism provoke intense public anger not only because of the inconvenience and high cost involved, but also because of the affront that such offences cause to the owners of these much-valued possessions. It is also notable that the largest proportion of car thefts and vandalism (67 per cent in 2004/5) occurred within or adjacent to the boundaries of properties owned or occupied by vehicle owners.

In relation to punitive public attitudes towards crime, and thus also towards the punishment of crime, the perceptions of the average citizen in relation to crime rates become a crucial issue. In Britain today, more than sixty *per cent* of respondents to a British Crime Survey investigation expressed the view that overall levels of crime had increased over the immediately preceding two years. Of these respondents, almost half believed it to have increased significantly, and such perceptions have remained remarkably constant since 1996.[17] In fact, both the British Crime Survey data and the overall number of offences recorded by the police over the past decade (1997-2007) indicate a consistent *decrease* in total offending to the point at which this stands presently at approximately two-thirds (or 60 *per cent*) of the levels recorded in 1997.

The point of this discussion is now, perhaps, a little clearer. Public confidence in the effectiveness of the criminal justice system in Britain in a number of key areas of justice delivery is at least very uncertain if not worse. In the 2004/5 British Crime Survey analysis of public attitudes:

- only 42 *per cent* of those surveyed considered that the system was very or fairly effective in bringing offenders to justice;
- only 38 *per cent* believed that the system was very or fairly effective in reducing crime;
- only 34 *per cent* considered that the system was very or fairly effective in meeting the needs of victims of crime; and,
- only 28 *per cent* of respondents considered the system was very or fairly effective in dealing with young people accused of crime.[18]

---

16. The same BCS (2006) indicates that in 1995 the level of all vehicle related crime was recorded as 3,511 thousand offences. In 2002/3 this figure had decreased to 2,365 thousand, and in 2004/5 to 1,886 thousand. Source: *Ibid.* Table 9.6, p.133.
17. See: BCS (2006), Figure 9.4 and explanatory text at p.132.
18. See: BCS (2006), Figure 9.20 and explanatory text at p.141.

But in the face of such widespread misunderstanding over whether or not rates of overall crime have actually risen or fallen, can these statistics be trusted other than as indicative of naïve public *perceptions* as to the effectiveness of criminal justice administration? The combination of public punitiveness and misinformation is undoubtedly fostered by media sensationalism of serious crime and disingenuous political attitudes towards telling the truth about crime, offenders and offending. Put bluntly, it suits the contemporary political agenda (predominantly for reasons of electoral credibility) to display attitudes and pursue policies that are 'tough on crime', if for no better reason that these reinforce both the prejudices of a misinformed public and the profits of a sensationalist media.

In such a perverse climate of opinions, public confidence in community sanctions cannot be other than minimal, and it becomes almost inevitable that infatuation with incarceration will continue into the future. This means that expansion of community penalties to enable a reduction in the prison population is unlikely to be viewed favourably by either the public or by politicians – that is, unless a reasoned and potentially effective alternative strategy becomes available. The critical question is: does such a strategy exist, and if so, how effective would it be?

The answer to this question is that a potentially effective alternative strategy does exist in the form of restorative justice, but it requires a fundamentally different approach to the way most 'Western-style' democracies operate their criminal justice systems *and* a willingness on the part of the public, politicians and the media to give it serious consideration. As we shall see in the chapters that follow, restorative justice is not new, it is not some fanciful idea dreamed up in the ivory towers of academia, and it is far from 'soft on crime'. It does, however, approach the problem of crime and offences from a different perspective, and has emerged from the hard-gained experience of criminal justice practitioners throughout the world who recognise the need to provide better justice for offenders, victims of crime and communities. In *Chapter 2* we shall examine what restorative justice is actually about, and what exactly it has to offer in terms of fairer and more effective justice.

But to return to the question that forms the title of this chapter, we can now see why so many criminal justice systems are presently in crisis. The main reason is that these systems are stuck in a form of 'time warp' in which punitive attitudes to criminal offending held by a widely misinformed public, and reinforced by media sensationalism of crime, drive politicians who want to retain power to adopt criminal justice policies that inevitably result in ever-increasing punishment for public protection. Given that all the rational and practical assessments of this situation indicate that such punishment 'does not work' in spite of the huge cost invested in it, the argument for change becomes difficult to resist.

CHAPTER 2

What is Restorative Justice, and What Does it Offer?

It would be encouraging to think that the reader who has perused and considered the content of the preceding chapter might now have some misgivings about continuing to do justice in the way that we, in Britain and many other democracies of the world, have become accustomed to doing it over the past 60 years or so. Futility, cost, failure, wastefulness, vindictiveness, inhumanity, carelessness, unconcern, inflexibility and even arrogance all spring immediately to mind as being to one or another extent contributory to the present penal crisis. Why, then, should it be any different if we were to adopt the concept and principles of restorative justice as a central motivation for delivering better criminal justice?

DIFFERENT JUSTICE OR BETTER JUSTICE?

This brief chapter describing restorative justice would be incomplete without some mention of how the concept came into being and where it stands at the present time. Contrary to what may widely be believed it is not new in terms of age, having developed progressively during the closing two decades of the previous century and into the new millennium. On the other hand it is new insofar as it presents an entirely different and reasoned approach to justice which makes it in some respects appear threatening to those who would protect the *status quo* against all incursions.

One of the main strengths of restorative justice lies in the fact that it has been 'practitioner-led', its development deriving predominantly from the practical experience of correctional officials and academics with a comprehensive understanding of penal systems in operation. Frustrated to some extent by the 'Nothing Works' analysis and by the subsequent drift towards punitive justice, these 'pioneers' brought their 'What Works' experience to bear on the identification of a more humane, equitable and practical means of delivering a form of justice that was altogether more likely to meet the needs of offenders and victims and, at the same time, reduce reoffending.

The restorative justice movement grew steadily during the 1980s from small beginnings in the field of victim-offender mediation (VOM) launched in Canada in 1974.[1] Interest in the concept became widespread during the late 1980s and 1990s

---

1. The first practical application of restorative justice principles was evident in the Victim Offender Reconciliation Program (VORP) in Kitchener, Ontario in 1974. This was followed by several similar initiatives in North America and Europe, and in the USA at Elkhart, Indiana, in 1978. See: M. Umbreit,

on a worldwide basis, particularly in Europe, Australia and New Zealand, and in 1994 the American Bar Association endorsed VOM on a voluntary basis. Six years later, the United Nations Congress on Crime Prevention developed a draft proposal for *UN Basic Principles on the Use of Restorative Justice Programmes in Criminal Matters* (United Nations, 2001), and this proposal was formally adopted in 2002 (United Nations, 2002). In Europe, the Council of Europe in 1999 adopted recommendations on the use of VOM by member states, and in 2001 issued a policy directive that mediation in criminal cases should be incorporated within the domestic law of member states by 2006. (Umbreit et al., 2005:260-261).

In Britain, the government responded to this initiative in July 2003 with a consultation document entitled *Restorative Justice: The Government's Strategy* (Home Office, 2003a)[2], and this was followed in the same year by a further policy document *A New Deal for Victims and Witnesses: National Strategy to Deliver Improved Services* (Home Office, 2003b)[3]. In 2006 the Youth Justice Board for England and Wales published an Action Plan for implementing restorative justice practice within the juvenile and young offender sector.[4]

However, in spite of all this apparent activity, progress towards actually implementing restorative justice principles into mainstream criminal justice practice is slow, and limited to youthful offenders at the present time. The reason for this is that to incorporate restorative justice to any meaningful extent requires systemic change to the criminal justice system as a whole, and this does not sit easily alongside the overtly punitive strategies towards offenders pursued by the British government over recent years.

As we shall see in the subsequent chapters of this book, restorative justice robustly challenges the *status quo* because it seeks to do justice both differently *and* better. But this single fact may prove at present, to be its 'Achilles' heel' because, as Susan Sharpe (2004) has suggested, it has developed widely but in a piece-meal fashion, and there is still no universal agreement on the extent to which its various agendas (VOM, group conferencing, healing circles, etc.) fit together in a coherent and unambiguous manner within criminal justice systems.[5] Gerry Johnstone (2004), within the same volume of collected papers on restorative justice, raises an important issue about

---

B. Vos, R. B. Coates and E. Lightfoot (2005), 'Restorative Justice in the Twenty-First Century: A Social Movement Full of Opportunities and Pitfalls', *Marquette Law Review*, vol.89, no.2, pp.254-263.
2. This document is available at http://www.homeoffice.gov.uk/documents/rj-strategy-consult.pdf.
3. See: http://www.cjsonline.gov.uk/home.html (July).
4. Youth Justice Board (2006), *Developing Restorative Justice: An Action Plan*, London: YJB, and see: http://www.rjb.gov.uk/rdonlyres/F475830A. The consultation led to the publication in 2008 of a cross-government initiative, the Restorative Justice Strategy Group: see Home Office, Ministry of Justice, Cabinet Office and Department for Children, Schools and Families (2008), *Youth Crime Action Plan*, London: Home Office/YJB, and YJB (2006), *Developing Restorative Justice: A YJB Action Plan*, London: YJB.
5. S. Sharpe (2004), 'How Large Should the Restorative Justice "Tent" Be?' in H. Zehr and B. Toews (eds), *Critical Issues in Restorative Justice*, Monsey, NY: Criminal Justice Press and Cullompton, Devon, UK: Willan Publishing, pp. 17-31.

the development and application of restorative justice up to the present time. This concerns whether (as John Braithwaite and Heather Strang (2001) have suggested) restorative justice is busily pursuing two quite different outcomes within criminal justice simultaneously: *process* change in the way justice is done, and *value* change in the motivations that presently underpin criminal justice policy-making.[6] If it is predominantly the former then issues of punishment rationale, sentencing and trial procedure need to be addressed: if the latter, considerations relating to quality and outcomes of justice become paramount. If both, then there is a long climb ahead.

A CHANCE TO THINK DIFFERENTLY ABOUT JUSTICE

In his book *Changing Lenses: A New Focus for Crime and Justice* written as long ago now as 1990, and subsequently in his (2002) work *The Little Book of Restorative Justice*, Howard Zehr, frequently referred to as the 'father of restorative justice', set out an admirably clear vision of what restorative justice proposes.[7] Stated in the briefest of terms it is this:

> Restorative justice requires, at minimum, that we address victim's harms and needs, hold offenders accountable to put right those harms, and involve victims, offenders and communities in this process. (Zehr, 2002: 25),

This single statement, more perhaps than any other in the entire and now extensive literature of restorative justice, provides us at one and the same time with the key to the door of restorative justice and a comprehensive analysis (by implication and extension) of the defects of contemporary criminal justice. It therefore gives us an indispensable starting point for the discussion within this chapter.

First and foremost, our definition focuses on holding offenders to account for the harm that criminal offending causes, primarily to victims, but also to the good order of the wider community and to the authority of the law and the state. Secondly, we find an unequivocal requirement that in order to be reintegrated into the wider community having caused harm, offenders must do something substantial to repair that harm. Third, we are presented with a *process* through which victims, offenders and communities have a recognised and legitimate stake in the outcomes of justice.

---

6. G. Johnstone (2004), 'How, And In What Terms Should Restorative Justice Be Conceived?' in H. Zehr and B. Toews, *op. cit.*, pp.5-15. And see also J. Braithwaite and H. Strang (2001), 'Introduction: Restorative Justice and Civil Society' in H. Strang and J. Braithwaoite (eds), *Restorative Justice and Civil Society*, Cambridge, UK: Cambridge University Press.
7. See: H. Zehr, (1990 and 1995), *Changing Lenses: A New Focus for Crime and Justice*, Scottdale, PA: Herald Press, and H. Zehr, (2002), *The Little Book of Restorative Justice*, Intercourse, PA: Good Books. For the reader who requires a concise summary, a most helpful article is to be found in H. Zehr and H. Mika, (1998), 'Fundamental Principles of Restorative Justice', *Contemporary Justice Review*, vol.1, no.1, pp.47-55.

But there is much more to the definition than may be apparent at first sight. Here we are given only a *minimal* requirement that does not rule out (in holding offenders accountable) an appropriate element of punishment, but which does not insist upon it or impose it for its own sake. We are also obliged to look, primarily, at who rather than what has been harmed, and how this can be put right as a matter more important than punishment. This places victims at the heart of the justice process, and places an obligation on offenders to make reparation.

For too many years past we have been accustomed to definitions of crime that rest predominantly on the fact (or supposition) that the law has been broken, and that whoever has done this must be punished. While it may indeed be true that a wrongful act has infringed the law and that some action is necessary to deal with this, there also remains, as Howard Zehr has helpfully indicated, the important fact that the wrongful action has caused *harm* to people (whom we normally call victims) and to relationships between people. And while the violation of the law must always constitute an abstract technicality, the real and possibly more important violation lies in the extent of the harm done by perpetrators to victims.

A NEW APPROACH TO GUILT AND HARM

We have traditionally become accustomed to the idea that violation of the law (if proven) implies guilt, but that the guilt relates more to the breach of the law than to the harmfulness of the act and the effect of that harm upon the victim. I would like to suggest that it may be helpful to view this rather differently, along the lines that the harm caused not only creates an obligation on the part of the offender to 'put it right' (as Zehr quite rightly insists), but also that it alienates the offender from the community *until* something substantive is done to restore the situation of the victim.

The English language is not necessarily the most precise and effective means of conveying this concept of harm and guilt, possibly because of the traditional legalistic interpretations placed on both terms. However, in the German language we find the words *Schaden* which means 'damage' or 'harm', and *Schuld* which is an active representation of the term 'guilt' implying fault – and by extension responsibility and obligation. Viewed in such a context, it becomes possible to separate the notion of *Rechtschuld*[8] (or law guilt) from that of *Schadenschuld* (or harm guilt) in a most helpful manner.

---

8. Here it will be noted that the German language uses the terms *Recht* and *Gesetz* in slightly different contexts of the word 'law' within its legal literature. The former (literally translated as 'right') conveys an active embodiment of law in the sense of an entitlement as a citizen to protection from harm, freedom from interference, and the like, whereas the latter relates more closely to the legal enactments of the law in terms of ordinances, proscriptions, and provisions.

The concept of *Schadenschuld* conveys very effectively the essence of what restorative justice is all about. In contrast with *Rechtschuld* it is more concerned with the effects of crime on those harmed, establishing who is responsible for this harm, and what can be done to put it right. In so doing, it holds offenders primarily responsible for accepting the wrongfulness of their actions and places an obligation upon them to do something about the harm caused as a pre-condition of being restored to full social status. Thus, acceptance of guilt, taking responsibility for it, and making reparation for harm done, become the key components of a justice system that demonstrates appropriate respect for all parties to criminal offending – victims, offenders and communities.

Traditional justice as it is widely practiced today makes no such demands upon offenders, largely ignores the situation and needs of victims of crime, and is obsessive about punishing in relation to a notion of guilt that has more to do with the law being broken than harm having been caused. It is for all these reasons that the penal crises described in the previous chapter continue to recur. This outmoded form of justice finds itself obliged to punish to sustain its own 'integrity', and to punish with increasing severity because the methods of punishment used do little to change offending behaviour other than for the worse.

All of this brings us back to the need to re-examine the purposes of criminal punishment in modern societies, and, in particular, to look at how restorative justice deals with the central issues of retribution and 'rehabilitation' – whatever the latter concept means in relation to criminal offending. These issues become the focus of attention in *Chapters 3* and *9* respectively.

For the moment, however, we are concerned with the question of what restorative justice is, and what it has to offer that is preferable to the form of justice that prevails under existing circumstances. Thus far, we have noted the need to take a more constructive approach to dealing with offenders, giving victims of crime a central place within justice processes, and the potential advantages of thinking differently about harm and guilt. Returning to the definition set out earlier, it will be evident that what restorative justice proposes is an *inclusive* process of justice administration that involves offenders, victims and communities in working together to heal the harms caused by criminal violations. Such a process differs markedly from the *exclusive* process of incarcerative justice noted in *Chapter 1*, and the reasons for this deserve mention at this stage of the discussion.

INCLUSIVE JUSTICE

Restorative justice offers the potential to establish a range of stakeholders within the process of justice administration, each of whom has an important contribution to make to its outcomes for all the parties concerned. Zehr (2002 *op. cit.*:27) clearly identifies the immediate victims of crime and offenders as the 'key stakeholders', along with community members and close others who, as 'secondary victims' may have been directly affected by the commission of offences and the aftermath of them. I have argued elsewhere (Cornwell, 2007 *op. cit.*: 73-5) that this definition appears somewhat confining, since within a concept of 'obligations', the state also has a direct responsibility for making available the means by which victim reparation can be made. As a matter of preference and of clarity I propose the somewhat different approach to the identification of stakeholders that is illustrated at *Figure 2:1*.

The illustration highlights three distinct 'clusters' of interest in criminal justice that are described as the 'governmental', 'correctional services' and 'public interest' clusters respectively. The primary stakeholders are identified as the state government, offenders and victims of crime because these are the immediately involved parties in a restorative justice setting. The location of the courts within the illustration spans all three clusters because courts directly affect outcomes of justice for all the entities within the clusters. Similarly, offenders span both the 'correctional services' and 'public interest' clusters because their needs and interests are common to both.

'Beneficiary' (or secondary) stakeholders is the term used to describe those interest groups that should derive some direct benefit from the outcomes of criminal justice, but who are not primary stakeholders. 'Enabling' stakeholders are those organisations within the spectrum of criminal justice agencies that give operational effect to criminal justice and have a professional interest in the effectiveness of the justice system. As the diagram indicates, all three clusters have an overlapping involvement in the delivery of criminal justice, but somewhat different primary interests in the outcomes of the justice process.

The main purpose of the illustration is to indicate the breadth of involvement in the delivery of criminal justice within many different national jurisdictions, the nature of the relationships between the clusters, and thus the difficulty of making justice 'inclusive' unless there is a clear view of which interest groups have a reasonable claim to centrality within the wide complex of agendas that necessarily become involved. Importantly for our discussion in this work, the 'beneficiary' stakeholders (communities, close others and the general public) are given an evident status within a restorative and reparative justice model, and are not consigned to a peripheral or incidental place within the margins of the justice process as too frequently becomes the case with the 'traditional' justice model. It is this form of inclusiveness that is the hallmark of restorative justice.

Inclusive justice involves recognition of all the legitimate interests within the justice process, and evident acknowledgement of this legitimacy. It is for this reason that I believe that Zehr's analysis, although helpful, is actually incomplete. The role of the state within restorative justice should be central since it determines criminal justice policy, employs the officials who put policy into practice, and has a direct

What is Restorative Justice, and What Does it Offer? 47

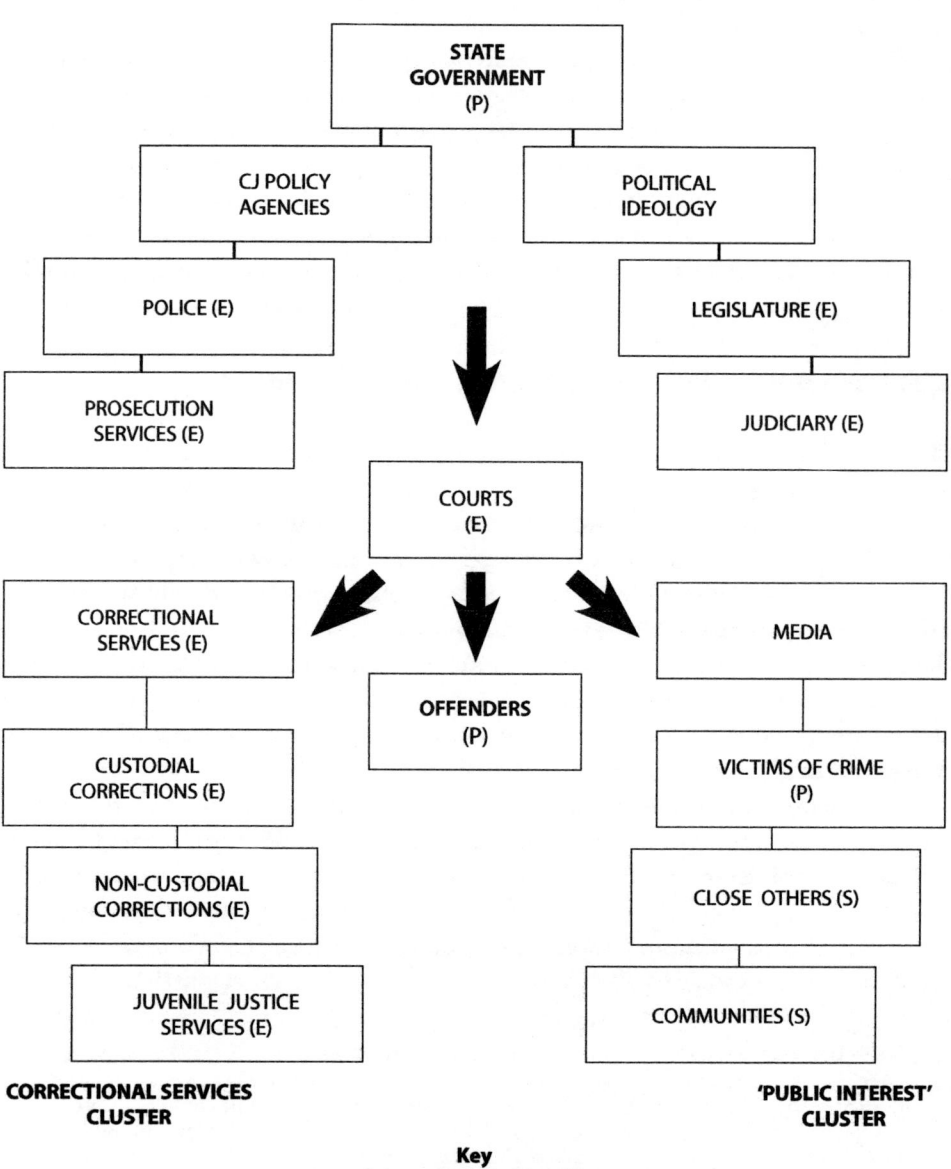

Figure 2:1 A 'Stakeholder' Model of Restorative and Reparative Justice

responsibility for providing the resources that make practice operational. Given this extent of direct involvement, it is difficult to perceive how the state can be other than a primary stakeholder.

Inclusiveness does, however, go beyond this, particularly within a restorative justice model of corrections. For while it is self-evident that offenders and victims of crime have the primary involvement in the commission of offences, the 'beneficiary' stakeholders within the 'public interest' cluster ultimately pay for, and are thus at least entitled to receive, outcomes from the criminal justice process that are socially beneficial. As we have seen in *Chapter 1*, it is at the least doubtful whether an incarcerative model of justice delivers substantial social benefit other than short-term public protection, and it is altogether certain that it is considerably ineffective in reducing reoffending.

COMMUNITY INVOLVEMENT IN JUSTICE

The term 'community' has widely different meanings depending upon the context in which it is used.[9] The title of this book assumes that within any democratic society there exists a 'centre-ground' within the population that is reasonably informed and questioning in matters of the public interest, moderate in a political and intellectual sense, and willing to enter into debate without preconceptions about the outcome. These are the passengers on the Clapham Omnibus. As we shall see in later chapters, however, there is an aspect of 'community' in relation to the operation of prisons and non-custodial sanctions that has a more immediate territorial proximity to correctional facilities with which a level of co-operative involvement might benefit the purposes of criminal justice.

An essential feature of restorative justice is its aim to make the processes of criminal justice more purposeful and understandable to ordinary citizens, to enable offenders to take responsibility for their actions and their lives, and to give victims of crime the consideration that they deserve. These purposes cannot be fulfilled in an exclusive penal vacuum that effectively denies the existence of the wider public

---

9. For instance, Howard Zehr (2002 *op. cit*.: 25-6) identifies communities of 'space' such as towns and precincts in which people live and interact, and communities of 'care' or the micro-communities of family, kinship and close others immediately involved with them. Then there are communities such as religious groups and associations that have common purposes or interests beyond a territorial or relationship affinity. Other forms of 'community' tend to be of a more abstract nature described in terms such as 'the general public' that assumes a homogeneous identity that may be deceptive. There is also, however, a sense of 'community' as it is found in the more ancient cultures of First Nation and Aboriginal peoples throughout the world in which commonly shared values, language, customs and ideals provide the cohesive force that maintains a communitarian ethos. Within this work the term is used to identify that element of any society with a legitimate and reasonably informed public interest in the operation and outcomes of criminal justice exemplified by the 'passenger on the Clapham Omnibus'. Such an approach excludes (by implication) the holders of views of an extreme, immoderate or fundamentalist nature, the excessively punitive, and those penal 'abolitionists' whose preference is for the abandonment of all or any forms of custodial corrections.

community, because to act in such a manner subjugates the humanity of offenders to state power to a less than reasonable extent. The vast majority of offenders sentenced to custody return to the communities from which they were removed, and those made the subject of non-custodial corrections are required to fulfil the terms of their sanctions within the community environment. For these reasons alone, and for others that will become evident later, local communities should have an actively participative role in the delivery of criminal justice.

Paul McCold (2004: 162) helpfully reminds us that 'offenders harm more than their victims. They damage their relationships with their communities of care by betraying trust and create a negative relationship with the victim's communities of care.'[10] He further points out that these important micro-communities are often and in many respects the strongest influences that shape and maintain the attitudes and life patterns of offenders. Thus, particularly in the field of juvenile justice but also more generally, it is important to include members of these micro-communities in restorative justice practices such as family group conferencing (FGC) and VOM.

As will become evident in *Chapters 11* and *12*, community involvement in justice can also be encouraged through the work of voluntary groups such as Independent Monitoring Boards (IMB)[11] in prisons, access to the counselling services of organisations like the Samaritans, and by the involvement of charitable groups that specialise in addiction therapy and counselling, marital relationships, and the like.[12] Most UK prisons also have accredited Prison Visitors recruited from within local communities and sponsored by the Faith Centre (or Chaplaincy) who befriend inmates who have no close relatives to visit them on a regular basis.

Within the non-custodial sector of corrections, communities have the potential for even more extensive involvement and innovation, as we shall see in *Chapter 13*. However, within a restorative and reparative concept of corrections, much closer links may be envisaged between the custodial and non-custodial sectors. This development is as critical for the social reintegration of offenders within communities as it is for the reduction of reoffending. Indeed, if restorative justice is to achieve its true meaning, then reparation, restoration and reintegration must combine in a sequential manner to enable ex-offenders to lead law-abiding lives. This is the process formerly described as 'rehabilitation', but which lost its meaning in the wake of the 'Nothing Works' era of the 1970s and 1980s previously noted in *Chapter 1*.

---

10. P. McCold (2004), 'What Is The Role Of Community In Restorative Justice Theory And Practice? In H. Zehr and B. Toews (eds), *Critical Issues in Restorative Justice*, Monsey, NY: Criminal Justice Press and Cullompton, Devon, UK: Willan Publishing, pp.155-172.
11. Independent Monitoring Boards (IMBs) have replaced the former Boards of Visitors (BOV) in prisons in England and Wales. Each prison establishment (including Young Offender Institutions – YOIs) must have a Board appointed by the Ministry of Justice. Boards comprise voluntary membership charged with general oversight of the management, inmate custody and conditions aspects of day-to-day operation.
12. Notable among such agencies are Alcoholics Anonymous (AA), Turning Point for drug addiction and abuse, and RELATE which specialises in relationship counselling.

A RE-ASSESSMENT OF CAUSES AND EFFECTS OF CRIME

One of the main shortcomings of the traditional model that restorative justice seeks to address may be summed up in the term 'justice as fairness'. Fairness in this context has a wider meaning than merely that of 'even-handedness' and impartiality, of equality and the absence of bias – admirable and necessary as such qualities may be. Being 'tough on crime' is only acceptable if it is accompanied by a genuine resolve to be equally 'tough on the causes of crime'. This means not just punishing wrongdoing because it is identified as criminal by law, but by fashioning responses to offending in a manner that addresses the social disparities that give rise to crime and the social deficits of offenders, and make future illegal behaviour less likely.

It is a more or less taken for granted fact that in most modern societies the major proportion of all crime is committed by that element of the total community which is less affluent, educationally under-achieving, lacking in social and emotional skills, and which lives in areas of relative deprivation in terms of housing, health, and access to amenities. People thus marginalised do not remain so out of choice, but because such conditions become a way of life from which escape is difficult, if not almost impossible, unless some form of intervention occurs to alleviate the situation.

In such circumstances, resort to criminal activity becomes little more than a culturally accepted means of redressing the outcomes of relative deprivation and lesser eligibility by the commission of acts that the law defines as illegal.[13] However, because these acts infringe the law they become punishable, and within a retributive mode of justice *must* be punished because the law has been violated rather than, necessarily, because harm has been done. Thus the law is requited, but those harmed remain injured and those who harm them remain 'criminal'. Meanwhile, nothing of substance is done to change the circumstances of either of the parties – other perhaps than for the worse.

Restorative justice perceives this state of affairs as an unjust, 'no-win' situation. Those offended against have little or no status within the process, and frequently no redress other than through recourse to civil justice, while those who offend have no opportunity to make amends for the harm caused, and neither are they necessarily required (or expected) to acknowledge any responsibility for that harm. Thus within the 'traditional' concept of justice neither the causes nor the effects of crime are addressed other than symbolically through the process of retributive punishment.

As we shall see in *Chapter 3*, such a situation is strictly avoidable and, in fair-

---

13. See here, for example, explanations within the work of David Garland and Peter Young (1983), *The Power to Punish*, London: Heinemann, and previously, of Paul Wiles (1976), *The Sociology of Crime and Delinquency in Britain*, London: Martin Robertson. Many of the earlier accounts of deviance written during the 1960s and 1970s reflect a similar theme (e.g. Howard Becker (1963), David Matza, (1964 and 1969), Edwin Lemert, (1967); Steven Box, (1971), and, later, Keith Bottomley, (1979)).

ness to all concerned, should be avoided. Whether or not this absolutely requires a retreat from retributive punishment becomes an interesting matter of debate. As we shall also note, however, these difficulties are made worse when punishment is used for purposes other than dealing strictly and equitably with the harm caused by offences: where, for instance, it is used in what John Blad (2003 and 2006a) has so aptly described as an 'instrumental' manner to pursue other social policy objectives other than justice.

We see evidence of this tendency in the singling out of specific forms of offending for exemplary punishment justified by the supposed need for 'public protection' deriving from assessments of individual dangerousness that may have no basis in reality, and may, in fact, be entirely unsubstantiated. In Britain, this form of sentencing is particularly prevalent in relation to sexual offences, and the arrangements for it that have their origins in legislative activity dating back to 2000 as we shall see in *Chapters 3* and *4*.[14] Worse, such measures stand a significant risk of being falsely predicted and may be entirely unjustified (see, e.g. Bottoms, 1977; Cornwell, 1989; Matravers and Hughes, 2003: 52-3). They are, however, among the 'effects' of crime in addition to the dysfunctional nature of the collateral social damage that an excessively punitive and retributive culture of punishment imposes on offenders, victims and communities as we shall see as this work unfolds.

Where, then, does this leave restorative justice in its quest to provide better justice that is 'fairer' to offenders, victims and society? John Blad (2006b) provides the following telling analysis:

> The *functional* reasons for a restorative culture to develop are all related to the socially destructive, dysfunctional and often even counter-productive consequences of over-criminalisation and over-penalisation. So there are good reasons for expanding restorative practices. But if we want to continue to maximise the application of restorative practices in the field of criminal justice and still keep their restorative integrity, the process of defining restorative practices into the punitive–cultural and structural framework can only be counteracted by developing, communicating and safeguarding a very clear identity of restorative justice, differentiated from the identity of punitive justice. We should strive for an integration of restorative practices within the criminal justice system *understood* as restorative practices and *not* as punitive practices. In view of the dominance of [the] punitive culture this is not an easy task. (Blad, 2006b: 113).

As we shall see, and indeed as a central theme running throughout the remaining chapters of this work, restorative and retributive approaches have to reach an accommodation at both the philosophical and the practical levels. *Chapter 3* provides a basis for understanding the complexity of this need both in theory and in practice.

---

14. See here the White Papers: *Review of Sex Offences, Setting the Boundaries* (Home Office 2000); *Criminal Justice: The Way Ahead*, (Home Office 2001a); the *Review of the Sentencing Framework, Making Punishments Work* (Home Office 2001b); *Protecting the Public*, (Home Office 2002b); *Justice for All* (Home Office 2002c); and, ultimately, the Criminal Justice Act 2003.

CHAPTER 3

Does Restorative Justice 'Do Away' With Retribution?

In the concluding part of his analysis of how, and in what terms, restorative justice should be conceived (mentioned in the previous chapter), Gerry Johnstone (2004 *op. cit.*) made the following somewhat contentious observation:

> It is an act of power to direct social resources and people's minds towards waging battle against 'crime' as officially defined, as opposed to preventing and remedying the distress, poverty and inequality that frequently arises from 'lawful' social policies and practices. A serious charge against the movement for restorative justice is that instead of questioning the power-based act of defining and prioritising social problems, it restricts itself to the question of how the battle against crime should be waged. We might well agree that it is better that, in the battle against crime, it is both more ethical and more effective to deploy restorative justice than retributive justice. Yet, to the extent that the movement for restorative justice has so far put the spotlight on crime, as officially-defined, and deflected it from other forms of social harm, it is open to the charge that it is itself acting inconsistently with the principles of restorative justice. (Johnstone, 2004:14) (parentheses omitted).[1]

There are a number of points that need to be made about this accusation which affect the discussion within this particular chapter. First, restorative justice does not at all content itself with crime as 'officially defined' as we have already seen in Howard Zehr's re-definition of criminal and restorative justice (Zehr, 2002 *op. cit.*:19-21). Secondly, as I have pointed out in other work which, admittedly, Johnstone's commentary pre-dates, restorative justice is conscious of the fact that 'it is morally and socially irresponsible and unreasonable to continue to exclude victims of crime from due consideration; it is pointless to incarcerate offenders without addressing their social deficits or enabling them to make reparation; and it is mindless to be "tough on crime" without being equally energetic about redressing the causes of crime.' (Cornwell, 2007 *op. cit.*: x). Thirdly, as this chapter will make clear, the ultimate choice is possibly not *between* restorative and retributive justice, but rather about the extent to which a retributive element in criminal punishment is, or is not, consistent with the aims of restorative justice.

And fourthly in relation to Johnstone's conclusions, restorative justice is, as its name implies, primarily (though not solely) concerned with delivery of better justice rather than changing the entire political discourse of social policy. While it does not, in any sense, condone the dysfunctional outcomes of 'lawful' social policies and practices, it can only, at best, indicate the deficiencies of such, and the

---

1. G. Johnstone (2004) *op. cit.*

effects of these deficiencies on offending and offenders. Moreover, to do so is entirely consistent with its fundamental principles as articulated by Zehr and Mika (1998).[2]

LEGALLY PUNITIVE RESPONSES TO CRIME

One of the most intriguing aspects of the many learned and excellent books that have been written on the subject of criminal punishment is the persistent disagreement about what it is, precisely, that this practice - so widely used – is actually designed to achieve. Stated in the broadest of terms, the argument seems to be polarised into two quite different approaches that have historically become regarded as the main 'justifications'[3] of punishment as a response to crime.

To those of a retributive disposition, the answer appears to be deceptively simple. Punishment is necessary (and moreover essential) because a law has been broken, and justice requires that the person found guilty of the offence should suffer, and indeed *deserves* to suffer, to an extent at least in some reasonable proportion to the seriousness of the wrongdoing and the harm that this causes. This is the essence of what has, in the past, been described as the 'classical' approach to crime and punishment that emerged in the mid-eighteenth century and has cast a long shadow over criminology to this day.[4] Thus stated, the process of punishment – however severe or lenient – is an inevitably retrospective (or backward-looking) one that upholds the integrity of the law, but which may, co-incidentally, be instrumental in persuading other would-be offenders to refrain from similar wrongdoing.

A different approach was adopted by those moral philosophers and criminologists usually described as being of the 'utilitarian'[5] tradition, and who in the mid-nineteenth century and onwards attempted to present a different view of criminal punishment based upon its social usefulness (or 'utility') in relation to offenders, victims and the general population. The utilitarian position was based in the belief that retributive punishment served little purpose in a social sense, did even less to encourage reformed behaviour in offenders, and, ultimately, was detrimental to the general well-being of the wider population. Put another way, the utilitarians believed that punishment could only be justified if it promoted a greater social benefit than merely inflicting pain for the sake of the law being upheld.

Without doubt, the apparent persuasiveness of the utilitarian argument served

---

2. H. Zehr and H. Mika (1998) *op. cit.*, pp. 47-55.
3. Here I use the term 'justification' to mean the moral and philosophical reasoning process that makes the socially unusual or unpleasant process of punishment acceptable in the interests of justice and fairness.
4. Exemplified particularly in the writing of Caesare Beccaria (1764) in his treatise *On Crimes and Punishment* (translated by H. Paolucci), Indianapolis: Bobbs Merrill (1963).
5. A tradition of thinking about crime and punishment in terms of its socially beneficial effects, characterised in the writing of Thomas Hobbes (1973), Jeremy Bentham (1830, 1962), John Stuart Mill (1859 and 1951), and later John Rawls (1955 and 1958) and H. L. A. Hart (1968).

more to muddy rather than clarify the waters of a developing criminological science throughout the twentieth century. For while it made possible the proposal of a rehabilitative approach to dealing with offenders in both their own and the wider social interest, its ambiguity towards promoting social benefit through the process of punishment was widely evident and exploitable by those of a retributive inclination. This was particularly marked in relation to the supposedly beneficial effects of general deterrence[6] through the exemplary imposition of penal sanctions.

Few would dissent from the view that when criminal and harmful acts are committed, those who offend and cause the harm should be brought to account for their actions. The question that arises from such an assertion is: what under-pinning rationale best allows sanctions to be devised and imposed that will be of moral and practical usefulness to all the parties affected by the act of wrong-doing? These parties, as we have noted earlier in *Chapter 2*, are the 'stakeholders' in the criminal justice process, and include (at the least) offenders, victims and communities in addition to the wider public and the state. Each of these stakeholders has legitimate expectations of the punishment process and its outcomes, though it is in all respects predominantly desirable that crime reduction should result from it. Let us first of all deal with the case that can be made for relying upon retributive justice.

RETRIBUTIVE JUSTICE 'UNDRESSED'

Within the popular understanding of the term 'retribution' there is, at the least, some notion of a process or practice that 'pays back' a person – and in this sense it must be assumed someone who has done wrong – in some measure of unpleasant consequence[7] for the harm caused by an offence. This apparently reciprocal activity is usually deemed to be morally justified to that extent (only) which bears some evident relationship to the degree of the harm occasioned, and thus it is argued, the 'seriousness' of the wrongful action. Here we may already perceive a number of conceptual and definitional difficulties, but at this point it should be noted that the use of punishment for such a purpose is clearly dependent upon an offence having been committed, and a person (or persons) having been adjudged guilty by a competent authority of committing the offence in question.

The discussion so far leads us to a need to confront at least three very difficult

---

6. The concept of general deterrence suggests that through the process of punishing those guilty of offences, others who might be tempted to offend similarly will be persuaded to refrain from unlawful conduct for fear of the same consequences. There are, however, significant difficulties in measuring the actual effects of general deterrence as I have explained in some detail in earlier work: see D. J. Cornwell (2006) *op. cit.*, at *Chapter 4*, pp.53-65.
7. In much of the criminological literature the term 'pain' is evident in a definitional sense here, though I would prefer to avoid such usage on the basis that it encourages a notion of vindictiveness that is not necessarily consistent with a reasonable concept of reciprocity – and hence of desert.

issues: first, the matter of 'inevitability'; secondly, that of proportionality; and third, the notion of desert. We might also have added a *proviso* within the definition to the effect that it would only be morally justifiable to punish persons deemed to be mentally competent to distinguish between right and wrong actions, and who had, in the course of their offending, acted with *mens rea* (wrongful intent) or culpable negligence.

As to the first issue of 'inevitability', the concept of retributive justice effectively compels us to punish to a far greater extent as a consequence of the law having been broken, than out of concern for who has been harmed, and how badly. In fact, we punish because a failure or unwillingness to do so would, in the retributivist view, weaken the moral status of the law. This compulsion to punish frequently proves to have a spiralling effect because it is evident that many offenders, and indeed would-be offenders are not deterred as a result of sanctions being imposed, and thus increasing 'doses' of punishment are presumed to be necessary to secure their unwilling compliance. This means that penalties increase in severity to the extent that more and more offenders end up in prison custody, and for longer and longer periods of time.

Allied to the situation just described is the difficulty of deciding how much punishment is strictly necessary or proportionate to the harm caused by offences, and that of maintaining this notion of proportionality between different forms of offending. In England and Wales during the past decade, and in particular since the enactment of the Criminal Justice Act 2003 (CJA 2003), there has been a marked increase in the number of people in prisons serving indeterminate sentences.[8] In fact, the number of people detained indefinitely in England and Wales is greater than in all the other member states of the European Union together.[9] This increase in the use of indeterminate sentences clearly signals a decreasing emphasis on proportionality in sentencing since those so sentenced will remain in custody until deemed by the Parole Board safe to be released, rather than for a finite period of time deemed necessary to mark the seriousness of their offences.

Increasing use of indeterminate sentencing is not, however, the only sign that the principle of proportionality in sentencing has been eroded significantly over the past decade in Britain – or indeed elsewhere. During the decade 1995-2005, use of

---

8. The CJA 2003 made provision for offenders guilty of committing serious violent and/or sexual offences after April 2005 to be sentenced to a new indeterminate public protection sentence, and kept in prison until the Parole Board deems them safe to be released. Between February 2007 and March 2008 the number of prisoners serving IPP sentences increased by 56%, from 2,300 to 4,050. The total number of prisoners (including those sentenced to life imprisonment serving indeterminate sentences) stood at 12,143 in February 2009, an increase of 13% on the February 2008 total of 10,754. During the same period a total of 7,648 people were serving sentences of under 12 months duration in February 2009, a decrease of 14% on the February 2008 level of 8,859. Source: Ministry of Justice (2009), *Population in Custody*, London: NOMS (February).
9. Prison Reform Trust (2007a) *Life Sentence Prisoners* (Briefing Paper) available in html and pdf format at http://www.prisonreformtrust.org.uk/subsectionaspd?id=345.

imprisonment as a punishment for indictable offences in England and Wales rose by 25 *per cent*, and the average length of such sentences similarly increased by 26 *per cent*.[10] Within a sentencing climate dominated by considerations of retribution and deterrence, these statistical measures become clear indicators of an increasingly more punitive approach to offending adopted during the past ten years. The provisions within the CJA 2003 specifically singled out violent and sexual offences for increased severity of sentencing for the purposes of public protection rather than, necessarily, as a measure of the seriousness of such crimes.

Although the principle of proportionality has long been held to matter within criminal punishment and sentencing philosophy, it is evident that it amounts to little more than a good intention in a practical sense. How, in any precise manner, does the sentencing official weigh the seriousness of one rape against another, or one burglary against another, in terms of the extent of the sanction deserved? We might argue that this can be achieved in part through sentencing *maxima* and *minima*, but the same outcomes may vary markedly as between different courts. Is a rape or robbery committed ten years ago more or less serious than a rape or robbery committed today? Indeed, if either or both are or were similarly harmful, how can we justify a considerable increase in the severity of punishment other than on the basis of a preference for more retributive sanctions? These are some of the questions that have to be answered if the case for retributive and deterrent punishment is to be sustained.

As to the concept of desert, supporters of retributive justice (e.g. Mundle, 1954: 65-82, and Postscript 1968; Baier, 1955: 130-137; and Armstrong, 1961: 138-158) have traditionally maintained that punishment is justified on the basis that it is deserved entirely because the actions that provoke us to punish (crimes) are both morally and legally wrong.[11] So far, so good, the observer might be tempted to respond, but there are other equally important issues to be weighed in this discussion. While the argument for desert may be sustainable in principle, it does not tell us in any particular instance *how much* punishment is either necessary or reasonable. Indeed, the principle of parsimony (or frugality) in the infliction of punishment advanced originally by Jeremy Bentham (1948)[12] urges us to impose the *minimum* amount of sanction consistent with adequately censuring the seriousness of offences. Thus, it might be argued, the widespread use of indeterminate sentences is not only disproportionate but also undeserved.

Now as John Blad (2006a: 137) has so perceptively argued, we are in an era

---

10. Source: Home Office (2007), *Sentencing Statistics 2005*, London: Home Office Research, Development and Statistics Directorate at: http://press.homeoffice.gov.uk/press-releases/sentencingstatistics/2005?version=1
11. All three of the authors cited here made significant contributions to the compilation by H.B. Acton (ed) (1969), *The Philosophy of Punishment: A Collection of Papers*, London: Macmillan at the pages indicated.
12. J. Bentham (1948), *An Introduction to the Principles of Morals and Legislation*, London: Basil Blackwell, in chapter xv, section xi.

in which 'penal instrumentalism' reigns, and criminal punishment of a predominantly retributive nature has become a powerful instrument of social policy that deliberately ignores the limits that should be imposed on its use.[13] This means, in effect, that the processes of criminal justice have been harnessed to the pursuit of social control objectives that are far removed from the concept of 'justice as fairness'. Worse still, perhaps, retributive justice contrives to largely ignore the situation and needs of victims, and contributes little, if anything, towards changing the offending behaviour of criminals.

What retributive justice does achieve, albeit very expensively, is the social incapacitation of offenders and a (temporary) means of public protection through excessive use of custodial punishment. Such is, however, an entirely false economy that merely postpones reoffending rather than addresses its root causes in any practical manner. In so doing, retributive justice creates extensive collateral damage within the social structure, punishing not only offenders excessively, but also those immediately dependent on them who have not committed offences. Such a form of 'punishment by proxy' might be regarded by some as an unintended consequence of penal instrumentalism, but there is no escaping its vicarious nature.

RESTORATIVE PENOLOGY: A 'NEO-REHABILITATIVE' APPROACH?

As we have already seen in *Chapter 2*, the restorative approach to criminal justice is a far cry from the retributive model identified in the previous section of this chapter. Some critics of restorative penology have argued that it amounts to a thinly-disguised attempt to return to a rehabilitative era of justice, but without the implicit disadvantageous characteristics that led to its abandonment in the 1970s. I believe this criticism is erroneous for a number of reasons that I shall indicate briefly in the paragraphs that follow within this section.

At the outset it is reasonable to agree that a restorative penology has far more in common with the former rehabilitative ethic than it has with a retributive concept of criminal punishment and corrections. This much said, however, restorative justice does not countenance the use of sentencing indeterminacy[14] either for the purposes of 'treatment' in prisons, or as an indefinite form of custody for public protection. The former practice became widespread in the 1960s and 1970s within a British parole system that made release from life and long determinate sentences contingent upon professional judgements and assessments that therapeutic interventions had reduced dangerousness to an acceptable level within a quasi-medical treatment

---

13. J. R. Blad (2006a) op cit., 'The Seductiveness of Punishment and the Case for Restorative Justice: The Netherlands', in D.J. Cornwell (2006), *op. cit.*, pp. 135-148.
14. Other, perhaps, than in the existing circumstances in Britain in which life sentences are a mandatory form of sentence for the crime of murder.

model. The latter has been discussed earlier in this chapter and requires no further elaboration here.

It is also the case that a restorative model of corrections seeks the reintegration of offenders back into the community as a result of experiencing penal sanctions – whether custodial or non-custodial in nature, but having addressed the causes of their wrongful behaviour, and having made reparation to victims of crime. A restorative approach to correctional practice implies the improvement of offender life and social competencies as a means towards adopting a crime-free lifestyle, enhanced employability, and social acceptance. It does, however, acknowledge that some offenders may decline the opportunity to participate in reparative and restorative correctional regimes, and is able to accommodate this within a bifurcated approach to sentencing and custodial management.[15]

Unlike either the retributive or the former rehabilitative model, restorative justice recognises and acknowledges the status and needs of victims, and makes a deliberate effort to address these in a practical way as part of the process of offender reintegration within their communities. Indeed, reintegration is, in a restorative correctional sense, contingent upon victim reparation having been made. This stands in stark contrast with a retributive penology that produces overcrowded prison conditions and regimes within which it is entirely unrealistic to believe that attempts to rehabilitate inmates have other than the most superficial meaning.

Many correctional practitioners, and particularly those who work in prisons are sceptical about the entire concept of rehabilitating offenders within a custodial environment that allows minimal, if any, access to the community beyond the perimeter. For although educational provision can be of great assistance in increasing basic literacy and numeracy, the 'one size fits all' nature of the majority of cognitive behavioural programmes does little to address the individual pathology, deficits or needs of offenders other than in the most general sense. We shall return to these issues in greater detail in *Chapters 9* and *10*. Adoption of a law-abiding lifestyle and avoidance of repeated offending require a much closer relationship amounting almost to partnership between prisons and their immediate communities if social reintegration of those imprisoned is to be successful. This, the former rehabilitative model never either envisaged or encouraged.

Penal policies based in retributive incapacitation and general deterrence derive more from the perceived need to manage social risk than to change offending behaviour. High rates of recidivism reveal very clearly that 'prison doesn't work', and that large numbers of predominantly young, embittered, unimproved and criminally more sophisticated people return to their communities from prisons without employment prospects and to a life of 'drifting' that makes them an easy prey to reoffending.

---

15. For an explanation of this approach, see Cornwell (2007), *op. cit.*, at pp. 133-135.

Also, unlike the prevailing retributive or the former rehabilitative model, restorative penology requires offenders to take responsibility for their offences, for the harm caused to victims, and for their own behaviour and improvement. As we shall see in the chapter that follows, this can be very demanding, but it can also make prisons much easier and safer places to manage effectively. The same is also the case with community sanctions operated within a reparative and restorative model of corrections, even though it is undeniable that this ethos brings with it an element of social risk that sits uneasily alongside the risk-averse nature of the public protection model of penology that prevails widely in contemporary societies.

Thus, in relation to the question of whether a restorative penology amounts to a re-visited form 'rehabilitation by stealth', it should be evident that it would, if adopted, pursue a very different approach towards the re-socialisation and reintegration of offenders and communities from that of the rehabilitative model of the previous century. And although the philosophical purposes of both might appear to display superficial similarities, the restorative penology acknowledges an element of social risk that the rehabilitative 'treatment' model was unwilling and indeed unable to contemplate.

IS RESTORATIVE PENOLOGY ANTI-RETRIBUTIVE?

The answer to this important question, like the answers to so many of the more complex issues in moral philosophy and contemporary criminology, is unavoidably ambiguous. In a strict sense, restorative justice accepts and accommodates the necessity for an element of retributive philosophy and practice as a response to criminal wrongdoing. It does so on the basis that crime, in the majority of its presenting forms, violates people and causes them harm and suffering. To this extent it is entirely reasonable to insist that those who perpetrate crime should suffer unpleasant consequences as the social response to their offending behaviour.

This stated, however, restorative justice does not countenance retributive punishment of an excessive nature used instrumentally for purposes other than strict justice. It differs from retributive justice insofar as it is essentially forward rather than backward looking, seeking to 'put wrongs right' and heal broken relationships instead of focusing predominantly on the need to punish for punishment's sake. Restorative justice is strongly opposed to the use of indeterminate sentences, insisting that it is every offender's right to know the extent of the punishment imposed upon them, and for this punishment not to be arbitrarily extended for the purposes of social protection. But perhaps the main point of difference is that restorative justice acknowledges the situation and needs of victims and attempts to do something to alleviate the harm done to them: retributive justice largely ignores victims and focuses almost entirely on offenders and offences.

However, as Howard Zehr (2002 *op. cit.*: 58) has pointed out in quoting Conrad Brunk[16], 'retribution and restoration are not the polar opposites that we often assume.' He continues:

> In fact they have much in common. A primary goal of both retributive theory and restorative theory is to vindicate through reciprocity, by evening the score. Where they differ is in what each suggests will effectively right the balance ... Both retributive and restorative theories of justice acknowledge a basic moral intuition that a balance has been thrown off by a wrongdoing. Consequently, the victim deserves something and the offender owes something. Both approaches argue that there must be a proportional relationship between the act and the response. They differ, however, on the currency that will fulfil the obligations and right the balance. (Zehr, 2002 *op. cit.*: 58-9).

Here once again, we are confronted with the issue of proportionality, though in a somewhat different context from that previously discussed. Retributive justice theory places emphasis on the need for punishment to be proportionate to the gravity of crime (e.g. Hart, 1968; von Hirsch, 1976: 66; Galligan, 1981; Hudson, 1987: 40-41)[17], but then frequently ignores this by imposing 'incremental' or indeterminate punishment for reasons external to the seriousness of the action.

Another issue that proponents of restorative justice have to address is that of whether, and to what extent, reparation should (or can) be proportionate (Wright, 2003:17). For just as it is evidently difficult to equate harm and culpability with the extent of the punitive response in an accurate and consistent manner, so also it is problematic to determine with any certainty the amount of reparation that is appropriate in individual cases and between similar cases. The issue of proportionality is, therefore, potentially a difficult one for both retributive and restorative justice, though for different reasons.

Historically, criminal justice within all the major democracies of the world has displayed a remarkably pendulum-like movement since the end of World War 2. Throughout this period spanning more than sixty years the centrality of retribution within criminal punishment has remained the most consistently maintained of its supposed justifications.[18] Though during the heyday of the rehabilitative era of the 1960s and early 1970s a lesser emphasis was placed on retribution as a dominant

---

16. C. Brunk (2001), 'Restorative Justice and the Philosophical Theories of Criminal Punishment' in M.L. Hadley (ed), *The Spiritual Roots of Restorative Justice*, Albany, NY: State University of New York Press, pp. 31-56.
17. Here see in particular the accounts provided in A. von Hirsch (1976) *op. cit.*, at p.69, and B. Hudson (1987) *op. cit.*, at pp.38-41. Galligan's contribution to this general debate is an interesting one, written as it was in 1981 at a time when the tide had already turned against rehabilitation, but the so-called 'justice model' on which von Hirsch's work (cited above) made a major impact had but recently become accepted in an operational sense. See: D.J. Galligan (1981), 'The Return to Retribution in Penal Theory', in C.H.F. Tapper (ed), *Crime, Proof and Punishment* (Essays in Honour of Sir Rupert Cross), London: Butterworth, pp.144-171.
18. These being retribution, deterrence (both general and specific), reform and rehabilitation.

purpose of punishment, this quickly changed with the emergence of the desert-based justice model of the late 1970s and 1980s. It was, however, during the 1990s that matters changed dramatically with a much more explicit and punitive brand of retributivism dominating the criminological landscape. This 'naked' retributivism was born of frustration with increasing serious crime in increasingly affluent societies, combined with high rates of recidivism that clearly indicated the fragility of deterrence as a major component of criminal justice policy formulation.

However strong the emotional appeal of the 'moral rightness' of retribution may be within the popular mind and political conceptions of justice, the more moderate analyst of crime and justice still retains strong reservations when retribution (almost alone) becomes both the dominant and oppressive guiding principle and component of criminal justice policies. Its oppressiveness stems from its capacity to adopt a draconian 'toughness' on crime and criminals without addressing either the causes of crime in affluent societies or its victims. It is these reservations that have led to the search for a way of 'doing justice better' through the more humane and constructive concept of restorative justice.

Thus we arrive at the answers to both the question posed at the start of this section and the question that forms the title of this chapter. Restorative justice is not fundamentally anti-retributive, but it is firmly opposed to excessive reliance on retributivism as the guiding force within criminal justice. Retribution has its rightful place within the overall aims and purposes of criminal punishment, but that punishment becomes morally degraded by excessive resort to retributive policies and practices.

And as to the second question, there is no doubt that restorative justice has to accommodate a retributive element within its own punishment philosophy, since without it the concept of sanctions for wrongdoing has no intelligible meaning. In this respect, therefore, restorative justice cannot 'do away' with retribution but it can moderate its influence and genuinely seeks to do so. Proponents of restorative justice hope that a day will come when justice will be more purposeful and even-handed to all the stakeholders that it should legitimately consider. These, it will be recalled, are principally offenders, victims and communities.

The point made by John Blad in the concluding part of the previous chapter (p.51 *supra*) is, however, profoundly important. For although restorative justice cannot ignore that element of retributive action that is inherent in all punishments and sanctions, it has to create not only its own unambiguous identity, but also be *understood* to insist that its primary motivations are to *repair* the harm done by offending and offences, ensure that *reparation* is made to victims of crime, and thus *restore* offenders to their place in communities having made an attempt to put right the harm caused by their offences. This is very different from punishing for the sake of it, for the sake of being seen to do so, and frequently to an unnecessary extent.

Within a world in which the 'climate' of criminal punishment has become increasingly hostile towards offenders – at least from the vantage point of the moral high ground occupied by those who make laws or who refrain from offending – the idea of punishing less or differently will pose difficulties. The most frequently encountered reason for maintaining or increasing severity of sanctions is that not to do so would 'increase public risk'. In the chapter that follows we examine this assertion and assess its validity, since it may contain more superstition than substance. If such were to be the case, then it would make a restorative and reparative penology much more easily understood.

CHAPTER 4

Would Wider Use of Restorative Justice Increase Public Risk?

I have deliberately chosen to include this very difficult question at this stage of the discussion within this book because it seems to epitomise the complex dilemmas that impinge upon the way in which criminal justice policies are formed as responses to the politically sensitive issues involved in crime and crime control. In Britain, as in so many other countries of the world, politicians anxious to retain their electoral credibility cannot afford to disregard the 'mood and temper' of the public in relation to crime, but yet fashion crime control policies that seldom reflect any accurate analysis of what the average citizen *really* knows about criminal offending or the processes of justice.

The situation is not helped by the constantly high profile afforded to crime – and in particular violent or sexual crime - by the mass media whose primary interest lies in maintaining circulation and profit, and for whom the sensationalism of crime is a powerful means of attracting readership and audiences. Indeed, it might be argued that the influence exerted by the media in contemporary societies is as pivotal to the formation of political opinions as it is to that of public opinion – whatever that actually is.

This fascinating triangle of 'interests' is completed at intervals in which electoral considerations dominate the political discourse and those seeking to gain or retain the power to govern have to rely on the majority support of the voting public. It is, therefore, no surprise that issues relating to crime and criminal justice occupy a prominent position within the hierarchy of electoral manifesto pledges and initiatives devised by political parties to secure voter allegiance.

The difficulty with all of this is that it is very questionable whether there is any such thing as an identifiable consensus within what is called 'public opinion', or whether what is perceived as constituting 'public opinion' is to any significant extent accurately informed about criminal justice issues. A considerable amount of research evidence points to the contrary[1], and this is unfortunate since where *mis*information also occurs, it opens wide the door for politicians and their advisers to construct policies based on populist appeal and dogma rather than on criminological evidence. (e.g. Indermaur and Hough, 2002; Hough and Park, 2002).

---

1. See, for example, the work of M. Hough and J. Roberts (eds.) (1998), *Attitudes to Crime and Punishment: Findings from the British Crime Survey*, Home Office Research Studies 179, London: HMSO, pp.1-79, and the account of S. Maruna and A. King (2004), 'Public Opinion and Community Penalties', in A.E. Bottoms, S. Rex and G. Robinson (eds), *Alternatives to Prison: Options for an Insecure Society*, Devon, UK: Willan Publishing at pp.83-112.

CRIME AND PUBLIC RISK

If the officially published statistics on crime in England and Wales (Home Office, 2007b)[2] can be said to be reliable, there has been an overall decrease in total crime of the order of 42 *per cent* during the years between 1995/6 and 2006/7. More specifically, over this period as analysed by the British Crime Survey (BCS), the most notable reductions have occurred in the crimes of vehicle theft (61 *per cent*), domestic burglary (59 *per cent*), and inter-personal violence (41 *per cent*).[3] Other forms of theft have also reduced significantly with household theft and non-specific theft showing a 47 and 41 *per cent* decrease respectively. The same data analysis suggests that the risk of being a victim of violent crime increased by a single percentage point between 2005/6 and 2006/7, but remains 16 *per cent* lower that it was in 1995/6 at 24 *per cent* as against 40 *per cent*.

Insofar as crimes reported by the police are concerned, a broadly similar pattern of decrease becomes evident, and a 'snap-shot' comparison of the percentage changes in recorded crime for the July – September periods in 2005 and 2006 reveals marginal increases in criminal damage, robbery, non-injurious assault and drug related offences, but an overall reduction across all offence groups of four *per cent*.[4] It is also of interest to note that the BCS data spanning the decade in question and the police data, though not statistically comparable, reveal consistently similar trends of overall crime decrease during a period in which, as we noted in *Chapter 1*, the prison population of England and Wales has risen from a daily average of 65,000 to one of over 80,000.

It is of course the case that criminal offence statistics, however reliable or otherwise, tell only part of the story that concerns us here. From a crime and public risk perspective we also have to take into account what is known with any extent of accuracy about public perceptions of crime and the likelihood of becoming a victim of crime. A current and wide-ranging analysis compiled under the auspices of the European Commission makes available a European System of Social Indicators, a number of which relate directly to crime and public safety. Two of these indicators provide interesting international comparisons of perceived crime risk of burglary and assault respectively by population age groups and gender, extracts of which for the UK, The Netherlands, Finland and USA are reproduced below:

---

2. These are contained in the Statistical Bulletin: Home Office (2007b), *Crime in England and Wales 2006/7*, 4th Edition (S. Nicholas, C. Kershaw and A. Walker (eds.)), London: Office for National Statistics. The document brings together statistics from the British Crime Survey and crimes reported by the police in a single volume.
3. The categories included within the range of violent crime include domestic violence (-59%), acquaintance violence (-53%), stranger violence (-11%) and mugging (-6%).
4. This information is available at: http://news.bbc.co.uk/1/ni/uk_politics/6297715.stm and the detailed increases were criminal damage (+1%), robbery (+4%), violence without injury (+7%) and drug offences (+9%). All other offence groups showed reductions consistent with the BCS data discussed earlier.

Age Group	UK	NL	FIN	USA
60 +	39.5	17.1	27.2	16.0
45- 59	32.3	25.5	31.1	16.5
35 – 44	35.3	15.3	31.9	17.4
25 – 34	36.3	22.9	20.5	13.2
15 - 24	35.4	17.5	15.7	11.3
All Females	38.7	20.7	26.6	15.7
All Males	33.1	20.0	25.7	15.2

Table 4:1: Perceived Percentage Crime Risk for Burglary or Break-in at Home
Source: European System of Social Indicators[5]
Life Domain: Crime and Public Safety
Measurement Dimension: Personal Crime Attitudes
Sub-Dimension: Expectation of Being Victimised
Indicator: M2121 - Perceived Crime Risk for Burglary within 12 months

The information within the Table is notable for the fact that the perception of risk among all age groups within the United Kingdom is consistently higher than for each of the other countries, and matched most closely by that in Finland. Comparative rates between The Netherlands and the United States display some similarities, but are considerably lesser than those for the United Kingdom and Finland. It is also interesting that the perception of risk among females is higher in each nation than that of males, though only marginally other than in the United Kingdom.

Age Group	UK	NL	FIN	USA
60 +	27.6	16.7	24.7	12.6
45- 59	28.2	21.0	26.9	11.5
35 – 44	29.6	15.8	36.2	8.2
25 – 34	33.3	28.3	28.7	13.2
15 - 24	45.1	29.4	30.7	22.9
All Females	34.4	18.1	27.8	11.1
All Males	29.3	26.0	30.2	15.0

Table 4.2: Perceived Percentage Crime Risk for Assault Against the Person
Source: European System of Social Indicators
Life Domain: Crime and Public Safety
Measurement Dimension: Personal Crime Attitudes
Sub-Dimension: Expectation of Being Victimised
Indicator: M2122 – Perceived Risk of Assault within 12 months

---

5. Compiled by the European Commission, Social Indicator Department, ZUMA, Mannheim, Germany (2007).

This table demonstrates a much closer similarity of perceptions between the United Kingdom, Finland and The Netherlands, with the highest values being found in the 15-24 year age group in all four of the countries identified. Only in the United Kingdom do females perceive themselves to be more at risk of assault than males to a significant extent, as was the case in the previous Table for Burglary. Moreover, in the United Kingdom the markedly higher perception of risk of assault among the youngest age quintile may amount to a clear reflection of what has been termed the 'yob culture' of anti-social behaviour that has emerged during the past decade, and most particularly within the major cities of the United Kingdom.

If, as Maruna and King have indicated, research on public opinion in Britain (and probably also elsewhere) suggests that the public is sceptical about crime statistics, however collected, it is interesting to speculate on how perceptions about crime are formed and maintained, and what accounts for the significant differences between levels of perception within the United Kingdom and the other nations identified in the tables above. For as these writers point out:

> At the same time, there is considerable public interest in all aspects of crime and justice and a seemingly insatiable appetite for often highly distorted tales of 'true crime', 'reality' police dramas and the like.[6] Furthermore, individuals hold very strong beliefs regarding issues of justice and punishment and have no great concern that these beliefs are not founded in criminological science. (Maruna and King, 2004: 87)

The issue of prison overcrowding in Britain has been maintained in a high profile in all areas of the mass media, particularly over the past two years or so. This is a recurring problem that dates back to the riots and disorder at Manchester and elsewhere in the Spring of 1990 and cast a long shadow over the penal system throughout the past decade. Public lack of confidence in the penal system and perceptions of risk are also enhanced by speculative front page articles in leading newspapers indicating that the government may be considering reducing the jail terms of 'thousands of criminals' as a means of creating space in overcrowded prisons and avoiding a risk of further mass disorder over prison conditions.[7]

---

6. This 'appetite' extends also to repeated and long-running series of television dramas depicting prison life that caricaturise custodial corrections, of which 'Porridge' and 'Bad Girls' provide vivid examples. It is also reinforced by an almost daily diet of televised Crime Scene Investigation (CSI) programmes originating in Britain and the United States.
7. An example of this situation may be seen in two recent articles in *The Times* newspaper normally noted for its moderately responsible approach to journalism. In late October 2007 the paper printed an article by its crime correspondent Richard Ford under the banner headline: 'Big Rise in Dangerous Criminals Reoffending While on Probation', and amplified by sub-headlines: Murder and Rape Were Among Their Crimes', and 'Supervision Failed to Stop Determined Sex Offenders'. *The Times*, October 23, p.4. In a second article by correspondents Frances Gibb and Richard Ford under the headline: 'Criminals Must Have Terms Cut in Full Jails' and a supplementary headline 'Shorter Sentences Will Ease Pressure on Jails', *The Times* indicated that: 'Thousands of criminals could have their jail terms cut after one of Britain's most senior judges said that courts were justified in giving lower sentences where prisoners faced

TRUTHS, MYTHS AND PUBLIC ATTITUDES

As we have previously noted in *Chapter 1*, it is a relatively small element of the total population[8] that persistently commits possibly up to half the volume of recorded serious crime, and some 20,000 such individuals are in prison custody at any one time, the prospect of extensive use of premature release is hardly one to boost public confidence. It is also notable that in recent years Britain has developed an almost paranoid attitude towards sexual offenders that has been encouraged by considerable and much publicised government activity, and by what Matravers and Hughes (2003: 51-79) have described as 'unprincipled sentencing' provisions[9] in response to sexual offences.

Given all these different factors, it is scarcely surprising that what passes for 'public opinion' in Britain is to a considerable extent 'conditioned' by a very sensationalist media treatment of crime, by a plethora of criminal justice legislation over the past decade, and by a traditionally ill-informed and attitudinally fixed approach to crime and criminal offenders. It is, however, towards sex offenders that the most vituperative and immoderate expressions of media, public (and also governmental) prejudice are directed. This is strange because as Matravers and Hughes indicate:

> Firstly, there is no reason to suppose that sex offenders present an increasing problem. Sex offences continue to account for less than 1 per cent of all recorded crime and the number of offenders found guilty or cautioned for sex offences has been falling for a decade (Home Office 2002c). In particular, there has been no increase in the sorts of offences that worry the public most: murders of children by sexual predators have remained remarkably constant and mercifully rare, at some five or six per year since 1980. Although rapes have doubled since 1987, this is generally attributed to a greater willingness by victims to report, particularly among complainants whose accounts do not follow the contours of the 'classic' stranger rape, and of the police record (see Harris and Grace, 1999).
>
> Secondly, 'dangerous', that is predatory violent individuals form only a tiny minority of sex offenders. While public and media attention focus on serious crimes committed by offenders who are strangers to their victims, some 80 per cent of sex offences against children take place in the home of the victim or the offender. It is estimated that between 25-40 of offenders have a fixated sexual attraction to children and therefore fit within the category of 'paedophiles'. The majority of child molesters, however, are people who are known to their victims, in many cases fathers, stepfathers and other family members (Grubin, 1998). (Matravers and Hughes, 2003: 53).

---

overcrowded jails.' *The Times*, November 5, pp.1 and 2.
8. Estimated (see p.34 *supra*) at 100,000 offenders of whom at any time 20% are held in custody in England and Wales. This would account for up to 20,000 of the average daily prison population of 81,000 at the time of writing.
9. Particularly within the Criminal Justice Act 2003 that emerged from the Review of Sex Offences *Setting the Boundaries* (Home Office, 2000), the Review of the Sentencing Framework *Making Punishments Work* (Home Office, 2001b), the Sex Offences White Paper *Protecting the Public* (Home Office 2002b), and the White Paper *Justice for All* (Home Office, 2002c).

Evidently, it is easy to overstate the extent of serious crime and certainly of 'dangerousness' among offenders[10], and in so doing send shock waves of alarm through any population. It is also easy for governments to indulge in what Zimring *et al.* (2001) have described in terms of a similar situation in the United States as 'populist political decision-making'[11] as a means of retaining or seeking electoral approval. But perhaps the most powerful influence on public opinion in relation to perceptions of crime risk remains that of constant media exposure that tends to be uncritically accepted as truth by many members of the public.

Whether politicians favour punitive responses towards crime as a means of gaining popularity or as a means of deflecting attention from other social problems is a matter for speculation. There are, however, within the British parliamentary tradition over the past twenty years, numerous instances of what David Garland (2002:132-3) has so aptly described as 'acting out' behaviour on the part of senior politicians in relation to criminal justice policy and legislation.[12] But even this in itself becomes contradictory in an era in which there has arisen a demonstrable need to limit the size of the prison population, and yet in which legislation has allowed for mandatory minimum sentences, extended sentences, and wider use of indeterminate life sentences that result in offenders spending longer and, in some instances, indefinite periods in custody.

Public attitudes towards crime and offenders are extremely difficult to identify with any clarity, other, obviously, than in relation to sexual offending. Passengers on the Clapham Omnibus are far from all the moderate, well informed and fair-minded being alluded to in the legal literature. Some undoubtedly have punitive motivations towards offenders, but as Warr (1995: 296) has noted, 'public opinion on crime and punishment encompasses such a wide variety of issues and attitudes that it is pointless to attempt to describe it in any one adjective or phrase.'[13] Thus to allege that the public is inherently punitive 'as if there were such a thing as "the" public and it had a single opinion about anything become, as Maruna and King (2004:89) suggest, largely an exercise in futility.'

---

10. I have discussed this issue in some detail in former work. See: D.J. Cornwell (1989), *Criminal Dangerousness and Its Punishment: Beyond the Phenomenological Illusion*, D. Phil. Thesis: University of York, pp.201-222.
11. See: F.E. Zimring, G. Hawkins and S. Kamin (2001), *Punishment and Democracy: Three Strikes and You're Out in California*, New York: Oxford University Press.
12. In D. Garland (2002), *The Culture of Control: Crime and Social Order In Contemporary* Society, Oxford: Oxford University Press. As I have noted elsewhere (Cornwell, 2007, *op. cit.*, p.40), the most notable of these was the 'prison works' tirade delivered by Michael Howard as Home Secretary to the Conservative Party Conference in October 1993.
13. Quoted in Maruna and King (2004), *op. cit.*.

RESTORATIVE JUSTICE AND PUBLIC RISK

If a restorative penology were to replace the clearly discredited retributive and incarcerative model of justice that presently dominates the world of corrections, would the transition carry with it an unacceptable element of public risk? This is, perhaps, the key question that lies at the core of the evident reluctance of politicians and their advisers to implement restorative practices in other than a piecemeal fashion within contemporary criminal justice systems. For while it is easy to criticise the manifest failures of existing approaches to crime and its punishment, it is an altogether different matter to implement significant change that could be claimed to threaten community security to a greater extent than is presently the case.

In attempting to answer this question, some measure of 'devil's advocacy' may be inevitable because the apparent vulnerability of restorative justice propositions has to be overcome to an extent at least sufficient to make adherence to the *status quo* an unreasonable option. Such is not to suggest that restorative justice is conceptually flawed, but rather that its difference of approach to justice is so marked as to raise legitimate concerns over its claim to deliver better and more effective justice. Indeed, critics of restorative justice and some of its most convinced proponents have questioned the robustness of its credentials and ability to withstand the inevitable counter-arguments that might be deployed against its acceptance both in principle and in practice.[14]

Restorative justice, as we have seen in *Chapter 2*, certainly asks different questions about offences and offenders, and proposes an alternative view of stakeholders within the processes of justice. Further, as we have noted in *Chapter 3*, it is not ultimately anti-retributive, but is resolutely opposed to excessive reliance on retribution as the primary justification of criminal punishment. This means that it is inherently more economical with sanctions for wrongdoing, and perceives the reparation of victims by offenders as the primary route towards offender reintegration within communities.

A restorative penology does not seek 'decarceration'[15] as a principal objective, but would adopt an entirely different approach towards the use of prison custody on the basis that it should be strictly reserved for those offenders for whom no other option is reasonable. Thus less reliance on short-term prison sentences would be a priority, as would be the abandonment of indeterminate sentences for public protection

---

14. Here, for example, see James Dignan's (2004) comprehensive analysis in 'Restorative Justice and the Law: The Case for an Integrated, Systemic Approach' in L. Walgrave (ed), *Restorative Justice and the Law*, Devon, UK: Willan Publishing, pp.169-190, and M.S. Umbreit *et al.* (2005), *Opportunities and Pitfalls Facing the Restorative Justice Movement*, University of Minnesota Centre for Restorative Justice and Peacemaking.
15. Meaning here the abolition of custodial punishment through imprisonment as proposed by writers such as Rothman (1973) and Scull (1977). For a broader explanation see D. Walsh and A. Poole (eds) (1983), *A Dictionary of Criminology*, London: Routledge and Kegan Paul, pp.65-6.

other, possibly, than for murder. A move away from the use of short-term (less than twelve months) prison sentences is consistent with the recommendations in the Halliday Report (Home Office 2001b: iv) and the government's own White Paper *Justice for All* (Home Office 2002c: 92 and 102) that such sentences are 'usually ineffective and increase the chances of reoffending'.

Discontinuing the use of indeterminate sentences (and extended sentences) for the purposes of detaining offenders for periods longer than that strictly deserved and for public protection is a matter of principle and of justice. Such practices lead to excessive use of punishment that is unjustifiable and arbitrary, and make release contingent upon an executive decision making process that is more likely to be wrong than right in relation to future similar offending.[16] For these reasons it is suggested here that other than possibly in relation to the crime of murder (though even then it remains morally questionable), a system of entirely determinate (or fixed duration) sentences is preferable to the present arrangements.

Changes of this nature may appear to be both radical and far-reaching, but it has to be remembered that the present sentencing situation was reached in a radical and reactive manner over the years of the past decade, and has contributed in a significant way to the present penal crisis. It also has to be reiterated that at the present time almost *seventy per cent* of all offenders released from prison custody re-offend within two years, largely because prisons, as these are currently operated, fail comprehensively to change offending behaviour. As we shall see in the next chapter and those within Part Two of this book, this situation could be different and victims of crime would get a much better deal than they do at present.

If, for the present, we follow what might be termed the 'hard core' theory of offending mentioned in *Chapter 1*, and allow that of the estimated 100,000 or so persistent and serious offenders in England and Wales some 20,000 are in custody at any one time, these, if any, are the persons for whom imprisonment might be said to be largely unavoidable, and who pose a public risk at least through reoffending. However, the following Table shows a broad comparison of the prison population of England and Wales in custody between September 2005 and February 2009:

---

16. For an explanation of the 'false-positive' argument in relation to criminal dangerousness, see A.E. Bottoms (1977), 'Reflections on the Renaissance of Dangerousness', *Howard Journal of Criminal Justice*, vol. XVI, no.2, pp.70-96, and D.J. Cornwell (1989), *op. cit.*, pp.212-3.

Type of Custody & Sentence	September 2005	February 2009
Total Population in Custody	77,807	82,993
Remanded in Custody	13,500	12,854
Sentenced Prisoners	62,680	68,072
Up to 6 months	6,125	5,021
6 to 12 months	2,575	2,447
12 months to 4 years	21,587	23,930
Over 4 years (excluding life)	26,378	24,224
Life / Indeterminate Sentences	6,568	12,143

Table 4:3: Prison Population (England and Wales) by Type of Custody and Sentence Length September 2005 and February 2009

Sources: National Offender Monitoring Service (September 2005)[17]
Ministry of Justice (May 2009)[18]

From the extracted information it is evident that though there was a decrease in people remanded in custody between the two periods, the sentenced population had risen by some 5,186 by February 2009, and that the majority of this increase was in the categories of prisoners serving sentences of between one and four years (+2,343) and life or other indeterminate sentences which almost doubled in size (+5,575). The fall in the over four years category of prisoners may be explained by the fact that the provisions for indeterminate sentences within the Criminal Justice Act 2003 only came into operation for those convicted after April 2005.

A restorative justice penology would undoubtedly impose more stringent criteria on the use of remand in custody to prevent its use as a 'taste of prison', and on the basis that some 40 *per cent* of those so dealt with are found not guilty at trial, or, if found guilty, are given non-custodial penalties. Applying such a proportion to the February 2009 remand population as an approximation, it might be possible to reduce the remand population by at least 5,000 prison places. Further sizeable reductions might also be made in the 7,500 or so prisoners serving up to 12 months, and even a few of those serving sentences of between 12 months and four years. In such a manner, it might be suggested that without undertaking any major risks and by applying reduction strategies to only the low-risk (short sentenced) element of the prison population, at least 15,000 prison places, and very possibly even more[19], could easily be reduced.

---

17. Available at: http://www.reform.co.uk/filestore/pdf/Population%20%custody%20%20september%2005.pdf
18. Available at: http://www.justice.gov.uk/docs/population-in-custody-february09.pdf (09)
19. More because of the fact that a significant number of prisoners in (say) the 12 month to four years sentence band would be in the final part of their custodial sentence periods, and, as we shall see in *Chapter 8* , would be eligible to serve the terminal part of their sentences within the community.

Though a strategy for reduction of the use of prison custody such as that outlined above is clearly speculative and approximate, it is indicative of the type of approach that restorative penology would adopt without taking unwarranted risks with public safety. To this might be added the possibility of devising an altogether less punitive sentencing structure, and placing a finite limit on the total number of 'uncrowded' prison places to be provided, and which could not be exceeded. By way of further reduction of the use of custody, a restorative approach to criminal punishment would (as we shall see in *Chapter 5*) seek actively to divert from custody wherever possible those offenders who accept guilt for their offences and voluntarily opt to make reparation to victims of crime in a substantial manner within their communities.

As I have indicated in former work, reductive strategies are far from impossible to implement where there is both the political will and the social tolerance to make them work effectively as the Finnish experience has proved most conclusively.[20] Between the 1950s and 2006 the Finnish government reduced its incarceration rate from 187 offenders per 100,000 of its population to 66, and without a significant threat to either public safety or national security. The Dutch government acted in a similar fashion during the twentieth century, and by 1975 was imprisoning only 17 per 100,000 of its population. But in the 1980s its government returned to a more punitive approach to the punishment of crime and a correspondingly increased penal population (Blad, 2006a:136; van Ruller, 1986). These examples alone indicate that reduction of prison populations is achievable, but it requires a sustained political will to make it happen.

BALANCING THE CUSTODY: COMMUNITY EQUATION

While unnecessary and excessive use of imprisonment is self-evidently wasteful of national financial, penal and human resources, it will be evident to the reader that a reduction in the prison population requires an increase and a strengthening of the provisions for sanctions within the community if public risk is to be minimised. In some respects, the greater the reduction that can be made in the use of prisons, the more the potential exists to enhance the effectiveness of community based measures. Community penalties are inherently less expensive to operate than imprisonment, simply because these do not have to operate throughout every twenty-four hour period of each week and year, and for the obvious reason that there is no residential cost involved and community sanctions are much less staff-intensive.

This much stated, however, in order for community penalties to be effective, they have to be demanding on the offender, demonstrably purposeful, strictly enforced

---

20. See D. J. Cornwell (2007), *op. cit.*, at *Chapter 6*, pp.138-163, and the work of M. Joutsen, R. Rahti and P. Pölönen (2001), *Criminal Justice Systems in Europe and North America – Finland*, Helsinki: Academic Bookstore.

 **Shows why we should never give up on the capacity of people to change**

Jim Hopkinson, Bradford Children's Services

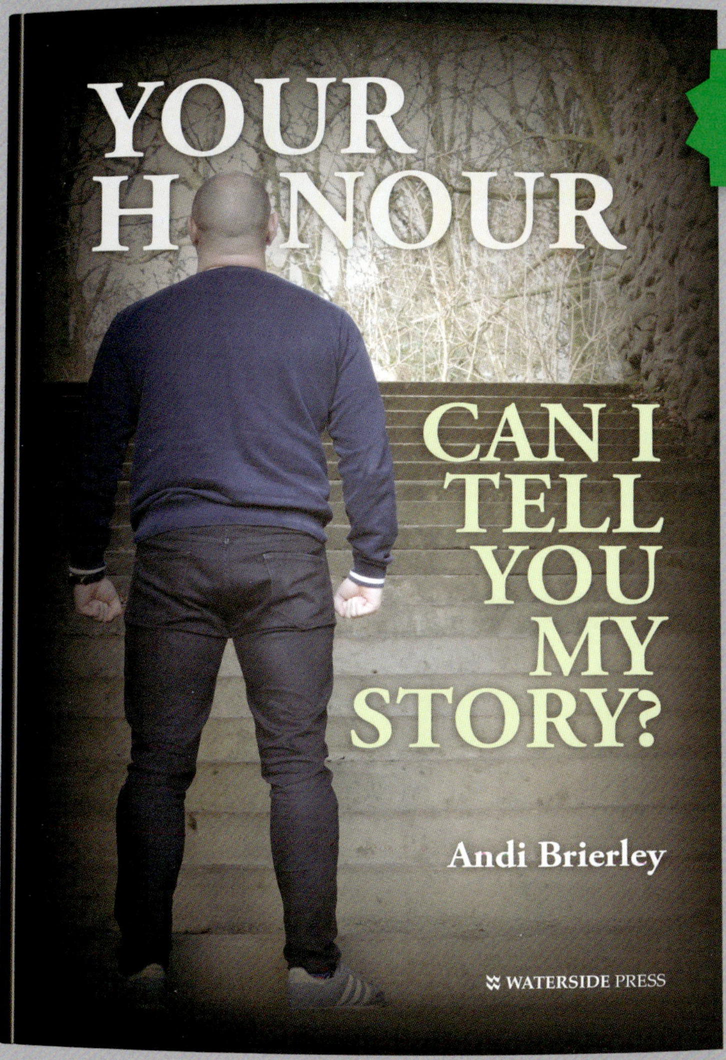

YOUR HONOUR
CAN I TELL YOU MY STORY?

Andi Brierley

NEW

WATERSIDE PRESS

Free UK Delivery

WatersidePress.co.uk

Turn Around Stories

Your Honour Can I Tell You My Story?
by Andi Brierley

Andi Brierley's story of his progress through care, prison and social rejection to youth justice manager in Leeds contains countless clues for those who work with troubled young people. It begins with failures to deal with his chaotic early life moving from place to place, fragmented parenting and poor role models. In a family home encircled by criminality, drugs, violence and baffling adults he ended up first in a young offender institution then in prison.

There he learned how to act and think as a prisoner for his own survival, something that only made matters worse when trying to re-adapt to the world outside on his release. Caught in a downward spiral, hooked on drugs, partying, not strong enough to resist negative influences and his well-being deteriorating, the book shows how small things made a difference.

Until he regained self-worth and rescued his life. Important for the messages it contains for professionals and young people in trouble with whom he has forged a remarkable connection.

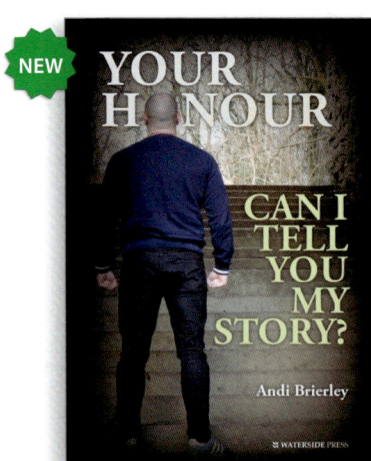

As featured in the *Yorkshire Post* and the Association of YOT Managers *Bulletin*

Available in paperback & ebook
(inc Kindle, Apple and Google)
258 pages | Published in April 2019
ISBN 978-1-909976-64-1
Price £19.95

More details at www.WatersidePress.co.uk

WATERSIDE PRESS

Turn around stories
Writing as a route out of crime and towards a better life

Prison writing is a valuable two-way process. Education aside many prisoners have changed their lives using writing as a bridge to a new life and career. Our first book in this genre was Bob Turney's acclaimed *I'm Still Standing* back in 2002. Recommended personally by Lord Longford, Bob the one-time prolific burglar turned author actually went on to become a probation officer! Ex-offenders who followed his lead include Alan Weaver (who became a social worker, *So You Think You Know Me?*), Ben Ashcroft (young offender to youth worker, *Fifty-one Moves*) who tells of his constant changes whilst in care and Justin Rollins (ex-graffiti artist and now motivational speaker, *The Lost Boyz* and *Street Crhymes*) whose books have been adopted as set texts on degree courses in Birmingham and elsewhere.

Another ex-prisoner turned author whose book has been widely used in education is Frankie Owens whose *Little Book of Prison* also made the final of the People's Book Prize. There is also a book, *Recovery Stories*, about those who have survived addiction.

Actor Stephen Fry's turn around story was included in a collection called *Going Straight* along with that of the train robber Bruce Reynolds whose life changed after being released from his 25 year sentence. Andi Brierley (opposite) who went from prisoner and heroin addict to manager of a youth justice unit in Leeds is the latest in this considerable line-up. Each of these books centres on identifying the changes, choices and threads that led from being an offender to law-abiding citizen.

Further details, information and reviews of these and other key texts are available at our website.

WatersidePress.co.uk

Free UK Standard Delivery on Every Order

Bob Turney's *I'm Still Standing* is the book that established the turn around genre with Waterside Press. Will Phillip's *A Good Man Inside* is a diary of the impact of imprisonment on a white collar offender telling how he survived it before returning to normal life.

Order Online
WatersidePress.co.uk
Call +44 (0)1256 882250
or ask at all good bookshops

Payment by invoice — for multiple copy orders only, we may invoice your firm/institution (at our discretion). Please place an order via our website and select "Invoice With Order" as your payment method.

Free UK Delivery

- UK Standard Delivery is **FREE** for all orders and takes 2–5 working days.
- First Class starts at £2.00 rising by £1 per additional book to a maximum of £5.95 for 5+ books.
- **In stock items are typically despatched within 24 hours.**

International Delivery

- For rates see www.WatersidePress.co.uk/delivery

  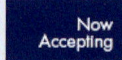 

Ebooks

Most Waterside Press titles are also available as ebooks. These can be read on a variety of devices, including **Kindle**, **iPhone/iPad**, **Android**, **Nook** (and many more). You can buy them through online retailers, including **Amazon**, **Apple** and **Google Play**. Search the web, or see our website for details and links. Our ebooks are also available to institutions via **library agreements** — ask your supplier or contact us for more details.

Available on

Amazon, Kindle and all related logos are trademarks of Amazon.com, Inc. or its affiliates. The Apple logo is a trademark of Apple Inc., registered in the U.S. and other countries. Apple Books is a service mark of Apple Inc. Google Play and the Google Play logo are trademarks of Google LLC.

Waterside Press
Sherfield Gables, Sherfield-on-Loddon,
Hook, Hampshire, RG27 0JG. Tel. 01256 882 250

and supervised, and professionally operated. We shall return to these fundamental requirements in the concluding part of this book. More important at this stage of the discussion is the need to be clear about the extent to which any system of community sanctions implies some measure of public risk, and balance this against the potential benefits that increased use of such measures might make available.

There have traditionally been two opposing trends of thinking about the visibility of offenders undertaking non-custodial sanction projects within communities. The first is that it is entirely appropriate for them to be clearly identifiable through the wearing of high visibility outer clothing or a distinguishable uniform as a matter of public security, and for the areas in which they to work to be notified to the public in advance of their arrival. The opposite view is that to impose such requirements 'stigmatises' offenders and makes them vulnerable to public abuse, and that such tasks as they undertake should be discreetly handled with a low level of visibility and little, if any, prior public notification.

In the event that a considerable expansion in the use of reparative community sanctions were to envisaged, it would be logical to argue that a sizeable proportion of those thus sentenced might otherwise have been imprisoned under existing circumstances, and would thus have attracted a measure of stigmatisation as a result of that experience. If, in addition, the final element of custodial sentences were to include a period spent working in the community on probationary release, then additional numbers of those sentenced to custody would, in any event, be present working within communities as a matter of course.

A third consideration is that although it may be impossible to quantify with any accuracy, there may be some incidental value in terms of general deterrence in making offenders work visibly within communities, and that as a matter of public security making them readily identifiable is an issue of social responsibility and accountability. Finally, it might be argued that a significant increase in the use of community sanctions would, inevitably, be accompanied by a proportion of 'failures' or further offending, and that public confidence needs to be re-assured that all reasonable steps are taken to safeguard both local people and offenders.

All things considered, the custody: community equation is inevitably a delicate one to balance. Fewer people sent to prison, more extensive reparation made to victims, and the potential amenity value of well-organised and planned community projects all weigh heavily on the positive pan of the scales. The increased presence of offenders at large – even though adequately supervised, the inevitability of some 'failures', and the unquantifiable element of public risk combine to provide a counter-balancing effect. Proponents of restorative justice would argue strongly that fewer people sent to prison results in fewer damaged families and dependents who suffer indirectly from imprisonment; reparation vindicates victims and offenders in a real and positive manner; and that well-planned and executed projects hold out the potential for skills acquisition and subsequent employability. The sceptically minded would insist that the supposed benefits are uncertain, that the attendant public risks cannot lightly be discounted, and that if such initiatives were shelved victims would be no worse-off than they are at present.

The decisive factor in the equation is whether or not more extensive use of community sanctions, and in particular of reparative projects previously subsumed under the general category of 'community service' would reduce subsequent reoffending.[21] As Gill McIvor (2004: 175-8) points out, 'while prison sentences and community-based disposals have similar reconviction rates (e.g. Barclay and Tavares 1999), offenders on community service often have lower reconviction rates than would be predicted by their criminal history, age and other relevant characteristics (Lloyd et al, 1995)'. Also, May (1999) found that reconviction rates for community service were better than predicted even when factors such as unemployment and drug use were taken into account. And, as McIvor further points out, in a Swiss study of community service outcomes, Killias et al. (2000) found lower reconviction rates among offenders sentenced to community service than among those given short prison sentences.[22]

Indeed, in earlier work, McIvor also made the following telling observation in relation to the effectiveness of community service:

> ... community placements which were viewed by offenders as most rewarding – and which were associated with reductions in recidivism – might best be characterised as reintegrative and as entailing a degree of reciprocity or exchange. In many instances, it seems, contact with the beneficiaries had given offenders an insight into other people and an increased insight into themselves; the acquisition of skills had instilled into them greater confidence and self-esteem; and the experience of completing their community service orders had placed them in a position where they could enjoy reciprocal relationships – gaining the trust, confidence and appreciation of other people and having the opportunity to give something back to them in return. (McIvor 1998: 55-56).

Here, at least, there seem to be some positive signs of hope for the future. For although the case for restorative justice cannot be in any sense claimed to be proven and accepted, it might at least be said that lesser use of imprisonment and extended use of robust community sanctions would almost certainly not increase reoffending, might well reduce it, and the social benefits to victims, offenders and communities are potentially much greater than those of maintaining the *status quo*.

As to the question that forms the title of this chapter, 'Would Wider Use of

---

21. The point here is that the former sanction of community service, which originated in the USA in the 1960s, was introduced into England and Wales in 1973 (and subsequently in Scotland in 1977), and was re-named community punishment under the legislation within the Criminal Justice and Court Services Act 2000 effective from April 2001. Its traces now feature in a requirement of 'unpaid work'.
22. See: G. McIvor (2004), 'Reparative and Restorative Approaches' in A.E. Bottoms *et al.*,(eds.), *op. cit.*,pp.162-194.

Restorative Justice Increase Public Risk?', it would be disingenuous to suggest that such a transition to wider use of restorative and reparative sanctions at the expense of short prison sentences could be made without an element of additional public risk, but the risk: gain calculus undoubtedly falls in favour of doing so. As we shall see later, prisons simply cannot provide the opportunities for change identified so clearly in McIvor's analysis, and victims deserve greater consideration as will become evident in the chapter that follows.

Chapter 5 provides the final discussion of 'Issues of Principle' that form *Part One* of this work. It is devoted to an analysis of the situation of victims of crime as matters stand in England and Wales at the present time, and in many respects represents a 'bridge' between this part and that which follows in which the focus of attention turns to discussion of prisons and ways of making these institutions more effective. The situation of victims of crime is one of the central strands that run throughout this book, and substantial change to the extent to which victims are afforded proper understanding and support is in many respects dependent upon resolving many of the other issues that have been raised in this and the foregoing chapters.

CHAPTER 5

Could Restorative Justice Give Victims of Crime a Better Deal?

The present decade began with a blossoming of hope that restorative justice principles and practices were attracting serious consideration at governmental level in the United Kingdom and in many of the other leading democracies of the world. This was particularly the case in relation to the claims of restorative justice to give crime victims a more substantial place in justice processes, and the formal endorsement of restorative principles by the United Nations and the Council of Europe respectively. (Cormier 2006: 160, fn.11).[1]

GREAT EXPECTATIONS: MEAGRE OUTCOMES

Of all the contentious issues that the development of restorative justice has raised over the past two decades, the status it affords to victims of crime is surely the most controversial for criminal justice practitioners, politicians and academics alike. In retrospect, the year 2003 might have been a watershed within the United Kingdom for it saw the publication of the government's consultative document *Restorative Justice: The Government's Strategy* (Home Office (2003a) in the Foreword to which the (then) Home Secretary David Blunkett stated:

> The Government is committed to placing victims' needs at the centre of the Criminal Justice System. We also want a system that encourages responsibility, so that offenders face up to what they've done, and make amends. And we want the wider community to be involved in finding positive solutions to crime and anti-social behaviour. (Home Office 2003a: 4).

And within the promotional literature heralding the strategy, we find promissory statements such as: 'the Government aims to maximise the use of restorative justice in the Criminal Justice System as it works well at both addressing the needs of the victim and in reducing offending.' More than this, we find the claim: 'Evidence suggests that restorative justice can help to deliver key objectives across the CJS: improving victim satisfaction, reducing crime and reoffending, delivering justice effectively and building public confidence.' (Home Office 2003b:1).

Later in the same year the government introduced its Criminal Justice Bill (subse-

---

1. United Nations (2002 *op. cit.*), *Resolutions and Decisions Adopted by the Economic and Social Council 2002*, (E/2002/INF/2/2) and (United Nations (2001 *op. cit.*) *UN Basic Principles on the Use of Restorative Justice Programmes in Criminal Matters*, (ESOSOC Resolution 2001/12). See also Articles 10 and 17 of the European Union Framework Decision of 15 March 2001.

quently to become the Criminal Justice Act 2003), an extensive document by any standards with its provisions for 'custody plus', 'custody minus' and 'intermittent custody' among a plethora of other arrangements, but of restorative justice there was little trace other than in the provision for 'conditional cautions' by the police which 'might include restorative interventions' (CJA 2003, Part 3, Section 22). At much the same time as the Criminal Justice Bill was published, the government launched yet another initiative under the title: *A New Deal for Victims and Witnesses: National Strategy to Deliver Improved Services* (Home Office 2003b), a consultative exercise that ultimately resulted (some two years later) in the publication of no less than three associated government initiatives relating to victims of crime.[2]

The publication of the Criminal Justice Act 2003 could have provided an excellent opportunity to introduce restorative and reparative measures into the British criminal justice system, particularly since two years earlier the Auld Report[3] had recommended the introduction of conditional cautioning, and this had been reflected in the White Paper *Justice for All* (Home Office 2002b) in advance of the (then) Home Secretary's comments indicated above. What in fact the new Act did was to provide a much more punitive basis for the 'mix and match' arrangements for 'custody plus and minus', the underlying motivation for which, one suspects, was as much 'laced' with punitive public protection as it was with any belief that a reduction in reoffending would result from it.

Now six more years on, not much has moved forward to place crime victims 'at the centre of the criminal justice system' or to 'maximise the use of restorative justice'. Indeed, as Gavrielides (2003) pointed out, 'the provision of restorative and reparative initiatives [in the United Kingdom] is currently uneven and is characterised by the inclusion of a number of fairly disparate initiatives. There is also evidence that, possibly because so many different schemes have been brought under its umbrella, the practice of restorative justice is somewhat removed from its underlying theory.'[4] This is unfortunate because it would appear that some of the more valuable aspects of restorative justice principles and practices have effectively been 'cherry-picked' to support other initiatives, leaving its central tenets languishing at the margins of the Criminal Justice System.

---

2. These were: Home Office (2005a), *Victims' Rights*, available at http://www.homeoffice.gov.uk/crime-victims/victims/Victims-rights/?version=1, Home Office (2005b), *The Code of Practice for Victims of Crime*, London: HMSO, (October), and Home Office (2005c), *Re-building Lives- Supporting Victims of Crime*, CM 6705, London: HMSO (December).
3. This report was named after its author Lord Justice Auld (2001), *Review of the Criminal Courts of England and Wales: Report*, London: The Stationery Office.
4. See: T. Gavrielides (2003), *Restorative Justice Theory and Practice: Mind the Gap!* available at http://wwweuroforum.org/readingroom/Newsletter/Vol.4Issue.3.PDF.

WHAT DO VICTIMS REQUIRE FROM CRIMINAL JUSTICE?

Becoming a victim of crime, and particularly of serious violent, sexual or other mentally or physically injurious crime, is frequently a sudden, unexpected and traumatising situation. Its effects can be long lasting, causing problems that extend beyond a physical recovery period, and which can require medical, psychological and even psychiatric intervention. Moreover, apart from the more obvious effects of trauma, victims can suffer prolonged inability to pursue their employment, a very real fear of repeated victimisation, and severely diminished quality of life, all and often, it might be said, for 'being in the wrong place at the wrong time.'

Apart from the unfairness of all this and the justifiable anger that it can provoke, there seems to be a widespread misunderstanding (or misappreciation) of what the majority of victims need most from the criminal justice process as a response to their situations. Of course, some victims will be vindictive towards those who harm them, and rely upon the courts to exact vengeance on their behalf that may even be disproportionate to the harm they have suffered, but this seems to be far from universally the case. In a short but extremely perceptive analysis of this situation Heather Strang (2004: 96-105), in reviewing research in this area[5], suggested that when asked about their needs, victims widely identify the following factors:

- a less formal court (or adjudication) process where their views are actually considered;
- the ability to participate in their case;
- more information about both the processing and outcome of their case;
- fair and respectful treatment throughout the criminal justice process;
- material restoration (which may include reparation);
- but most importantly of all, emotional restoration, including an apology.

In amplification of this view, Strang offered the following explanation, the poignancy of which will not escape many proponents of restorative justice:

> It is plain that the court-based Criminal Justice System is remarkably unsuited for delivering almost all of these benefits to victims. Victims turn out to be the most unimportant of all the players in formal criminal justice processing. The state also assumes the role of the injured party and leaves victims to play no part beyond that of witnesses. So, little wonder that no provision is made for addressing any of these needs within the formal court system. The injustice of this state of play is self-evident to every victim caught up in the court system, and the lack of a legitimate role comes as a shock to almost all of them. Certainly there is little opportunity for victims to put their side of the story or to participate in a meaningful way in

---

5. Strang refers here to the work of Shapland *et al.* (1985), Mawby and Gill (1987), Waller (1989) and her own contribution in Strang (2002).

the manner in which their case is dealt. Because their role is so meagre, little attention is given to keeping them informed of progress in their case. Even when legislative amendments require the victims to be kept informed, let-out clauses such as 'as far as possible' or 'whenever feasible' have meant that the police, the prosecution and the courts fail to give victims the information they need. As a result, most victims feel that, at the end of their encounter with the various branches of the Criminal Justice System, they have not been taken seriously, that no one has responsibility for representing their voice, and that no one is interested in repairing the harm they have suffered. (Strang, 2004: 96-7)

Trenchant though such a criticism may appear to be, Strang is absolutely correct to make it. British government's utterances on the subject, *A New Deal for Victims and Witnesses: National Strategy to Deliver Improved Services* (Home Office (2003b), and *Code of Practice for Victims of Crime* (Home Office 2005c), echo its accuracy entirely.[6]

Now while at first sight the 'hierarchy' of victims' needs indicated by Strang may seem unexceptionable, it does raise a number of issues that make acceptance and implementation less than straightforward. These matters require brief explanation here. First, the perceived need for a less formal process is entirely understandable since many who come into contact with the Criminal Justice System in the courts find the procedures and modes of behaviour – and in particular within the adversarial process – both archaic, impersonal and largely incomprehensible. And since victims are, at least in present circumstances, confined largely to the role of interested observers without a right of participation other, possibly, than as witnesses, there is little reason why they should find the process 'user friendly'.

As to the second issue of participation which I have discussed in some detail in earlier work[7], there arises a considerable divergence of opinion as to the extent to which this is desirable and practicable. On the one hand many members of the legal profession and some academics regard victim participation to the point of 'allocution'[8] as inappropriate almost to the point of impropriety (e.g. Ashworth, 1993a: 284: 1993b: 505; Cavadino and Dignan, 1997 *op. cit.*: 237-8). On the other hand the most ardent proponents of victims' interests perceive any lesser extent of participation as an arbitrary curtailment of what might be regarded as a fundamental right. On balance it seems reasonable to suggest that there is a potential for compromise between these extreme positions, allowing, in addition to the right of victims

---

6. If for no other reason that these initiatives deflect the victim from the court processes towards complaint to external agencies (e.g. the police, Victim Support, and the Parliamentary Commissioner (Ombudsman)) rather than making it an implicit obligation of court procedures to meet victims' needs and expectations other than as witnesses.
7. Here see Cornwell (2007, *op. cit.*) at *Chapter 3*, pp.73-90.
8. That is to say the opportunity for victims to make personal verbal statements to the court about their situation, feelings about being victimised, and, some proponents of victims' rights would insist, the form or extent of punishment they might consider appropriate.

to make victim impact statements (VISs) or victim personal statements (VPSs)[9], a measure of personal hearing, but *excluding* any opinion as to the form or extent of sentence they might believe justifiable in the circumstances.

Insofar as the matter of respectful and fair treatment is concerned, it might be contended that this arises in part out of the issue of allocution mentioned above, and in part also in relation to the procedural formality of the court process alluded to earlier. Once again, within an adversarial method of trial, it would be difficult to see how an oral statement made by a victim, other than as a witness, could not be subject to cross-examination unless such were to be specifically precluded. This being the case, it would place a victim in the unenviable position of being challenged by the defence as to facts, motives, pre-dispositions and the like. Perhaps even worse, a victim who was not also a witness would be placed in the invidious position of becoming what might be termed a 'witness by default', and find this experience both distressing and traumatising.[10]

There is little doubt that most victims would welcome material (or financial) restoration without having to pursue civil litigation for compensation, since many defendants in criminal cases might decline or have no resources to make reparation, and court-awarded compensation schemes are – at least in the United Kingdom – strictly limited in extent and resources.[11] Many victims are, however, less concerned with receiving financial compensation than they are that the offender should take responsibility for his or her wrongdoing and apologise for it. In addition, as Strang points out, more value is placed by victims on any financial reparation made by offenders as part of their acceptance of responsibility than on its financial worth (Strang, 2004: 98).

The existing Code of Practice does require what are termed the 'service providers'[12] within the Criminal Justice System to inform and update victims (whether

---

9. Victim impact statements (VISs) originated in the United States as a means of allowing victims to inform courts of their situations in a formal written submission dictated to police or legal advisers. The equivalent in the United Kingdom is the victim personal statement (VPS) introduced in October 2001 within a *Practice Direction* by the Lord Chief Justice of England and Wales – *Practice Direction (Crime Victim Personal Statements)* (2001) 4 All ER 640 : III. 28). For additional information see: Home Office (2001c), 'Victim Personal Statements' (Circular 35/2001), London: Home Office.
10. As the UK organisation Liberty points out in relation to the rights of victims in court hearings: 'A victim of crime is not a party to any criminal proceedings, has no legal status, and has no right to legal representation in court. Other than as a witness, a victim's involvement is normally limited to, at most, receiving compensation (where duties are placed on the court to consider this), making a victim impact statement (VIP) (aka a victim personal statement (VPS)) and participating in reparation schemes if appropriate and available. He or she should also receive the support of both Victim Support and the nationwide Witness Service. There is also a Criminal Injuries Compensation Scheme re violent offences where recompense is not forthcoming as a result of adequate court-based compensation: see http://www.cica.gov.uk
11. See here the explanation offered by Cavadino and Dignan (1997 *op. cit.*), pp.215-218. Courts in England and Wales have the power under the Criminal Justice Acts of 1972, 1982 and 1988 and the Powers of the Criminal Courts Act 2000 to make compensation orders, but have proved reluctant to do so because many offenders do not have the resources to make them effective even though compensation should take precedence over a fine if an offender cannot afford both. (Moxon *et al.*, 1990).
12. Among which are the Police, the Crown Prosecution Service, the Courts Service, the Criminal Injuries

witnesses or not) of matters relating to the processing and outcomes of their case at each stage in the justice process. The entire process is, however, predicated on the implicit assumption that victims are also witnesses, and, more importantly, witnesses who have made VPSs that become part of the official prosecution documentation disclosed to the defence in criminal proceedings. Thus a victim of crime who, for whatever reason, declines to give evidence and thereby become a witness, has no legal status whatsoever within the criminal justice process.

One further factor needs to be considered before we can determine whether restorative justice might improve the situation outlined in the preceding paragraphs. The nature and conduct of the adversarial court process is such as to significantly reduce the likelihood, once a case comes to trial, that the offender will admit guilt and offer to make reparation, and thus that victims of crime will feel vindicated by the justice process. This means that under existing circumstances restorative justice practices such as group conferencing, victim: offender mediation, diversion and the like are confined to minor offences at the pre-trial stage, and are effectively excluded from the more serious range of criminal offences that almost invariably arise from arrest, charging by the police, and a decision to proceed with a criminal prosecution. This seems to be one of the principal reasons for restorative justice being confined, as hitherto, to the periphery of the criminal justice process.

CAN RESTORATIVE PRACTICES IMPROVE JUSTICE DELIVERY?

If restorative justice is to move from the margins and into the mainstream of criminal justice in the foreseeable future, the present climate of 'expressive punitivism' has to be replaced by a more rational response to criminal offending than the prevailing incarcerative model of public protection. Crime is not ultimately amenable to reduction by 'managerialist' dictates or political posturing, since neither addresses the causes of crime or the genuine needs of those affected by it. The re-definition of crime as Zehr (2002: 23) has proposed it is a starting point, moving us away from pre-occupation with the law and the state and towards the violation of people and relationships. This allows victims, offenders and communities to become stakeholders in justice, and their differing needs to be met through justice.

And if, as Maruna and King (2004: 84), Wright (2003: 12), and others have suggested, the public within most democracies are not as punitive as sentencers, politicians and public officials assume them to be, and there is compelling evidence to suggest that such is the case (e.g. Roberts and Stalans 1997; Roberts et al., 2003),

---

Compensation Authority, the National Offender Monitoring Service (including the Prison and National Probation Services) and Youth Offending Teams.

then either the latter choose to remain ignorant about public opinion or deliberately act perversely. There is little excuse for politicians and their advisers to remain unaware of public opinion when factual evidence is available to them from the research of academics and correctional professionals:[13] there is no excuse for ignoring the evidence for the sake of electoral expediency.

There is also no doubt from what has been indicated earlier that the British government has maintained an entirely ambivalent attitude towards restorative justice over the past decade. Putting restorative justice 'at the heart of the criminal justice system' (Home Office, 2003a: 4) is simply incompatible with the legislation within the Criminal Justice Act 2003 in relation to 'punishment within the community'. The more cynically disposed would contend that the *Code of Practice for Victims of Crime* (Home Office, 2005b) was little more than a thinly veiled initiative based not in a desire to expand the use of restorative justice, but rather to persuade more victims to become witnesses and thus enable the issue of 'victim allocution' to be conveniently shelved.

But wherever the truth lies in these matters, there is little evidence of a political willingness to promote restorative justice throughout the British Criminal Justice Systems at the present time, or to giving a higher profile to meeting the *actual* needs of crime victims upon which it is predicated. This is surprising since in the words of the Minister for Victims (Fiona Mactaggart) in a press release announcing the publication of the consultative document *Rebuilding Lives – Supporting Victims of Crime* (Home Office 2005c):

> Even relatively minor crimes can be traumatic, but the most serious crimes cause enormous emotional and physical harm. That is why better support for victims is at the heart of our vision for improving the criminal justice system.
>
> We are well-placed to make these reforms now. The number of people who are victims of crime has fallen by 40% compared to ten years ago. (Home Office, 2005c: 1).

It is interesting to note that the 'consultation' period allocated by the government for comment on the document extended for a week less than three months,[14] and that as far as can be ascertained, during the twenty months since the closing date to the time of writing the Victim and Confidence Unit of the Office for Criminal Justice Reform has made no public response to such comments as may have been received.

---

13. David Garland (2002, *op. cit.*: 151) has provided a telling criticism of this situation, and the way in which, since the late 1970s and 1980s the influence of criminal justice professionals within policymaking has been eroded and transferred to managers and accountants.
14. From 7 December 2005 to 1 March 2006 (Home Office 2005d: 4).

A STAKEHOLDER APPROACH TO VICTIM VINDICATION

A truly restorative approach towards improving the support of victims of crime would envisage what might be termed a 'quadripartite' approach to their situation that would bring together the principal stakeholders (victims, offenders, communities and state government) each with their own needs and resources in collaboration. This approach is illustrated in *Figure 5:1*, and it will be noted that the entire focus is on victims (as opposed to witnesses) and the forms of resources that might be brought to bear on their legitimate requirements.

The illustration recognises that each of the stakeholders brings to the collaborative arena both needs and resources, and that these can be used through restorative and reparative dialogue to the benefit of all the parties. One of the main criticisms of contemporary criminal justice made by victims is that the process is dominated by considerations relating to offenders and the legal process, and frequently at the expense of victims themselves. The approach outlined here recognises the importance of maintaining a balance between all the participants, using as far as possible the resources that they can provide towards meeting the needs of each other.

By way of example, victims as we have already noted have needs for healing, apology, reparation and support. Healing may in some respects result from resources that offenders can offer in terms of remorse (including apology), understanding, and the making of reparation. Local communities and close others can be instrumental in supporting victims and aiding healing, and are thus a resource to them. Local communities that can also provide restorative justice facilitators to assist victims and offenders to recognise each others' needs also contribute an essential resource through victim: offender mediation, group conferencing and participation in healing and other circles.

Offenders also have needs for forgiveness that victims can meet, and for the means of leading law-abiding lives that both the state and local communities can provide in terms of life skills, employment opportunities and social reintegration. They also need the support of close others who can be an invaluable asset in encouraging the making of reparation and apology to victims.

Communities have needs in the form of security, crime reduction, social cohesion and a lesser fear of crime. These can be met in part by offenders who make reparation to victims and opt for a crime-free lifestyle, and also in part by the state through the resources of the Criminal Justice System and the presence of law-abiding citizens. Communities can (as we shall see later) provide employment opportunities to offenders and receive reparative amenity in return through projects funded by the state and locally on which offenders can be employed and learn valuable life and employment skills.

84 *The Penal Crisis and the Clapham Omnibus*

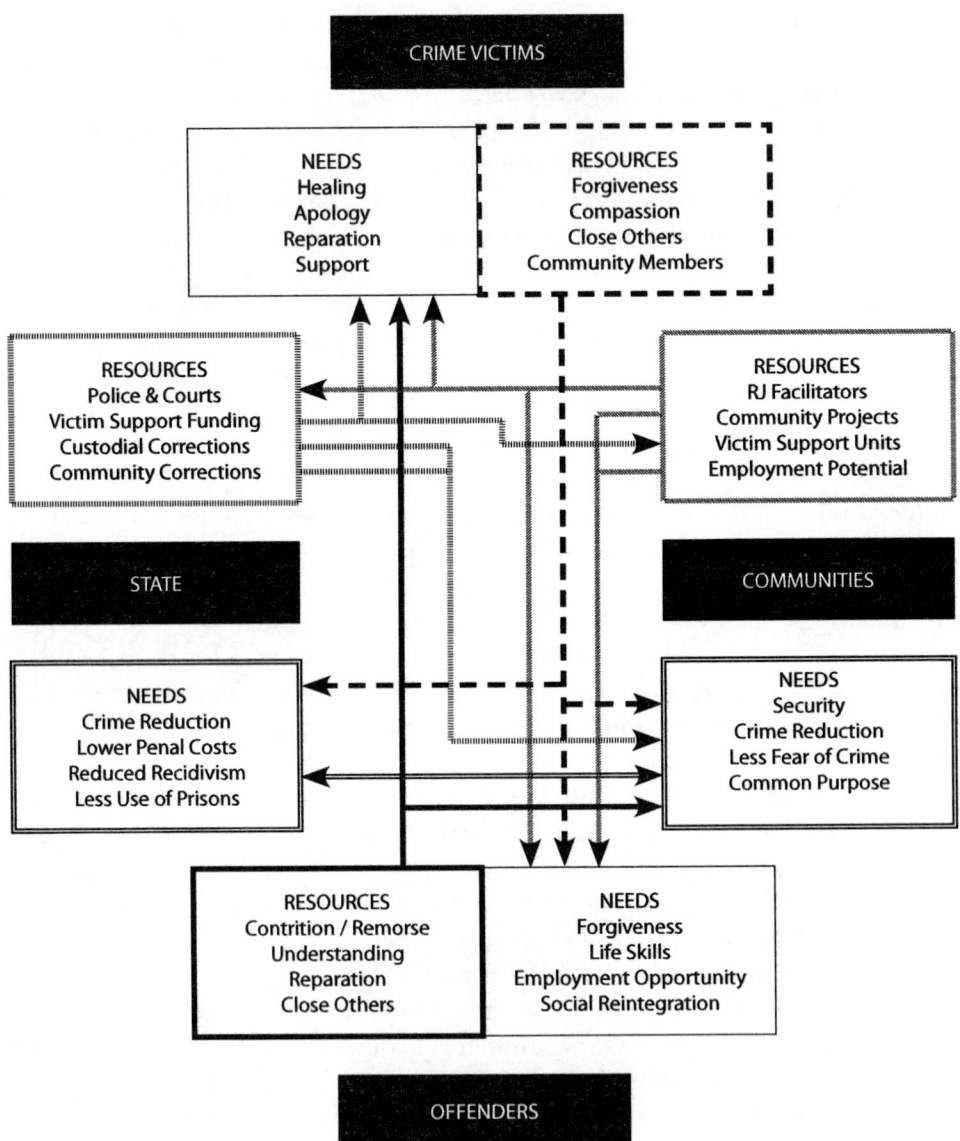

Figure 5:1: A Quadripartite Approach to Restorative and Reparative Dialogue

The state also has needs for crime reduction, lower penal system costs, reduced recidivism and lesser use of prisons. An increase in the use of community sanctions can meet these needs and provide reparation for victims of crime by using the resources that offenders can bring to community sanction projects. More constructive use of custodial corrections also contributes significantly to community wellbeing and the needs of government.

Restorative justice might be said to be the 'fuel' that could add a motive force to this collaborative enterprise in a number of different respects. First, the ethos of restorative justice, as we have already seen in *Chapters 2, 3* and *4*, enables a different conceptual approach to be taken towards the punishment of offenders, the use of custodial and community corrections, the reparation of crime victims and the involvement of communities in delivery of justice. Secondly, the various forms of restorative justice dialogue (victim: offender mediation (VOM), conferencing and the use of circles) provide a means of communication between the stakeholders in an attempt to meet their needs and employ their resources to best effect. Third, these same forms of dialogue enable a more *inclusive* form of justice to be envisaged by making diversion from the full and formal criminal justice process possible in relation to less serious crime where victims and communities are reconciled with offenders who accept guilt, apologise and make appropriate reparation. And perhaps most important of all, these forms of dialogue reveal both high offender and victim satisfaction rates combined with reductions in recidivism. (Umbreit *et al.*, 2006).[15]

The advantages of such a situation may readily be seen in the possibility of abandoning the present *exclusive* model of incarcerative punishment that is predicated on the supposed benefits it brings for social protection, and replacing this with a restorative model that seeks the best outcomes for all the stakeholders within criminal justice. Moreover, by using custodial punishment only when it is strictly unavoidable (as the Finnish experience cited in *Chapter 4* illustrates[16]), and by using it more constructively as we shall see in the chapters that follow, considerable fiscal resources can be saved and re-directed towards providing effective community sanctions. This can be achieved without undue additional social risk, without the collateral damage that imprisonment imposes on the dependents of offenders, and without the present neglect of their legitimate needs suffered by victims of crime and those close to them.

Restorative justice offers, in a very direct and collaborative sense, the means of adopting what Mary Achilles (2004: 66-67) has described as the need for a more holistic approach to justice, and towards the markedly different requirements of

---

15. In *Restorative Justice Dialogue: Evidence-Based Practice* (2006), Mark Umbreit and colleagues provide a comprehensive analysis of VOM, group conferencing, circles and other forms of RJ intervention based on research evidence from a wide range of countries. This research indicates high rates of participant satisfaction, and, in some instances, clear evidence of reduced recidivism through offender participation.
16. See *Chapter 4*, p. 71.

victims and offenders.[17] Heather Strang (2004) has asked the important question: 'Is restorative justice imposing its agenda on victims?' By way of an answer she concludes that:

> I have suggested that if we are in accord with Howard Zehr's view of restorative justice as, among other things, a means by which victims' harms and needs are addressed, then the central role played by victims means they are integral to the process...
>
> Restorative justice provides the time and space for victims and offenders to talk about more than the price to be exacted for the wrong-doing, and much of it is more salient and important to all players than the question of punishment. But the need for censure and reparation through the voluntary undertaking of a burdensome action should be seen for what they usually are: the signal of an offender's remorse and an acknowledgement of the victim's suffering. (Strang, 2004: 103-4)

The title of this chapter asks, 'Could Restorative Justice Give Victims a Better Deal?' In Britain at present and under the existing circumstances in which the Criminal Justice System operates, victims are clearly not afforded a high priority in response to their needs and concerns. A restorative and reparative penology would give victims of crime a much more central place within the justice process, while at the same time making it clear to offenders that the onus is on them to take responsibility for the harm caused and to do something substantial to 'put wrongs right'. In this sense, and where this challenge was met, victims would get a 'better deal', and offenders would earn the right to full social reintegration. More than this even, justice would be more civilised, more purposeful, and arguably more effective.

It is, however, important to re-iterate at this stage that the process of victim vindication is four-dimensional, with each of the stakeholders (state, offenders, victims and communities) having legitimate needs to be met and contributions to make towards fairer justice. The fact that offenders have resources to offer within this equation is frequently overlooked, and almost entirely so by retributive justice. The state has a duty as a principal stakeholder to ensure that the process is properly resourced as we shall see in Parts Two and Three of this book. Communities, given an opportunity to do, so can also make a valuable contribution towards victim reparation and support, but all too often at the present time their potential involvement is ignored by both the state and its correctional services. It is insufficient for the state to rely upon voluntary organisations to provide adequate and appropriate victim support as is largely the practice in contemporary Britain (Home Office, 2003b, 2005b, c and d).

---

17. Here see: M. Achilles (2004), 'Can Restorative Justice Live Up to Its Promise to Victims?' in H. Zehr and B. Toews (eds.), *Critical Issues in Restorative Justice*, Devon, UK: Willan Publishing, and Monsey, NY: Criminal Justice Press, pp. 65-73.

And, lest it be forgotten, both the state and communities also have needs in the form of crime reduction and lesser levels of recidivism. This means that correctional services need to be effective in enabling offenders to desist from crime, and a restorative and reparative penology is better placed to achieve this than a retributive one, as will become clear in the chapters that follow. However, within the chapters that contribute to Part Two of this book we shall examine practical issues and dilemmas within the field of custodial corrections, and the ways in which restorative justice might enable prisons to be more effective than at present in terms of changing offending behaviour and making a substantial contribution towards victim reparation.

Societies have a right to know that prisons are safe, secure and purposeful places that provide constructive regimes on a 'value for (taxpayers) money' basis. They also have a right to expect that people released from prisons will be less likely to re-offend, and that the experience of prison custody will have had a positive rather than a damaging impact on the lives of those who are thus sentenced.

CHAPTER 6

Why Are Prisons as Presently Operated So Ineffective?

Just over twenty years ago Andrew Rutherford, a former prison governor turned academic wrote a most influential book describing the prison crisis in England and Wales in the early 1980s during the period of retreat from rehabilitation and the surge towards the so-called 'justice model' of criminal punishment.[1] At the time the prison population had risen to an all-time record high figure of 47,000 from an immediately post-war level of just over 20,000, and a similar pattern of expansion was evident in the United States and a number of the other democracies within the Western world. Re-reading Rutherford's work at the present time cannot fail to fill the observer of the contemporary penal system with the most profound sense of *déjà vu*, recording, as it did, the deep sense of concern felt by correctional professionals, penal reform groups, academics and religious leaders. In Rutherford's words:

> A new and virulent gaol fever is now endemic in many societies, including some which set high store on democratic values and aspirations. Imprisonment is being used more extensively and the apparatus of the prison system being greatly expanded despite, in some instances, stated government policy that parsimony should guide decisions to impose custody. The new gaol fever has every appearance of being out of political control. . . As the prison system expands the ultimate values of democratic society are threatened. (Rutherford, 1986:3)

Those with memories of the penal system stretching back far enough will recall that 1986, the year in which Rutherford's book was published, marked the start of a wave of prison disturbances in the United Kingdom that was to continue into the early 1990s with the 'riot of all riots' at Strangeways Prison in Manchester in April of that year. Though there had been major disturbances prior to 1986 (notably at Parkhurst 1969 and 1979, Albany 1971 and 1972, Gartree 1972 and 1978, Hull 1976 and 1979, and Wormwood Scrubs 1979)[2], these were more about prisoner dissatisfaction with the regimes and conditions within high security and uncrowded prisons than with the pressures caused by overcrowding in prisons of lower security status. The same post-rehabilitation era also saw a similar pattern of disturbances in the United States from the mid-1970s onwards, with those at Attica in 1971, and Santa Fe in 1980 being perhaps the most notorious. (Adams, 1992:87-103).

Such is not to suggest that the present penal crisis of 'numbers' within England

---

1. A. Rutherford (1986), *Prisons and the Process of Justice*, Oxford: Oxford University Press.
2. Here see J. Ditchfield (1990), *Control in Prisons: A Review of the Literature*, Home Office Research Study No. 118, London: HMSO at pp.3-4, and R. Adams (1992), *Prison Riots in Britain and the USA*, Basingstoke, UK: Macmillan Press at pp.155-169.

and Wales necessarily threatens a new wave of prison disturbances, but it has to be said that overcrowding of correctional establishments has always held the potential for concerted disorder, and the reasons for this need to be recognised. Overcrowding and indifferent management are the main reasons why correctional facilities become ineffective, and that is what this chapter is about.

MANAGEMENT OF PRISONS: ORDER, AMENITY AND SERVICE

John DiIulio, one of the most influential writers on prison management in recent years, has insisted that the presence and quality of three principal aspects of prison life ultimately determine whether such facilities are effectively managed. These he describes as order, amenity and service respectively. (DiIulio, 1987: 50). Now while the need for order in prisons may be self-evident, the way in which it is approached and imposed becomes a critical factor in the stability and safety of daily life for prisoners and correctional officials alike. Amenity, in DiIulio's terms, means the extent and diversity of arrangements within the prison regime for keeping inmates occupied in a purposeful manner, for providing adequate outlets for recreation and self-expression, and for making available opportunities for self-improvement that might encourage a law-abiding lifestyle. Service constitutes the reliability and invariability of the delivery of those important aspects of prison life (such as food, medical treatment, mail, visitation, and the like) upon which those in custody rely for their reasonable comfort and subsistence.

As I have indicated elsewhere (Cornwell, 2007: 125-130), effective prison regimes rely absolutely upon the maintenance of safety and security as the bedrock conditions in which daily life can be tolerable and constructive for all those – both staff and inmates – who form the daily population within prison perimeters. Ensuring good order and safety require that measures of control are imposed to enable adequate supervision of inmates in manageable sized groups with acceptable standards of behaviour at all times. Because of the fact that criminal offenders (unlike hospital patients or residents within other institutions) are detained involuntarily, the internal and external security of prisons has to be sufficiently robust to prevent them from leaving lawful custody. However, over-intrusiveness of security systems and routines can equally become an oppressive and depressive factor of custodial life, and needs to be sensitively matched to the level of risk (both external and internal) posed by the inmate population.

Effective prison management requires that careful and consistent attention is given to ensuring that adequate numbers of staff are on duty at all times to create a safe and secure environment. Too many staff on duty is wasteful of resources and creates an oppressive atmosphere, while too few staff in attendance leads to lax supervision and unreliable delivery of routines. The Direct Supervision model of staff detailing, pioneered in the United States and now used in a number of other jurisdictions[3], is more likely to result in correct manning levels within prisons, and a more flexible use of the staff resource throughout each working day.

The Direct Supervision model of staff detailing and deployment has never been adopted in British prisons because, in spite of its evident advantages in economy and flexibility, it has been opposed in principle by the traditionalist stance of the Prison Officers' Association (POA), the trade union that dominates the employment practices of the Prison Service.[4] (Hawkins, 1976: 167-173; Thomas, 1972: 220-221; Lewis, 1997: 130-132). The model has, however, been introduced very effectively in the first privately operated high security prison in the Republic of South Africa which was designed, built and commissioned by the British-based consortium Group 4 and subsequently Global Solutions Limited.[5] We shall return to the operational method and merits of Direct Supervision in some further detail in *Chapter 8*.

Beyond having a formal role[6] and appropriate security systems provision to maintain order and prevent escape or concerted indiscipline, every prison needs a clear statement of its 'custodial vision' or operational purpose. The term 'correctional' service implies that within every convicted prison regime there is a deliberate and structured emphasis on the examination of offending behaviour, the acquisition of skills and competencies that will encourage a law-abiding life style, and preparation for release and social reintegration. Beyond these essential components, the requirement of 'amenity' dictates that proper provision is made for physical well-being, recreation, religious observance, visitation, healthcare, and the like. As we shall also see in *Chapter 8*, prisons operated within a restorative justice ethos would make specific provision for victim reparation in addition.

---

3. Direct Supervision staffing levels are closely related to the architectural design, regime delivery and security requirements of correctional facilities to ensure safety and supervision without wasteful or neglectful practices becoming widespread. For an excellent architectural resource, see P. Krasnov (1998), *Correctional Facility Design and Detailing*, New York: McGraw-Hill.
4. The difficulty of changing the attendance systems of staff to implement Direct Supervision in British prisons could only be overcome by a deliberate policy change and imposition, or by convincing the POA that it would be in the direct interests of its members (financially and professionally) to embrace the change. For reasons that will become clear in *Chapter 8*, the traditional resistance to change within the POA and its adherence to 'custom and practice' is so entrenched that only a considerable financial incentive would be likely to succeed.
5. The facility is known as Mangaung Correctional Centre at Bloemfontein in the Free State Province of South Africa. It is a 3,000 bed prison opened in July 2001, and is operated on the Direct Supervision model of inmate management and control. The author was the consultant operations adviser to the prison throughout the building, commissioning and first two years of operation. Global Solutions Limited was part of the former Group 4 organisation, subsequently Group 4/ Falck, and currently Group 4 Securitas (G4S).
6. That is to say a statement of what type of prison it is, whether an adult or young offender facility, a remand or convicted offender establishment (or possibly both), and its level of security (maximum, medium or minimum – however expressed).

The requirement for a clearly stated 'custodial vision' is an essential means of focussing the attention of inmates and staff on what it is that the facility seeks as the *outcomes* of the custodial process in a 'correctional' sense. This custodial vision must be expressed in terms of indicators (or measures) of performance that are achievable, and against which both the extent and quality of performance can be audited and assessed at specified intervals. Only in such a manner can it be said that the operation of the custodial process is 'managed' in terms of its effectiveness and its use of human and material resources. There is, however, a danger that the requirements for audit and assessment become a burdensome and self-serving process that can divert attention and resources away from performance and towards the satisfaction of bureaucratic ends. Managerial effectiveness demands that such systems be kept as simple as is consistent with obtaining measurable outcomes.

Within his assessment of the nature of prison management, DiIulio suggests that much of the success (or otherwise) of correctional practice depends upon the ethos within each facility developed by its front-line staff whose working lives are lived in the closest proximity to inmates, and the essential difference of approach between treating those in custody as 'incarcerated citizens' or as 'criminal offenders'. (DiIulio, 1987: 182). This difference is, I believe, profoundly important in shaping the custodial vision of any prison, since it ultimately determines whether inmates are treated as potentially responsible human beings, or as a form of social sub-class to be controlled and subjugated while in custody.

Such is not to suggest that prison managers from the Governor (or Director) downwards do not have an immediate responsibility for setting the 'tone' and standards of conduct and the nature of the daily relationship between prison staff and inmates, but it does imply that, if left to itself to develop, the quality of this relationship and the manner in which it is given operational effect will be fashioned by front-line staff with the tacit approval of their immediate superiors. Whether this will result in what DiIulio so aptly describes as a 'keeper' mentality, or in the development of a 'responsibility' model of governance and relationships, is ultimately a matter of the managerial 'style' and example adopted and insisted upon by senior management. We shall return to this important issue in due course.

The concept of 'service delivery' within prisons is no less important than those of security, control, 'amenity' and staff: inmate relationships. Prisons, like hospitals and other 'consumer' dominated organisations, face a challenging logistical task in providing the essentials for the daily maintenance of those in their charge in an efficient and effective manner. Whether it be meals, mail, opportunities for visitation, access to healthcare, daily recreation or any of the other necessities of prison life, delivery has to be achieved reliably and to acceptable (if not better) standards of quality and reliability. The routine nature of daily life in prisons makes each of these aspects of delivery an 'event' anticipated by inmates as an essential feature of their well-being and conditions, and failure to meet these expectations is the most common cause of prisoner unrest and indiscipline.

Meals, and the quality, variety and nature of the food provided in prisons, are amongst the most sensitive issues of custodial life, particularly for a predominantly relatively young and active population. It is also one of the anomalies of prison life that many inmates received into custodial facilities have a history of poor and irregular dietary consumption when at liberty within their communities, and yet quickly develop expectations of, and come to rely upon, relatively high standards of catering while in custody. In addition, to this sensitivity has to be added the need, in recent years, to provide that range of diets that is consistent with the ethnic, religious, and the medical needs of increasingly diverse populations.

Now while the need for routines to ensure reliable delivery of inmate services in prisons is evidently essential and thus an important component of sound management practice, it is also a potential source of friction between inmates and prison staff. It is also the case that the higher the standards of quality and reliability of provision become, the higher the expectations of the 'consumers' also become, and the greater their perceived sense of grievance when these are not fully met. On the other hand, prison staff required as a matter of good practice to maintain these standards can easily come to perceive themselves as being, to some extent, the vulnerable 'domestic servants' of those in their charge, and driven by the (sometimes unreasonable) expectations of the latter. In management terms, therefore, this is a delicate balance to maintain, and one that inevitably consumes a considerable amount of effort and attention.

In addition to the aspects of prison management described briefly in the foregoing paragraphs, it further has to be stated that the operation of contemporary correctional facilities has become increasingly complex over recent years. Part of this complexity derives from the budgetary regulation of such facilities to meet what might be termed 'value for public money' considerations; part from the increasingly professional nature of human resource management and employment law provision in relation to correctional employees; and part from the markedly greater extent of public, political and media scrutiny of the operational conditions and standards of correctional services almost universally.

On balance it seems reasonable to suggest that it is this increasing managerial complexity and the nature of the competing demands made upon those charged with the direction of correctional services that calls for particular skills and personal attributes. Correctional management has moved beyond the era of the 'competent generalist' with certain defined leadership and humanistic skills, and into an age in which an ability to 'juggle' the competing priorities effectively leads to professional success. Whether this amounts to an art or a science I leave to the reader to decide. One thing is, however, certain: those who do not have an ability to lead and handle *people* within an enclosed, potentially stressful and demanding environment, are unlikely to manage prisons well. Competent bureaucrats they may be, but success in the correctional enterprise demands a 'feel' for the constantly changing temperature in a potentially volatile and unstable environment.

PRISONS, IDEOLOGY AND REALITY

We have noted in the preceding part of this chapter the need for prisons to have a clearly defined 'custodial vision' in order to be manageable and effective. This is, however, rather in the nature of 'putting the cart in front of the horse', since if the entire prison system of any country has no discernible ideology[7] to guide its correctional processes, or adopts an inappropriate concept of penology, then it is altogether unlikely that the outcomes of criminal punishment will be favourable in controlling crime or reducing reoffending.

In Britain, as in other countries across the world, what has been termed 'the retreat from rehabilitation' described in *Chapter 1*, and the abandonment during the late 1980s of the 'justice model' as it was originally proposed (American Friends Service Committee, 1972; von Hirsch, 1976; Hudson, 1987; Cornwell, 2006:33-35)[8], created a void that could only be filled by a return to retributive and deterrent concepts of criminal punishment. Thus the present 'crisis of numbers' that has progressively escalated since the mid-1990s might be said to have arisen because of the lack of a coherent ideology *and* the adoption of inappropriate punishment concepts based on a return to retribution and deterrence in pursuit of 'tough on crime' policies.

This could have been foreseen, for as Rubin pointed out as long ago as 1979: 'The issue is *not* punishment or reformation but whether we will have a prison crisis in addition to the crime problem' (Rubin, 1979: 8). Paradoxically, however, even this analysis has proved to be to some extent incorrect since in the past decade we have endured, and still endure, a prison crisis during a period in which (at least in Western Europe) crime has generally reduced - as we have already noted in *Chapter 1*.[9]

The coincidence of the factors described above, combined – at least in England and Wales – with a distinctly impetuous and eclectic quality of penal policy-making has resulted in the custodial penal system becoming full above its operational capacity, many individual prisons being overcrowded, and no substantive plans

---

7. That is to suggest in this particular context a broadly consensual set of ideas that form the basis for the formulation of effective penal policies and their implementation.
8. This situation has been commented upon at some length in earlier work, but the move away from a 'just deserts' model of criminal justice to a form of 'neo-retributive' justice caused what I have described as a political vacuum in the 1990s that led to the escalation of prison populations due to deliberately adopted 'tough on crime' policies.
9. See *Chapter 1*, pp. 38-9.

(other to increase long-term capacity) being in place to reduce the pressure. This lack of an evident ideology, caused presumably because of a perceived dearth of alternatives other than to continue in the same upward punitive spiral, means that prisons can have no custodial vision other than that of 'containing the pressure' and warehousing excessive numbers of prisoners.

To the Clapham Omnibus passenger this must appear to represent a penal system out of control, the brakes having failed and the engine still propelling the vehicle forward. To those charged with the management of prisons some form of collision must seem inevitable because for them the vehicle has neither brakes nor steering, and it is carrying more passengers than is strictly admissible. But if a collision occurs, who will carry the blame at a subsequent inquiry? Do the wheels have to fall off before this runaway vehicle can be brought to a halt?

The answer to these questions lies within the arena of contemporary penal politics. There can be no coherent ideology without a reasoned analysis of the realities and outcomes that have resulted from the pursuit of political expediency rather than penological pragmatism. At this stage of the penal crisis it matters little what the political complexion of the government looks like, but much more how, and to what extent, that government is prepared to weather the storm of media and public criticism that must inevitably accompany the remedial measures necessary to bring the penal system back under control.

The use of executive early release of prisoners towards the end of their sentences is one means of speedily reducing excessive prison populations, but it brings with it an immediate and deafening cacophony of media accusations of endangering public safety. A moratorium on the imposition of short prison sentences for an indefinite period is another means of ensuring that fewer offenders are sentenced to custody in the first place, but it is liable to the same chorus of opprobrium. Placing strict criteria on sentencing *maxima* is a further way of curbing excessive custodial punishment, but it alienates the judiciary from the executive and creates political tensions within government. None of these measures, however, buys more than short-term relief, and neither do they provide any guarantee that similar situations will not recur in the future.

However, as I have indicated in former work (Cornwell, 2007: 165-6), penal history provides us with evident examples of the way in which Finland, Germany, The Netherlands and North Carolina in the United States have all, at different times and for different reasons, made significant reductions in excessive prison populations when faced with the need to do so, and as a matter of political expediency.[10] In addition, The Netherlands, Denmark and Norway have, in times past, imposed

---

10. Here see also the explanations of Lappi-Seppälä (2001) in relation to Finland in the 1950s, Wiegend (2001) in relation to the (then) West Germany in the 1960s and 1970s, and Tonry (2003) and Wright (2002) in relation to North Carolina in the 1980s and 1990s).

strict limitations on the admission of offenders to prisons operating at, or above, full capacity. (Tak, 2001; Kyvsgaard, 2001 and Larsson, 2001). There are, therefore, a number of precedents for such actions given the political determination to act in a reductive manner. Ideally, Britain should follow these examples.

In England and Wales the Prison Service has a Statement of Purpose that was designed to guide its work within the criminal justice system. It is:

> Her Majesty's Prison Service serves the public by keeping in custody those committed by the courts. Our duty is to look after them with humanity and to help them lead law-abiding lives in custody and after release.

Though the first part of this statement may be unexceptionable, it is very difficult to see how a considerably overcrowded organisation like the Prison Service can hope to fulfil its duty in delivering the requirements of the second part. The widespread use of cells designed for single occupancy to house two people is far from humane, and the retention in use of sub-standard accommodation due to the need to house excessive numbers of prisoners is similarly unjustifiable – other than as a means of providing public protection. The use of police and court cells to house those for whom there is no room in prisons is an unacceptable practice, and should be forbidden in a humane and civilised society.

Overcrowded prisons cannot deliver constructive regimes to assist inmates to lead law-abiding lives because of the lack of resources and space to do so. For similar reasons, prisons filled to (or above) their operational capacity are obliged to keep prisoners locked in their cells for many hours a day because there is no purposeful work for them to do and the pressure on educational and recreational facilities is greater than can be met. Thus however potentially well such places might otherwise be managed, and however clear the 'custodial vision' that they may aspire to achieve, it becomes impossible for them to do much more than warehouse prisoners for the periods of time specified by the courts that commit them to custody. These are the reasons why prisons managed under existing circumstances of overcrowding are failing institutions that are not 'fit for purpose'. But there are reasons other than those associated with overcrowding that render prisons, as presently managed, ineffective.

THE ROOT CAUSES OF PRISON INEFFECTIVENESS

Whenever, as is increasingly the case, it is claimed that prisons are ineffective, it becomes necessary to ask the question: In doing what? In other words, what is it that can reasonably be expected of prisons that such institutions cannot deliver effectively? In order to answer such questions we have, in the first place, to have some measure of agreement about what socially exclusive places like prisons can do *beyond* the fulfilment of a public protection role. After all, locking people away from the society within which they would otherwise live is a serious matter: to do so for longer than strictly necessary is injurious, and to do so without some beneficial purpose is both aimless and possibly cruel.

Mechanistic imprisonment supposes a non-correctional dimension for penal custody that admits a retributive warehousing function, possibly in conditions of decency, but little else. Correctional imprisonment, on the other hand, supposes that the experience of custody should legitimately provoke changed behaviour, and that the enterprise fails if this does not occur. But how legitimate is it to hold out expectations of change, particularly if offending is a matter of free-will choice; and how, in any case, can we know if and when this change has occurred?

These are troublesome questions not infrequently avoided by those who make penal policies that result in citizens, sometimes in large numbers, being deprived of their liberty. We might reasonably curtail the debate at the warehousing point, but in order to do so with any sort of justification we would need to be certain beyond reasonable doubt how long a period spent in the warehouse is strictly permissible on the basis of desert. It seems that we have never been able to arrive at this degree of certainty, and in any case have confused the issue completely by attaching other agendas (such as deterrence) to the calculus.

If the requirement for change is anything beyond a (perhaps) worthy aspiration we seem to be in deeper trouble still since it carries with it the risk of the widespread use of indeterminate and extended sentences of which strong criticism has been made in *Chapter 4*. Moreover, to make release from custody contingent upon such subjective criteria as 'reduced public risk', 'decreased dangerousness', or 'evidential attitudinal change' is highly questionable in both a moral and an operational sense.

A number of reputable commentators on criminal justice have, since the demise of the rehabilitative ideal, questioned whether it is possible to 'rehabilitate' people in a closed custodial environment. (e.g. American Friends Service Committee, 1972; Cross, 1971; Allen, 1981; Hudson, 1987), and from my own experience of working in prisons both for adults and young offenders I concur with such reservations. In addition, if contemporary recidivism statistics in Britain provide any reliable guide, then it would seem that what little is attempted in the name of rehabilitation in contemporary prisons is significantly ineffective (Cornwell, 2006: 66-79).

Yet, as we shall see in *Chapter 8*, a reparative and restorative model of penology, and in particular the use of prisons within such a context may offer us some respite. It will, however, as matters currently stand, be a long march uphill. For as Margery Fry, the penal reformer of an earlier era, wrote as long ago as the middle of the last century:

> One only has to propose some change in our penal laws to become aware at once that ages of traditional emotion, of obscure thinking, of desire for vengeance, of terror of 'bad men', of distrust of authority, of religious doctrine, of sadism, of love of power have woven around the subject a complex tangle of motives and beliefs ... At the present moment it is no exaggeration to say that the greatest obstacle to the revision of our penal administration is this mass

of confused thought and emotion in the public mind. Old rules, old buildings, old cruelties are protected by this thicket of unanalysed fears and prejudices. (Fry, 1951: 161 quoted in Hawkins, 1976: 161)[11]

And so it is presently with many of the initiatives within criminal justice that have emerged during the past decade and the one that preceded it. Prisons as we currently use them have been largely emasculated from serving any social usefulness other than the 'containment of the wicked' largely because the purpose of such places has remained ambiguous and their aims confused. The confusion arises not because prisons are what they are, but because the criminal justice system that they serve is equally uncertain in its goals, and remains at the mercy of political whim and external pressures imposed predominantly by a mass media that thrives on the sensationalism of crime and the vilification of offenders.

If it is true as Hawkins insisted way back in 1976 that: 'Even in situations where the rehabilitative ideal has been embodied in correctional practice the evidence from the empirical studies that have been made in recent decades is overwhelmingly negative'[12], and as Conrad three years before had argued: 'It is not possible to continue the justification of policy decisions in corrections on the supposition that such programmes achieve rehabilitative objectives'[13], then it is unreasonable to judge the performance of prisons on these bases. But to continue to pretend, for inexplicable reasons other than of presentational expediency, that prisons retain this function is at best hypocritical and at worst disingenuous. Thus, then, prisons are inevitably to be perceived as ineffective by politicians, the public and the media that so greatly influences them.

The situation in relation to the rehabilitation of prisoners within the custodial correctional setting has not changed since 1976, and is altogether unlikely to do so in the foreseeable future. Therefore, if the offending behaviour and attitudes of criminal persons are to be changed towards the adoption of a law-abiding life as a result of criminal sanctions, then this has to be achieved by other means and for other reasons. Until this happens, prisons will remain an ineffective vehicle for such an endeavour, but restorative justice opens the door to a new approach that could transform the lives of many offenders, as we shall see in the chapters that follow.

THE NEED FOR A NEW CUSTODIAL VISION

In view of all that has been suggested in the foregoing discussion it is clear that a new meaning has to be given to the way in which criminal justice is presently

---

11. M. Fry (1951), *Arms of the Law*, London: Gollancz.
12. Hawkins, 1976, *op. cit.*, p.51.
13. J. P. Conrad (1973), 'Corrections and Simple Justice', *Journal of Criminal Law and Criminology*, vol.64, pp. 208-217. The quotation is at p.209.

administered in Britain, and, indeed, in a number of other democracies in which similar penal crises are being experienced. Experience indicates that the traditional belief systems relating to the punishment of offenders, and in particular the use of imprisonment, have failed because rates of reoffending do not decrease as a result of existing penal policies grounded in them. It is also doubtful whether what has hitherto been described as 'rehabilitation' is a viable concept within the constraints that prison custody imposes.

Moreover, as we have seen in *Chapter 5*, the present approach to criminal justice does little to improve the situation of victims of crime, and neither does it in any particular sense encourage offenders to take responsibility for their wrongdoing and do something to repair the damage that this causes to victims and communities. Insofar as prisons as institutions are concerned, it would be desirable to move away from a 'warehousing' mode of operation simply because this serves little prospective purpose and is probably more damaging to offenders and those persons close to them than beneficial in any social sense. Use of prisons as at present may incapacitate offenders from further offending for the duration of sentences, but this is only 'using time to buy time'.

It will always be necessary to have prisons because the seriousness of some criminal offences can only adequately be punished by the perpetrator(s) of them being removed from society for an appropriate period of time. This stated, there is evidently a need to create a custodial correctional system that has the capacity and the resources to provide regimes that allow for behavioural change *and* enable offenders to make good their debt to victims and the wider community. This inevitably means outlawing the practice of overcrowding prisons beyond their reasonable operational capacity, and, ideally, avoiding sending to prison those for whom imprisonment is not strictly necessary.

But prisons do not (or at least should not) exist in some form of social vacuum, although there has been a tendency in the past to locate and design such places as though this were, in fact, the case. As we shall see in later chapters there is a strong case for making prisons much more integrated within the communities that surround them, and create an infinitely stronger link between custodial and non-custodial corrections. Moreover, if the often-alleged public fear of offenders is to be overcome, and in any event almost all offenders eventually return into communities, there is much to be gained from a wider involvement of local communities in the work of prisons.

All of this calls for a new concept of corrections that casts off the shackles of past thinking and is open to innovative approaches and greater transparency in operational terms. The present situation is professionally frustrating and motivationally limiting for correctional officials and largely purposeless for offenders in custody. Given the enormous cost that prisons impose on national resources, reasonable prudence alone dictates that this important social service should be delivered with greater economy and effectiveness.

It is of historical interest to note that in 1980 in a Britain that was then facing a situation of significant prison overcrowding[14], the Parliamentary All-Party Penal Affairs Group (PA-PPAG) published a report under the chairmanship of Robert Kilroy-Silk MP entitled *Too Many Prisoners*. The report examined the ways in which the prison population might speedily be reduced, and made a number of far-sighted recommendations to the incumbent conservative government. In his response the (then) Home Secretary William Whitelaw said in an address to the Conservative Central Council at its conference in Bournemouth on 21st March:

> It is no use continuing to over-burden the staff who have to run the system, too often in antiquated and inadequate buildings, with petty offenders who can be dealt with just as well in other ways ... we must ensure that prison is reserved for those whom we really need to contain in custody and that sentences are no longer than necessary to achieve this objective ... We shall need, and in this the courts have their part to play, to see that the prisons are not allowed to remain cluttered up with trivial and inadequate offenders who are no real threat to anyone, except possibly to themselves, but whose presence helps to create the extremely acute pressures which afflict our prisons today and all who work in them. (PA-PPAG, 1980: 2)

Since that time the prison population of England and Wales has almost doubled and the same problems continue to confront the prison authorities. In the event, the 1980 crisis was eased by a considerable prison building programme rather than by sending less offenders to prison and expanding the use of non-custodial alternatives. The same situation recurred in the 1990s and was similarly resolved. Now, again, a further crisis is being dealt with by again expanding the capacity of prisons rather than by reducing the number of prisoners. It might be considered that failure on three occasions should prompt government to take alternative strategies seriously, but it seems that there is no limit to the number of offenders it is prepared to lock away, many of whom do not pose a significant public risk or merit the cost of being imprisoned.

If ever a new custodial vision were needed it is at the present time. Prisons as presently operated are ineffective because there are once again too many prisoners and the purposes of imprisonment, beyond that of social protection, are demonstrably unclear. In the chapter that follows we shall examine how a restorative penology might assist in resolving this situation and contribute to the possibility of creating a new custodial vision for the future.

---

14. The prison population of England and Wales in mid-March of that year had reached an all-time high of 44,800 housed in certified normal accommodation (CNA) of 38,500. Parliamentary All-Party Penal Affairs Group (1980), *Too Many Prisoners: An Examination of Ways of Reducing the Prison Population*, Chichester and London: Barry Rose Publishers (June).

CHAPTER 7

Does Restorative Justice Propose Less Use of Prisons?

In the preceding chapter we have discussed a number of the reasons why prisons – and particularly overcrowded prisons – become largely ineffective in reducing reoffending. It is also clear that as these institutions are presently managed, in both the strategic and the operational sense in Britain and elsewhere, it is unlikely that offenders will accept the challenge held out by restorative justice to take responsibility for their offences and make practical amends for them because there is little, if anything, to encourage them to do so. This situation achieves nothing for victims of crime, and much the same amount for offenders and the communities to which most of them return on release from custody.

The concept of restorative justice does provide an opportunity to adopt an entirely new way of looking at this situation, but this implies significant change in the way that criminal justice is administered in most Western-style democracies as we have noted in *Chapter 2*. Given the huge costs involved in maintaining excessive prison populations it seems altogether remarkable that in the present era we seem to be content to accept little (if any) control being exercised over the number of people in custody *and* the fact that prisons are so evidently ineffective in changing criminal behaviour. This reduces prisons to the social role of warehousing offenders for the purposes of public protection, but little else of consequence.

But what if we were to say: 'enough is enough?' What if we were to insist: 'we simply cannot afford to do this any longer'. What, if we were to ask: 'why are we doing this when other nations find it unnecessary to do so?' These, surely, are relevant questions and issues to which discerning members of the public are entitled to seek reasonable answers. Put another way: is it reasonable for the taxpayer to meet the cost of keeping people in prison at the rate of more than £40,000 each *per* year when to do so may be entirely avoidable? Let us suppose that it might be possible to do this differently.

RE-SETTING THE PRISON POPULATION PARAMETERS

A broad comparison of the total average daily prisoner population of England and Wales between 1981 and 2007 indicates a rise of 98 *per cent* from some 42,000 to just over 81,000. Throughout this period the proportions of prisoners held on remand in custody and those sentenced have remained relatively similar, though the sharpest period of overall growth took place between the years from 1993 onwards.[1] This prompts the question of why, when in 1993 an average daily prison population of around 46,000 was adequate, do we presently need one of over 80,000?

As we have already noted (in *Chapter 4* at p.71 *supra*), of the daily average contemporary prison population of around 83,000, the ratio of sentenced to unsentenced prisoners is in the order of 81% to 19%, and of those sentenced some 53% (36,367) are serving sentences of more than four years to life in duration, and a further 35% (23,930) sentences of 12 months up to four years. This leaves a residue of almost eleven per cent serving up to 12 months (7,468), and some 13,000 prisoners held on remand. It will also have been noted that since 2005 there has been a significant rise (55.5%) in people serving life or indeterminate sentences (from just over 6,500 to 12,143) as a result of the Criminal Justice Act 2003.

Now for the sake of discussion here we might suppose that it would be prudent to set a finite limit of 55,000 on the total prison population for the next decade, but with a view to a further reduction to (say) 45,000 thereafter. This would mean that a reduction of some 25,000 places from the present population might be envisaged in combination with a legislated moratorium on exceeding the 55,000 maximum remaining places under any circumstances. The question then becomes: how might this be achieved?

First, we might insist that other than in truly exceptional circumstances it would be entirely reasonable to divert all those presently serving sentences of 12 months or less[2] in custody to alternative community sanctions. This would provide a reduction of more than 8,000 places almost immediately, leaving a further 17,000 reductions to be found. The rationale for doing this lies within the present government's own recognition expressed in the Halliday Report (Home Office, 2001b *op. cit.*) and the White Paper *Justice For All* (Home Office 2002b:102, *op. cit.*; Roberts and Smith 2003:182) that such sentences are largely ineffective and may even encourage reoffending.

Second, it might be proposed as I have suggested formerly (Cornwell, 2007 *op. cit.*: 129-130) that every determinate sentence should include a period of time spent working in the community on trial prior to release. Though we shall return to this proposal in more detail in *Chapters 10* and *11*, depending on the proportion of a custodial sentence considered reasonable for 'conditional release', the arrangements could result in a significant number of those presently completing their sentences in custody being released to undertake community sanctions. In the event that one-third of those (23,530) currently serving sentences of over 12 months and up to

---

1. In 1993 the average daily prison population had only risen to some 46,000 from the 1981 figure of 42,000, thus the significant increase of 80.9% has occurred during the period 1993 to 2007. Source: National Statistics Online, Home Office, available at http://www.statistics.gov.uk/cci/nugget.asp?id=1101.
2. Which results in six months or less being spent in custody under present release arrangements.

four years[3] became so eligible, a further 7,500 prison places might be relinquished, leaving 10,000 now to be identified.

Third, the same principle might be adopted towards those prisoners serving more than four years (excluding life and indeterminate sentences), but who were also nearing the point of release.[4] If a quarter of those (25,658) so sentenced at present were approaching the mid-point of sentence and were considered suitable for discretionary conditional release (see fn.4 below), it is possible that a further 6,000 places might be saved. This possibility leaves a further 4,000 (or so) prison places to be considered for inclusion in our reduction programme.

The fourth and final area for potential reduction lies within the remand prison population that presently stands at some 12,865 people in custody. It is difficult to estimate with any precision how many of these individuals are detained unnecessarily, but it is apparent that up to 50 *per cent* will, when tried in the courts, be found not guilty or, if found guilty, be given non-custodial sentences.[5] Thus if more stringent rules were to be applied to those being remanded in custody and excluded the use of remand in all cases in which a sentence of 12 months imprisonment or less were to be contemplated, it becomes more than likely that at least 4,000 places could be saved in the remand sector of the prisoner population.

The important point to note about these proposals is that the criteria upon which they are based lie *within* present legislative arrangements. In the cases of all those prisoners serving custodial sentences of 12 months or more (excluding life and indeterminate sentences), all that is suggested is an advancement of the date upon which those prisoners would, in any event, be released from custody *under present provisions*. The question that remains is that of what element of risk would be taken if such a practice were to be adopted. Moreover, if we were to agree that short (six months or less) prison sentences could profitably be replaced by more demanding community sanctions and without a significant element of public risk, then there might also be a reduction in reoffending in addition.

It has, of course, to be stated that the figures used illustratively in the preceding paragraphs are speculative to the extent that we cannot know how many existing

---

3. A maximum of 24 months in custody (50% of sentence period) followed by a further 12 months on 'automatic conditional release' (ACR) on licence under supervision (25% of sentence period) on a four year sentence at present. The remaining one quarter of the sentence period is, in any event, spent on 'unconditional release' (UR) within the community.
4. Such prisoners presently serve a minimum 50% of their sentence period in custody, but this period may be extended to the two-thirds point if they are not selected for 'discretionary conditional release' (DCR) under parole arrangements. Between the two-thirds and three-quarters period of a sentence these prisoners are treated in the same way as those mentioned in fn.3 above, and become eligible for ACR. Thus a prisoner sentenced to six years imprisonment (72 months) would serve 36 months and up to 48 months in custody if not granted DCR, followed by 12 months on ACR and 12 months on UR. See also the *Glossary* at the end of this work for these items and explanations of other terms, etc.
5. Source: Information published under the auspices of the Prison Reform Trust (2007b), in *Prison Fact File*, available at http://www.prisonreformtrust.org.uk/subsection.asp?id=10708fact=75.

prisoners in each of the categories serving 12 months or more are, at any time, close to the mid-point in their sentences, and would thus become eligible for consideration. However, assuming a reasonably even spread, the numbers indicated seem far from improbable. There is, in addition, a further objection that might be levelled at such proposals, and this concerns the manner in which it could be said that they interfere with the sentencing protocols of the courts to an unacceptable extent. This requires brief explanation.

Traditional and present sentencing arrangements in Britain allow the courts considerable discretion to decide on the duration of sentences for most offences other than murder. As Cavadino and Dignan (1997, *op. cit.*: 87-90) have pointed out there are statutory maximum penalties for some offences, 'but these were devised so long ago and in such different circumstances, as to render them largely irrelevant for the control of judicial sentencing today.' (1997: 89). Sentencing officials are also aware of the way that determinate sentences of imprisonment are subject to *de facto* reduction in terms of the periods actually spent in custody as we have already seen. It is, therefore, understandable that the length of a custodial sentence decided upon in the court will bear a relationship to the mid-term of that sentence served in practice. Thus the equivalence of desert to the seriousness of offences (however inexact such a concept may be) is tempered to some extent by the prevailing arrangements for release under the automatic unconditional release (AUR)[6], automatic conditional release (ACR)[7], and discretionary conditional release (DCR)[8] schemes respectively within the provisions of the Criminal Justice Act 1991.

The proposals made here for those convicted would affect only that balance between the sentence period spent in custody and that on the various forms of release within the community, and thus might be viewed as a form of commutation of sentence (or executive release) for purposes other than those of strict justice, desert or commensurability. This much admitted, however, for reasons that will become clear in subsequent chapters, it seems a price well worth paying insofar as those concerned would stand to be released in due course anyway. Balanced against this is the fact that at least in terms of public protection, those afforded the opportunity of community release would, in the event of further offending or failure to comply with release conditions, be subject to recall to custody where necessary.

The advantage of placing a 'cap' figure on the prisoner population would be that in the event of all available prison places being fully occupied, those prisoners closest to their normal release dates and deemed suitable for community project work would be discharged first in order to create places for the newly convicted. As I have indicated elsewhere (Cornwell, 2007, *op. cit.*: 164-5) such a strategy has been

---

6. Applying to sentences of less than 12 months.
7. Applying to sentences of between 12 months and less than four years.
8. Applying to sentences of four years or more, excluding life and indeterminate sentences.

adopted in The Netherlands, Norway and Denmark in recent times and has worked effectively. There is also no specific evidence to indicate that to act in such a manner results in an escalation of public risk or of reoffending.

Taken together, the reductive measures suggested here would seem to provide a reasoned basis for adopting a bold and determined approach towards decreasing the size of excessive penal populations, but it would require a corresponding increase in the nature and range of community sanctions. This particular issue is discussed at some length in Part Three of this work. Such an approach would also be accompanied by significant cost reductions, part of which could be devoted towards making community sanctions more robust, demanding and effective.

Reducing the size of prisoner populations does not, as we have seen here, specifically require a penology based on restorative justice principles, but incorporation of these principles could, as we shall shortly discover, lead to an even more positive and permanent climate of corrections that would make re-escalation of reduced prison populations far less likely or appropriate in practice. The most important issue for this analysis is that once the concept of reduction is accepted as both practicable and necessary, then the application of restorative and reparative initiatives within criminal justice could deliver infinitely more humane and effective justice for all the stakeholders involved.

BUILDING TOWARDS REDUCTION: A RESTORATIVE APPROACH

As has been indicated earlier, the principal strengths of restorative justice lie in the fact that it requires offenders to take responsibility for their wrongdoing, is victim-focused, and offers each offender the opportunity to 'put wrongs right'. Contemporary criminal justice within most of the 'Western-style' democracies is offender-focused, makes no demands on offenders, and is more concerned with punishing crime than vindicating victims of crime. In adopting and maintaining its present offender-focused approach, traditional criminal justice propels itself towards maintaining high prisoner populations simply because it does little to address the causes of offending or provide offenders with the potential to avoid reoffending: it is thus scarcely surprising that so many former prisoners appear repetitively before the courts.

A penology based on restorative justice principles would propose that from the time a criminal offence is committed and someone is identified as the perpetrator of the offence, there arises a relationship (however fractured) between all the parties affected by the event. These parties we have already described (in *Chapter* 2) as the 'primary' stakeholders within the criminal justice process.[9] Though the dynamics within this relationship may be far from cordial or even antagonistic, the relationship exists because the stakeholders have reasonable expectations of the process that will investigate the commission of the offence, anticipating that it will be at the least fair, constructive and appropriately vindicating.

The existence of this relationship is significantly at odds with the rationalisation within the contemporary mode of justice that an offence has been committed because a law has been broken, someone is responsible for this, and when identified must be punished. How much he or she must be punished will be determined to some extent in relation to the perceived seriousness of the offence, and also to some extent in relation to the prevailing aims of punishment: but punished he or she will be. This makes the infliction of punishment inevitable more to maintain the integrity of the law than to reconcile the harm that the offence has caused. The stakeholders within such a process thus become the state whose law is transgressed, the courts that are empowered to distribute punishment, and the offender who deserves it.

It is the fact that restorative justice offers offenders the opportunity to make amends to victims that is its hallmark quality, and it is this attribute that makes possible the healing of the relationship breakdown caused by offending. This may (and indeed need not) be accomplished in a direct manner between individual offenders and victims, but it can be done in an indirect way by structuring within both custodial and non-custodial sanctions the means by which offenders can work to provide reparation for victims of crime. However, as we shall see in subsequent chapters this implies that prison regimes are specifically designed to provide demanding, useful and productive work that generates revenue for victim support, and that community sanctions are similarly organised, supervised and challenging.

The starting point in the reparative process begins at the time the offence is discovered and the perpetrator is identified. Whether the outcome of the offence adjudication will be a prison sentence or a community sanction, the first step must be to ascertain from the alleged offender whether or not he or she is prepared to accept responsibility for the harm, apologise, and commit to putting it right as far as possible. In cases of minor or less serious offences this may involve victim: offender mediation (VOM) on a face-to-face basis or through intermediaries. Where more serious offences have been committed, and in particular those involving physical violence or rape, it may be entirely inappropriate for such direct contact to be considered other than through third parties, in order to protect victims from further anguish and trauma.

Such a starting point opens up, within a restorative penology, options for dealing differently with offenders willing to accept guilt and make reparation from those

---

9. Here, see *Chapter 2* at pp.47-48 and Figure 2-1 *supra*.

unwilling to do so. This is important because it enables us to move away from a retributive and desert driven justice process towards one that is more compassionate towards victims and responsive to offenders in looking towards their eventual social reintegration. The sanctions that derive from such a penology can be constructively rather than destructively devised, both in prisons and within the community, to provide opportunities rather than mere penalties that work to the benefit of all the stakeholders rather than to their detriment.

In cases of much minor, first-time and juvenile offending the achievement (through VOM or other restorative practices[10]) of a measure of reconciliation between victims and offenders can result in the diversion of offenders away from the full and formal court processes towards a speedier and more effective outcome. This saves much valuable time and expense while at the same time proving more satisfactory to victims of crime. Even in more serious cases, acceptance of guilt by offenders and willingness to make reparation can result in non-custodial sanctions becoming preferable to the custodial alternative. However, as Michael O'Hear points out, care must be taken to ensure that there is a public (and legal) understanding and acceptance of the desirability of such practices, and that these are not perceived as some form of plea-bargaining or 'out-of-court dispute settlement process more commonly found in civil litigation.' (O'Hear, 2005: 322-3).

From the viewpoint of custodial corrections, reduction in the size of the penal population would enable prisons to be less crowded and deliver more effective regimes, and possibly fewer prisons to be necessary in the longer term. This much stated, however, it will be evident that a restorative penology would envisage different types of prisons being operated for offenders willing to take responsibility and make reparation to victims, as opposed to those unwilling or declining to do so (Cornwell, 2007 *op. cit.*: 112-138).[11] Though we shall return to this proposition in *Chapters 8* and *9*, it may be useful to add some elaboration of the reasons for the suggestion at this point in the discussion.

First, under existing circumstances within many jurisdictions, there is no necessary requirement that those imprisoned accept guilt, examine their offending behaviour, or undertake any substantive work in reparation of victims of crime. Those who elect not to do so are treated identically with others who may wish to do so, but there is no particular incentive (other perhaps in self-interested privilege terms) to encourage such participation. Second, few contemporary prisons - at least in Britain - have the resources to provide the quality of work that would generate a sustained and substantial revenue for victims of crime, and neither have the prison authorities afforded such provision any specific priority. Third, most UK prisons

---

10. Such as group conferencing involving families and close others, and healing circles (see, e.g. Umbreit *et al.*, 2005a, *op. cit.*: 251-304; McIvor, 2004 *op. cit.*:162-194; McCold, 2004 *op. cit.*: 155-172)
11. Here see my explanation of a restorative approach to prisons in Cornwell (2007), op. cit., at *Chapter 5* entitled 'Making Prisons Reparative and Restorative: Designing for Outcomes in Custodial Corrections.'

struggle to attract quality work of a purposeful nature to employ every prisoner for a full working day at least five days in each week. Much of the better quality work that is available in these places is devoted to meeting the internal needs of prisons themselves, and thereby defray to some extent the escalating costs of maintaining an excessive prisoner population.[12]

Fourth, levels of prisoner pay are so low in British prisons[13] that most inmates spend what little they earn on their own needs for toiletries, tobacco, stationery and the limited range of confectionery items permitted within prison shops. Many also rely on contributions of private money from their families and friends to make their lives more comfortable in custody. Fifth, within the traditional culture of British prisons it is a normative expectation that most inmates will comply only reluctantly with the requirements of prison employment and constructive cooperation within the regime, and most will do so only to the minimum acceptable level. Finally, prisoners who deny guilt and feel aggrieved at the extent of their punishment tend to be also the least cooperative, and the most disruptive towards correctional staff and those inmates prepared to cooperate. This makes the operation of single regimes (or prisons) for reparative and traditional custody not only undesirable, but also altogether unlikely to succeed.

For all these reasons and for others that will become clear in subsequent chapters, a restorative penology would advocate a twin-track prison system that dealt differently with those prepared to accept guilt and make reparation as opposed to those who declined to do so. It is very probable, as we shall also see, that reparative prisons could be operated with lesser capital[14] and staffing costs, since those permitted to serve their sentences within them would have a vested interest and incentives to comply fully with regime requirements. Such prisons would also have much closer links with their local communities which would be actively encouraged to participate in regime provision linked to community projects.

---

12. This type of work generally tends to be confined to making inmate prison uniforms and other clothing, a limited range of furniture, and where space permits, growing of produce for consumption by inmates. Most other work is of a mundane nature made to relatively low levels of quality assurance, and requiring no particular aptitude, skills or concentration. Though there are exceptions to this situation, these tend to be sporadically available in long-term prisons, and employ relatively small numbers of inmates who have the aptitude and motivation to participate.
13. Information from the research of the Prison Reform Trust indicates an average wage level of £8 per week in prisons in England and Wales in 2006/7 – http://www.prisonreformtrust.org.uk/subsection.asp?id=10708fact=75.
14. That is to say costs incurred in providing high levels of security, CCTV surveillance, and similar systems, the savings on which might be diverted to the provision of high quality workshop, vocational training and production facilities.

THE MORALITY OF PRISON REDUCTION

The incentive towards a reduction in the prison population in many countries of the world today is not driven entirely by financial considerations, even though these may be compelling in their own right. There are also some strong reasons of a moral or ethical nature that *should* encourage a lesser use of imprisonment, or, at the very least, change the way in which prisons are presently operated. Most of the democratic nations have abandoned use of capital punishment altogether, though a few retain the death penalty for the most heinous forms of murder, and this leaves the process of imprisonment as the most serious form of punishment available in modern societies.

Some years ago now at the time of the decline of the rehabilitative ideal, Hugh Klare, a former secretary of the Howard League for Penal Reform, made some penetrating observations on the nature of the imprisonment process. In his words:

> 'Offenders', wrote the late Sir Lionel Fox, Chairman of the Prison Commission, 'are sent to prison *as* a punishment and not *for* punishment'. . . Many of them come from a background of social and psychological deprivation. Deterrence, which works well for the haves, works most uncertainly for those who have never had a stake in society, . . Many prisoners are deeply convinced of their own worthlessness. . . Prison deprives offenders of their liberty. It should not also take away from them what little dignity and self-respect they may possess. Work should not be demeaning but constructive and, where possible, socially useful. Prison officers must fulfil their custodial duties. But they, too, need the chance to be positive, to enter into relationships, to be helpful, to take pride in their job. (Klare, 1976, reproduced in Blom-Cooper and Drewry, 1976:87-8)[15]

To many correctional practitioners and others with knowledge of life within modern custodial penal systems, Fox's statement has a somewhat hollow ring. For though at the theoretical level it may be unexceptionable, there is no doubt that in spite of recent advances in international standards and building provision, prisons remain oppressive and depressive institutions within which people are detained against their will, and often in impersonal and squalid circumstances.

While the long-running debate on the causes of criminal offending continues largely unresolved, there is no doubt that many people who find themselves in prisons do come from socially deprived and traditionally delinquent areas in which unemployment, poor health and diet, housing and education are widespread. The following facts recently published by the Prison Reform Trust[16] reinforce such a contention:

---

15. The full title of Hugh Klare's article was 'The Reformer's Dilemma: Striking a Balance in the Fight Against Crime', reproduced in L. Blom-Cooper and G. Drewry (eds.) (1976), *Law and Morality: A Reader*, London: Duckworth, at pp.86-88.
16. Source: Prison Reform Trust (2007b *op. cit.*), *Prison Fact File*, London: PRT.

- 50% of all prisoners sent into custody are not registered with a General Practitioner before reception into prison;
- 48% of prisoners on reception have a reading age of 11 years or less, and 82% a writing ability of the same age;
- of the 16 to 20 year age group received into prisons, 85% show signs of personality disorder, and 10% of psychotic illness;
- only 20% of prisoners have the ability to fill in a job application form completely;
- 50% of all prisoners lack the skills required by 96% of jobs;
- around 33% of women prisoners lose their homes and often their possessions while in prison, and 66% of female prisoners have dependent children under 18 years old. In addition, 30% of the children of female prisoners are taken into Local Authority care; and,
- some 30% of all prisoners will be homeless on release from custody.

These statistics provide a grim reminder of the accuracy of Klare's analysis, but more than that remind us of the probability that the causes of criminal behaviour may lie as much within the social structure as within individual pathology. The use of imprisonment in punishment of the already socially disadvantaged represents the most extreme penalty when resources are so badly needed to alleviate the symptoms of social inequality and lesser eligibility that the statistics reveal.

The morality of prison reduction is not tied specifically to the case made in this work for a restorative penology, but more to the premise that the use of imprisonment should be a measure of last resort in civilised societies, and used with the utmost parsimony. Restorative justice may assist us to use prisons more rationally and effectively where custody is simply unavoidable, but it does not resolve the unnecessary use of imprisonment with its highly undesirable outcomes for the already disadvantaged.

The further point is that there is no merit in implementing restorative and reparative prison regimes in penal systems that are already overcrowded through excessive use of the custodial sanction. This means that the case for a restorative penology is contingent upon the need for reduction having been accepted as a prior course of action. As in all matters of difficulty and change within the field of law and morals, some actions have to be taken simply because it is 'right' that they should happen, and 'right' not because of majority acceptance, but because it would be wrong for them not to do so. As Blom-Cooper and Drewry have indicated:

> The abolition of capital punishment [in Great Britain], as with most penal reform, would never have come about (at least when it did[17]) if the 'man on the Clapham omnibus' had been

---

17. The Murder (Abolition of the Death Penalty) Act 1965 came into force on 9 November 1965, though capital punishment for high treason and piracy continued. In December 1969 an affirmative resolution of

the final arbiter on the matter... Clearly as J.S. Mill so clearly recognised, collective morality is something which cannot be identified just by counting heads any more than by canvassing the opinion of the mythical 'average' man. (Blom-Cooper and Drewry, 1976, *op. cit.*: xiii). [Parenthesis those of the present author].

This seems to me to be as true of capital punishment back in 1965 as it is of the need for prison reduction in 2007. Certainly the British media, some 'hawkish' politicians and many members of the general public would (and do) argue a case for the *status quo* on the basis that to use imprisonment less would increase public risk. This does not, however, amount to a substantial argument against the moral case for using imprisonment less because it is used excessively and in a manner that is operationally unreasonable and unacceptable in a civilised society.

LESS PRISONERS AND BETTER PRISONS

As has been noted in the foregoing discussion, adoption of a restorative penology would greatly assist in enabling fewer offenders to experience imprisonment, but would not, of itself, lead to a significant reduction in prison numbers unless (and at the same time) a different approach to sentencing and the use of sanctions were to be implemented. Moreover, to avoid a subsequent 'regression' it would be desirable to accompany a reductive strategy with a finite limitation on the number of prison places that might not be exceeded, and the means of ensuring this.

Though decreased use of imprisonment would undoubtedly result in an increased demand for capacity in the community corrections sector in addition to a simplified and more demanding range of sanctions, the potential savings on the former would almost certainly enable the latter to be implemented, albeit with a measure of increased public risk which is difficult, if not impossible to quantify. Similarly, a reduction in the use of custody for remand purposes would require clear policy direction and implementation to ensure that it was only used as a measure of last resort and necessary public protection. Use of custodial remand on the suspicion that accused persons *might* abscond or fail to attend for trial, or *might* interfere with witnesses has long been a speculative and contentious issue (e.g. King and Morgan, 1977; Fitzgerald and Sim, 1979 *op. cit.*; Home Office, 1979; PA-PPAG, 1980 *op. cit.*), and its use as 'a taste of prison' frequently criticised.

A reduced prisoner population in statutorily 'uncrowded' prisons would make a restorative and reparative penology considerably easier to implement, and the necessary linkage between the custodial and non-custodial sectors of corrections could become a more coherent strategy. It would also enable prisons to be set aside in

---

both Houses of Parliament decided that the 1965 Act should remain in force without time limit. Capital punishment was effectively outlawed in the UK for any remaining purposes (e.g. its use in wartime) in 2004 when the UK ratified Protocols 6 and 13 to the European Convention On Human Rights.

their entirety for delivery of reparative regimes without the risk of 'contamination' by offenders who declined the opportunity to participate within them, or who were deemed unfit to do so because of their disruptive behaviour.

Models of reparative prisons are slowly beginning to appear in unlikely places such as the Tihar Jail in Delhi, India (*The Times*, October 26, 2007: 46), which, though grossly overcrowded, has pioneered a regime in which a proportion of prisoners' pay is deducted and credited to a central fund for victim reparation. Workshops are designated for making woven cloth, bread, school furniture, and stationery items for government departments, in addition to mustard oil and soap which are marketed through shops, mail order and a retail website.[18] The regime has also resulted in a considerable increase in workshop productivity since the inmates also enjoy an incentive scheme for exceeding production targets that have increased six-fold a year.

Though the 'Tihar experiment' is in its early stages of operation and has had to be set in place in the worst possible conditions of overcrowding and structural provision[19], it demonstrates that such initiatives are possible where there is a determination to attempt them. The 'Victim Fund' is administered by a prison committee, and makes monthly payments directly to victims or, if they are deceased, their closest relatives. As we shall see subsequently, this may not be the ideal way of administering victim reparation, but at least it is in operation and provides a model for discussion.

Reduction in prisoner populations is a widespread need in many areas of the world, and yet has been approached by a few nations with considerable success. Restorative justice, while seeking to avoid, at all costs, sending offenders to prison other than as a last resort, is not necessarily a cornerstone of reductive strategies that can be delivered without it. It is, however, a powerful force for making better use of those prisons that have to be retained, and for improving both the status of victims and the life chances of offenders. There will always be some offenders who remain unrepentant, oblivious to the needs of their own lives, to those of victims, and wholly uncooperative with prison regimes: these are facts of life within custodial corrections that have to be faced squarely and dealt with appropriately. There are, on the other hand, no good reasons why such persons should irreparably damage the prospects of those who are repentant and willing to 'put wrongs right', and whose lives thereafter might be constructive and law-abiding. These are the important issues that form the basis for discussion in the chapters that follow.

---

18. This development is described by Ashling O'Connor (2007), 'Jail Where It's Always Payback Time', *The Times*, London, 26 October, p.46. Prisoners participating in the regime forego a quarter of their wages weekly for the reparation of crime victims.
19. The Tihar facility occupies a sprawling site in the outskirts of Delhi housing 12,500 inmates at twice its designated capacity. Its inmate population is the largest in Asia, of which some 80% are unconvicted. Many spend years awaiting their trial: making the jail a target for human rights campaigners in India.

CHAPTER 8

Can Prisons Rehabilitate Offenders Effectively?

This very 'vexed' question has tormented correctional practitioners, academics and penal policy-makers for at least the past sixty years, and shows no signs of being resolved satisfactorily in the present era. Much, it has to be conceded, depends upon what precisely the term 'rehabilitation' amounts to both historically and within the contemporary penology, and how its purposes are defined in an operational sense. Certainly in times past there was a widely held belief that offending behaviour, like an 'illness', could be 'cured', but little consensus about precisely how this was to happen. By the closing years of the 1970s, disillusionment with the apparent failure of the 'treatment model' to reduce reoffending had become so widespread that its demise had become a pragmatic inevitability (see, e.g. Home Office, 1979 *op. cit.*: 4,27; Bean, 1981: 53-68; Hudson, 1987: 16-36; Fitzgerald and Sim, 1980: 82-3 and 1982: 156-8).

The sheer volume of the critical academic literature that emerged as a result of the decline of the rehabilitative ideal, particularly in the United States and the United Kingdom, provides singular evidence (if such were needed) of the profound effect that it had on subsequent penal policies and practices. With hindsight, however, it may be argued that the penological vacuum that the retreat from rehabilitation created was more notable for the supposed justifications of punishment that it left unchallenged than for the regimen of coercive treatment and bureaucratic control that it sought to abandon. This much stated, it is also clear that the reasons for this abandonment lay as much in the spectrum of political and professional interests that impact upon penal systems, as in the nature of the systems themselves and the failure to curb rising rates of recidivism.

WHAT IS PENAL REHABILITATION?

Francis Allen, one of the most prolific contributors to the academic debate about rehabilitation in the penal setting has offered the following explanation:

> The rehabilitative ideal is a complex of ideas which, perhaps, defies completely precise statement. It is assumed first that human behaviour is the product of antecedent causes. These can be identified as part of the physical universe, and it is the obligation of the scientist to describe them with all possible exactitude. Knowledge of the antecedents of human behaviour makes possible an approach to the scientific control of human behaviour. Finally, and of primary significance for the purposes at hand, it is assumed that measures employed to treat the convicted offender should serve a therapeutic function, that such measures should be designed to effect changes in the behaviour of the convicted person in the interests of his own

happiness, health, and satisfactions and in the interest of social defence.

Although these ideas are capable of rather simple statement, they have provided the arena for some of the world's most acrimonious controversy. And the disagreements among those who adhere in general to these propositions have been hardly less intense than those prompted by the dissenters. This is true, in part, because these ideas possess a delusive simplicity. No idea is more pervaded with ambiguity than the notion of reform and rehabilitation. Assuming, for example, that we have the techniques to accomplish our ends of rehabilitation, are we striving to produce in the convicted offender something called 'adjustment' to his social environment or is our objective something different from or more than this? By what scale of values do we determine the ends of therapy? (Allen, 1972: 209-210)[1]

The central importance of Allen's analysis lies in its insistence that the notion of rehabilitation is predicated on a raft of assumptions rather than on scientific fact, that its motivations are, at the least, ambiguous, and that it should work to the social benefit of offenders *and* the enhancement of public safety, rather than the satisfaction of therapeutic professionalism. Though he does not say so implicitly, there is no doubt that the idea of coercion lies behind the therapeutic approach, and that this is the primary objection to medical models of 'treatment' and 'cure' in the custodial setting.

Rehabilitation, whatever else it means, implies a process through which offenders are enabled or, in the modern parlance, 'empowered' to resume their full place within society and live law-abiding lives thereafter. This, as Shlomo Shoham (1972) has pointed out, is fraught with difficulties:

> This mechanistic approach to the treatment of offenders may be necessary but it is certainly not sufficient. In order to achieve true reformation it is not enough to 'neutralise' the criminogenic factors in a given offender's personality or social background; it is necessary, in plain language, to provide the offender with a new set of norms and to strengthen his moral resistance against committing offences. The crucial problem, however, is that we do not have a reasonably defined set of norms and values to offer the offender. We, the treatment men, come to the offender as representatives of a chaotic (and sometimes almost non-existent) normative system. We represent a value vacuum where honesty in business, altruism, selfless devotion to a cause and even common decency are often regarded as archaic relics to which people may pay lip service but seldom adhere. (Shoham, 1972: 202)[2]

The problem here is that to Shoham and to many others who are anxious to steer

---

1. This quotation is originally to be found in F. A. Allen (1959), 'Criminal Justice, Legal Values and the Rehabilitative Ideal', *Journal of Criminal Law, Criminology and Police Science*, vol.50, no.226, a text reprinted as 'The Rehabilitative Ideal' in R. J. Gerber and P. D. McAnany (eds.) (1972), *Contemporary Punishment*, London and Notre Dame: University of Notre Dame Free Press, pp. 209- 218. However, for a more lengthy and comprehensive account of Allen's approach following the decline of rehabilitation, see: F. A. Allen (1981), *The Decline of the Rehabilitative Ideal*, London and New Haven: Yale University Press.
2. Also reprinted in Gerber and McAnany (eds.) (1972), *op. cit.*, pp.200-208 as an excerpt from the original text *Crime and Social Deviation*, published by the Henry Regenery Company in 1966.

clear of deterministic[3] explanations and approaches to offences and offenders, the empowerment process is essentially an educative one within which offenders have to be 'taught' new norms and values and accept these as both legitimate and preferable to those previously held by them. Within the custodial sector of corrections, as Barbara Hudson (1987) and others point out, this pedagogic approach causes considerable difficulty, and is open to the criticism that rehabilitative initiatives are used more for control and disciplinary reasons than for therapeutic ones' (Hudson, 1987, *op. cit.*: 34-5).

On the other hand there have been proponents of what has been termed 'state obligated rehabilitation' that derives from the notion that offenders have a 'constitutional right' to be provided with such programmes as an integral part of the punishment process (e.g. Cullen and Gilbert, 1982; Rotman, 1986). Though such a 'right' has never been recognised in either Britain or the United States, it has been acknowledged in some European countries, notably Italy, Germany and Spain, and also in Argentina, as falling within the spirit of the United Nations Minimum Rules for the Treatment of Prisoners (United Nations,1955).[4]

Ernest van den Haag, in his own interpretation of the notions of reform and rehabilitation, raises the interesting question of whether or not the concept of 'rehabilitation' includes an element of intimidation. He suggests:

> The intimidation, or rehabilitation, of the convict is expected to lead him to law-abiding conduct upon his release. 'Rehabilitation' is meant to change the offender's intent, motivation, or even character toward law-abiding conduct. 'Intimidation' causes avoidance of offences because of fear of punishment. Whereas rehabilitation affects the offender's wish, intimidation leaves the wish unchanged – only it is not carried out because of fear ... Since internal motivations and restraints are not directly observable, the distinction between rehabilitation and intimidation cannot easily be made on the basis of statistical data. Sometimes, too, it is impossible to tell what has produced law-abiding behaviour in an individual .. Nonetheless, the distinction is of some importance in penology; policies aimed at intimidation differ from policies attempting rehabilitation or merely incapacitation. (van den Haag, 1975: 58-59).

This, surely, is the crux of the difficulty presently confronting those countries with excessive penal populations that wish to pursue penal policies of incapacitation and social protection, but at the same time invest their justifications for doing so with a 'rehabilitative respectability'. For although van den Haag's analysis may

---

3. A term within criminology that has its origins in the Italian *Scuola Positiva* or Positivist School whose adherents believed that crime was largely a problem of heredity and other causative factors over which offenders have only limited control. Thus the notion of the 'free will' offender who makes rational (even if illegal) choices of action becomes at odds with the concept of crime as largely predetermined. For a further explanation see Cornwell (2006), *op. cit.*, pp.29-30, and Walsh and Poole (1983) *op. cit.*, pp. 67-68.
4. In Italy in the Costituzione (Cost.) art.27; in Spain in the Constitución (Const.) art.25; and in the former West Germany in a judgement of 5 June 1973, Bundesverfassungsgericht (W. Ger.), 35 Bundesverfassungsgericht (BverfGE) 202. The situation in Argentina is set out in E. Zaffaroni (1983), 1 Tradato de Derecho Penal 63-65.

appear at first sight to be to an extent self-evident and unexceptionable, from the viewpoint of this work it is of profound significance.

The reasons for its importance are threefold: first, if we mean to rehabilitate offenders we have to be able to change their life-style preferences from crime as an occupation to that of the normally law-abiding citizen; secondly, if we propose to intimidate them into refraining from offending we can do so by means other than 'rehabilitation'; and third, if we cannot know what does or does not motivate law-abiding behaviour, the case for rehabilitation in a custodial context becomes at best speculative and at worst abusive.

If we were to admit the possibility of changing offenders through intimidation, that is to say the instillation of a fear of returning to custody, then the door opens wide to the provision of poor, degrading and crowded prison conditions of precisely the type criticised in this work. Further, such levels of provision would be legitimised by a 'tough on crime' agenda that was ultimately incarcerative but nothing more. As history reminds us only too well, these are the 'bottom-line' ingredients for unrest, prison violence, riots and disorder. Worse, perhaps, in addition to having a 'crisis of numbers' such a course of action would lead to an additional 'crisis of legitimacy'.[5]

Crises of legitimacy are not confined to the perceptions of unjust and unreasonable prison conditions held by those held in custody alone, but extend to the entire Criminal Justice System. Those working as correctional practitioners and prison staff lose a sense of purpose, professionalism and dedication, sentencing and court decisions are constrained by lack of options and a reluctance to make a bad situation worse, and the general public perceives the entire system as in disarray and out of control. Ultimately, such crises lead to a loss of public confidence in the nature of justice, and towards ambivalent attitudes in relation to offending.

PRISONS AND REHABILITATION

It seems strange to recall that in spite of the apparent retreat from rehabilitation during the 1960s and 1970s, the rise and fall of the 'justice model' of criminal punishment during the 1980s and 1990s, and the increasing resort to incarceration during the 1990s and into this millennium, the term 'rehabilitation' has been retained, re-packaged, and re-branded at intervals throughout almost sixty years. The persuasiveness of rehabilitation, particularly within custodial corrections has proved remarkably obdurate, almost to the point that without it penal systems somehow lack both credibility and legitimacy.

Indeed, at just the time that the justice model seemed to have achieved its

---

5. Here see for example the explanations provided by Cavadino and Dignan (1997 *op. cit.*: 21-22) and Fitzgerald and Sim, (1982: 23).

ascendancy in the early 1980s there arose a 'neo-rehabilitative' movement within criminal justice in Britain, the United States, Europe and Australia that deliberately challenged the 'just deserts' fundamentalism of the new punishment paradigm. (Hudson, 1987 *op. cit.*: 170-176; Cullen and Gilbert, 1982 *op. cit.*). It therefore seems that rehabilitation, at least as a concept if not as an operational agenda, will simply 'not lie down'.

The reasons for this may be speculative, but they merit brief discussion here since prisons have retained at least a vestigial interest in rehabilitation in spite of an evident inability to exercise any profound effect on reoffending following custodial sentences. Most modern organisations employing significant numbers of professionals trained specifically to deliver a 'service' (as opposed to a 'product')[6] find the need for a prospective purpose to sustain their professional beliefs and momentum. If this is the case, then deletion of a rehabilitative ethos, however fragile or tentative, removes from prisons the potential to view their task in a prospective manner, if only because the remaining justifications for criminal punishment are retrospective in nature.[7]

It is also evident that high rates of recidivism within short periods of release from custody have brought into question the effectiveness of rehabilitative programmes in prisons almost universally. These rates of reoffending become a matter of political embarrassment to governments, and a source of public concern inflamed by media coverage of serious acts of a criminal nature committed by ex-offenders. The same statistics also encourage 'tough on crime' policies that tend to drive the more punitive and less humanitarian forms of penal policy-making.

Somewhat later in his work discussed in the previous section of this chapter, Ernest van den Haag advanced three main reasons for the failure of rehabilitation in the custodial setting of prisons. In his words:

> First, only diseases can be cured by treatment. Few offenders are sick. There is no convincing independent evidence that convicts are more sick than non-convicts...Theoretically, it seems likely that many offences are rational acts on the part of the offender; to minimise offences one must change not the offender but the cost-benefit ratios that cause offences to be rational.
>
> Secondly, even offenders who are clinically sick – some certainly are – are not likely to be rehabilitated coercively...The comforts of the prisoner and the duration of his incarceration

---

6. Here I differentiate between commercial enterprises whose effectiveness is generally measured in terms of profit margin and resource management, and those of a public sector nature (e,g, Health, Education, and Prisons) charged with delivery of a service with lesser emphasis on what might otherwise be described as measurable 'value for money'. Though the latter organisations are expected to exercise effective budgetary control, it is generally the case that they are considered to be consumers of resources rather than generators of financial profit.
7. It will be noted that retribution in combination with individual (or specific) deterrence focuses on the past nature of criminal acts, and the notion of reform has largely lapsed into desuetude or has been subsumed within the concept of rehabilitation.

must be entirely independent of his acceptance of a treatment programme, which should be addressed only to those who want it.

Third, rehabilitative treatment is necessarily ineffective, unless it follows or is part of independent retributive punishment for another reason as well. When a person decides *sua sponte* to undergo psychotherapy (or for that matter medical treatment), he does so because he is dissatisfied either with his state of mind ... or with his own behaviour ... He seeks treatment to help him decide what he wants and to help him achieve it. (van den Haag, 1975: 190-191).

All of which makes the very important point that treatment or therapy should be voluntary and not used as a pre-condition of normal or early release. This, in turn, tends to militate against widespread use of indeterminate sentences, and parole procedures that make release contingent upon treatment having been accepted and improvement achieved. In a contemporary sense in England and Wales also, such criteria run counter to the provisions for extended sentences for sexual or violent offences within the Criminal Justice Act 2003 (Tonry, 2003: 17-18).

Another raft of problems related to rehabilitation programmes in prisons emerges when a differentiation is made between programmes of a medical, psycho-therapeutic or cognitive-behavioural nature, and those designed to enhance life skills in an educational or vocational context. This is particularly the case in relation to serious forms of offending[8] which attract longer sentences that include parole-type decision-making over release. There has always been a tacit acceptance, particularly among long-term prisoners and many prison staff, that the parole decision-making process was loaded in favour of those who 'played the game' (e.g. Shoham, 1972 op. cit.: 205; Fitzgerald and Sim, 1982 op. cit.: 102-106) and most evidently complied with the control and regime requirements of prisons.

Indeed, as early as 1975, it became clear that the parole system was to some extent devised both as a pragmatic means of reducing the size of the prison population *and* as a means of enhancing control of inmate behaviour in prisons. In guidelines issued by the Home Secretary to the Parole Board in 1975 we find the following direction:

If a prisoner shows, commonly by bad prison behaviour, refusal to co-operate with anyone trying to help him ... then he must be regarded as having forfeited parole by his current conduct and attitude (Home Office, 1975: para. 30).[9]

However, the more important point is that once in operation the parole system added both a measure of indeterminacy and bifurcation into the criminal justice

---

8. Notably of a violent or sexual nature, but also drug-related offences. The parole system in England and Wales was introduced under the provisions of the Criminal Justice Act 1967 though variants of such systems had much earlier been established in some European jurisdictions and in the USA.
9. The passage quoted here is extracted from the *Report of the Parole Board in England and Wales, 1975*, London: HMSO, paragraph 30.

process, and, without much doubt when considered in conjunction with prevailing provisions for remission of sentence, led to a trend towards increased lengths of sentences imposed by the courts (Cross, 1971; Bottomley, 1979 *op. cit.*: 126-7; Fitzgerald and Sim, 1982 *op. cit.*: 104-5). In addition, for our purposes here, it created a two-tier approach towards rehabilitation that operated in favour of the compliant and to the direct disadvantage of those unwilling to conform within the 'treatment and training' regimes of prisons.

DO THE FACTS OF CUSTODIAL LIFE RULE OUT REHABILITATION?

There would be little doubt in the minds of most people who have spent significant parts of their lives working within prisons and similar custodial penal institutions that such places are unnatural and intimidating places. The inevitability of the close proximity within relatively confined spaces of many angry, sad, lonely, and unwilling occupants, some of them suffering from or bordering on mental disorder, others socially inadequate and an easy prey for the predatory, is quite unlike any situation encountered outside of the penal world – other, perhaps, than in the former asylums for the insane. In fact, prisons represent an artificial environment created specifically for the unusual purpose of separating those within them from the free world of choice beyond the perimeter. Daily life within these institutions is regulated, regimented, observed, controlled and dictated by the need to maintain order and provide as safe an environment as is possible in the circumstances.

Unlike the outside world of the wider community, hundreds of same sex persons are herded together with little opportunity to express personal choices, make significant decisions, or exercise any real control over their lives. Days of identical pattern become weeks that in turn become months and often years of captivity. Though domestic accommodation, food, medical care, opportunities for work, recreation and religious observance are all usually provided, these have to be accessed in the constant company of others, and under the supervision of cameras and custodial staff.

Now, while the need for prisons is not disputed – at least in this work – the reductivist argument advanced in *Chapter 7* is important if decent prison conditions are to be delivered. One of the main criticisms levelled at prisons almost universally is the seemingly inevitable 'institutionalising' effect they have upon those who spend protracted periods of time within them. The term 'institutionalisation', though psychologically recognised and widely acknowledged to exist, is difficult to define precisely. It has much to do with the 'sameness' of days indicated above, much to do with the pressures to conform imposed by prison authorities, and also what is frequently described in the literature of prisons as the 'inmate sub-culture' (see, e.g.

Sykes, 1958; Cloward, 1960; Parker, 1970; Cohen and Taylor, 1972 and 1978; and particularly Sykes and Messinger, 1960).

Institutionalisation conditions the mind of inmates towards acceptance of all the dysfunctional aspects of prison life, depersonalisation[10], and loss of freedom of choice and movement. It also creates its own 'normality' insofar as the inmate comes, over time, to perceive the restricted and routine life in prison as 'normal', and become dependent on this 'sameness' for stability and reassurance. Those inmates who most actively resist the effects of institutionalisation and insist on maintaining their individual identities frequently find themselves regarded by prison staff as arrogant, uncooperative and disruptive, while those who do not tend to be perceived as compliant and better disposed towards the regime.

It is generally accepted that the longer a person is exposed to the effects of prison life, the greater the extent to which he or she becomes institutionalised and out of touch with the realities of life beyond the prison perimeter. This, in turn, makes readjustment to life within the wider community more difficult for the prisoner on release, and to some extent increases the likelihood of reoffending. Donald Clemmer identified the same situation in the United States as early as 1940, and described it as 'prisonization' in a seminal work on inmate communities and the effects of imprisonment (Clemmer, 1940).[11] Quoting Clemmer's words, Hawkins notes:

> According to Clemmer, every prisoner was subject to 'certain influences which we may call the universal factors of prisonization.' These factors include such things as the acceptance of an inferior role, accumulation of facts concerning the organisation of the prison, the development of somewhat new habits of eating, dressing, working, sleeping, the adoption of local language and the recognition that nothing is owed to the environment for the supplying of needs. He described the process of prisonization as being such that even if no other factor of the prison culture touches the personality of an inmate of many years residence, the influences of these universal factors are sufficient to make a man characteristic of the penal community and probably so disrupt his personality that a happy adjustment to the community becomes next to impossible' In the course of assimilation into the culture of the prison community the inmate became subject to 'influences' which breed or deepen criminality and antisociality and make the inmate characteristic of the criminalistic ideology in the prison community. (Hawkins, 1976 *op cit.*: 60).

Now, however much we may dislike such an analysis and its implications, these are the plainly stated 'facts of prison life' and they have been well-known to all those

---

10. Which here means strictures like the surrender of identity and autonomy in such matters as having a prison index number used on all correspondence, being addressed most frequently by the surname, and strict limitations on the extent to which personal space in cells can be individualised with the inmates' own identities. In addition, the prisoner has to 'request' or queue to receive visits, mail, replacement clothing or cell equipment, and to make telephone calls to friends and relatives on an 'approved list' of contacts maintained by the prison authority.
11. Donald Clemmer recorded his observations in a work entitled *The Prison Community* published in New York by Rinehart & Co. in 1940. It is regarded as the first authoritative explanation of the effects of the prison culture on the behaviour of inmates.

who have worked in the correctional field since Clemmer recorded them. Prison architecture may have changed over the intervening decades, regimes may also have become more developed, conditions within prisons may have improved, and relationships between staff and inmates may be less oppressive and more enlightened, but the 'universal factors' of inmate community life remain unchanged. These factors are infinitely more powerful than any others in influencing prisoner adjustment to the realities of incarceration.

It is against the background of these same unchanging factors that the entire notion of rehabilitation has to be assessed in the custodial correctional setting. Though it is, as Glaser and Stratton pointed out somewhat later in a critique of Clemmer's analysis, difficult to be certain of the extent to which prisons are actually 'criminalising' institutions, but the potential for this effect is certainly present and widely acknowledged to be so by sociologists and criminologists alike (Glaser and Stratton, 1961: 381). Moreover, as Sutherland and Cressey subsequently recorded, 'Because it causes prisoners to identify themselves as persons quite different from non-criminals, even contact with the 'universal factors' will render difficult any effort at clinical treatment' (Sutherland and Cressey, 1970: 538).

The idea of rehabilitating people in prison has retained an enduring idealism since the 1970s, even against the tide of the justice model and the subsequent decline into an era of incarceration for public protection. However, if the facts are squarely faced, this idealism is probably more a need of correctional practitioners and penal policy makers to give the process of custodial punishment a benign and humane appearance than any deeply held conviction as to the efficacy, or even the practicability, of substantially changing criminal behaviour in the isolation of prisons. Such is not to suggest that some inmates will not 'go straight' because they simply will not wish to re-visit the prison experience, but that is the unquantifiable effect of individual deterrence, and not what rehabilitation is about. Prisons, as we shall shortly see, may achieve some success in re-socialising inmates, particularly within a reparative and restorative penology, but rehabilitation ultimately has to be achieved beyond the walls of custodial institutions.

IF NOT REHABILITATION, THEN WHAT?

Having concluded that it is difficult to see how prisons can rehabilitate in the secluded circumstances in which such institutions operate, this is not quite the end of the matter. Those whose offences make custodial sentences inevitable, provided that they have the motivation and the incentive to resist the effect of the 'universal factors' previously described, can purposefully use the time spent in prison. In order to make this possible, however, prison regimes have to be re-structured in a much more coherent and effective manner that encourages willing rather than reluctant inmate participation. In the final section of this chapter I shall suggest what this means in practice, and how it might be approached.

At the outset it is necessary to be clear about the 'penal context' in which prisons are constrained to operate, and the extent to which such places can contribute towards the encouragement of attitudinal change that is an essential ingredient in the re-socialisation of offenders sentenced to custody. The point here is that if the prevailing penal rhetoric is evidently predominantly punitive, then the responses of offenders to custody are likely to be negative since they will perceive themselves to be 'instrumentally' punished.[12] This means that their punishment is imposed by those who legislate and sentence more as a matter of demonstrating that the law has teeth that bite, than of strict or proportionate justice. The 'legitimacy' of prisons in the view of those confined within them is, therefore, inextricably linked to the extent of fairness that the law exhibits within the sentencing process.

In addition, a 'just' penal system would regard it as an indispensable moral obligation that in addition to punishing by the deprivation of liberty, something substantial is done to address the social deficits and antecedent conditions that contribute to offenders committing crime in the first instance. Though this need not amount to a case for 'state obligated' rehabilitation as proposed so elegantly by Lewis (2005) and by others such as Doyal and Gough (1991) and Rotman (1990, *op.cit.*), it reinforces Carlen's contention that 'the state's right to punish rests on its contractual obligation to address the social problems that cause lawbreaking' (Carlen, 1994: 310)[13].

A reparative and restorative approach to imprisonment would open up for those offenders who opted to comply with its regime requirements the opportunity and assistance to examine their offending behaviour and its causes, the nature and extent of the harm caused to victims, and the means of making apology and substantial reparation to victims of crime. More than this, however, such an approach would insist that offenders spent time working within local communities on projects of amenity value, learning and putting into practice skills and competencies that would ultimately enhance their employability (Cornwell, 2007, *op. cit.*: 120-133).[14] In such a manner, the period spent in custody has a specific purpose for each offender, and is perceived from the day of admission to be part of the process of eventual release

---

12. Here see John Blad's explanation of 'instrumental' punishment as a means of pursuing social policy objectives in his contribution: 'The Seductiveness of Punishment and the Case for Restorative Justice' in D. J. Cornwell (2006), *op. cit.*, at pp. 137-8.
13. See P. Carlen (1994), 'Crime, Inequality and Sentencing', in A. Duff and D. Garland (eds.), *A Reader on Punishment*, Oxford: Oxford University Press, at p.310.
14. I have set out proposals for the design and operation of reparative prison regimes at some length in earlier work, and thus do not repeat these here. The important feature of such regimes is, however, that they provide a clear link between prisons and communities, and that as part of the custodial period offenders spend a transitional period working in the community on trial to test their commitment to regular work, law-abiding behaviour, and compliance with the conditions of their temporary release from custody.

into the community within which the offender has to become re-integrated. There is thus an *incentive* for all participants in such regimes to use the experience in a positive and purposeful manner that will assist them to stay 'crime-free' on release.

In the course of preparing this book I have become aware of, and have been considerably impressed by the work recently undertaken in relation to serious sexual offending and its therapeutic treatment by Ward and Stewart (2003) and Ward *et. al.* (2007) in Australia and New Zealand within their Good Lives Model (GLM) and its extended formulation.[15] There has been a need for some time to move away from the 'one size fits all' approach to the treatment of sexual offenders as an homogeneous group, and towards an individualised therapeutic methodology that treats each individual as a specific case for intervention to identify causes and reduce future risk. Though Ward *et. al.* promote this as a 'rehabilitative' model over which, in the custodial setting I have expressed reservation, it is clear its risk reductive approach (once completed) fits within the general framework for offender re-socialisation described here.

This specific model of offending behaviour analysis is highlighted here because of the particular profile occupied by sexual offenders in the mass media and the public mind, and the tendency within many jurisdictions to punish their offences in a manner both different from and more extensive than those of other offenders who may cause equal harm, but who are, in the public perception of offending, seen as less 'dangerous'. It would seem, moreover, that the GLM-C model of disciplined analysis and intervention has the potential for adaptation in other forms appropriate for dealing with relapse prevention and risk reduction in violent and drug-related offending.

And since the starting point of reparative and restorative regimes is the deliberate focus on analysing offending behaviour and its causal factors in each individual case, there is much potential merit in following a similar pattern of intervention model providing that this can be achieved within a determinate sentencing framework. Further still, that subsequent release should not become dependent upon some or another notion of 'cure', or delayed indefinitely until the 'treatment' is deemed to have been sufficiently effective in terms of risk reduction.

Emphasis has been laid in the latter part of this discussion upon the need to ensure that participation in reparative and restorative custodial regimes is a matter of deliberate choice for offenders. In the chapter that follows it becomes necessary to consider how best to deal with those offenders who will, inevitably, decline

---

15. Two particularly useful accounts of the GLM and its later extended formulation into the Good Lives Model – Comprehensive (GLM-C) are to be found in T. Ward and C.A. Stewart (2003), 'The Treatment of Sex Offenders: Risk Management and Good Lives', *Journal of Professional Psychology: Research and Practice*, vol.34, no.4, pp. 353-360, and T. Ward, R.E. Mann and T.A. Gannon (2007), 'The Good Lives Model of Offender Rehabilitation: Clinical Implications', *Journal of Aggression and Violent Behaviour*, 12, pp. 87-107.

to participate, or who might be considered unsuitable, and who might well prove disruptive of such regimes given an opportunity to do so.

If prisons cannot realistically rehabilitate offenders, then this as we have noted here does not necessarily remove from such places a prospective purpose in re-socialising offenders and preparing them more constructively for reintegration within communities. This prospective purpose does, however, need to be reflected in more flexible sentencing arrangements that combine both custodial and community elements. The underlying principle is already established in the origins and development of parole and temporary release protocols, and requires extension rather than regression if more effective justice is to be delivered. Effective justice, in the sense implied here, comprises a sustained attempt to avoid unnecessary use of custody, and an equally deliberate attempt to use it more effectively for the reduction of recidivism and an improved quality of life for former criminal offenders.

CHAPTER 9

Reparative and Restorative Prison Regimes: Pipedream or Paradigm?

In the concluding section of the previous chapter there have been sketched in the briefest possible outline a number of principles that stand at the heart of the concept of reparative and restorative regimes in prisons. These were, in key-word form: voluntarism, responsibility, participation, self-analysis, reparative action and social reintegration. Within the scope of this chapter I shall attempt to describe how these attributes come together to provide an holistic approach to prison regime management informed and under-pinned by the principles and goals of restorative justice.

There is not yet, as far as I am aware, a prison in existence that is designed to operate entirely in accordance with these principles, or which maintains a regime given over entirely to reparative and restorative operational concepts. Susan Sharpe (1998) identified three main goals of restorative justice as: putting key decisions in the hands of those most affected by crime; making justice more healing and, ideally more transformative; and reducing the likelihood of future offences.[1] In commenting on these goals, Gill McIvor has suggested:

> Proponents of restorative justice argue that it is inappropriate to restrict assessment of its effectiveness to measures of recidivism since they embrace broader aims and give priority to different sanctioning objectives in the response to crime (Bazemore and Umbreit, 1995). Indeed reducing reoffending is perhaps the goal of restorative justice least likely to be achieved because of the limited ability of most approaches to exert an impact on the wider factors that contribute to and sustain offending behaviour (Wundersitz and Hetzel, 1996; Ervin and Schneider, 1990; Umbreit, 1996). (McIvor, 2004 *op. cit.*: 178)

It would be preferable to be able to suggest that this view is questionable in relation to the reduction of recidivism, but at the present time and in the absence of any valid statistical evidence to refute it, the situation must remain equivocal, at least, insofar as prisons are concerned, until a substantive effort has been made to implement and validate reparative and restorative regimes.

It is, of course, as important to address the underlying causes of crime as it is to analyse the nature of, and harm caused by the criminal act. Prison regimes cannot, however, redress the socially dysfunctional environments from which many offenders originate, but it is possible to equip prisoners with the abilities and moti-

---

1. S. Sharpe (1998), *Restorative Justice: A Vision for Healing and Change*, Edmonton, Ontario: Offender Mediation Society, quoted in Zehr (2002), *op. cit.*, p.37.

vation to resist reoffending.[2] In addition to this, being brought to an understanding of the harm caused to victims, and being given the opportunity to make apology and reparation can enhance the self-esteem of offenders and the self-confidence of victims.

THE IMPORTANCE OF VOLUNTARISM

As we have already noted in *Chapter 6*, one of the foremost ingredients of effective prison management is the need for a clear and unequivocally defined 'custodial vision'. There is no doubt that the move away from rehabilitation previously discussed blurred the custodial vision of the 1960s and 1970s, however imperfect that vision may have been, and has continued to do so to the present day. In addition, the riots and disorder within the British prisons of the 1980s and early 1990s created a deep-seated and persistent fear of loss of control that has pervaded the development of custodial penal policies into this millennium. This, as Roger Houchin (2003) has identified. results in a conflict of purposes within the imprisonment process that has proved difficult to resolve:

> The unreconciled pursuit of conflicting aims is particularly strong in our current penal environment. At a political level, a discourse emphasising the exclusionary, incapacitative and expressive potential of prison is pursued alongside that advocating respect for individual rights and the promotion of social inclusiveness. At a managerial level, structures and procedures premised on a perceived need to control and which regulate access to necessary developmental opportunities and psycho-social supports, persist notwithstanding the articulation of policies that prioritise the responsiveness of the institution to the needs of its clients ... At each level there is a fundamental contradiction between conceptualisations of the prisoner as, on the one hand, a threat to be isolated, controlled and corrected, and on the other, someone with whom we intend to engage. It is unsurprising, in a climate of such pervasive policy ambivalence, that the prison system has been unsuccessful in generating a sense of shared purpose sufficiently robust to give direction to and to validate individual reform initiatives. (Houchin, 2003: 146).

The dichotomous relationship between control and regime delivery has been a persistent issue for three main reasons: first, the traditional and deeply embedded culture of reluctance among prisoners to comply other than nominally with prison regimes; second, an equally traditional and embedded reluctance of uniformed custodial staff and their trade union associations to contemplate more progressive methods of control that do not rely solely upon mechanistic regimentation; and third, a widespread failure to invest in the provision of regimes and facilities that completely and purposefully occupy all prisoners for at least the equivalent of a

---

2. It is for this important reason that the structure of custodial sentences within reparative and restorative regimes proposed in this work includes a period spent under supervision within the community prior to release. This would enable correctional professionals within the community to assess and address aspects of the offender's home (or other lifestyle) circumstances that might encourage further offending.

normal working day.³

True progress in each of these areas requires significant cultural change, but prisons are notoriously change-resistant organisations (Lewis, 1997 *op. cit.*: 130-132). Such change must necessarily alter the attitudes of prisoners towards the use of time spent in custody, of prison staff towards a more professional and flexible image and behaviour, and the government and prison authorities in resolving the ambiguities so correctly identified by Houchin. Each of these forms of change involves a considerable and inevitable element of voluntarism.

But voluntarism within the operation of regimes for offenders in custody has a somewhat different meaning. A 'custodial climate' has to be created within which, from the viewpoint of offenders, it is acceptable and indeed preferable to take a full and active part in the processes of offending behaviour analysis, remedial counselling, self-improvement and victim reparation. Neither is it inappropriate for there to be incentives to adopt such a choice of action, since to do so gives meaning to the correctional agenda and opens up the possibility of subsequent crime-free lifestyles. The starting point for this endeavour has to be a pre-conviction identification of offenders willing and suitable to take part in such regimes, and the development of prisons (or other institutions for young offenders) specifically set aside for the operation of reparative and restorative regimes.

Once offenders (and prison staff) perceive that action has been taken to exclude from these regimes those who would be disruptive and unwilling to comply with basic rules and requirements of daily conduct, the way is open to develop a 'responsibility model' of custodial practice within which each individual has a part to play and there is an absolute expectation that he or she will do so. Under ideal circumstances regimes of this nature become largely self-regulating once acceptable standards of inter-personal conduct and behaviour have been agreed by all concerned as desirable and necessary. As I have indicated in earlier work (Cornwell, 2007 *op. cit.*: 127-130), the 'direct supervision' model of inmate behavioural control becomes a most useful baseline element of regime design.⁴

---

3. In recent years there has developed a tendency in British prisons to 'measure' the effectiveness of regime delivery in terms of 'time out of cell'. The failure to deliver regimes that provide purposeful full-time daily occupation results in other activities (such as recreation, education and supervised association) becoming part of this calculation, simply because inmates are 'unlocked' but are not necessarily at work. In addition, wasteful and inflexible attendance patterns insisted upon by prison staff and their unions frequently prevent provision of a full eight hour working day for inmates, even if sufficient occupational places were available.
4. The direct supervision model of correctional management was first introduced in the United States in 1974 and has been developed over the intervening years to the present time. It is widely used in the American Criminal Justice System for all levels of security and control provision, and has proved most effective in reducing the levels of inter-personal violence and rule infraction in prisons. At the same time, research and comparative evaluative assessment indicates that it is more staff-efficient, cost-effective and safer than the regimes in traditional jails. For a detailed analysis of the benefits of direct supervision, see Richard Wener (2006), 'Effectiveness of the Direct Supervision System of Correctional Design and Management: A Review of the Literature', in *Journal of Criminal Justice and Behaviour*, Vol.33, No.3, pp.392-410.

The key to success in operating regimes of this nature is firstly that inmates volunteer to participate within them, and secondly that levels of staff supervision can be reduced simply because offenders have a vested interest in compliance with the 'ground rules', and because it is seen as desirable to do so. The 'fall-back' position in the event of repeated non-compliance is that the inmate is demoted from the regime level, its incentives and earned privileges, its provision for self-improvement and its more relaxed environment, to one of lesser status and greater supervision. In serious instances of indiscipline the inmate may be transferred to other facilities operated on the more 'traditional' model of prison administration.

RESPONSIBILITY AND PARTICIPATION

In addition to the evident value of voluntarism within the direct supervision model of custodial correction, the attributes of respect, responsibility and participation become the driving forces that provide its credibility in practice. Central to this situation is an absolute insistence that all dealings between offenders and staff are conducted on the basis of mutual respect for the individual, for the consideration of others, and for the manner in which the regime operates. Front-line staff employed within direct supervision regimes need not only innate and well-developed interpersonal skills, but also the ability to communicate clearly, assertively and sensitively with inmates (Parrish, 2005:3; Wener, 2006).[5]

The 'ground rules' governing daily life within living units and elsewhere within the establishment require inmates to take responsibility for their own behaviour, for compliance with 'house rules', for the cleanliness of themselves and their living space, for their individual contribution to the daily life of the residential unit, and for following the 'compact' or agreement made during their induction period and setting out their personal targets or standards to be achieved. Lapses of performance in these basic aspects of the regime are met in the first instance with verbal correction, in a second instance with a written (and recorded) 'notice of improvement', and on any subsequent occasion with a disciplinary interview with a unit supervisor or more senior manager.[6]

Misconduct amounting to an infraction of Prison Rules invariably results in

---

5. David Parrish's (2005), *Commission on Safety and Abuse in America's Prisons*, pp.2-3, at http://www.prisoncommission.org/statement/parrish_david.pdf+direct+supervision+in+prisons+USA&hl=endct=clnx&cd=128gl=uk.
6. The model of direct supervision described briefly here is that in operation at the Mangaung Correctional Centre (MCC) outside Bloemfontein in the Republic of South Africa operated by Group 4/ Securitas based in the United Kingdom. MCC is a 3,000-bed facility designed to maximum security standards, and was the first privately managed prison to be commissioned by the Department of Correctional Services RSA. The author spent some five years between 1999 and 2004 as the operations adviser to the prison during the building, commissioning, staff training and build-up to full operation of the establishment. He continues to act as a consultant to the director and management of the prison when requested to do so.

a formal disciplinary hearing before the prison director or deputy director[7], with recourse to a scale of sanctions agreed with and authorised by the Correctional Services Authority. In instances of serious misconduct (assault, drug trafficking, or other criminal offences) the offence may be referred to the police with a view to prosecution in the courts. In either of these events, and invariably in the latter instance, the offender will be liable to transfer out of the establishment.

These formally necessary provisions noted, however, the emphasis on personal responsibility and respect is modelled by custodial staff, and is overwhelmingly reciprocated by those in their charge. This simple fact assists in making inter-personal relationships between inmates and staff more relaxed, enhances staff professionalism and confidence, and builds trust in the commitment of the prison towards the welfare and future lives of those held in its custody.

In addition to reasonable compliance with 'ground rules' there is an equally robust expectation that every inmate will participate to the best of his or her ability within the regime, and will also use the time spent in custody purposefully in terms of personal development and preparation for a law-abiding life on release. This is reinforced by the fact that each inmate has a sentence plan or 'compact' setting out personal goals and standards to be achieved with time boundaries for completion. Compacts are agreed between the inmate and the casework professional (or mentor) to whom he or she is assigned, and meets at regular intervals to review progress and update the compact. The mentor is also the person (in addition to direct supervision staff) who is the first point of reference in the event of problems arising during the period spent in custody.

Active participation within the regime is encouraged in all aspects of activities such as sport and recreation, evening classes involving music, art, drama and basic education, and religious observance outside of the core working day. In addition, since many inmates have relatively low literacy and numeracy skills on admission to custody, remedial education may have to precede (or be undertaken in conjunction with) the primary phase of offending behaviour analysis and counselling. Such education may also be necessary before vocational or skills training can take place in order for reparative work to be completed, and may thus form part of the core day activity.

The continuous presence of direct supervision officers (DSOs) within houseblock units throughout the day not only provides inmates with constant supervision, but also a source of advice and guidance when personal difficulties arise. Some prisons operate personal officer schemes in addition to the presence of casework professionals, within which small groups of inmates are assigned to the general over-

---

7. Or, in some prison systems in which private sector management is a permitted practice, by an official appointed by the Correctional Authority to undertake disciplinary hearings as a 'magistrate' or 'controller' whose role is also to monitor compliance with regime delivery conditions agreed with the authority in contractual terms.

sight of a nominated unit staff member for the purposes of their general welfare and the resolution of personal problems and difficulties. This tends to free the time of caseworkers to be devoted to the professional aspects of offence analysis, counselling and pre-release planning and assessment.

In return for full participation within the regime it is customary for privileges to be set at different levels depending on the assessed trustworthiness and effort displayed by each individual inmate. This system also provides a structure of informal sanctions that can be applied by unit supervisors and managers in cases of rule infraction of a non-serious nature. Inmates normally receive a basic level of privileges at the admission and induction stage, raised to an intermediate level once their participation has reached a satisfactory standard. For those who comply fully or better with all aspects of the regime on a consistent basis, an 'enhanced' (or upper) level of privileges maintains the impetus of the sentence planning process. Compliance with unit 'house rules' is under-pinned by the operation of an 'intermediate treatment' (or referral) unit within the prison to which those persistently reluctant to comply with these rules are liable to be returned to repeat the induction process on a basic level of privileges. The intermediate treatment unit is not a punishment unit, but rather a unit in which the 'ground rules' are re-explained and enforced, and inmates have to demonstrate regime compliance before re-entering the mainstream population of the prison's house-block units.

SELF-ANALYSIS AND REPARATIVE ACTION

Within custodial facilities managed on the direct supervision (or similar) model of operation, once an inmate has completed the admission and induction phases of sentence[8], he or she will normally spend a short period of personal assessment in the intermediate treatment unit (ITU) to ascertain willingness to abide by regime requirements and identify any potential problems that may affect subsequent life within the House-block units of the prison. The ITU may be co-located with the induction unit or an extension of its regime, but it represents the first stage in the process of analysing offending behaviour and the extent of support that the inmate will need in order to undertake this task in conjunction with professional counselling and therapy.

Once admitted into house-block unit life, the process of analysis will continue under the guidance of casework professionals (and personal officers) in conjunc-

---

8. These are normally of between two and four weeks in duration, depending whether any initial programme work is undertaken to identify offending behaviour causes and determine the extent of support, educational, medical or therapeutic needs that the inmate will require to be met during the early stages of sentence. The induction phase should, however, conclude with at least the formulation of an initial 'compact' agreed with the inmate as the basis for the initial period spent within the mainstream houseblock units of the facility.

tion with meeting educational needs and allocation to vocational training or daily employment. Each inmate having previously been considered suitable for participation within the prison regime should have had little difficulty in negotiating an initial 'compact', and agreeing to a proportion of his or her prison earnings being deducted for victim reparation. This means, however, that wage structures within the prison have to be sufficiently realistic to enable inmates to be able to make reparation *and* retain sufficient earnings to meet their reasonable needs in custody.[9] It also means that most forms of work need to create products of a marketable nature outside the prison in order to generate the revenue to purchase raw materials and pay increased wages on a productivity basis. With imagination and pro-activity this is possible to achieve as we have noted with the Tihar Experiment described in *Chapter 7*, at p.111 *supra*.[10]

Within reparative and restorative regimes assisted analysis of offending behaviour is as important as the development of a consistent personal work ethic and the acquisition of skills and competencies that may lead to regular employment on release from custody. For this reason it is expected that offenders will have accepted guilt for the harm done in their offences, and have started down the road of understanding the reasons why their offences occurred in the first place. This understanding may develop from 'one to one' counselling and examination of past life-styles, dysfunctional influences, individual pathology and the like, or from participation in group therapy in which offenders may come to perceive that their peer group members have encountered similar experiences. The most important factor is that each offender should be confident that their particular needs and behaviours are being addressed in a manner that will enable them to opt for a crime-free life in the future.

In many important respects retaining a sense of individuality and of the future is as important as being clear about what went wrong in the past and the reasons for this. This is one of the principal strengths of the Good Lives Model that envisages just this form of approach, as opposed to the Relapse Prevention (RP) and Risk-Need Models (RNM) that preceded it, and have formed the basis of many of the cognitive-behavioural programmes presently in use. In dealing with sexual offenders and their offences in particular, Ward *et al.* suggest:

> [Third,] in the GLM there is an important emphasis on the construct of personal identity and its relationship to sexual offenders' understanding of what constitutes a good life. In our view, individuals' conceptions of themselves directly arise from their basic value commitments to pursue human goods, which are expressed in their daily activities and lifestyle. People acquire

---

9. These needs include the purchase of toiletries and stationery, small quantities of personal food items, tobacco (where this is permitted), and the like.
10. For the reader who requires to research further the American concept of direct supervision, see, for example: P. M. Carlson and J. S. Garrett (2005), *Prison and Jail Administration: Practice and Theory*, Sudbury, Massachusetts: Jones and Bartlett Publishers, and G. F. Cole and C. E. Smith (2004), *Criminal Justice in America*, (4th Edition), Belmont, California: Thomson Wadsworth.

a sense of who they are and what really matters from what they do; their actions are suffused with values. What this means for therapists is that it is not enough to simply equip individuals with skills to control or manage their risk factors, it is imperative that they are also given the opportunity to fashion a mode adaptive personal identity, one that bestows a sense of meaning and fulfilment. (Maruna, 2001)

[Fourth,] in our view the concept of psychological well-being (i.e. obtaining a good life) should play a major role in determining the form and content of rehabilitation programmes, alongside risk management. Thus a treatment plan needs to incorporate the various primary goods (e.g. relatedness, health, autonomy, creativity and knowledge) and aim to provide the *internal* and *external* conditions necessary to secure these goods. This necessitates obtaining a holistic account of an offender's lifestyle leading up to his offending, and using this knowledge to help him develop a more viable and explicit good lives plan. (Ward *et al.*, 2006, *op. cit.*: 90-91). (Italics in original)

Working to make reparation to crime victims is one means of enabling offenders in custody to have a feeling of self-worth, take responsibility for the past, and do something substantial to 'put wrongs right'. However, it is also a means by which skills can be acquired with a view to purposeful employment in the future, and, in conjunction with participation in community work projects towards the end of a custodial sentence, forms a most effective 'bridge' between the prison and the community. As we shall see in the concluding section of this chapter, the entire purpose of reparative and restorative custodial regimes is to return into their communities ex-offenders as little damaged by the experience of custody as possible, and with a genuine chance of surviving the temptation to re-offend in the future.

It is important that the process of making reparation should extend beyond the symbolic, and genuinely offer offenders and victims of crime the real opportunity to regain their self-respect and confidence in the future. Within reparative regimes it should be expected that following a period of self-analysis the offender may wish to offer an apology to his or her victim(s), having been enabled to perceive the nature of the harm done, and the extent of personal suffering that may have resulted. Though it may be altogether unlikely that offender and victim may have face-to-face contact in the custodial setting, and, indeed, this may not be at all desirable in cases of violence or sexual crime, the potential healing that an apology can assist should never be overlooked. Some victims may, however, have no wish to be contacted by those who have offended against them, and this also is entirely understandable. There will, notwithstanding, be instances in which it is possible and desirable for offenders to make a written apology to victims through third parties such as external probation supervisors or relatives who might approach the families or close others of victims to ascertain whether such an apology would be acceptable. For some victims, receipt of an apology and explanation is more important than the fact that an offender has been punished, and can be a powerful restorative influence in the psychological recovery of the victim.

Work done in custody to contribute financially to victims of crime should be of a productive nature as we have previously noted, and preferably be marketed beyond the prison where possible. Ideally, also, it should have a skill-acquiring value that will enhance the employability of offenders on release from custody. It is also important, as suggested in the concept of the Good Lives Model discussed previously, that from a holistic point of view offenders should know the value and extent of their contributions to the reparation of victims for the reasons already outlined in *Chapter 5*.

Making reparation is the starting point on the road to social reintegration, preparing offenders for more demanding and less intensely supervised tasks within the community. It also contributes to the vindication of victims of crime whose situation, at least in contemporary Britain, receives far too little attention and support other than at a rhetorical level. Making reparation to some extent balances the harm done and the need for forgiveness: in so doing it represents an acceptance of responsibility for 'putting wrongs right'.

SOCIAL REINTEGRATION

The reader will recall Gill McIvor's (2004:178) comment included at the beginning of this chapter concerning the possibility that reduction of recidivism is, perhaps, the goal of restorative justice least likely to be achieved in practice. I should like to suggest at the outset of this part of the discussion, and in relation to the forms of custodial correctional regime embracing restorative principles proposed here, that this comment might in fact be both speculative and also somewhat sceptical. The real question that arises is that given the inevitable nature of the imprisonment process both presently and within a possible future restorative penology, which is the more likely to have an impact on reoffending? As will have become evident in the foregoing sections of this chapter, at the least a restorative penology addresses the issues involved in offending with considerable thoroughness, seeks actively to redress individual deficits, focuses on the legitimate needs of victims, and envisages a period at the conclusion of each sentence in which the effectiveness of these activities can be tested in practice.

In fact, of course, the type of custodial regime outlined in this work goes considerably further than that: it removes those offenders deemed suitable to participate within it from the criminalizing effects of the traditional prison model, challenges them to take responsibility for themselves and their offending, and does the most possible to equip them to live law-abiding lives and re-integrate into society as useful citizens. The manner in which it seeks to achieve these purposes is altogether more humane, holistic and structured than any regime followed by the incarcerative model of criminal punishment.

Furthermore, by McIvor's own admission somewhat earlier in the same analysis:

> Community service may, it appears, have a positive impact upon recidivism even though it has not traditionally been regarded as an explicitly rehabilitative disposal (McIvor 2002). Comparisons of recidivism between different sanctions suggest that while prison sentences and community-based disposals have similar reconviction rates (e.g. Barclay and Taveres 1999), offenders on community service often have lower reconviction rates than would be predicted by their criminal history, age and other relevant characteristics (Lloyd *et al.* 1995). May (1999) found that reconviction rates among offenders given community service were better than predicted even when social factors such as unemployment and drug use were taken into account. A Swiss study, Killias *et al.* (2000), found lower reconviction rates among offenders sentenced to community service than among those given short prison sentences. (McIvor, 2004:175-6)

A study into the attitudes of offenders and the perceived effectiveness of community service by Rex and Gelsthorpe (2002) within the Pathfinder projects set up under the Home Office's Crime Reduction Programme in 2000[11] produced a number of encouraging conclusions. Allowing that many of the offenders sentenced to community sanctions were probably of lower public risk than others who might have served short prison sentences, three-quarters of those surveyed were considered by supervising staff as unlikely to re-offend, and a similar proportion considered that community service had made them less likely to re-offend. Importantly, however, the aspect of the experience most strongly associated with changed attitudes among offenders was whether they felt the work they had done was of value to themselves and those for whom it was performed (McIvor, 2004 *op. cit.*: 178).

If our ultimate aim within the criminal punishment process is to cause the least damage to offenders consistent with expressing adequate social disapproval of wrongful acts, then the main emphasis must lie in equipping them to be decent citizens. This implies that from the moment that a sanction is imposed by the court we should (other than in exceptional cases[12]) actively contemplate the return of the offender into society at large. Given the difficulties of achieving this within the custodial setting described in the preceding chapter, the shorter the time spent in custody the better, probably, the prospects for social reintegration must become.

---

11. The legislation within the Criminal Justice and Court Services Act 2000 became effective in April 2001, renaming the existing community service order as the community punishment order. A number of 'Pathfinder' projects were established within the existing Probation Service areas to evaluate offender's reactions to the new order and the manner in which it is administered. The results of this evaluation were published in S. Rex and L. Gelsthorpe (2002), 'The Role of Community Service in Reducing Offending: Evaluating Pathfinder Projects in the UK', in *Howard Journal of Penal Reform*, vol.41(4), pp. 311-324
12. Such, for instance, as in cases in which serious offenders are sentenced to 'whole life' custody on the basis that they will never be released from prison. In most modern democracies such sentences are truly exceptional since the offender thus sentenced has no incentive towards remorse or attitudinal change, and, some would assert, might reasonably blame the state rather than him/herself for this situation.

Moreover, as Eugene Ostapiuk has noted:

> It is, therefore, worrying that emphasis is still placed by the 'law and order' lobby on unproven methods based on punishment and deterrence, and institutional incarceration. (And, quoting Schur (1965)), there is no evidence that probation is better than institutions, that institutions are better than probation ... [so] much of what is now being done about crime may be so wrong that the net effect of that action may be to increase rather than decrease crime ... none of the researches concluded to date answers these questions. (Ostapiuk, 1982: 135)

Though these words were written a quarter of a century ago, neither prevailing political attitudes nor the traditional model of custodial punishment have changed significantly over the intervening years, and the observation retains some considerable validity.

Social reintegration is an adaptive process that ultimately requires a community setting in which to take place. Swimming cannot be learned without entering water of sufficient depth to enable the body to float unaided, and much the same must be said of the re-integrative process for offenders. That a measure of social risk inheres in such a situation is to some extent unavoidable, but this risk has to be weighed against that of doing little or nothing to improve each offender's chances of adopting a law-abiding lifestyle. Thus the choice may not ultimately lie between prison *or* probation, but become one rather of prison *and* probation.

This is, of course, the 'nub' of the problem that has to be faced by politicians, the media and the passengers on the Clapham Omnibus alike: the former are risk-obsessive, the media are risk-assertive, and the latter are generally risk-attentive only to the extent that they are influenced by the other two. However, as has been indicated in *Chapter 4* (at p.72 *supra*), and more extensively in earlier work[13], the Finnish experience of the 1950s and onwards clearly indicates that prison populations can be massively reduced and the use of community penalties similarly extended without significant public risk or increase in offending (Joutsen *et al.*, 2001 *op. cit.*). Thus, when it is suggested here that every determinate sentence served within a reparative and restorative regime should include a period spent in the community work setting, this is nothing more than an elaboration of the same principle. Indeed, in the Finnish situation, legislators were far-sighted enough to avoid sending many offenders to custody in the first place.

However, as we shall see in the chapter that follows, this transition depends upon making prisons more 'community friendly' and empowering communities to play a more extensive role in the life of prisons and of offenders. This means that prisons have to cease to be the bastions of exclusion that they presently represent, and communities have to become more actively engaged in the social reintegration of offenders. Meanwhile, a case remains for those offenders who do not (or cannot)

---

13. Cornwell (2007), *op. cit.* at *Chapter 6*, pp.156-8.

participate within the restorative framework to be dealt with in a more traditional model of custodial corrections. Maybe the day will eventually come when those prisoners opting to participate in reparative and restorative regimes will outnumber those declining to do so: it can only be hoped that this will be so.

CHAPTER 10

How Can Prisons Become More 'Community Friendly'?

It was always anticipated in the planning of this work that this chapter would be the most challenging of all of those within this book to write. Challenging because the entire nature of the 'prison: community divide' has traditionally been one of separation and introspection on the part of prisons, and of seclusion and isolation on the part of local communities. The massive and fortress-like designs of the Victorian penitentiaries and convict prisons still, to this day in Britain, cast long shadows over their immediate environs in many major cities, signalling in the most forceful manner possible the stark reality of the state's unfettered power to punish.

More modern prisons with extensive perimeters of metal clad fencing, though less architecturally imposing, provide a visible reminder of the different worlds within them and without. Illuminated brightly by night within the open landscape surrounding them, such places are an ever-present reminder – if indeed one were needed – that the process of criminal punishment is ceaseless within our societies. However, as Andrew Coyle has indicated:

> Prisons as we know them today are based on the notion of exclusion from society. Such a notion sits very uneasily with the concept of a society which is integrated and in which everyone is meant to contribute to the good of others. It is naïve of us to assume that by excluding large numbers of people from our society behind the high walls of a prison for a specified period of time we will somehow turn them into better citizens. The successful experiments which are now emerging from other countries about restorative justice and community penalties give us real reason to hope that there may indeed be, in Vaclav Havel's words, 'a better way of coming to terms with things.' This alternative is not an easy way. It is a very difficult way. But eventually it will be a much more successful way. (Coyle 2001:4)[1]

Writers such as Coyle and Daniel Van Ness (2005)[2], with considerable experience of the difficulties of narrowing the 'prison: community divide' through the introduction of restorative practices within prisons, have stressed the importance of adopting a fresh approach towards the involvement of communities in the daily work of prisons. This is, however, within correctional and political circles a difficult message to convey, since, as we shall shortly see, a careful balance needs to be main-

---

1. Also quoted in Cornwell (2007 *op. cit.*: 137-8). The passage is extracted from Andrew Coyle's (2001) address entitled 'Restorative Justice in Prisons' delivered to the International Prison Chaplains' Association (Europe) in May of that year, the full text of which is available at www.icpa.net
2. Here see also Daniel W. Van Ness (2005), 'Restorative Justice in Prisons', paper presented to Session 204 of the *Symposium on Restorative Justice and Peace*, at Columbia, California, 9-12 February, PFI Centre for Justice and Reconciliation: Prison Fellowship International.

tained between the desirability of wider community involvement and the evident requirements of prison security.

BALANCING RISKS: TAKING A BROADER VIEW

In the preceding chapter and its discussion of prison regimes, some care was taken to suggest that reparative and restorative regimes might only be introduced successfully in circumstances in which offenders would volunteer to participate, and that such participation should not be vulnerable to disruption by others whose willingness was questionable or whose behaviour was un-cooperative or subversive. There is also a question concerning the extent to which it is either reasonable or appropriate to include within such regimes (at least during the period immediately following upon conviction) those prisoners whose offences were so serious as to result in a considerable period in custody.[3] In the same chapter it was also proposed that in ideal circumstances entire prisons should be set aside for restorative regimes, rather than attempt to operate both these and traditional regimes with the same perimeter.

These considerations would combine to suggest that at least in the early stages of the adoption of a restorative penology, such regimes should be operated in prisons holding offenders serving shorter sentences and requiring lesser conditions of physical security than those necessary for more serious offenders serving long terms of imprisonment. There should, however, be no reason why the latter, having served specified periods of longer sentences, should not eventually be transferred to restorative and reparative prisons towards the end of their custodial periods if they volunteered to do so, and were to be considered appropriate to participate within these regimes.

Balancing public risk and the evident need for both more enlightened use of prison custody and victim reparation with that of creating a correctional environment ultimately more likely to reduce reoffending and encourage the social reintegration of offenders is a critical criminological issue. To suggest, in addition, a wider involvement of local communities in the operation of prisons produces a further dimension of potential uncertainty. This stated, however, each aspect of this conceptual 'pyramid' is, in fact, ultimately interdependent, and the reasons for this deserve brief explanation.

It will be evident from the representation of this dynamic illustrated in *Figure*

---

3. Or, at the least, a period of several years before such offenders might be deemed to represent a reasonable public risk of avoiding similar reoffending in the future, and to have served the minimum period in custody consistent with the seriousness of their offence(s). In sentencing terms, therefore, it would be desirable for the court to express a view (when considering imposing terms of imprisonment greater than (say) of five years) as to the minimum period that it perceived should necessarily be spent in prison custody. Such a view should take into account prevailing arrangements for remission of sentence and for conditional release.

10:1 that the greater the demand for public and custodial correctional re-assurance about the risks inherent in community involvement in prisons and the delivery of regimes, the greater the impact upon the nature of these regimes will become. Yet without community involvement the regimes themselves cannot be operated in a manner that will fully test the intentions and ability of offenders to lead law-abiding lives not only during conditional release from custody, but also subsequently under the circumstances of unconditional release. In addition, unless or until prison regimes are operated in a more enlightened and testing manner offenders will remain vulnerable to reoffending, and the risk to the public due to their recidivism is ultimately enhanced.

It would therefore seem reasonable to suggest that if reduction of recidivism is the *ultimate* purpose of the correctional process, then some diminution in present public and correctional levels of demand for assurance concerning public risk has to be accepted if enhanced community involvement in corrections is to be envisaged with a view to reducing reoffending. Moreover, since the 'testing' process cannot be implemented without a greater than present level of community involvement, and the *actual* increase in public risk from this involvement cannot easily be quantified, it becomes unreasonable for assumptions (or public perceptions of risk informed by media pressure) concerning any such increase to dictate the manner in which the correctional environment operates.

Furthermore, given the indications (discussed in *Chapter 9*) that restorative practices do appear to reduce recidivism, and that offenders serving sanctions in the community rather than in prison do better than might be anticipated in terms of reoffending, it would seem absurd to continue to diminish correctional regimes on the basis of such assumptions since both the Finnish experience and that of other nations supports such an approach.

THE CUSTODY: COMMUNITY EQUATION

It will be evident from the illustration at *Figure 10:1* that there is a tension between the publicly perceived issue of risk from offending, the media handling of criminal activity, and the political responses of governments – particularly in Britain – to both in the form of criminal justice policy formulation. The tension may, in fact, be more imaginary than real, but the outcomes of its interpretation and articulation in 'tough on crime' policies that have an overtly punitive intent have significantly affected the operation of custodial sanctions (Grimshaw 2004; Prison Reform Trust 2004).[4] As Grimshaw points out:

---

4. Particularly in the form of mandatory minimum sentences involving drug trafficking and domestic burglary, and including life imprisonment for repeated serious offences. The mandatory minimum sentence for a third drug trafficking offence is seven years imprisonment, and three years for a third offence of domestic burglary. Serious offences include causing grievous bodily harm, arson and rape, among others.

THE CUSTODY: COMMUNITY EQUATION

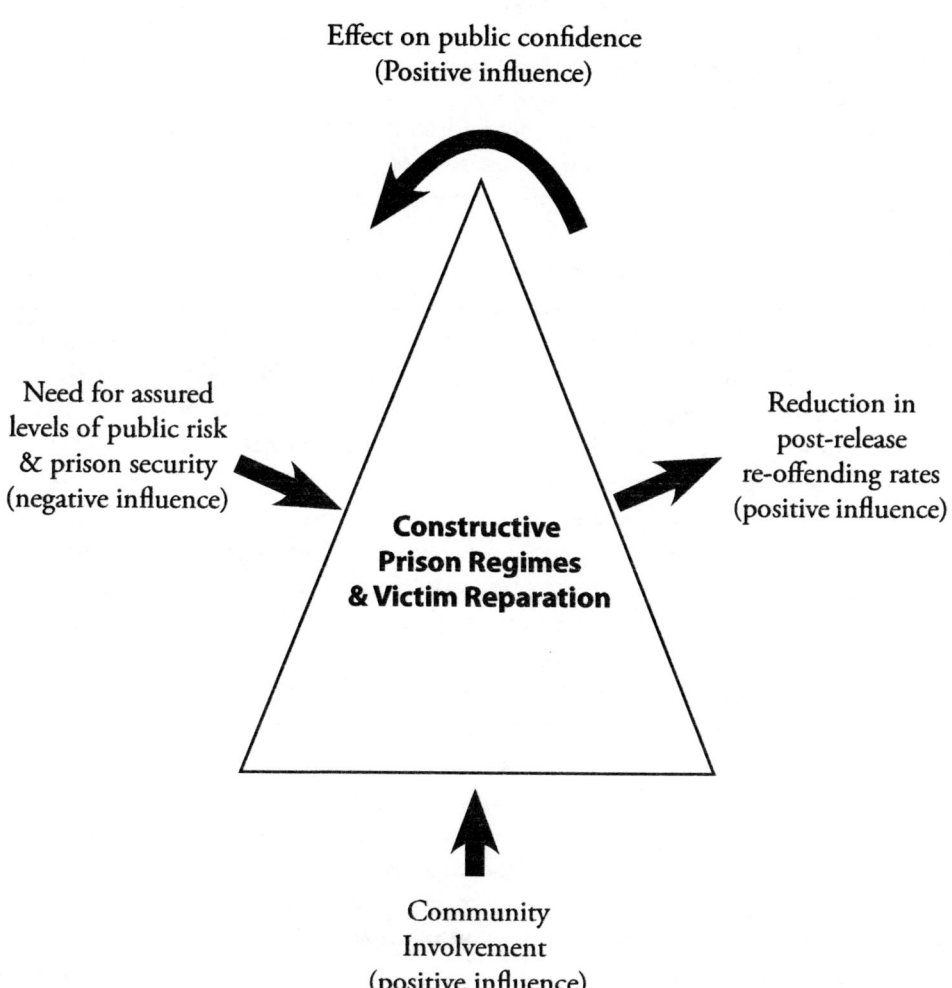

Figure 10:1: The Custody: Community Equation

> 'Toughness' implies robustness, but it is also – and more significantly – a codeword for punitiveness. By 'punishment', we usually mean the infliction of pain or loss. There is now a familiar history of punitive political interventions beginning in the mid-1990s that made imprisonment into a bleaker and more constrained experience, and at the same time promoted imprisonment as a punishment with a positive value, instead of merely a last resort (Downes and Morgan 2002; Liebling and Arnold 2004). (Grimshaw 2004: 2-3)

Not only is this situation confusing and contradictory, but it has also had the dysfunctional effect of increasing the prison population to unmanageable levels during the past decade, and of crippling the delivery of change-provoking custodial regimes. This development has, in its turn, affected both the incorporation of restorative practices into mainstream criminal justice and the wider involvement of communities within the correctional process. Tough and robust the policies may have been, but their effect on recidivism has been at best marginal, and in many respects actually counter-productive. The difficulty that such policies create is that they become extremely difficult to reverse due to the emphasis that is placed on severity (see e.g. Pratt 2002a; Tonry 2004), within a new managerialist culture of centralised government that perceives severity as a powerful tool for reducing or eliminating all forms of public risk.

Taking a broader view of the prison: community relationship implies the replacement (or at least reduction) of the overt punitiveness mentioned previously with a more progressive and enlightened approach to justice delivery that seeks to put 'correction' back onto the penological agenda. This means, in effect, adopting a more communitarian approach to the *outcomes* of the justice process, rather than perceiving that process as an end in itself. Prisons cannot function satisfactorily in a social vacuum simply because they deal in people who come from, and return to communities in which they have to learn to survive legitimately. Moreover, since victims and communities are those stakeholders in justice most affected by criminal acts, it is at the least arrogant for governments to withhold from them the potential to participate within the justice process to the extent that is both reasonable and appropriate. However, as Grimshaw further indicates:

> A major obstacle to progress in increasing democratic participation has been ignorance of a kind exploited by an irresponsible press and media. Consultation initiatives have foundered on the rocks of misinformation and suspicion based on citizens' distance from a powerful centre (Hough and Roberts 2004a and b). Yet people in diverse and deprived communities can show an awareness of crime that is far from simplistic (Roberts et al. 2003 *op. cit.*; Scheingold 1995). What are needed are more tool-kits that show communities how their members can administer justice and prevent crime without falling into the traps of populist punitiveness and control. (Grimshaw 2004 *op. cit.*: 11-12)

CREATING A DIFFERENT CUSTODIAL IMAGE

In an era in which the failings of the punitive agenda within criminal justice are so manifestly evident in its ineffectiveness in achieving the purposes of crime reduction, prisons, if such places are to serve a social purpose, have to be empowered to undertake a 're-branding process' of some considerable magnitude. Not only does this need for change depend upon placing the concept of 'correction' at the forefront of the custodial agenda, but also upon demonstrating an awareness of the social context in which an effective imprisonment process should operate in the interests of the global community that prisons serve.

To whatever extent the intentions of the criminal justice system are overtly punitive, there is no reason for that punitiveness to extend into a process within which deprivation of liberty is already the primary expression of censure. Put another way, perhaps, it should not be expected or permitted that the process of imprisonment should impose further pain or suffering that the deprivation of liberty entails, and particularly not in instances in which offenders have accepted guilt and taken responsibility for it, are prepared to address their offending behaviour, and make substantial reparation to victims of crime. This means that it is necessary to think again about how prisons should be operated to maximise positive aspects of changing lives for the better, and minimise the secondary effects of institutional confinement to the greatest extent possible.

Within the inevitable constraints that enforced custody imposes[5], and its 'deformative risks' sometimes described as the effects of 'prisonization' (Cross 1971 *op. cit.*; Hawkins 1976 *op. cit.*: 56-80)[6], one outcome of the process is undeniable: this is that in the majority of cases protracted imprisonment results in moral, physical and psychological deterioration. For this reason alone imprisonment should be used to the least extent possible, and consistent with the seriousness of offences. Moreover, where imprisonment is strictly unavoidable, the conditions in which sentences are served should be such as to minimise this deterioration and not, as is so often the situation in so many contemporary societies, to exacerbate it.

The most powerful means of minimising the dysfunctional effects of prison life lie in the measures that can be taken to break down the 'custody: community gap' by involving local communities in the daily regime of correctional facilities to the maximum extent that is consistent with the reasonable requirements of security.

---

5. That is to say custody imposed by the courts as a sanction designed to remove offenders from public circulation for specified periods of time against their will. It is a widely held view among correctional practitioners that the impact of imprisonment diminishes significantly after a relatively short period of time, and that thereafter the majority of prisoners undergo a process of acculturation that involves the development of coping strategies to make the process of incarceration less onerous (see e.g. Hawkins 1976 *op. cit.*: 72-3; Irwin and Cressey 1969: 141; Glaser 1964: 118).
6. A term first evident in the criminological literature in the work of Reimer (1937) and Clemmer (1940 *op. cit.*).

This means viewing every day of a custodial sentence, from the day of admission, as one of preparation for release, rather than as one during which the offender is denied liberty and the public is protected from his or her presence within the community. Seen thus, it becomes easier to envisage the prison as a perimeter *within* which as many *normal* events as possible occur by virtue of the fact that members of the community are actively involved in the work, training, offence-analysis, recreational and educational aspects of regime delivery.

Within a reparative and restorative custodial regime for offenders who have acknowledged the harm caused by their offences and accepted responsibility, the errors of the past are infinitely less important than the prospects for the future. Work done to make reparation to victims has a prospective purpose; vocational training undertaken with a view to enhanced employability is an investment for the future; remedial education to achieve normal levels of literacy and numeracy can be seen as a foundation for vocational training as much as for better citizenship; understanding the impact of offences on victims removes a focus of self-pity and encourages one of empathy and willingness to make apology. In each of these areas of activity, and in a number of others such as theatre, music, discussion and addiction counselling, and faith-related groups, it is both possible and advantageous to involve local community members in participation.

Of course it is necessary that members of communities admitted into prisons to become involved in regime activities have to satisfy the reasonable requirements of police checks or similar 'vetting' to verify their good character, but this is far different from the assumption, so frequently encountered within the British prisons tradition, that all of such persons represent a potential security threat and should be excluded unless their presence is strictly unavoidable. Indeed, it may be possible for groups of local crime victims to become regular participants in discussion groups with offenders to reinforce the work done in offence-analysis, and do so to their own improved psychological well being in addition to that of offenders.

In exactly the same manner that visitation facilities are customarily located in areas adjacent to the entry building of most custodial correctional establishments, it is possible to envisage a 'prison: community' building or zone that permits access from either side for regime activities, but does not necessitate the admission of community members into the domestic 'core' of the complex. The most important feature of functional correctional facility design is that of having a clear vision for the purpose of the establishment and enabling this purpose to be met reliably, efficiently, and with the most effective use of the staff resource.

In prisons designed to deliver reparative regimes and facilitate offender reintegration into communities effectively, it is important that provision is made for the 'hostel-type' accommodation of offenders released daily from custody to undertake work on community projects, but returning to the establishment at night. Once again, such accommodation should be located in an area adjacent to the perimeter of the facility from a security viewpoint, and enable 'out-workers' controlled access and egress for the purposes of attending their employment with minimal staff supervision. It is also essential that this 'trusted' population should be accommodated separately from the resident population in order that they cannot be placed under duress by the latter to import or 'smuggle' unauthorised items into the main prison complex.

Viewed in such a context, we are already able to envisage a 'new-generation' custodial and semi-custodial correctional facility that has infra-structural links with its local community designed into its spatial footprint, while at the same time conforming to the necessary requirements of public safety, custodial security and a restorative vision. Such a design is enabling of a regime that combines to fulfil a custodial purpose with an additional potential to provide conditional release on a soundly structured basis. Just as importantly, however, such a design concept begins to break down the dysfunctional aspects of custodial life, and overcome a number of the 'deformative risks' so aptly described by Rupert Cross and discussed earlier.

CHANGING THE TRADITIONAL CUSTODIAL CULTURE

Correctional services world-wide, like police services and other similar large public bodies establish over time an organisational culture that is to an extent definitive of their role, but also expressive of the manner in which that role is perceived and performed by employees. In his seminal study of prison management in the United States, John DiIulio (1987) has defined this, in prisons, as the 'keeper philosophy'[7], though it is described in a broadly similar manner by a number of authoritative writers on prisons and their organisational cultures (e.g. Thomas 1972 *op. cit.*; Hawkins 1976 *op. cit.*; Fitzgerald and Sim 1982 *op. cit.*; Fleisher 1989 *op. cit.*; Lewis 1997 *op. cit.*). The philosophy, it is claimed, 'derives from a common body of beliefs' held by correctional officials, which fashions their responses and approaches to the daily task of dealing with those held in custody within a structure of bureaucratic rules and regulations (DiIulio 1997 *op. cit.*:166-7).

The organisational culture of prisons themselves is undoubtedly characteristic of a number of factors, foremost among which are the prevailing mode of correctional practice[8], the extent to which prison management at all levels sets and imposes standards of behaviour for both staff and inmates, the manner in which prison staff approach their custodial duties, and the way in which prison inmates respond to

---

7. For an explanation of this approach see: J. J. DiIulio Jnr. (1987), *Governing Prisons: A Comparative Study of Correctional Management*, New York: The Free Press and London: Collier Macmillan, pp.167-174.
8. By this term I mean the purposes and the manner of implementation of penal policies formulated by governmental agencies and subsequently expressed in the 'mission statement' or similar declaration of the operational practices to be adopted in correctional establishments.

their treatment by both management and correctional employees. Though this is, at first sight, a complex dynamic, to a considerable extent the culture will ultimately be indicative predominantly of the latter two factors since both are key determinants of the stability of daily life within each penal facility.

It is a fact, however, that the daily working lives of 'front line' correctional officials are considerably influenced by the necessity for routine practices to be carried out methodically, in conformance with procedures, and reliably in terms of the standards required. To some extent this makes the work of these officials repetitive and sometimes mundane, particularly in relation to the recurring routines of feeding, exercising, escorting and supervising inmates on a daily basis, listening to their complaints, and dealing with their seemingly endless demands and requests. These duties have to be carried out in circumstances in which relationships are often less than cordial, and in which staff can feel relatively isolated – and even at risk - due to the preponderance of inmates around them.

The manner in which correctional staff members behave both individually and collectively towards inmates in prisons is in many respects critical. The task requires high levels of inter-personal skills, an ability to exercise authority fairly, to avoid discrimination of any sort, and to persuade in circumstances in which compliance is far from automatic or willing. It also involves an ability to deal with persons whose behaviour can be aggressive, uncontrolled, abusive, and not infrequently conditioned by personality disorder and even severe mental impairment. It thus becomes scarcely surprising that correctional officials develop 'coping strategies' as a group and individually for dealing effectively with the considerable and often stressful demands placed upon them.

Given the unusual nature of the task, it is only to be expected that correctional officers rely heavily upon a feeling of 'belonging' to the staff group, upon a corporate approach to the demands of their work, and solidarity in their relationships for dealing with both those who manage them and with inmates. In some countries this has led to the development of strongly trade unionised and change-resistant correctional workforces whose relationship with their national management authorities have – particularly in Britain – been historically fragile and even turbulent (Vorenberg 1972:67; Hawkins 1976 *op. cit.*: 170-173; Lewis 1997, *op. cit.*: 130-142).

The reasons for which correctional employees tend to be stereotypically described as change-resistant tend to differ between nations and penal organisations. In England and Wales as Thomas (1972) has recorded, the development was a complex one based primarily upon a perception held widely by prison staff during the period he described that their status and authority were being undermined and eroded by the employment of considerable numbers of 'specialists' from the Probation Service and the academic discipline of psychology to undertake casework with prisoners. (Thomas 1972 *op. cit.*: 199-208). Within a workforce that was traditionally heavily recruited from ex-military and police sources with a strong authoritarian and rank-conscious bias, this influx of 'specialists' was resented as a deliberate move to reduce the status of the prison officer to that of the 'turnkey' of the Victorian era.

Be that as it may, the Prison Officers' Association (POA) of England and Wales has accumulated a reputation for obdurately opposing significant change in the working practices of prisons, and, as Derek Lewis observed:

> The fact that the Prison Service and its staff do not enjoy the support or admiration of the general public reflects to some extent the state it was in at the start of the 1990s. No public service with such a poor record for security, humane treatment of prisoners and operating efficiency deserves to be held in high regard, despite the heroic efforts of many individuals.
>
> Part of the blame for this must be laid at the door of the Prison Officers' Association. Its stubborn defence of restrictive practices, coupled with its belligerent and often threatening demeanour, resulted in deep public prejudice against prison officers, and an image of a service rooted in the past. The POA must have been the last bastion of 1960s trade unionism. (Lewis 1997 *op. cit.*:130).

In all fairness, however, much has changed since the early 1990s, and the implementation of the Fresh Start Agreement of 1987[9] paved the way for a more professional approach to working conditions and practices for uniformed members of the Prison Service. It was subsequently accompanied by a management process setting key indicators of performance for prison establishments, and standards of delivery that are auditable and considerably more accountable to the government and the public.

All of this stated, the Prison Service of England and Wales remains to this day a deeply unionised organisation within which the POA still exercises excessive power to resist change at both the local and national levels. This resistance has become a seemingly embedded aspect of the organisational culture because it is actively encouraged by the traditional negotiating methods of the POA and prison management[10], by the reluctance of national management to risk industrial action, and by a disputes resolution procedure that is archaic by modern management standards.

---

9. The 'Fresh Start' Agreement implemented from 1987 brought about a significant change in working practices within the Prison Service of England and Wales. It ended the use of paid overtime hours worked and placed all uniformed grades on a salaried basis. In addition to reducing working hours to a reasonable level (basically 39 hours per week), it set out procedures for resolving disputes over working conditions at both a national and local level, and arrangements for repaying additional hours worked by uniformed staff by granting time off duty *in lieu*.

10. Normally involving fixed monthly and *ad hoc* meetings between the local POA committee and prison management that are frequently combative rather than cooperative in nature. As a former prison governor I recall a series of such meetings on the agenda of which was a revised system of attendance for uniformed staff more resource efficient and in keeping with the regime of the prison than that at the time in use. The negotiations lasted for 12 months due to the filibustering tactics of the POA committee, and ended with them withdrawing from further discussion by resort to a 'Failure to Agree' notice that escalated the entire negotiation to a national level. In the event the initiative had to be abandoned because the industrial relations 'climate' at the national level was too fragile for the support of the prison management to be assured. The POA committee hailed this as victory for local democracy!

Prison governors seeking to introduce new initiatives or working practices still have to secure the prior agreement of their local POA committees, and this process can take months (and even years) to negotiate before change can be implemented. The negotiating process is underpinned by reliance upon the *status quo ante* that prevents change being implemented and also provides a mechanism for filibustering negotiation of change unless or until union agreement is secured.

Correctional facilities need a vibrant and progressive organisational culture to remain effective and innovative in a professional sense. This means that there has to be a sense of shared purpose between management and employees to seek and deliver a service of excellence rather than of any lesser standard. It also means that there has to be a high perception of self-belief in the professional nature of the work done in prisons that extends beyond the 'keeper' rationalisation of the task. All too frequently at present, however, correctional officials find themselves trapped in an ambivalent culture and role conflict that is uncertain about what the purpose of the organisation *actually* is, and thus also about the extent to which the work that they do is valued by governments and the public whom they serve.

This ambivalence is entirely unnecessary and avoidable if government policies are coherent and the purposes of corrections are explicit beyond a concept of punitiveness. The punitive and incarcerative agenda feeds the 'keeper philosophy' and at the same time places significant limitations on the professional aspirations of correctional staff. Small wonder, then, that these people become frustrated and change resistant. A reparative and restorative penology holds out the prospect of changing the culture of prisons from one of ambivalence to one of much clearer and constructive purpose. If for no other reasons, and there are many cited in this work, such a change in the penal culture deserves the most serious consideration.

ENCOURAGING COMMUNITY STAKEHOLDERS

Within the closed situation in which most prisons operate, correctional staff can all too easily become remote from the community beyond the perimeter due to their focus upon their work and the secluded nature of the prison environment. Moreover, as we have noted earlier, many correctional officials perceive community involvement in prisons as in some senses an intrusion into their specialised world of work, and one that can easily be resisted for apparent reasons of security. In addition, it may also be probable that some staff will view such involvement as a diminution of their authority as was the case in the attitude adopted towards the introduction of casework 'specialists' in the 1960s and early 1970s. How, then, can such reluctance be overcome?

In a more enlightened penal climate it would be appropriate to suggest that the present sharply defined divide between custodial and non-custodial correctional services, and particularly between custodial officials and probation officers might profitably be closed to a significant extent, and to the benefit of both parties. For as we shall see in Part Three of this work, and have also discussed in earlier chapters[11], lesser use of custody and increased use of community sanctions would require a robust form of supervision to ensure that actual or perceived public risk did not jeopardise the transition. It might, therefore, be worth considering whether some correctional officials presently employed solely in prisons might not usefully be re-deployed to increase the effectiveness of, and compliance with, the requirements of community sanctions.

Such a transition would have the benefit of broadening the professionalism of the present prison officer role, particularly in the supervision of offenders released conditionally from prisons to undertake community projects prior to unconditional release. It would also provide some respite to the presently considerably over-burdened National Probation Service (NPS) in England and Wales, and might well also assist in bringing the two main arms of the present National Offender Management Service (NOMS)[12] closer together with a sense of genuinely shared purpose.

It is also possible to suggest that from the viewpoint of the public and of victims of crime, a more closely controlled and supervised operation of community sanctions might inspire greater public confidence in the correctional process, and at the same time encourage wider public or community participation in the selection of projects and the delivery of these to a state of completion. Local communities have potentially much to gain from an expansion of non-custodial sanctions that could bring much-needed amenity value to their areas, and enable projects to be planned and completed which might otherwise remain unidentified, unfunded and otherwise overlooked for lack of resources. We shall return to this possibility in the chapters that follow.

Within this chapter we have explored in a broad sense a number of the reasons why prisons remain remote places of exclusion, and how the nature of the work done within them by correctional officials tends to make these places and their staff somewhat introspective and resistant to change. If delivery of effective justice is to become a reality there is a need for greater community participation in the way that

---

11. Particularly in *Chapter 4* and *Chapter 7* in which mention has been made of the need for a better balance between custodial and non-custodial sanctions, and a significant expansion of the latter to deal with those offenders who might otherwise serve very short prison sentences.
12. The National Offender Management Service (NOMS) came into being as a result of legislation within the Offender Management Act 2007 which received the Royal Assent on 26 July 2007. NOMS is part of the newly formed Ministry of Justice, which includes the Prison Service and the National Probation Service. It comprises ten regional areas in England and Wales, and a detailed description of its organisation and tasks can be found at: http://www.noms.justice.gov.uk/documents/MofJ_org_charts_01_08.
The Ministry of Justice also sponsors and funds the Youth Justice Board (YJB), an executive non-departmental public body, which reports to the MOJ and the Department for Children, Schools and Familes. The YJB was formed under the Crime and Disorder Act 1998, and originally reported to the Home Office. See http://www.direct.gov.uk/en/D12/Directories/DG_10012305.

prisons operate, and, in particular, for a narrowing of the presently marked extent of separation between custodial and non-custodial sanctions. Narrowing this gap will be no easy task, but it is one that could bring real and lasting change to the manner in which correctional services are conceived and operated. It could also lead to an enhanced level of public confidence in the Criminal Justice System that is sorely needed at the present time.

The 'public', however that term is interpreted, pay considerable sums in the form of taxes for the delivery of justice, and should be confident that these sums are well used in providing safety and reducing crime and reoffending. A restorative penology would allow a more enlightened approach to sanctions to be adopted, particularly for the many offenders who regret their criminal acts, are prepared to take responsibility for them, and would be willing to make real and substantial reparation to victims of crime. Such a penology could also entirely change the face of contemporary prisons in an exciting and constructive way, but this requires that prisons must become more 'community friendly' and communities must take a greater interest and stake in the processes of justice.

In the final part of this work the focus of attention is placed on the operation of sanctions within the community, and the ways in which it might be possible to make these measures more effective and useful while at the same time increasing the likelihood that offenders would opt for a law-abiding life as a result of being thus sentenced. Within this process it will be necessary to suggest how the transition of imprisoned offenders from custody to community might best be managed, and thereby, eventually, make lesser and better use of imprisonment. As we shall see, communities have much to offer to criminal justice that is presently overlooked or disregarded. As stakeholders in justice these same communities have both rights and responsibilities within a concept of delivering justice with a more vibrant and socially conscious ethos.

CHAPTER 11

What Should Be the Real Purposes of Community Corrections?

The final Part of this book is entirely devoted to a discussion of how sanctions or penalties for criminal offending might be operated within the community and, at the same time, contribute towards making restorative justice a central feature of the penal system in practice. In the previous chapter, reference was made to the stark nature of the 'custody: community divide', a phenomenon that has existed for decades past, and which has deeply affected attitudes towards offending and offenders that seem to have 'hardened' even further over the past decade in particular (Pratt, 2000a. *op. cit.*; Cullen *et al.*, 2000; 2002).[1] Neither is it a simple matter to separate attitudes that appear to be punitive from those of a retributive nature, since the two terms tend to become blurred within a number of otherwise informative research studies (von Hirsch, 1993; Walker *et al.*, 1988).

And if, as Maruna and King (2004 *op. cit.*:87-90) have suggested - in discussion of authoritative and reliable research sources - public punitiveness is more a myth than a reality, then there is something particularly cynical about the increasingly punitive nature of the criminal justice legislation that has been enacted in England and Wales over the past decade (Tonry, 2003 *op. cit.*:5-6). What seems equally likely, however, is that the manner in which the visual and written media sensationalise particularly serious crimes invokes a strong feeling of antipathy in the public towards those who commit them, and that this antipathy is interpreted in a populist manner by governments anxious to be seen to be 'tough on crime' (e.g. Stalans, 2002; Garland, 2001 *op. cit.*; Cullen *et al.* 2000 and 2002; Pratt, 2002b).

Further, it is possible to accept the inevitability of a measure of retributive denunciation within the punishment process without that process becoming predominantly or even exclusively retributive as has largely become the case in Britain, the United States, and a number of other countries within the contemporary world of penology. Indeed, it is the contention within this work that when such situations arise, it becomes difficult not to over-use the custodial sanction because sentencing practices escalate in some or another proportion to the extent in which retributive

---

1. For the purposes of the discussion here it becomes necessary to consider what is known about 'public' attitudes insofar as these can ever be determined with any accuracy, and what might be termed the 'official' attitudes that drive governmental responses to crime and the formulation of criminal justice policies. It would be tempting to suggest that clear linkages can be discerned between these two sets of 'attitudes' at the political level, the latter being responsive to the former, but as will be seen such may be to overstate the case considerably (e.g. Maruna and King, 2004 *op. cit.*; Mayhew and van Kesteren, 2002; Roberts, 2002; and Hough and Roberts, 1998 *op. cit.*).

punishment alone fails to have a discernible impact upon recidivism (Cornwell, 2006 *op. cit.*: 97-99; Gross, 1979: 4-5)[2].

If wider use of community sanctions is to have credibility, these also have to display a 'punitive bite' of a demanding proportion that convinces politicians, sentencing officials, offenders, victims and the public not only that such measures represent no 'soft option' in comparison with custodial punishment, but also that they are a *preferable* option where use of custody is strictly avoidable. This is quite different from making a case for 'decarceration', though, as we shall see subsequently, a measure of reductivism may, and ideally should, result from such a transition.

CONCEIVING A CHANGE OF PENAL DIRECTION

Within the discussion offered in preceding chapters, three principal themes have emerged in relation to the wider use of community sanctions. These are that in the first place it is both desirable and possible to send less offenders to prison than is the case at present. Secondly, that for many of the less serious offenders sentenced to medium terms in custody and who might be suitable to participate in reparative and restorative regimes, there should be a more coherent process of progression from custodial to non-custodial status within the overall sentencing framework. Third, that non-custodial sanctions must evidently be seen to be demanding of offenders, properly resourced and supervised, have a reparative outcome for victims of crime, be of amenity value to communities, and enhance, where possible, the subsequent employability of offenders themselves.

A fourth theme, contingent upon acceptance of the former three also became evident. This was that for those offenders, the seriousness of whose crimes make more extended detention in custody inevitable, or who might be unsuitable for participation within reparative and restorative prison regimes, a 'traditional' mode of imprisonment would need to be retained and operated alongside regimes of a reparative and restorative nature. Such is not to imply that at some stage the latter might not 'progress' to the former type of regime either later in a sentence or as a result of changed behaviour, but that the practicalities of custodial life and regime operation require a formalised process of bifurcation.

As to the first proposition, it must be acknowledged that a number of other countries have faced and overcome the need to reduce their excessive prisoner popu-

---

2. I have discussed this situation in greater detail in former work, and thus do not detain the reader with it at any length here. For a wider discussion of the issues involved see Cornwell, 2006 *op. cit.* and in particular in *Chapter 7* which bears the title: 'Criminal Punishment: Is there an Inclusive Theory?' at pp. 97-107. My colleague John Blad (2003 and 2006 *op. cit.*) has argued similarly, and in particular in relation to what he terms the use of 'instrumental' punishment within which excessive retribution is employed for purposes of wider social policy and control rather than the strict proportionality and appropriateness of sentences.

lations[3], and most (with the exception of The Netherlands) have maintained such reduction. In the particular instances of Spain and Canada significant reductions have been made by a slightly different route through the use of suspended sentences of imprisonment from the mid-1990s onwards: a trend entirely opposite to that of the British experience during the same period. (Cid, 2005:169-179; Roberts and Gabor, 2004: 100; Cormier, 2006 *op. cit.*: 153). This means that where there is a determination to reduce penal populations it is possible to do so, and in each instance mentioned it has been achieved without a significant increase in crime rates occurring.

The second proposition might, at first sight, appears to be more challenging since it proposes that where offenders accept guilt and are willing to make reparation to victims, the sentencing structure should allow for a two-phase approach to custodial sanctions in the form of reparative custody. The first phase spent in custody would include offence recognition, analysis and counselling in combination with vocational training and work to make reparation. This should, ideally, be followed by a second phase of conditional release to project work within the community, though the offender would return to prison hostel-type accommodation at the end of each working day. In the case of more serious offences that would need to be identified and specified[4], a third phase of community supervision might be added in place of the present practice of unconditional release.

The third proposition is central to the theme of this chapter, and raises a number of subsidiary issues concerning the nature, purposes and operation of community sanctions. It suggests that non-custodial sanctions, where these are used more widely as *alternatives* to custody, need to have a clear and visible structure and operational context that is evident to the public in terms of its value, supervision, delivery and demands upon offenders. This might be said to be vital as a means of securing public confidence in, and respect for both the Criminal Justice System itself and the credibility of community sanctions. As we shall see later (in *Chapters 12* and *14*), this may require a re-structuring of the existing penal system to provide both a custodial correctional service and a community correctional service under a single organisational structure with its officials professionally trained to deliver its tasks in either or both sectors. Correctional services for juvenile and youthful offenders might also be subsumed within the same overall Correctional Services organisation.

The main purposes of such a transition would be to create a wider public awareness of, and confidence in the aims of criminal justice in reducing reoffending, increasing public safety, reintegrating offenders into communities, and equipping them as far as possible to lead law-abiding and productive lives. At the present

---
3. Most notably Finland, The Netherlands, and Germany in Europe, and North Carolina in the USA, as previously described in *Chapter 6* at p.96.
4. Specifically, those offences that might entail an element of residual public risk such as sexual offences against minors, and repeated offences of serious violence, arson, or rape.

time in Britain in particular, but also elsewhere in many modern democracies, the conceptual and operational 'divides' between prisons and community sanctions are too wide to encourage public and judicial confidence in an expanded use of the latter which tend, in consequence, to be too frequently perceived as 'soft options'. There is no reason why this problem cannot be overcome provided that community sanctions are given a more coherent structure and made more demanding.

It will be noted that in this work a number of the traditionally used terms within (particularly the British) penal system 'nomenclature' have been specifically avoided. This is deliberate. Within a restorative justice penology it is pointless to speak of 'community punishment', 'rehabilitation', 'probation', 'parole', 'community orders', and the like, since these have all accrued failure-laden, outmoded or inappropriate images that contribute little if anything to public confidence in criminal justice. This does not mean that the well-intentioned and dedicated work performed by organisations like the present British Probation Service have no value, but rather that the image of that Service should extend far beyond the supervision of people who are subject to generic community sentences (or orders) which is but one aspect of the more important public role that it might so easily perform.

The purpose here is to propose the way in which criminal justice systems might be made more 'systematic' and cohesive, following a clearly defined purpose, and delivering a better quality of justice to the public. Community sanctions have a huge potential to change the values of the justice system providing that public confidence in their effectiveness can be improved. Well-planned, executed, supervised and completed community projects might have immense value to communities, while at the same time constructively engaging with offenders, meeting their social deficits, and providing better for victims of crime and their need for vindication. Simply locking away more and more offenders in prisons achieves none of these purposes and stores up further problems for the future.

The fourth theme or proposition identified earlier has to be explained at this juncture since it has a direct bearing on the 'deliverability' of each of those previously mentioned. It concerns what must, realistically, be done about those 'hard core' serious offenders whose crimes are heinous and whose detention for long periods for the safety of the public cannot be avoided. It also concerns those other offenders whose crimes are serious enough to warrant their imprisonment, but whose attitudes, behaviour and responses to the custodial process are disruptive and unacceptable. Here it has to be stated that the way in which many prisons presently operate is, in a number of respects, such as to breed resentment and disruptive behaviour because of the pointlessness of regimes, impersonal treatment, and a general failure to appeal to the reasonable responses in ordinary people confined within them.

These reservations stated, however, provision has to be made for long-term and behaviourally difficult prisoners for whom reparative regimes would be inappropriate, or who are so remorseless or disruptive that their participation in them would be entirely counter-productive. There is, it seems, no practical alternative other than to provide for such persons regimes along the more traditional lines that require basic compliance with prison rules, provide more limited facilities and privileges, and conditions that might be described in the words of a former British Home Secretary as 'decent but austere'.[5] This does not, however, imply that some long-term inmates might not be suitable for reparative regimes, but that it might be a matter of some years before, if at all, they could be considered for conditional release to work on community projects.

Suggestion of such a bifurcated approach to imprisonment is not without its difficulties since there will be some who would object to it on the basis of treating like offenders differently, or of denying the 'right' of equal access to circumstances or conditions that might improve their situations. The approach is, however, both pragmatic and utilitarian insofar as it is proposed in the greater interest of the reasonable majority of imprisoned persons, and with the genuine intention of enhancing the potential for their eventual social reintegration. In addition it might be said in countering objections such as those noted above that it is not necessarily the 'system' that treats intractable offenders differently, but their own choice of conduct that makes their inclusion inappropriate.

The manner in which such a system might work in practice is illustrated at *Figure 11.1*. From the illustration it will be noted that the pre-trial stage within a restorative justice model includes a mediation process which enables separation of those willing to accept guilt and make reparation from those unwilling to do so and thus effectively opting for the traditional mode of trial and subsequent court disposal. The process also enables minor offenders to be dealt with differently from serious offenders, and repetitive and non-repetitive offenders to be similarly differentiated. Due to the inclusion of the mediation process mentioned previously, it would be altogether likely and possible for those offenders opting (and deemed suitable) for the restorative justice model to be dealt with much more speedily by the courts than their counterparts opting for traditional trial and disposal.

Viewed 'side by side' the restorative justice and traditional models might appear to be entirely mutually exclusive, but the point was made earlier that for long-term offenders nearing the end of their custodial sentences it should be possible to transfer from the traditional to the reparative form of custody if experience and assessment indicate that to do so would be beneficial to all concerned. Thus long-term but cooperative prisoners would have the incentive to complete the later stages of their sentences as though they had, originally, been eligible for consideration for repara-

---

5. The term was originally used by Michael Howard in his speech as Home Secretary to the Conservative Party Conference in October 1993 in which he stated that he was determined to ensure that prison conditions were 'decent but austere'.

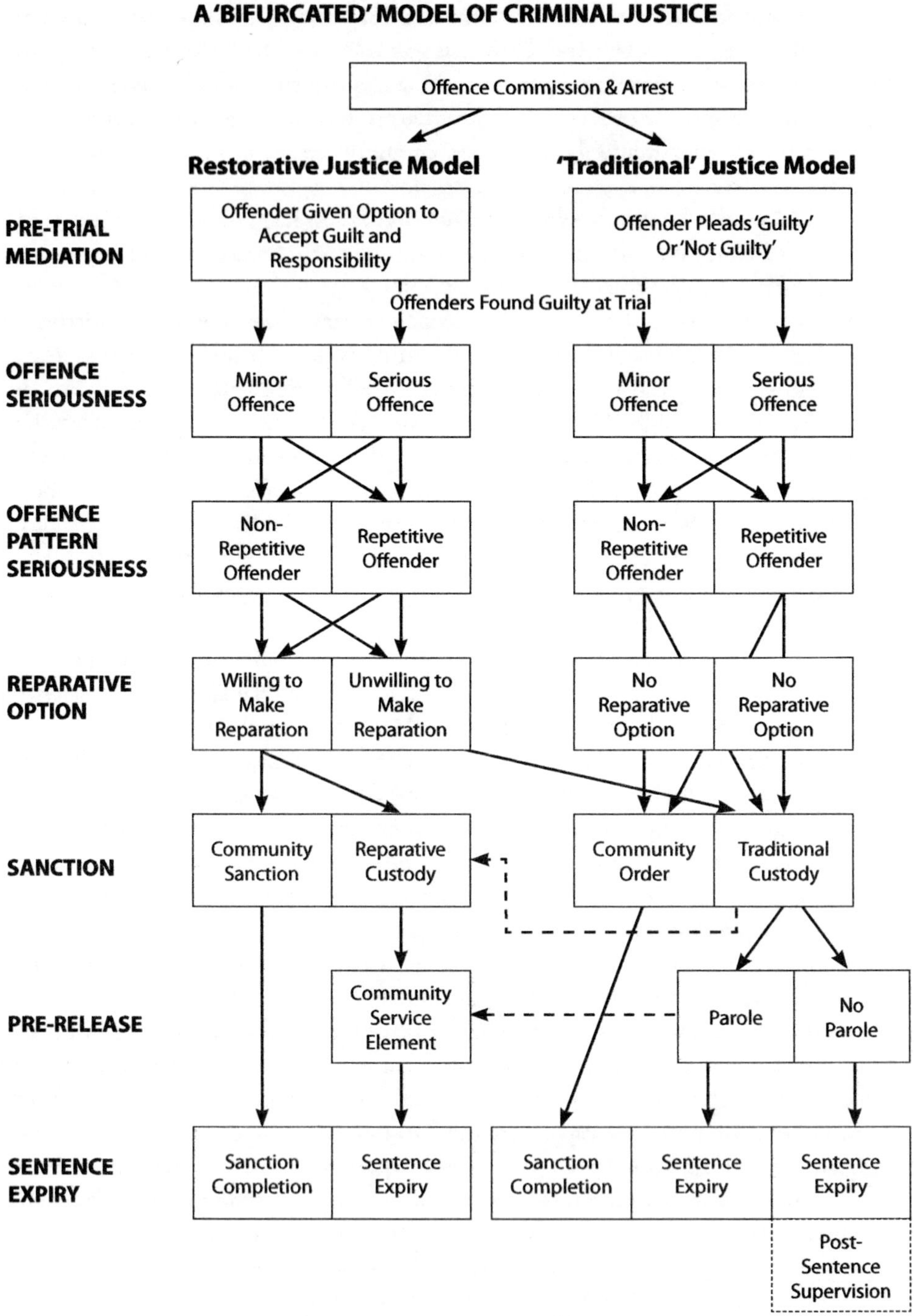

Figure 11.1; A 'Bifurcated' Model of Criminal Justice

tive custody combined with a pre-release community service element rather than traditional parole. This 'cross-over' point is indicated in the broken line between traditional imprisonment and reparative custody at the Sanction stage, and parole might be granted with a stipulation that it be served as community service.

IMPLICATIONS OF PENAL SYSTEM CHANGE FOR COMMUNITY CORRECTIONS

Clearly defining the purposes of community sanctions depends heavily upon shaping a penal system that will enable these sanctions to be delivered effectively and reliably. This means that the relationship between custodial and community justice has to be a coherent one, yet one that allows offenders sentenced in either 'penal direction' to have their opportunities for social reintegration maximised. Rather than placing a central insistence upon punishing those who offend in a manner that might ultimately lead to stigmatisation and marginalisation, it would be preferable for community sanctions to operate in an inclusive manner that results in offenders providing a service to the community whose relationships have been violated by the offending behaviour that creates obligations to 'put things right'. (Zehr, 2002 *op. cit.*: 21-23).

Viewed thus, community sanctions might be said to need to fulfil a number of different purposes that we might summarise as follows:

- indicating an expression of judicial censure for the wrongful act(s);
- provision of an opportunity for offenders to accept guilt and responsibility, express remorse for the harm caused, and offer apology to victims;
- creating opportunities for offenders to make reparation to victims of crime and the community;
- through these opportunities (and where necessary by providing support and/or training for them to be met in full) enabling offenders to improve their chances of adopting law-abiding lifestyles and addressing their social deficits;
- empowering victims and communities to feel vindicated as a result of seeing that offenders are purposefully sanctioned;
- enabling the public generally, and local communities in particular, to have confidence in the Criminal Justice System, and feel safer as a result; and,
- demonstrating that justice has a constructive rather than a destructive (or merely retributive) purpose, and that sanctions are designed to improve rather than diminish the prospects of reducing offending and recidivism.

When these purposes are viewed against the existing raft of legislation for community sanctions within the Criminal Justice Act 2003[6] it immediately becomes apparent that the punitive provisions of the Act in no sense reflect any such intentions. Indeed, far from pursuing the government's originally avowed aim of reducing the prison population by making greater use of what it termed 'community punishment', the 2003 Act with its provisions for custody 'plus', 'minus' and 'intermittent' opened wide the door for more offenders to experience short prison sentences. Moreover, the community order introduced by that Act includes 12 conditions or what are styled 'requirements' from which sentencing officials can select on a 'mix and match' basis, only four of which (compulsory or 'unpaid' work, participation in offending behaviour programmes, community supervision and the use of attendance centres for persons aged 25 years or less) bear any significant relationship to the requirements of community penalties. The remaining provisions provide means of restricting or prohibiting certain activities or behaviours more as a means of social control than of justice.

The provisions of the 2003 Act appear particularly bizarre when seen in the light of the recommendations of the Halliday Report of 2001 entitled *Making Punishments Work* Home Office, 2001b *op. cit.*) and the government's own White Paper *Justice for All* (Home Office, 2002 *op. cit.*) in which it was acknowledged that from available research evidence short prison sentences are not only 'usually ineffective' (p.92), but also 'increase the chances of reoffending (p.102). Furthermore, when the already high 'breach rates' for the former probation, curfew, community service and other miscellaneous orders are taken into consideration, the 2003 Act was more likely to result in setting offenders up to fail rather than to be improved by its provisions.

If, alternatively, we were to follow the example set by Spain and Germany among other nations and abolish altogether custodial sentences with an effective length of 12 months or less[7], and of the same countries, Finland, The Netherlands and Canada[8] in making available suspended sentences where otherwise up to two years imprisonment might be imposed[9], then the entire face of community justice would be propelled towards significant change and, it could be argued, change for the better.

---

6. I have described these provisions within the Criminal Justice Act 2003 for the community order, 'custody plus', 'custody minus' and 'intermittent custody' in some detail in former work (Cornwell 2007 *op. cit.*: 138-163, and particularly at pp.152-4). The same provisions are discussed in Bottoms *et al.* (2004 *op. cit.*) at pp.12-13.
7. Under present circumstances in England and Wales a sentence of up to 12 months imprisonment under the CJA 1991 provisions results in six months being spent in custody with no provision for post-sentence supervision under the terms of 'automatic unconditional release' (AUR). See also generally related explanations in the *Glossary* at the end of this work.
8. In Canada the term 'conditional imprisonment' was introduced in 1996 as the equivalent of a suspended sentence.
9. In Spain under the provisions of the Penal Code of 1995 the upper limit for suspended sentences of imprisonment was raised from 12 months (Penal Code of 1973) to two years. This resulted in an annual reduction of almost 10,000 prison receptions from 55,739 in 1997 to 41,768 in 2002. (Cid, 2005 *op. cit.*: 173).

Fewer offenders would be subjected to the damaging effects of prison custody, and the community corrections sector would inevitably have to be re-shaped to accommodate the increasing demands placed upon it.

In the process of re-vitalising community corrections to deliver the purposes identified earlier it would become possible to implement the intentions that the government set out in *Restorative Justice: The Government's Strategy* in 2003, and which was summarised in the following words:

> The Government aims to maximise the use of restorative justice in the Criminal Justice System (CJS) as it works well at both addressing the needs of the victim and in reducing reoffending.
>
> Evidence suggests that restorative justice can help to deliver key objectives across the CJS: improving victim satisfaction, reducing crime and reoffending, delivering justice effectively and building public confidence. (Home Office, 2003a. *op. cit.*: 1)[10]

When one considers that the statement quoted above appeared in July 2003, the same month and year as the Criminal Justice Act was brought before Parliament and subsequently received the Royal Assent on November 20 without any specific reference to restorative justice within it, there seems something curious and even tendentious about such utterances. And if the 'evidence' was sufficiently strong to justify the contention, then it must be that at the time the government was busy thinking about how the use of restorative justice might be 'maximised'. In the intervening years up to the time of writing there has been precious little indication of any intention to put such resolve into operation.[11]

Thus it might seem that the only aspect of the penal system of England and Wales that has changed significantly since the implementation of the 2003 Act is the size of the average daily prison population that has risen to almost 83,000 in February 2009 from the 2004 level of 70,861, and the even lower level of 65,298 during the year following that in which (May 1977) the present government took office. These stark facts, and the provisions for *punishment in the community* set out in the 2003 Act, have resulted in stifling any change within the provisions for community sanctions that adoption of a restorative justice based penology might have delivered.

But this would be to overlook two important recent innovations: the creation of the National Offender Management Service (NOMS) which eventually came into being in July 2007 (see pp.90-91 and fn.12), and of the Ministry of Justice

---

10. Summary Briefing Paper available at: http://www.crimereduction.gov.uk/workingoffenders42.htm.
11. In 2005 three government initiatives relating to victims of crime were circulated in the form of consultation documents: Home Office (2005a. *op. cit.*), *Victims Rights*, London: Home Office; Home Office (2005b. *op. cit.*), *The Code of Practice for Victims of Crime*, London: HMSO (October); and Home Office (2005c. *op. cit.*), *Re-building Lives – Supporting Victims of Crime*, London: HMSO (December). All three documents were, however, more concerned with procedural aspects of the support and handling of crime victims as witnesses and revision of the Criminal Injuries Compensation Scheme and its procedures.

(MOJ) in the same year. This legislation has, at least theoretically, brought under one organisational 'roof' the Prison and Probation Services and on a 'sponsorship' basis the Youth Justice Board within the Ministry of Justice, but the gestation period has been both lengthy and problematic. As one commentator has indicated:

> Few criminal justice reforms have been as riven with uncertainty and confusion as the creation of the National Offender Management Service. At a time when the reform of public services is apparently evidence-led, NOMS is an oddly non-evidence-based creation, conceived and implemented in haste and without the level of consultation that might have been expected. There has been much concern in the probation service at the lack of detail on fundamental issues such as the role of probation boards, the business case for NOMS, and the future role of probation officers. The recent announcement that the NOMS chief executive [then Martin Narey] – who was widely regarded as bringing much needed credibility and coherence to the new agency – is leaving 18 months after taking up the position, is likely to create further instability. (Bhui, 2005: 219)(parentheses added).

Traditionally the Prison and Probation Services of England and Wales have proved to be reluctant bedfellows due to widely held perceptions of the essential differences of ethos that have tended to separate them.[12] The combination (though not amalgamation) of the two services within NOMS does, however, offer an opportunity for a restorative penology to gain a greater foothold within criminal justice at the practitioner, even if not at the political level of justice considerations. It may, therefore, turn out to be the case eventually that this 'arranged marriage' can prosper, and that both custodial and community sanctions will become the beneficiaries of the union.

COMMUNITY CORRECTIONS WITH A NEW PURPOSE

In an ideal world the closer relationship between the Prison and Probation Services of England and Wales made possible by the creation of NOMS might be seen to offer a heaven-sent opportunity for the creation of a criminal justice system with core values grounded in a restorative penology. Indeed the title of the chief executive of NOMS as Commissioner of Correctional Services suggests that a much needed coherence of professional interests may be envisaged for the new agency, and the

---

12. This is to suggest that the perception of the Prison Service widely held within the Probation Service is that it is essentially a punitive organisation that struggles to accommodate the contradictory demands of punishment and containment on the one hand, and reconcile these with respect for human rights and rehabilitation on the other. The similarly widely (if mistakenly) held view of the Probation Service found within the Prison Service is that its ethos of befriending, counselling and rehabilitation of offenders is more appropriate in the community than the custodial setting, and that when imported into prisons it comes into a natural organisational conflict with the custodial 'keeper' philosophy. See here, for example: Bhui, 2003 *op. cit.*: 99-100; Houchin, 2003 *op. cit.*: 142-148. It should be stated that these are not views supported in this work, and that the author's experience of joint working between prison and probation staff does not support any such contention.

creation of probation areas with boundaries matching those of the Prison Service indicates an acknowledged potential for joint working.

This much stated, there remain questions about the motivations for creating such a monolithic agency in an increasingly 'managerialist' era driven overwhelmingly by the need to demonstrate efficiency and satisfy bureaucratic rather than humanistic objectives. It has also to be remembered that the new agency is the child of a government elected to be 'tough on crime', and which has demonstrated over a complete decade in power a relative carelessness about exercising any control over the size of the penal population. Leopards, so the fable tells us, do not change their spots, and it would seem altogether unlikely that these particular leopards would even wish to do so.

Indeed, as Cavadino *et al.* (1999) have suggested, it is questionable whether the application of managerialist techniques to organisations such as the Criminal Justice System - now exemplified by the new NOMS and MOJ - is designed to deliver better justice, or merely to make the *processes* of justice appear to be more resource-consciously administered. This is, however, probably far from the largest problem facing the new organisation that will struggle in the foreseeable future to create for itself an ethos that is embraceable by each of its two major partners. For as Andrew Rutherford has pointed out long before the creation of NOMS:

> The values and beliefs that shape the daily work and professional careers of criminal justice practitioners fall into three clusters. The first of these embraces the punitive degradation of offenders. The second cluster speaks less to moral purpose than to issues of management; pragmatism, efficiency and expediency are the themes that set the tone. Third ... there is the cluster of liberal and humanitarian values. (Rutherford, 1993: 3, quoted in Lewis, 2005 *op. cit.*: 129)

Insofar as the first of Rutherford's clusters is concerned, this clearly relates to the present methods of prison operation which, through overcrowding and an emphasis on containment result in degradation of prisoners, their lives, and those of others close to them. This is not to suggest that prison staff set out deliberately to degrade those in their charge in a punitive manner, but rather that the essential nature of the incarcerative process is punitively degrading in the way in which it operates. In a number of respects it seems not unreasonable to suggest that this is the way that the more 'hawkish' proponents of the 'law and order' lobby would wish it to be, secure in the belief that 'prison works' and in the moral 'rightness' of offenders being humiliated.

As to the second cluster, this would seem to resonate with the bureaucratic, centralised and somewhat monolithic management structures that oversee the functioning of both the prison and probation services within their geographic areas. These structures are staffed predominantly by civil servants with no necessary lifetime allegiance to either service, or particular knowledge or experience in operational practice at the point of delivery. Thus both services at the practitioner level perceive themselves to be managed by remote bureaucracies whose primary allegiances are to their senior officials and ministers rather than to those whom they manage.

The third cluster is descriptive of a perception of the Probation Service as an organisation whose practitioners traditionally received a professional training grounded in social work practice within the social sciences departments of universities. Over recent years this has changed significantly, and entrants into the Probation Service now complete a two-year part time Diploma in Probation Studies (DipPS) on an in-service basis that is managed through the nine probation area consortia in conjunction with institutions of higher education and NVQ assessment centres.[13] In the case of the Probation Service the image projected is of a caring and humanistic profession pledged to 'assist and befriend' offenders rather than to deal with them in the more controlling and dispassionate manner of the Prison Service.

When to this complex situation is added the fact that the Prison Service has traditionally relied on a quasi-militaristic uniformed rank structure within its prison officer grades to underpin its authoritarian image as a 'disciplined service', the dichotomous nature of the NOMS alliance becomes very apparent.[14] Small wonder, then, that the 'custody: community divide' described formerly extends into the organisational framework of criminal justice services.

In order to provide the correctional process with a new purpose these difficulties and differences of professional orientation have to be overcome, and the new organisation must somehow achieve for itself a 'seamless' image. It is the contention in this work that such a transformation is capable of achievement, and, moreover, that the restorative penology at the core of this account can provide the motive force for such a transition. It must also be stated, however, that the transition will require a measure of compromise in a number of different directions that include the philosophical, professional, managerial, organisational and operational aspects of criminal justice delivery as it is presently conceived in England and Wales.

---

13. Completion of the two-year programme leads to the award of the DipPS which comprises a BA honours degree in Community Justice and the National Vocational Qualification Level 4 in Community Justice. It is of interest to note that in Scotland there is no separate Probation Service. Social workers specialising in criminal justice are responsible for working with offenders. In Northern Ireland, probation officers are qualified social workers employed by the Probation Board for Northern Ireland. The Probation Service also employs probation service officers (PSOs) at a lower grade than probation officers, who assist in tasks such as supervising offenders, maintaining case files, helping to prepare court reports, and working with victims of crime.
14. The Prison Service's operational personnel structure at the establishment level is divided into governor grades that are non-uniformed, and prison officer grades that are uniformed. Governor grades are of five levels (from 1 to 5 in order of decreasing seniority), while prison officer grades are those of prison officer, senior officer and principal officer in ascending order. Additional uniformed staff are employed in the role of operational support grades (OSGs) who do not have the statutory powers of prison officers, but who undertake duties that do not involve the immediate physical and supervisory control of prisoners. The overall Governor of a prison may be of Grade 1, 2 or 3 status depending upon the size of the establishment and its inmate population, and/or its organisational complexity.

The creation of the role of 'offender managers' who are normally probation officers nominated to work with each offender throughout his/her prison sentence and while under supervision in the community is a most appropriate innovation. This development has the potential to provide a measure of continuity in planning for the release of prisoners from custody and assisting them during the critical phase of reintegration within their communities. It also enhances the case made in this work for the latter part of medium term custodial sentences to be spent on conditional release working within the community by those offenders sentenced to reparative custody.

It might, therefore, now be possible to perceive a new and more creative structure for community corrections that would embrace both the post-custody requirements of a reparative sentencing process *and* a simplified non-custodial corrections process under a single framework of supervision, operational control and accountability. Such would be a structure that would meet each and every one of the purposes identified earlier in this chapter (at p.155, *supra*), within the overall framework of an organisation such as NOMS.

TOWARDS A STRUCTURE FOR SOCIAL REINTEGRATION

One of the main difficulties in proposing change within penal systems is that of steering the discourse away from the ambiguities and prejudices of past or existing practices and the manner in which these are rationalised or 'justified'. It has been suggested earlier in this work (in *Chapter 8* at pp. 117-9, *supra*) that it makes little sense to speak of 'rehabilitation' in the custodial sector of corrections. This is because however well-intentioned efforts made in prisons towards preparing inmates for release may be, these must always be attempted in an environment that is entirely unlike that from which the offender came, and to which he or she must return: the community of origin.

In addition, for re-entry into society to be successfully undertaken by ex-offenders, particularly following a period of custody, they need the support and ability to overcome the contributory factors that led to offending, and a period of 'assisted transition' within which good intentions can be tested and actively encouraged. This period is at least, if not more important than the period deemed necessary to satisfy notions of retribution or censure, and should thus form an essential element of the sentence period.

Offenders sentenced to community sanctions also require the same support and encouragement to resist further offending even though they may have been saved from the prison experience. In many cases their lives, like those of their imprisoned counterparts, have been deeply affected by dysfunctional influences such as poverty, substance abuse and dependence, poor educational ability, homelessness, peer group delinquency, and the like. Many have a history of poor physical and/or mental health, inadequate or inappropriate diet, have never worked or sustained employment on a consistent basis, and are otherwise ill-prepared for social survival without recourse to reoffending. Punishing such disadvantaged people time after time without addressing their social deficits is not only pointless: it is also vindictive.

As we have already noted in *Chapter 8* (at pp.114-5), some countries have formally endorsed the idea of state-obligated rehabilitation as a right of offenders, though this has never been the case in Britain. This 'new rehabilitationist' approach emerged during the 1980s and has since attracted some respected criminological adherents (e.g. Cullen and Gilbert, 1982 *op. cit.*; McWilliams and Pease, 1990; Hudson, 2003). As we have noted, however, Hudson has been critical of attempts to rehabilitate in prisons (Hudson, 1987: *op. cit.*: 34-5), though she later indicated some willingness to accept the principle providing that sentences were both determinate and strictly proportionate to the seriousness of offences (Hudson, 2003:63).

However this notion is viewed, from both a utilitarian and a humanitarian perspective it seems altogether unreasonable not to make the identification of social deficits and criminogenic factors[15] an integral part of offender management, and to make deliberate provision to address these issues as a priority when offenders undertake community sanctions either as such, or as the latter part of reparative custodial sentences on conditional release from custody. Indeed, it might be claimed to be in the public interest that this should be done as a means towards reducing both public risk and the likelihood of reoffending. Though this does not necessitate embracing the principle of state-obligated rehabilitation, it should, as Lewis (2005 *op. cit.*: 125) has argued, 'form part of a social policy agenda that recognizes everyone's right to have their basic needs met.' This much stated, it is also important, as some commentators have insisted, that such a process should be free from coercion and voluntary, however strongly it might be recommended to offenders (Winick, 1991: 248; Bazemore, 1999: 183).

Within a restorative and reparative penology these issues fall relatively easily into place since it is implicit in its principles that offenders are expected to take responsibility for their wrongful actions, acknowledge the harm caused to victims, and make reparation. As a matter of reciprocity it is also reasonable to propose that in meeting these requirements, offenders should have the opportunity to have their

---

15. These are circumstances in people's lives that may be said to encourage criminal offending, though they may not necessarily be said to '*cause*' offending. Such factors include poor education, bad housing, unemployment, relative poverty, deviant peer group behaviour, and the like. The 'moral agency' theory of individual behaviour attributes to each citizen the choice between offending and desisting from doing so, and goes some way to explaining why persons in similarly (dysfunctional) circumstances offend while others do not. It is, however, widely accepted that the range of social disadvantages previously mentioned has an effect on the formation of attitudes to right and wrong actions, particularly in circumstances in which the individuals concerned consider themselves to be placed at unreasonable social disadvantage by comparison with others whom they see around them.

own needs addressed in order to help them to avoid further offending. These two propositions in particular provide us with a structure for social reintegration that is infinitely superior to, more purposeful, and more humane than the predominantly retributive and punitive approach to justice currently in vogue in Britain and many other nations worldwide.

As we shall discover in the chapter that follows, adoption of such an agenda would enable a more straightforward approach to be taken to the design of community corrections. Some existing community sanctions in Britain are designed more to prohibit or control illegal behaviour as a matter of public risk reduction rather than of addressing the causes of the behaviours themselves.[16] Others make compliance with specific forms of treatment programmes a pre-condition of avoiding custodial punishment, and could, therefore, be claimed to be coercive.[17] The motivations behind the prohibitive effects of such measures are as important for this discussion as are the restrictive and possibly counter-productive outcomes that may result from them. More importantly, perhaps, the general public, in exercising the judgement of 'reasonableness' attributed to the traveller on the Clapham Omnibus, needs to be assured that the purpose of such measures is ultimately of social benefit.

For the purposes of this chapter, however, it has become possible to identify both a structure and a methodology for the implementation of community sanctions that might operate 'in their own right' as non-custodial penalties, and as a 'bridge' to close the 'custody: community divide' for ex-prisoners conditionally released to project work within communities. This important step enables us to examine in the chapters that follow the ways in which restorative justice could enable a transformation within community justice and also deliver significant benefits to communities themselves.

---

16. Curfew orders, exclusion orders from places or activities, and prohibition from association with groups or persons might be cited as examples within this category of sanctions.
17. Such as drug, alcohol or substance abuse programmes designed to 'detoxify' offenders and reduce dependence. While such programmes are not necessarily to be criticised for their intention or methodologies, when these are reinforced by immediate custody in cases of 'breach' or failure it may be considered that a measure of coercion underpins their operation. Where offenders feel compelled to comply with these programme requirements they may agree and yet resent the compulsion, and either fail or derive little benefit from them (Winick, 1991 *op. cit.*: 248, quoted in Lewis, 2005 *op. cit.*: 124).

CHAPTER 12

Could Restorative Justice Transform the Community Corrections System?

In attempting to answer the question posed in the title of this chapter it is necessary to 'back-track' to the discussion in *Chapter 3* concerning the relationship between the retributive aspect of criminal punishment and the aspirations of restorative justice practices. For while it might be said that restorative justice is able to accommodate a measure of retribution as a seemingly inevitable aspect of the punishment process, it is also possible to question whether, in strict truth, retributive punishment (as the deliberate infliction of pain) is in any real sense a reasonable response to criminal acts. For if we were able to erase from our consciousness – even temporarily - the apparent *necessity* for retributive punishment, then it might be possible as Angela Davis (2003) has suggested, to 'envision an array of alternatives that will require radical transformation of many aspects of our society.'[1]

Indeed, one of the main difficulties with the legislation in England and Wales brought forward in the Criminal Justice Act 2003 is that the provisions for custody 'plus' and 'minus', 'intermittent custody' and community orders seem to attempt to meet entirely conflicting and irreconcilable objectives: provision of robust custody-related sanctions as evidence of governmental need to be seen to be 'tough on crime', and a reduction in the use of short custodial sentences (e.g. Tonry, 2003 *op. cit.*). We seem to have come to this confusing situation entirely because we cannot see beyond a criminal punishment system that is not primarily retributive, and because nothing short of overtly retributive punishment satisfies the 'tough on crime' agenda.

COMMUNITY JUSTICE SINCE THE 1960s

When one looks back on the developments in the search for alternatives to custody over the years since the 1960s a very curious pattern emerges. Until the early 1970s the main alternatives were the fine and the probation order. A few years later in the Criminal Justice Act 1967 the suspended sentence was introduced as a deliberate attempt to divert offenders from the (then) burgeoning prison population, and in the Criminal Justice Act 1972 the community service order (CSO) was provided as a reinforcement of the need for wider use of community-based sanctions. Thereafter, during the later 1970s and 1980s there appeared the plethora of attendance centre orders, curfew orders, combination orders, and in the 1990s the exclusion order, the

---

1. Angela Y. Davis (2003), *Are Prisons Obsolete?* New York: Seven Stories Press, and review by Richard Garside in *Criminal Justice Matters*, No.58, 2004 (Winter).

drug treatment and testing order, the drug abstinence order, and the reparation and action plan orders for young offenders.

Both the community service order and the suspended sentence proved widely popular with sentencing courts, but subsequently became used more as alternatives to the fine and probation order than as alternatives to custody. In 1975 the total number of community sentences imposed by the courts was (at almost 60,000) slightly greater than the number of prison sentences (55,300), but between 1980 and 1992 the use of suspended sentences of imprisonment had fallen from 40,000 to 20,000, and was to fall to only 4,000 by 1994 due to the expansion of alternatives then available, markedly decreasing use of the fine, and increasing use of custodial sentences (Bottoms *et al.* 2004 *op. cit.*: 1-12).

Though the provisions for the generic community order within the 2003 Act represent a logical attempt to sweep up under a single 'umbrella' sanction the entire range of existing community-based measures[2], it remains to be seen whether the 'menu' of options will not be so indiscriminately used as to create a situation in which many offenders will fail to comply with the multiple restrictive conditions imposed upon them, and thus become liable to 'breach' proceedings that might lead to re-sentencing or a custodial sentence (McKittrick and Rex, 2003: 144-5).

The important question that arises from all of these issues is not one of whether the present arrangements within the 2003 Act are good, bad or indifferent, but rather one of why such wide-ranging and specific provisions seem to have become so necessary as to create statute laws to provide for them. What has changed so dramatically within the social structure of England and Wales, or for that matter any other democracy perceiving its national situation to have similar criminal justice problems, that drives us into such a prescriptive mode of behaviour? If the fine and the probation order were adequate for the reasonable enforcement of community sanctions half a century ago, why are thirteen (or more) additional regulatory provisions so necessary today? More important for this work, perhaps, is whether restorative justice might enable us to 'do justice better'.

BACK TO BASICS: THE NEED TO LIMIT 'MANAGERIALISM'

The simple fact seems to be that over the years since the decline of the rehabilitative ideal in the 1970s and the rise and fall of the 'justice model' in the 1980s and

---

2. Of which no less than thirteen are retained. See: Criminal Justice Act 2003 (c.44) Part 12, Chapters 2, 3 and 4, and in particular sections 199 – 215. The main provisions are for unpaid work (s.199), the activity order (s. 201), the programme requirement (s. 202), the prohibited activity order (s. 203), the curfew requirement (s.204), the exclusion requirement (s.205), the residence requirement (s. 206), the mental health treatment requirement (s.207), the drug rehabilitation requirement (s. 208), the alcohol treatment requirement (s. 212), the supervision requirement (s.213), the attendance centre requirement (for those aged 25 or under) (s. 214) and in certain instances an added condition of electronic monitoring (s.215).

1990s, the emphasis within criminal justice policy formulation has been to attempt to 'control' crime and 'manage' its social risks by increasingly punitive measures and social surveillance, rather than to address the root causes of crime and attempt to reduce those dysfunctional social factors that encourage crime. This new 'managerialism', identified as early as 1992 by Bottoms and Stevenson (1992:37) in the wake of the English prisons crisis of 1990 and the subsequent Woolf Report (Woolf and Tumim, 1991), may be traced to a range of linked 'crises' within the penal system at the time: these crises have been described by Cavadino and Dignan (among others including Garland, 2001) as those of control, legitimacy and resources. (Cavadino and Dignan, 1997*op. cit.*: 22-25).

Moreover, as Cavadino and Dignan further indicate:

> This approach is based on the notion that modern managerial techniques, as used in private sector businesses, can be successfully applied to the problems of crime and punishment. (p.23) ... The tenor is one of smooth management rather than of moral mission (Rutherford 1993:13). Adherents [of this credo] are concerned to save resources (time and money) by maximising 'throughput' and efficiency generally, so the credo is associated with bureaucracy, pragmatism and a generally utilitarian attitude. The 'managerialist' approach to criminal justice can be appropriately characterised as [one] in which smooth and cost-efficient processing of offenders and suspected offenders takes precedence over the rights of individuals. (Cavadino and Dignan, 1997 *op. cit.*: 23 and 301) (parentheses those of the present author).

This is an interesting analysis if only because it may be said to have pervaded very significantly the behaviour of the New Labour government that has held office since May 1977, and its approach to penal policies and the delivery of criminal justice. The creation of a Ministry of Justice[3], appointment of a Commissioner for Corrections, and the creation of the National Offender Management Service (NOMS) are striking examples of bureaucratic pragmatism born out of the contemporary 'crisis of numbers' and a new 'crisis of legitimacy' which has been caused by the draconian provisions of the Criminal Justice Act 2003 in relation to custody 'plus' and 'minus', 'intermittent' custody, and the exemplary provisions for the extended punishment of sexual and other serious offenders. In addition, a renewed emphasis on 'punishment in the community' represents an appeal to placate the moral outrage of the media and a supposed lack of public confidence in the effectiveness of non-custodial sanctions.

---

3. Here see Frances Gibbs' (2007) analysis: 'Is this an Unseemly Rush to Change?' in *The Times*, London, 1st May, Law Supplement, p.1. It seems that the decision to launch the new Ministry of Justice was made without wide consultation with the judiciary, and that even on the night before the formal announcement was to be made in Parliament the Lord Chief Justice of England and Wales was unaware that that this was to be done. As Gibbs points out, the move marks 'a crucial shift in power away from their [the judiciary's] arm of the constitution- already the weakest when up against the executive and legislature.' (parentheses those of the present author).

Rutherford's succinct analysis noted in the preceding quotation is particularly apposite and penetrating in relation to the punitive 'law and order' ideology that seems now to be so deeply entrenched in the contemporary British penological psyche. The 'crisis of numbers' is a clear reflection of the outcome of punitive measures, over-use of custody, and the resistance of offenders to the experience of being punished repetitively, pointlessly, and now excessively. These factors create a new 'crisis of legitimacy' in which the penal system is perceived to be more concerned with managing the crisis than with its causes and outcomes. This will, in all probability, lead to a renewed 'crisis of control' because the solution to the 'crisis of numbers' will be sought in expanding the custodial sector of corrections even further in order to accommodate the increasing numbers of offenders sentenced to imprisonment. And so the upward spiral will move inexorably until eventually prisons become unmanageable and devoid of moral purpose.

Breaking into this cyclic and 'lemming-like' spiral requires exactly what Rutherford has identified: a renewed sense of moral mission in corrections. It means ceasing to punish in a deliberately retributive and excessive manner, and starting to put 'correction' back into the entire penal process. This is not a managerialist task that will be achieved by enlarging the bureaucracy or altering its administrative behaviours, but one that requires a return to human values and a strict limitation of the collateral damage caused by retributive responses to media-induced hysteria in relation to crime. It means thinking afresh about the causes of crime and being 'tough' on these dysfunctional aspects of contemporary society. It also means placing faith in the adage set forward by Alexis de Tocqueville: 'To render a people obedient and keep them so, savage laws inefficiently enforced are less effective than mild laws enforced by an efficient administration regularly, automatically, as it were, every day and on all alike.' (in Zetterbaum, 1967, and Auden and Kronenburger, 1962:210).

In strict fairness to his approach, Andrew Rutherford identified three quite separate credos concerned with criminal justice and its practitioners, of which that mentioned above was the second. The first credo concerned what he described as 'a powerfully held distaste and moral condemnation of offenders and the belief that as few fetters as possible be placed upon the authorities in the pursuit of criminals who, when caught, should be dealt with in ways that are punitive and degrading.' (Rutherford, 1993 *op. cit.*:11). This is ultimately the 'law and order' ideology previously mentioned. The third credo is a far more humanistic approach which Cavadino and Dignan (1997 *op. cit.*: 301) in paraphrasing Rutherford describe as a liberal credo seeking to minimise punishment, and including 'empathy with suspects, offenders and the victims of crime, optimism that constructive work can be done with offenders, adherence to the Rule of Law so as to restrict state powers, and an insistence upon open and accountable procedures' (Rutherford, 1993 *op. cit.*: 18).

Looking back on the discussion within the previous chapter, we may see each of these credos reflected in the various components of the contemporary British Criminal Justice System. Credo One is characteristic of the punitive stance towards offenders adopted by ministers and their advisers in response to a similar approach belligerently promoted by the tabloid media – particularly in relation to sexual offenders. It is reflective also of the provisions within the 2003 Act in relation to the extended incarceration of this group and of those deemed to present a public risk, and the provisions for custody 'plus', 'minus' and for 'intermittent custody'.

Credo Two exemplifies the 'managerialist' behaviour of the civil service element of the criminal justice system whose primary loyalties are to ministers and their senior professional colleagues, and only secondly to the effective oversight of the operational and procedural workings of the system components. The same credo also reflects the universalist 'manage all risks' approach to the provisions for community orders, and the threat of custody implicit in the breach procedures to be invoked in the event of non-compliance.

The operational element of the Prison Service sits very uncomfortably and precariously perched somewhere in between Credos One and Two, charged with delivering the outcomes of Credo One (in the form of a vastly over-loaded custodial system), yet managed on a day to day basis by officials identified more closely with Credo Two. It thus becomes an almost entirely reactive organisation, incapable of identifying a 'moral mission', and restricted to the pragmatic demands of containment and the mechanistic aspects of coping with the 'crisis of numbers'. This is an unedifying situation for its governor grades and other professional staff, and yet also one replete with opportunities for militancy and obduracy within the membership and leadership of the Prison Officers' Association (POA).

Credo Three has traditionally provided the professional basis for the work of the operational core of the Probation Service, and reflects the empathetic approach of 'befriending and assisting' offenders exemplified by field probation officers and their immediate superiors. Increasingly, however, the senior management of the Service has found itself in the same 'managerialist' situation that affects its counterparts in the Prison Service, and for almost identical reasons. Successive rafts of criminal justice legislation since the early 1990s (and even somewhat earlier) have served to dilute the sense of 'moral mission' within the Probation Service at the operational level, and have led to something akin to a 'crisis of identity' and exhaustion at the front line of the Service in recent years (Worrall and Hoy, 2005; Farrow, 2004: 206-220; Wargent, 2003:5; Nellis and Chui (2003: 273).

All of the considerations noted above conspire to make the *naissance* of NOMS appear little more than a marriage of the most extreme inconvenience and doubtful compatibility, but, perhaps worse still, more an exercise in administrative pragmatism and managerialist idealism that makes the potential for a resurgence of 'moral mission' appear decidedly fragile. The main reasons why both of these organisations find themselves in crisis can now clearly be seen to be threefold: first, the essentially punitive nature of criminal justice legislation over the past decade or so; second, the emasculating effect that this legislation has had on the ethos and core operational work of either Service; and third, the morale-sapping suspicion that the situation in either case is largely irreversible, and the implications of this for professionalism in an increasingly managerialist era.

Yet above all of this situation arches a more concerning and sinister reality: this is that unlike those of some other nations[4], the British government wields excessive executive power over both the judiciary and the legislature, and that this ultimately destroys any reality of consensus politics.[5] This same power in England is manifestly centralised, and maintained by the decline of cabinet government and the acquiescence of senior civil servants. Though the government's policies claim somewhat grandiosely to be 'evidence-led', it is clear from the experience of the Criminal Justice Act 2003, that the evidence is quickly discarded when it fails to prove to be consistent with a punitive managerialism.[6] The question that now has to be addressed is that of whether a revised penology based more upon restorative justice could play a part in overcoming the difficulties identified thus far.

ENVISAGING A DIFFERENT CONCEPT OF COMMUNITY JUSTICE

One of the most difficult aspects of conceiving a system of community justice based on restorative justice principles is that of being clear about what the term 'community' actually means, and the context in which its use is proposed. Much also depends upon the moral philosophical 'direction' from which this is approached, and therefore whether we adopt what might formerly have been described as a

---

4. Notable examples of which are America and France which maintain a greater 'separation of powers' between the executive, legislative and judicial elements of government, and a number of European countries such as Germany, Sweden and The Netherlands that rely more closely upon cross-party political consensus in the formulation of criminal justice policies.
5. This same point is elaborated in some detail by Michael Tonry (2003 *op. cit.*) in the opening chapter of his edited work *Confronting Crime: Crime Control Policy Under New Labour*. The chapter bears the most appropriate title: 'Evidence, elections and ideology in the making of criminal justice policy.'
6. The point here is that the evidence presented in both the Halliday Report (Home Office 2001b *op. cit.*) and subsequently in the Couslfield Report (Esmée Fairbairn Foundation, 2004) indicated very clearly that short prison sentences did little to reduce recidivism, and might have the opposite effect on offenders. This fact was apparently endorsed in the government's White Paper *Justice for All* (Home Office, 2002b *op. cit.*), and yet the 2003 Act and its subsequent implementation enacted provisions that run entirely counter to this evidence. See also Cornwell, 2007 *op. cit.*, pp. 152-156 for a further analysis of this situation.

predominantly 'liberal'[7] or a 'communitarian'[8] approach to our analysis.[9] (e.g. Duff, 1999). It is probably true to say that the entire concept of 'community' has changed with the passage of time in many democracies from an idealistic and close-knit local network of inter-dependent and often socially related individuals, towards a looser and less 'affinity-based' form of relationships between individuals and groups that share some common interests in co-existence at the least formal or structured levels of participation essential to acknowledged membership.[10]

Alluding to the general public as 'the community' makes little sense in criminal justice terms in most contemporary democracies since it is difficult to perceive any level of social inter-relationships within the public domain at which it might be said that common interests and defined values are widespread. The term is, however, widely used to convey a meaning and image of a wider society within which it might be imagined that the majority of its members share certain core beliefs and values at a minimal level. However, in some of the older and less diverse societies there remains a genuine culture of community in which strong ties of group solidarity, conformity to acknowledged norms, and collective concern and respect for all members and their welfare are maintained.[11]

Part of the difficulty within many modern democracies is that their criminal court systems tend to exist and operate in a manner that has developed a deliberate 'remoteness' or isolation from the daily lives of most of the citizens whom they are ultimately there to serve. This 'distancing effect' is enhanced by a number of factors such as the need for security, the procedural and linguistic complexity of trial processes, the traditional and sartorial protocols and formality of conduct and

---

7. The 'liberal' view of communities as defined by Duff (1999) and others is one in which individual freedoms of thought and action are a paramount consideration, making communities both diverse and optional from the viewpoint of individual and collective participation.
8. The 'communitarian' concept of communities is of a more structured nature based to a considerable extent upon social contract theory within which individuals consent to participate according to 'rules' decided by the community, and are prepared to an extent to mitigate their right to individuality in the greater (some would suggest utilitarian) interests of collective harmony and co-existence.
9. It is not suggested here that the 'liberal' and 'communitarian' conceptions of 'community' are mutually exclusive, but rather that both exist (as Duff, 1999: 38-9 suggests), and operate within a structure of commonly defined values to which the participants voluntarily subscribe, and to which they are prepared to adhere.
10. Here it is of interest to note that restorative justice is perceived to operate in its most effective manner within communities that still exist within a traditional structure of affinity and group (or tribal) loyalty. This is particularly the case in relation to aboriginal and 'first-nation' peoples in the Americas, Canada, Africa, Australia and New Zealand.
11. Examples may be drawn from the Maori national culture of New Zealand within which the term '*Whakawhanaungatanga*' is used to convey respect, fairness, interconnectedness, and harmony as fundamental elements and values of community living. (Hakiaha, 2007). In Southern Africa the word '*Ubuntu*' conveys a similar meaning involving a lifestyle or unifying world-view (or philosophy) of African societies based on respect and understanding between individuals. *Ubuntu*, from the Zulu '*umuntu ngumuntu ngabantu*' – a person can only be a person through others – embraces values of group solidarity, compassion, respect, human dignity, conformity with basic norms and collective unity. (Justice Mokgoro in *State v Makwanyane 1995 – at 308*, quoted in Anderson (2003: 7-8) and also in Hewitt (2002: 447-453) and Tutu (1999).

communication among legal practitioners and officials, and the combative nature of adversarial modes of trial. (Here, for example, see Pakes, 2004: 73-93). To many offenders brought before criminal courts, their trial assumes the nature of a theatrical performance in which they – *the accused* – become scarcely more than pawns within the disputatious and posturing dialogue conducted between the prosecution and the defence.

Another obstacle to the delivery of meaningful justice, particularly in Britain and other countries that have adopted similar adversarial trial processes, lies in the fact that once a decision is pending or made to prosecute an offender for an alleged offence, there is no formal provision for pre-trial mediation between the accused person and his (or her) accuser(s) who become the prosecuting authority representative of the Sovereign or the State. As Anderson points out in relation to the situation in South Africa:

> There seems to be a fairly general need to redefine traditional criminal justice procedures. The current Western criminal justice system that applies in South Africa creates many dilemmas. Often neither offender nor victim believe that justice has been done when a verdict is pronounced. The procedural system requires that an accused must plead either guilty or not guilty. When an accused pleads not guilty in circumstances where the victim knows that he is indeed responsible for the offence, this is seen as unjustly denying responsibility. The nature of the (accusatorial) criminal trial allows for little dialogue between the victim and the offender. Prosecutors and investigating officers, fearful that the offender may compromise the case often insist on stringent bail conditions prohibiting the offender from having any contact with the victim. The case is regarded as a 'legal battle' and interaction and participation between the two parties is stifled .... Restorative justice is a specific type of response to crime. 'Ubuntu' is much more than that – but both focus on restoring an imbalance created by someone's conduct and on building peace within communities. Both achieve this through co-operative efforts. (Anderson 2003: 10-11)

By way of contrast, many of the European nations that have followed post-revolutionary France in adoption of an inquisitorial mode of trial benefit from the structured provision for pre-trial mediation as a means of ascertaining the attitude of the accused towards the offence, the harm caused, and the situation of the victim(s). Such a starting point in the pre-trial processes of criminal justice is infinitely more consistent with the principles of restorative justice than is the adversarial mode.

Such is not to suggest that in order to implement a restorative penology it would be absolutely necessary in Britain and other countries that use adversarial trial procedures to change over to an inquisitorial process, but rather that the pre-trial stage of investigation would need to be handled somewhat differently.[12] This would open up

---

12. It should be noted here that within an inquisitorial system the accused person is not required to enter a plea of 'guilty' or 'not guilty' prior to the commencement of the trial proceedings. It is a matter for the court, in hearing the evidence advanced by the prosecution and the defence, to decide upon guilt and sentence accordingly, taking into account any exacerbating and mitigating factors (such as remorse, willingness to make reparation, etc.).

the possibility for a considerably greater extent of pre-trial conferencing involving the parties to the offence, those who support them, and mediators appointed for the purpose. It would also enable many less serious offences to be settled *outside* the formal court trial process through diversion, and require the court only to approve and record the outcome of the pre-trial negotiations, thus saving considerable time and expense.[13] Where, as in New Zealand in particular, but also elsewhere, such processes have been tried and adopted – principally in relation to juvenile and young adult offending – there has been considerable support for the transition (e.g. McElrea, 2002a and b; 2005; 2006: 119-134; Eaton and McElrea, 2003; Blad, 2006b: 93-117 McIvor, 2004 *op. cit.*: 178-181).

With particular reference to the non-custodial sector of corrections that tends, almost universally, to accommodate less serious forms of offending that do not warrant resort to imprisonment, the scope for use of reparative and restorative approaches seems to be real, and to offer some significant advantages by comparison with traditional justice. These advantages accrue to victims, offenders, and, potentially, the areas in which each of these parties and their close others reside. Criminal justice procedures and processes are, however, only part of a larger mosaic that, in terms of community corrections, embraces a number of other dimensions.

The reader will recall that in *Chapter 11* (at p.155), we identified a 'list' of purposes that non-custodial sanctions might be expected to fulfil. The forgoing discussion has to an extent explored better ways of enabling judicial censure to be expressed by providing opportunities for offenders to show remorse, accept guilt, express apology, and agree to make reparation to victims, but that still leaves other important issues un-addressed if our over-arching purpose is to reduce reoffending and thereby increase public confidence in criminal justice. The nature and potential effectiveness of non-custodial sanctions has to be such that these will be perceived as an *appropriate and an adequate* response to wrongdoing in the estimation of offenders, victims, the public, the media and politicians alike, while still contributing to crime reduction.

However, in order to *transform* community corrections, a restorative justice-based penology has to indicate why its prescriptions are operationally more desirable, qualitatively superior, more constructive, and potentially more effective in encouraging law-abiding behaviour than those presently in place. In terms of operational desirability these prescriptions have to be capable of straightforward implementation and encourage full offender participation; qualitative considerations include delivery of desired outcomes in relation to the essential 'inputs'; constructiveness

---

13. Here it will be noted that pre-trial mediation as proposed in this work would include provision for group conferencing involving accused persons, victims (or their representatives), officials of the prosecuting authority and the offender's legal advisors. It might also, where appropriate, be extended to the family or close others of both offenders and victims. See, for example, Marshall and Merry (1990); Sherman and Strang (1997); Umbreit *et al*. 2002, and in Britain, Miers *et al*. (2001) and Judge *et al*. (2002).

implies that the outcomes are socially beneficial to all the parties to criminal justice; and effectiveness has to be measurable in an auditable and accountable manner. These requirements are summarised and presented in Figure 12:1, and provide the basis for discussion in the final section of this chapter.

RE-FOCUSSING COMMUNITY CORRECTIONS

The reader will recall from the discussion in earlier chapters that the remit of community corrections proposed in this work embraces two separate groups of offenders: those sentenced to non-custodial sanctions by the courts on the one hand, and on the other those sentenced to prison custody who have participated in reparative regimes and have entered the final part of their sentence periods. Both groups, hereafter referred to as 'community sanction offenders' (CSOs), are regarded as a single entity within the subsequent discussion though, as will become clear later, the latter group may have somewhat different obligations to fulfil as a result of being released on conditional licence from custody.

As Gill McIvor has helpfully suggested, 'from a policy perspective . . the use of reparative and restorative interventions needs to be preceded by considering a number of key questions:

- what are these trying to achieve?
- at whom are they targeted and at which points in the criminal justice process should they be introduced?
- are they culturally appropriate?
- how are the interests of victim, offender and community represented and balanced and what safeguards are in place?
- how formalised should they be and should they be integrated with, or separate from traditional criminal justice processes?
- how might offender integration/rehabilitation be achieved without marginalizing victims and placing them at risk of secondary victimisation?
- what systems can be put in place to ensure that completion of agreements can be adequately enforced/ and,
- what resources will be required and how can these be most effectively deployed to maximise their potential benefit?

(McIvor, 2004 *op. cit.*: 185-6).

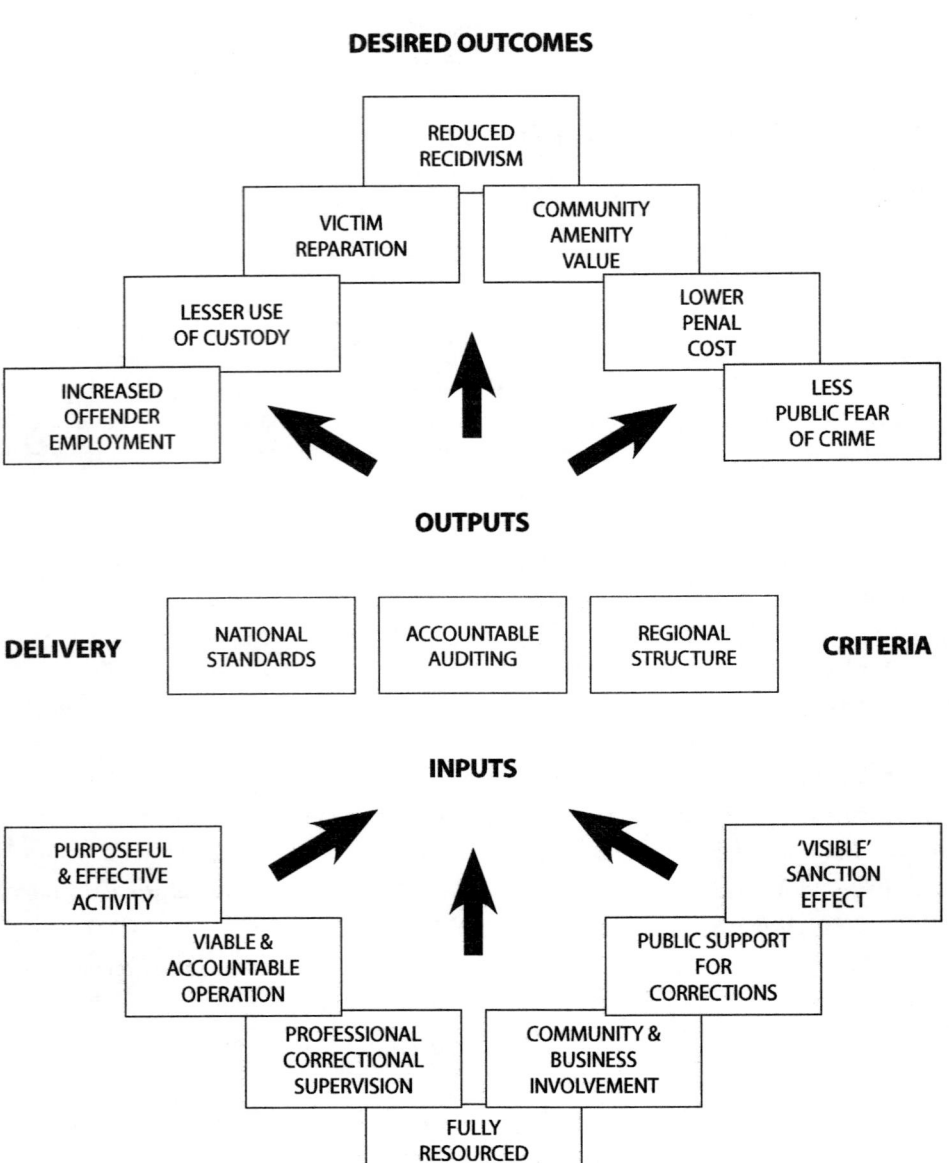

Figure 12:1: Refocusing Community Corrections

Some of these questions have been touched upon in the previous discussion, and are also evidently addressed in *Figure 12:1* in the form of 'outputs'[14] of the proposed community sanctions process. Others are considered in the form of 'inputs'[15] in the same representation, and form the basis of the discussion in the remaining chapters of this work. In this final section of this chapter we shall examine the issues relating to cultural appropriateness, stakeholder interests (with particular reference to those of victims), and accountability as represented in the 'delivery criteria' that have been placed centrally in the schema at *Figure 12:1*. In *Chapter 13* the issue of potential benefits to communities deriving from community sanctions becomes a focus for discussion, and in *Chapter 14* we shall address the question of how community sanctions might best be organised and supervised to provide maximum effectiveness in reducing reoffending, making reparation to victims and communities, and restoring public confidence in criminal justice.

Most modern societies, whether democracies or not, are culturally diverse, and exist with the different ethnic elements of their populations sharing in, and contributing to the day-to-day life of the state. Equality and freedom under the law are values cherished by most nations, and these are frequently constitutionally enshrined by legislation.[16] However, the conferring of these 'rights' carries with it duties and responsibilities of every citizen that are much less clearly expressed or universal. The most obvious duty for our purposes here is that of obedience to the law, in default of which offences are committed and sanctions deserved. This duty of obedience is, however, universal and not amenable to extension or reduction on the basis of ethnicity or other cultural criteria.

McIvor poses the question as to whether community sanctions within a reparative and restorative penology are culturally appropriate, and it must be assumed from the brief subsequent assertion that some restorative justice initiatives are 'culturally specific' that a reference is made here to projects such as the RISE programme[17] that had its origins in Australia in the early 1990s. (Braithwaite, 1989). In addition, some peacemaking, healing and sentencing circles based on restorative justice

---

14. The 'outputs' identified here are, effectively, the aims or purposes of community sanctions, and are described as 'desired outcomes'. Though these outcomes are not assigned a relative hierarchical value, the reduction of recidivism rather than the administration of punishment is the ultimate purpose of the correctional process.
15. 'Inputs' are the conditions and investment necessary to the effectiveness of community sanctions.
16. See, for example, Sir Alfred (later Lord) Denning's exposition in the 1949 Hamlyn Lectures (First Series) published under the title *Freedom Under the Law*, London: Stevens and Sons Limited, particularly at pp. 67-96 (Lecture 3 – 'Justice Between Man and the State).
17. The full title of which was the Re-Integrative Shaming Experiment developed by John Braithwaite in Wagga Wagga, New South Wales in 1991, and aimed at publicly shaming young offenders for their conduct and then re-integrating them into their communities. (Braithwaite, 1989; Moore and O'Connell, 1994). An adapted version of the same model was introduced into Britain by the Thames Valley Police in the mid-1990s for dealing with violent, theft and drink-drive offences. Subsequent evaluation indicates that it was significantly successful in reducing reoffending. (Miers *et al.*, 2001 *op. cit.*).

principles are specific to the more ancient cultures of North America, Canada and New Zealand, having their origins in the 'first nation' and aboriginal peoples and their community justice systems over many centuries. (See: Umbreit *et al*, 2005a. *op. cit*.:273-290; and, more generally: Coates, Umbreit and Vos, 2000: 26-29).

There is, perhaps, a broader matter of issue implicit in McIvor's question concerning cultural appropriateness, and this concerns the ability of politicians, policy-makers, the media, and senior practitioners within criminal justice systems to *adapt* their thinking processes that have been fashioned in 'traditional' justice mode to the very different frame of questioning implicit in Zehr's (2002 *op. cit.*) analysis of the principles of restorative justice.[18] This is no simple transition to make since it shifts the focus of attention away from crime as a violation of the state and its laws, and towards the violation of relationships, victims and communities. Culturally, countries such as Britain may be reluctant to abandon the 'safe haven' of traditional retributive justice simply because it is so entrenched in the national psyche, and because anything less punitive appears a 'soft option' by comparison.

As to the balancing of interests between victims, offenders and communities and the means of safeguarding these, there clearly has to be set in place a more comprehensive Code of Practice than the one published by the British government (Home Office 2005b, *op. cit.*) and subsequently followed up by the consultation document *Rebuilding Lives – Supporting Victims of Crime* (Home Office 2005c, *op. cit.*). Neither document is specifically oriented towards restorative practices, and both focus more on the support services that victims might expect to receive from (largely) voluntary agencies such as Victim Support, victim care units and the centralised Criminal Injuries Compensation Scheme.

Victims' rights in Britain have remained curiously unspecific since the first publication of the Victims' Charter in 1990, a document that is not legally binding on either the government or the courts. Little further specificity was added in the publication *Victims Rights* (Home Office 2005a *op. cit.*) other than the fact that the 2005 Code of Practice would become law in April 2006. Since, as we have already noted in earlier discussion, the initial interest in restorative justice displayed by the government in the early years of this decade has evidently waned very considerably with the enactment of the Criminal Justice Act 2003, there is little to give confidence that a revival of interest is imminent.

A very similar pattern of developments is evident in a number of other jurisdictions worldwide, and particularly in Australia in New South Wales (Findlay, 2004). By way of contrast, Canada and New Zealand have taken active steps to enshrine restorative justice practices within their criminal justice legislation (Cormier, 2006 *op. cit.*; McElrea, 2006 *op. cit.*). This noted, however, it is difficult to see how the

---

18. See: H. Zehr (2002 *op. cit.* 21-22) and my further explanation of the implications of these principles for 'traditional' criminal justice in Cornwell (2006 *op. cit.*: 166-7, and 2007 *op. cit.*: 58-59).

relative and quite different interests of victims, offenders and communities can be *balanced* other than by insisting on greater measures of fairness towards each of the three legitimate sets of interests within criminal justice.

For while as we have previously noted, offenders in Britain have no statutory right to 'rehabilitation'[19], we also identified what might, at the least, be said to amount to a moral obligation that the state should, within the process of punishment, address the causes of their offending and their social deficits with a view to reducing the likelihood of reoffending. In addition, a restorative penology opens up the opportunity for offenders to help both themselves and their victims by accepting guilt for the harm caused by their wrongdoing, taking responsibility for this, and making both apology and reparation to victims of crime.[20] To some meaningful extent this process acts as a balancing influence towards the vindication of victims and the social reintegration of offenders within their communities.

The primary interests of communities in relation to criminal offending lie in reductions in serious crime and reoffending, and in the need for confidence that victims of crime are appropriately and sensitively supported. High rates of reoffending, even in an era in which crime rates are falling generally, have been linked very clearly with crowded prison conditions and the over-use of short custodial sentences. There is, however, no reason why communities should not benefit extensively from well planned, supervised and executed project and amenity work undertaken by offenders. It may also be the case that the completion of such work would change public attitudes towards offenders, victims of crime would benefit, and offenders themselves would learn practical skills that would improve their chances of long-term employment and living law-abiding lives. This would, indeed, transform non-custodial justice, and it is to this particular aspect of community sanctions that attention is turned in the chapter that follows.

---

19. See *Chapter 8* at pp. 113.
20. See *Chapter 5* at pp. 83-4.

CHAPTER 13

Can Non-Custodial Sanctions Have Significant Community Benefit?

In the closing part of the previous chapter we have identified a range of factors relating to the organisation of non-custodial sanctions that would seem to be critical in relation to the potential effectiveness of such measures. Indeed, from *Figure 12:1* (see *Chapter 11*), these factors might be summarised as the 'essential operational attributes' (inputs), 'delivery criteria' (accountability), and 'desired outcomes' (outputs) respectively. To these factors we might add a number of desirable qualitative characteristics that would be likely to enhance the deliverability of these sanctions and make them beneficial to offenders and communities, such as:

- simplicity
- visibility
- value
- propriety
- reliability

Taken together, these factors and characteristics combine to provide what might be described as a functional correctional purpose.

Community sanctions, as these are presently operated, enjoy a relatively low level of support from the passengers on the Clapham Omnibus for a variety of reasons, some of which are based in ignorance, others in prejudice, and even more in acceptance of the emotive manner in which crime and the 'fear of crime' are highlighted in the mass media (Maruna and King, 2004 *op. cit.*: 100-101). Community benefit from non-custodial sanctions will, therefore, only be realised when there is a greater acceptance of the *relevance* of such measures, a lessening (and misplaced) belief in the effectiveness of imprisonment, and a greater tolerance of offenders within the community.

HOW CAN PUBLIC CONFIDENCE IN COMMUNITY SANCTIONS BE IMPROVED?

Setting on one side for the present the quite evident financial savings that would accrue from lesser use of imprisonment which is, in itself, an argument largely unsupported by considerable numbers of the public – and thus many politicians -

in terms of acceptability (Stead *et al.*, 2002: 3-4), and the collateral social damage that imprisonment causes, how may the potential benefits of increased use of non-custodial measures best be presented to a sceptical public and media whose attitudes influence so markedly the behaviour of politicians and policy-makers? Put another way, perhaps, what is it about the present vogue for 'punishment in the community' that is both publicly misunderstood and mistrusted?

It is evident that over the past decade or so there has been considerable academic attention paid, particularly in Britain and the United States, to attempts to discover how public attitudes towards crime and criminal justice are formed, and the extent to which these attitudes are amenable to change and how this might be achieved. One of the difficulties that seems to recur within this research is that by reason of public exposure to information presented – however accurately or inaccurately - within the visual media[1] and the printed news press, the public is generally more aware of the role of prisons than of the operation of community sanctions such as those formerly recognisable as probation, community service, and the like as explained in the *Glossary* at the end of this work. Moreover, it also seems to be the case that when the most serious forms of offending are removed from consideration, members of the general public are less enthusiastic about, or convinced in relation to the *effectiveness* of such measures in reducing crime and reoffending (e.g. Roberts 2002 *op. cit.*: 34; Hough and Roberts 1998a and b; Maruna and King 2004 *op. cit.*: 90-91).

There is also some evidence to indicate that when the public feel threatened by crime, or can be induced to feel so threatened by media sensationalism of crime, then attitudes towards criminal offenders tend to 'harden', and non-custodial alternatives consequently become viewed as a 'soft option' for dealing with other than the most minor forms of offending of a non-violent nature. This much stated, however, it is also important to indicate that as Stalans (2002 *op. cit.*: 20) has pointed out, research in this particular area of criminal justice relating to public opinion is far from conclusive, and frequently highly speculative.

There are, in addition, geographic, ethnic and cultural differences in public attitudes towards crime and sanctions within and between nations in Europe and worldwide that tend to confuse the account even further. Some of these differences are generationally inherited, others deeply embedded in religious tradition, and yet others appear to be related to the different extent to which communities in different geographic areas are prepared to tolerate criminal activity, and thus those who perpetrate crime within them. To say the least, broad generalisations about public attitudes towards crime and sanctions may be more misleading than helpful, and thus what politicians and policy-makers believe the public thinks about these issues

---

1. In television and film accounts of crime, policing and prisons in particular, and through reinforcement by coverage of crime in the printed output of the mass circulation newspapers almost universally.

may well be similarly uninformed. As Maruna and King further point out:

> Nonetheless, the relationship between recent policy developments and public wishes has been anything but direct. A considerable amount of 'populist punitiveness' (Bottoms 1995) – defined as 'allowing the electoral advantage of a policy to take precedence over its penal effectiveness' (Roberts *et al.* 2003:5) – seems to take place with only a caricatured understanding of the public's real views regarding crime and justice (Roberts *et al.* 2003). Considerable research suggests that the public is not nearly as punitive as sentencers, politicians and public officials assume they are. . .
>
> As such, systematic reviews of public opinion regarding crime and justice are an important corrective to this 'failure to communicate' between criminal justice and the public (Flanagan and Longmire 1996). As Roberts (1992) eloquently demonstrates in his review, not only is it important to dispel the misperceptions the public holds towards crime, but it is equally urgent to dispel the misperceptions that criminal justice experts and policy-makers have towards the public's opinion on crime and punishment. Dispelling myths about public opinion might be most crucial in the area of non-custodial sentences, as Flanaghan (1996) suggests that '*perceived* public opinion' (emphasis added) is the 'greatest obstacle' to the success of community-based penalties. (Maruna and King 2004: 84)

The 'failure to communicate' between criminal justice and the public identified in the foregoing quotation is, of course, a communication gap between government, its policy-makers and the citizen that is quickly filled by the mass media in a manner unhelpful to the expansion of community corrections. This situation is to some extent exacerbated in both Britain and the United States by what can only be described as a crisis of confidence and professional direction within the Probation Service[2] that has weakened the credibility of what was formerly the probation order (and later for a time the community rehabilitation order) as an effective non-custodial sanction in the eyes of many sentencing officials and informed observers of the criminal justice system (Dickey and Smith 1998; McKittrick and Rex 2003 *op. cit.*:151-2[3]). The latter authors draw particular attention to the breaching of probation orders by the commission of further serious and violent offences while under supervision: a matter reported upon in an editorial in *The Times* newspaper of 12 February 2001 in Britain. A remarkably similar article appeared in the *St. Petersburg Times* (Florida, USA) of 13 June 2004 alleging widespread breaches of federal probation orders by offenders in that state, many of these being of a seriously violent nature (Kreuger *et al.* 2004).

There will always be failures, in the same way that some prisoners released on parole will commit serious offences when freed early from custody. This much is

---

2. Here see the account of Kathryn Farrow (2004 *op. cit.*), particularly at pp.218-9.
3. In strict fact the criticism levelled by McKittrick and Rex related specifically to the lapses in reporting further (and sometimes serious) further offences committed by offenders while under the supervision of the Probation Service in the early years of this decade in England and Wales. Though procedures in this regard have been tightened, the matter became the subject of a highly critical editorial comment in *The Times* newspaper of 12 February 2001 that accused the Probation Service of deliberately 'under-reporting' such offences, and thus of public and governmental deception.

generally accepted, even by a sceptical public, and however reluctantly by politicians. There is, nonetheless, a need to promote a positive image of community sanctions that focuses upon the advantages to be gained from wider use of them, telling the truth about falling crime rates, and ensuring that such sanctions display the 'essential operational attributes' and qualitative factors identified in the opening part of this chapter. If the means can be found to incorporate these attributes and factors, then the counter-arguments in favour of continued excessive use of custody become infinitely less appealing.

This means, in turn, going back to the proposed use of a 'bifurcated' system of criminal justice outlined in *Chapter 11* (and illustrated in *Figure 11:1* at p.154). There can be no suggestion of expanding the use of non-custodial sanctions for serious offenders (at least during the early part of custodial sentences), or for less serious offenders who are unwilling to enter into a reparative process. Noting such reservations, however, it will be recalled (from *Chapter 4* and Table 4.3 at p.71), that in England and Wales in February 2009 the sentenced prison population by length of sentence displayed the following profile:

Prison Population (England and Wales) - February 2009

Type of Custody & Sentence	Prisoners
Total Population in Custody*	82,993
Remanded in Custody	12,954
Sentenced Prisoners	68, 072
Up to 6 Months	5, 021
6 to 12 Months	2, 447
Over 12 Months to 4 Years	23,930
Over 4 Years (excluding Life)	24, 224
Life / Indeterminate Sentences	12,143

Source: Ministry of Justice (February 2009)
*This total includes a small number of civil prisoners and people awaiting deportation.

It is clearly necessary to establish some threshold for consideration of those prisoners held in custody under present sentencing arrangements, but who might be considered potentially suitable to have their sentences converted to reparative custody providing that they were willing to accept the demands upon them that this would entail. It will also be recalled that the suggestion was made earlier (in *Chapter 4*) that all sentences of imprisonment of six months or less in *effective* duration[4]

---

4. Under present remission of sentence arrangements in England and Wales this means sentences of twelve months or less in duration that results in a maximum of six months in custody.

might be discontinued and non-custodial sentences imposed as an alternative. Such a transition would decrease the prison population (as at May 2007) by more than 8,000 places, but place the same volumetric burden on sanctions served within the community.

In addition, it would seem sensible to limit consideration for reparative custody to those prisoners presently sentenced to 12 months and up to four years imprisonment whose effective sentence lengths in custody become a maximum of two years or less. If such a policy were to be adopted, a further 22,820 prisoners (as at May 2007) would become eligible for such consideration if deemed suitable for such custody and they were prepared to abide by its requirements. Evidently not by any means all of these offenders would be suitable due to their previous records of repetitive offending, but if half of them were considered suitable and willing, a further 11,500 prison places might be saved. The combination of the two measures outlined above could ultimately reduce the prison population by almost 20,000 places *in the short term*.

On the other hand, the non-custodial sector of corrections would also have to be capable of expanding, absorbing and dealing effectively with a considerably increased workload in terms both of supervision and daily employment, though a proportion of those released to community project work from reparative prison custody would return to accommodation supervised by the correctional services at the end of each working day. Though the general public might be reluctant to accept an inevitable measure of additional 'risk' from such a transition within criminal justice, much would ultimately depend upon its perception of the extent to which a new range of community sanctions had sufficient 'penal bite', and whether the delivery of the 'qualitative factors' of simplicity, visibility, value, propriety and reliability matched critical expectations.

In the final analysis, and in a somewhat bizarre and unintentional manner, the proposals advanced here might well have considerably more popular appeal than might at first sight be anticipated. For if the public is not as punitive as many politicians and the media seem to believe it to be, then such a transition may be seen as a sensible means of arresting and ultimately decreasing the vast sums of national expenditure ('the tax-payer's money') spent on prisons and prisoners. Conversely, a bifurcated model of criminal justice might also have some appeal to the punitively minded insofar as it would appear that serious offenders would (within the 'traditional model' of imprisonment) be more harshly dealt with by comparison with those serving reparative custody. In addition, those sentenced in the latter manner might attract some extent of public compassion insofar as their actions exhibit remorse and a willingness to make reparation to victims of crime. Ultimately, the balance of public opinion will depend upon delivery of the 'qualitative factors' mentioned earlier, and whether these will in turn effectively achieve the 'desired outcomes' identified in *Figure 12:1* on page 173 supra.

DELIVERING EFFECTIVENESS IN NON-CUSTODIAL SANCTIONS

If the assessment of Hough and Roberts (1998 *op. cit.*) is correct and the public (in Britain and possibly elsewhere also) is to a considerable extent unaware of the manner in which existing community penalties operate in practice, then its attitudes towards community justice are likely to be shaped more by media influences than by explanations provided by the government or the criminal justice agencies themselves. However, it is also the case that non-custodial corrections receive infinitely less coverage than prisons, policing and the courts in routine *reportage*, and that what is reported is predominantly skewed towards the perceived 'failures' and shortcomings of non-custodial sanctions, and the perception of these measures as a 'soft option' by comparison with imprisonment.

From *Figure 13:1* it will be evident that the 'qualitative factors' combine in an essential manner to contribute to the effectiveness of community sanctions, and also that the desired attributes of facilitating change and making penalties demanding are also important determinants of effectiveness in the public mind. Thus if sanctions do not provide the possibility and potential for change towards law-abiding conduct, and thus contribute towards reduced reoffending, then their perceived and actual effectiveness will be diminished. Equally, there is a reasonable expectation that sanctions should be demanding of the offender and require genuine effort in terms of work done to make reparation to victims, and to contribute amenity value to communities.

The issue of *simplicity* in the design and operation of community sanctions is of considerable importance in making the nature of the measures and the requirements that are entailed evident and clearly understood by offenders, correctional officials and communities. Thus the smaller the range of sanctions and the greater the simplicity with which these are described, the more effective the sanctions are likely to become. For example, the Finnish Criminal Justice System has only four sanctions available to the courts: in ascending order of severity these are the 'summary penal fee'[5], fines calculated on the 'day fine' principle, community service and imprisonment (either suspended or imposed) (Joutsen *et al.* 2001 *op. cit.*). Conditions such as attending programmes for substance, alcohol or drug abuse, can be attached to community service orders or fines, but restrictive conditions such as curfew orders, exclusion orders, prohibiting activities, residential restrictions and the like are regarded as excessively proscriptive and socially undesirable.

---

5. The summary penal fee is used for 'on the spot' dealing with motoring offences, vandalism, littering and other minor misdemeanours, predominantly by the police. Failure to comply with the requirement to pay the fee within a specified period can (but rarely if ever does) result in imprisonment which is normally suspended in such instances (Joutsen *et al.* 2001 *op. cit.*: 30 31).

THE COMPONENTS OF EFFECTIVENESS IN NON-CUSTODIAL CORRECTIONS

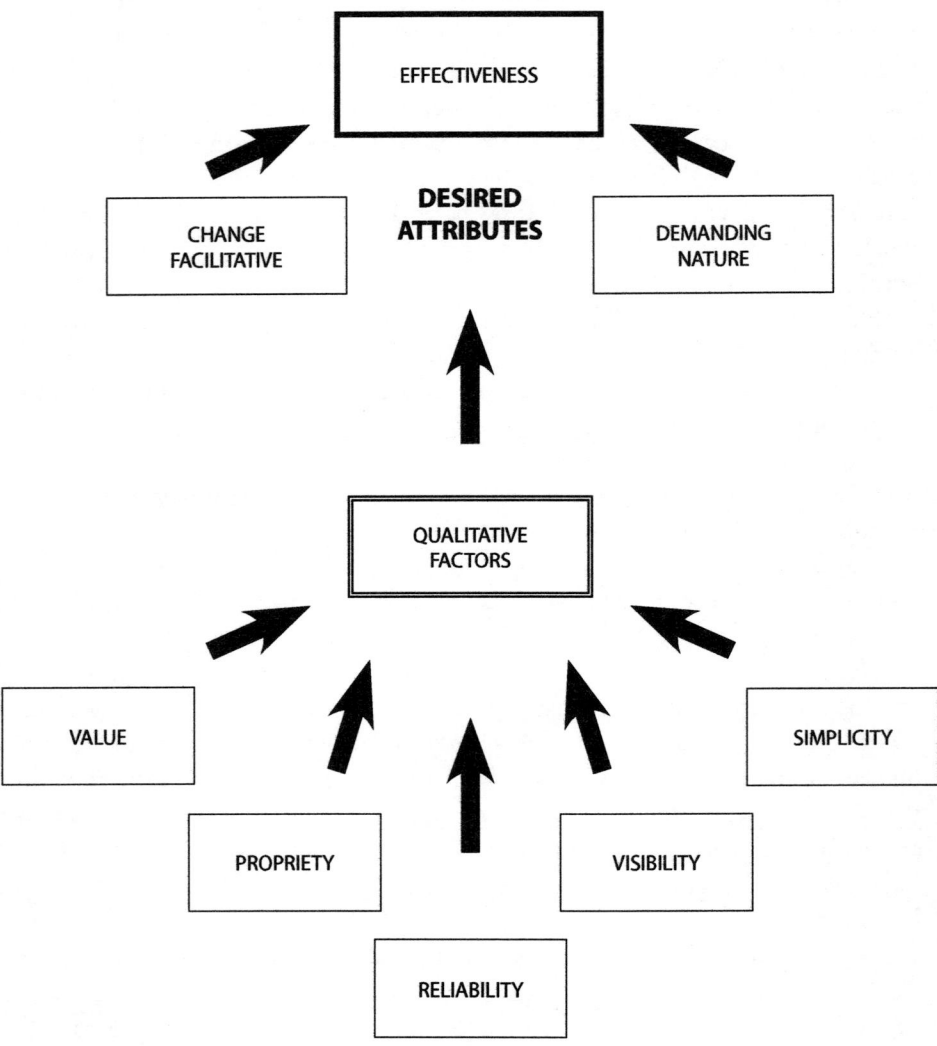

Figure 13:1: The Components of Effectiveness in Non-custodial Corrections

Visibility is also an indispensable aspect of community sanctions for a number of different reasons. First, it is an evident manifestation that justice is being done and that offenders are required to 'make good' the harm caused by their offences. Second, the fact that the penalty has constructive operational effect and is demanding *may* deter similar offending, but much more important, it evidences the fact that reparation is being made. Third, though there is a potentially 'shaming' aspect of community sanctions that some regard as an undesirable feature[6], there is also a reasonable case for the public to be aware of offenders working within communities as a matter of public safety. And finally, it can be argued that visibility is an important source of protection for offenders themselves to ensure that they are not subjected to abusive behaviour or worse while working within the vicinity of members of the public.

Reliability in the delivery of community sanctions is a key issue. It is essential that the work done by offenders is meticulously planned and resourced, that it is completed to high standards of quality, that it is effectively supervised at all times, and that it is evidently purposeful, demanding and socially useful. In fact, it might be maintained that reliability of performance is the key ingredient in the credibility and effectiveness of community sanctions, and that without it the entire purpose of such measures becomes questionable. Delivering reliability suggests strongly that the organisational structure for the operation of non-custodial corrections has to be of a professional and almost 'regimented' nature to ensure uniformity of outcomes and effectiveness. We shall return to this particular aspect of community sanctions in some greater detail in *Chapter 14*.

Linked strongly with the issue of reliability is the important requirement that non-custodial sanctions requiring offenders to undertake work or activities in the proximity of the public must be *appropriate*. This means that these must be purposeful and constructive, have a content that develops skills and competencies to enhance future employability, and not be of an entirely menial or degrading nature that further denigrates the status of those sentenced to undertake it. In this respect it is questionable whether, for example, setting offenders to work to clean graffiti from public places is appropriate other than when the offence(s) for which they were sentenced involved vandalism in the first place. Moreover, even if the offences were of such a nature, merely cleaning graffiti without any other skills enhancing instruction or training is altogether unlikely to enhance employability in the longer term, however socially useful such work might be seen to be.

The final 'qualitative factor' contributing to the effectiveness of community

---

6. This has proved a controversial issue in Britain in the past on the basis that offenders can appear to be 'officially scapegoated' for their offences and that this, as additional punishment, is unreasonable. The same objection has been used in relation to requirements for offenders undertaking community service to wear 'high visibility' clothing for the purposes of identification and supervision. The counter argument is that members of the public are entitled to be aware that offenders are working in public places, and that the wearing of distinctive clothing leads to a reduction of public risk.

sanctions is that of their *value* to society, victims, offenders and communities. The primary value to society must be evident in the reduction of crime and reoffending, but this will only occur if offenders are enabled through long-term employability to adopt a crime-free lifestyle and become law-abiding citizens. The value of community corrections for victims will depend on the financial resources that could result from the work done by offenders within communities from payment for which both offenders should be remunerated and victims compensated. Realistic levels of pay for offenders completing community projects to high standards of delivery, and from which contributions are deducted for victim reparation have two important effects for offenders: that of encouraging a work ethic; and, equally as important, that of enabling them to know that through their own efforts victims feel vindicated and communities have been recompensed for crime committed within them and social amenity improved.

There is now some documented research evidence that well selected and organised community projects not only enhance the employability of offenders, but also lead to lesser reoffending when offenders regard their sanction as 'fair'. (e.g. Killias *et al.* 2000 *op. cit.*; Rex and Gelsthorpe 2002 *op. cit.*; McIvor 1992 and 2004 *op. cit.*:176-7). This was particularly the case where offenders considered the work completed to be useful and skill-imparting, and relationships between themselves and the beneficiaries of their efforts had been consistent and encouraging (McIvor 1998: 55-56). Such outcomes make a strong case for expansion of the community service sanction (now a requirement of unpaid work) in particular at the expense of short and medium-term prison sentences.

COMMUNITIES AS BENEFICIARIES OF CORRECTIONS

In many respects the non-custodial sanction of community service (as opposed to 'unpaid work') - effectively operated - reflects all the main characteristics and principles of reparative and restorative justice in concentrating its focus on the main stakeholders in criminal justice who are offenders, victims and communities. However, as has been mentioned previously within this discussion, the state, as a stakeholder also, must take responsibility for the provision of resources to allow the sanction to be used to best effect. It has also been argued that the financial savings made by reducing the use of imprisonment could more than offset the cost of expanding the much less expensive and damaging alternative of community service.

It has been suggested in communication with professional colleagues who are supportive of restorative justice both in principle and practice that there is a need to distance it somewhat from the traditional nomenclature of criminal justice that clearly finds restorative justice to difficult to accommodate – particularly in relation to community sanctions. The main reason advanced for such an approach is the widely held concern among proponents of restorative justice that its agenda is susceptible to the 'cherry-picking' tendency of criminal justice policy-makers to select apparently attractive but low risk elements of restorative justice practice and implement these piecemeal while claiming to endorse its principles in their entirety. In such a manner, restorative justice can be deflected and consigned to the margins of criminal justice where it is less threatening to policy-makers, politicians and the sentencing officials of the courts. (e.g. Dignan 2002:187-188; McCold 2004 *op. cit.*; Umbreit *et al.* 2005 *op. cit.*:3-4). Such behaviour would also deprive communities of the potential benefits that reparative and restorative community justice could provide.

Both victims and communities are directly affected by crime, and each deserve reparation to some reasonable extent for the harm and distress that crime causes. Victims and those closely associated with them are those most immediately in need of support, and in addition to the services of professional counsellors, this support can be generated within communities where mutual cohesiveness is socially valued. Community corrections can enhance this support by providing the opportunity and the encouragement to offenders to understand and acknowledge the harm caused to victims, and to address the causes of their harmful behaviour. A simply and honestly expressed apology is frequently as much (if not more) valued and appreciated by a victim as any reparation that the offender may make.

The 'traditional' model of criminal justice, with its emphasis on retributive punishment, automatically and deliberately distances itself from both victims and communities in its pursuit of impartiality and judicial detachment. Restorative justice, in its pursuit of inclusiveness, acknowledges the needs of all the parties to criminal offending and seeks to meet these to the greatest extent possible. Above all, perhaps, it asks one vital question that traditional justices ignores as far as possible: what is more important – retribution or reconciliation?

Though we have acknowledged earlier that communities can benefit materially from work done by offenders in reparation to victims, this is only part of the potentially reconciling effect that a restorative penology can provide for societies. The different approach that it adopts towards offenders and victims makes the social reintegration of the former and the vindication of the latter much more likely to be successfully achieved. Though sanctions are necessary to express social disapproval of offences, these can be used in a positive manner and to the ultimate benefit of all the parties to criminal justice.

Wider use of non-custodial sanctions offers other potential benefits to communities in limiting what has been termed earlier in this work as the 'collateral damage' that excessive use of imprisonment causes to offenders, their immediate families and close others.[7] This damage is frequently evident in inflicting poverty on families, increasing the likelihood of permanent separation and divorce, reducing the long-term employment prospects of ex-offenders, and in the development of behavioural problems and affective disorders in children. Though the 'traditional' justice system can claim that these are the unintended or indirect consequences of imprisonment, such are, in reality, capable of anticipation and limitation to a considerable extent.

Families deprived of a main wage earner for considerable periods of time, and in which the remaining partner (as the primary carer of young children) may be unable to work or afford childcare costs, frequently become dependent upon state benefits for survival. This can lead to inadequate diet, poor health, housing problems and even homelessness in addition to the disintegration of relationships. In such circumstances also, dependency on alcohol or drugs to relieve distress can easily become an attractive option, and the spiral of disadvantage quickly worsens into one of despair. Lesser resort to custodial punishment - particularly that of women - and increased use of reparative and restorative community sanctions could help to reduce these dysfunctional effects within communities to a considerable extent.[8]

In early 2009 the penal system in England and Wales has reached a new crisis situation in which the daily average prison population now approaches 83,000 and the average annual cost of a prison place exceeds £40,000. The number of prisoners serving life sentences has almost doubled in the past decade to over 7,000, and more than 5,000 prisoners are now serving indeterminate sentences in addition. The average daily population of women prisoners presently exceeds 4,500 (Prison Reform Trust 2008). A decade ago, the average daily prison population was 61,114 of whom 2,066 were females, 3,721 were serving life sentences, and the average annual cost of a prison place in 1996-97 was £24,271 (White 1998).

Set against the huge contemporary costs incurred by increased use of imprisonment, the assessed cost in 2005/6 of supervising the community order or the

---

7. The term 'collateral damage' is used with some care within this work since it will be evident that the fact of imprisonment is bound to bring with it disadvantageous consequences for the families or close others of those sentenced to custody. The fact is, however, that these dysfunctional aspects of custody, however inevitable, constitute secondary (and additional) punishment of the offender and primary punishment of those affected directly by the sanction, but who have committed no punishable offence. The 'traditional' justice system is not required to consider in any formal sense such 'unintended consequences' within a tariff system of sentencing, though within a restorative penology these factors would be considered within the context of the principle that 'crime is a violation of people and relationships.' (see, e.g. Zehr 2002 op. cit.:19-22).

8. The imprisonment rate for women in England and Wales, at a daily average of some 4,500 in 2008, amounts to almost 6% of the total prison population. One third of these women had no previous convictions, twice the rate for male prisoners, and the majority were sentenced for non-violent offences. This population has increased by more than 100% in the past decade, and two thirds of the women imprisoned are mothers. It is estimated that more than 60% of imprisoned women have problems of drug dependency, 50% have suffered domestic abuse, and more than 33% sexual abuse. The median rate for female custody in Europe is 2.5% of national prison populations Source: Prison Reform Trust Factfile (January 2008). See: http://www.prisonreformtrust.org.uk/section.aspd?id=188fact.

suspended sentence order was in the region of £2,400 *per annum* for each offender thus sentenced.⁹ Reconviction rates in England and Wales within two years for offenders given community sentences have averaged around 55 *per cent* since 1997 (46 *per cent* for women), compared with those for offenders sentenced to imprisonment which exceed 60 *per cent* for all adults and 73 *per cent* for young offenders between 18 and 20 years of age (Crimeinfo.org.uk 2008:5-6).¹⁰ It would therefore seem no more that a prudent use of national fiscal resources to expand the use of non-custodial corrections, and divert the resulting savings towards reducing the root causes of crime within communities to the advantage of offenders, victims and communities themselves.

Put another way, both communities and other sources of social provision such as health, education and welfare services (including the development of statutory rather than voluntary agencies for the support of victims of crime) could benefit considerably from a moratorium on future prison building, and an eventual reduction of the custodial penal population. Plans are now being considered by the British government to add a further minimum of 9,000 places to the prisons estate by 2012 merely to keep in step with median population growth predictions and the present overcrowded numbers. The average cost of *each* additional place built since 2000 has been (reliably) estimated by the Prison Reform Trust (2008) to amount to £99,839, and the cost of such provision continues to rise year on year. If a moratorium were to be imposed in 2009, a saving of more than £900 million would be made with at least a five or more per cent lesser risk of recidivism through the increased use of community sanctions. These are measures that would be of real community benefit.

CREATING SPACE FOR COMMUNITY INVOLVEMENT

In the final part of this chapter it may be helpful to suggest, albeit briefly, a number of ways in which communities and local government structures might become involved in promoting an effective and expanded use of non-custodial corrections. Though these suggestions are modelled on a form of regional, county, district and city/town administrative structure that prevails in Britain, similar patterns of territorial administration should be broadly familiar to readers in other national situations.

The reader will recall from *Figure 12:1* (*Chapter 11*), that the delivery criteria

---

9. A community punishment order (CPO) (formerly the community service order ((CSO) had a minimum of 40 hours and a maximum of 240, now superseded by a requirement of 'unpaid work': see generally the *Glossary* at the end of this work. Such work is completed during the day, in the evenings or at weekends. The suspended sentence order (or 'custody minus") is technically a custodial sentence imposed on an offender who might otherwise have been sentenced to imprisonment for less than 12 months. The maximum period of suspension is two years, though the average is 17 months (Crimeinfo.org.uk 2008).
10. A comprehensive Fact Sheet on community sentences is available at: http://www.crimeinfo.org.uk/ servelet adding: factsheetservelet?command=printablefactsheet.html.

for maximising the inputs and outputs of community corrections were the need for national standards, accountable auditing of performance against standards, and a regional (or equivalent) structure to deliver the forms of community corrections most appropriate to the cultural and ethnic characteristics of the areas and communities in which these must operate.

A possible structure for achieving this is set out at *Figure 13:2* on p.192 from which the following points should be noted:

- at the national level correctional services would be separated into two distinct elements (custodial correctional services and community correctional services), the former including all forms of sentence involving deprivation of liberty, and the latter subsuming sanctions within the community including and semi-custodial penalties such as suspended sentences of imprisonment converted operationally to community service;
- the area coverage for both elements of correctional services should be identical both geographically and operationally, their boundaries being conterminous in every respect so as to provide a unified service;
- the same areas should, wherever possible, have boundaries that correspond with those of the district or county authorities that lie within them to avoid anomalies of geographical distribution within the communities served by them. Prisons, town and city authorities and Community Corrections Centres (CCCs) would thus fall within the same area and district boundaries for criminal justice purposes;
- Community Justice Forums (which are discussed subsequently) would serve their immediately proximate prisons, towns or cities and CCCs, of which one or more might be required within correctional services areas and geographic district (or county) administrative boundaries;
- Community Justice Forums would comprise those potential sponsors of community corrections projects, and employers willing to accept offenders serving community sanctions on a 'joint venture' basis with their immediately situated prisons, CCCs and local authorities, though under the oversight and operational control vested at the area and district or county level of civil administration;
- potential participant organisations might include (but not be limited to) any of the following:

    - Emergency Services (Fire and Rescue, Ambulance and Police);
    - Public transport providers;
    - Highways construction and maintenance authorities;
    - Refuse collection, disposal and re-cycling services;
    - Leisure centres, parks and public amenity authorities;

- Schools and colleges;
- Healthcare services, residential care facilities and hospices;
- Farms and horticultural centres;
- Environmental, countryside and forestry conservation authorities and agencies;
- River and waterways authorities;
- Local businesses involved in construction, factory production and allied trades;
- Voluntary services, faith groups, charities and community project groups.

The role of the Community Justice Forum (CJF) would be pivotal to the concept of Community Correctional Services suggested here. It brings together with the criminal justice and local government agencies all those potential sources of training and employment necessary to make community corrections visible, valuable and appropriate within a relatively simple structure that could lead to reliable delivery. It asks only of potential participant organisations the willingness to offer opportunity and employment to offenders to work within their supervision[11] for wages paid by central government at levels realistically above those paid to the unemployed.

Effectively, what is proposed here is that each Correctional Services Area[12] should enter into a 'Partnership for Crime Reduction' with the district, city and town Councils within its geographic boundaries, including within the membership of CJFs the prisons and CCCs also located within the same boundaries. This structure is shown within the double line links indicated in *Figure 13:2*. In this respect Area Correctional Services become the co-ordinators of the 'partnership' in conjunction with the higher tier local authorities, and the CJFs (comprising the lower tier local authorities, prisons and CCCs) become the 'driving force' and means of delivery of the work of the 'partnership'. We shall explore how this might work in practice in the chapter that follows.

Clearly it would not be feasible to provide a CCC in *each* town for reasons of economy, but a number of smaller towns in more rural areas might share a single CCC sited so as to provide convenient access for all participants. Similarly, in major

---

11. And that of the Community Correctional Services' professionally trained staff who would monitor attendance, participation and progress throughout the duration of the sanction period, and in addition provide the facilities for attendance on programmes of counselling, offending behaviour analysis and victim awareness on the FGC model that would include, where possible, offenders' family members and those of victims where this might be deemed beneficial to both parties.
12. Though correctional services at the area level are shown in *Figure 13:2* as comprising custodial and community services, it is envisaged that both would be under the operational control of a unified Correctional Services Headquarters at the area level. This is indicated in the broken line boxes and links in *Figure 13:1*.

A POSSIBLE STRUCTURE FOR DELIVERY OF RESTORATIVE AND REPARATIVE CORRECTIONAL SERVICES

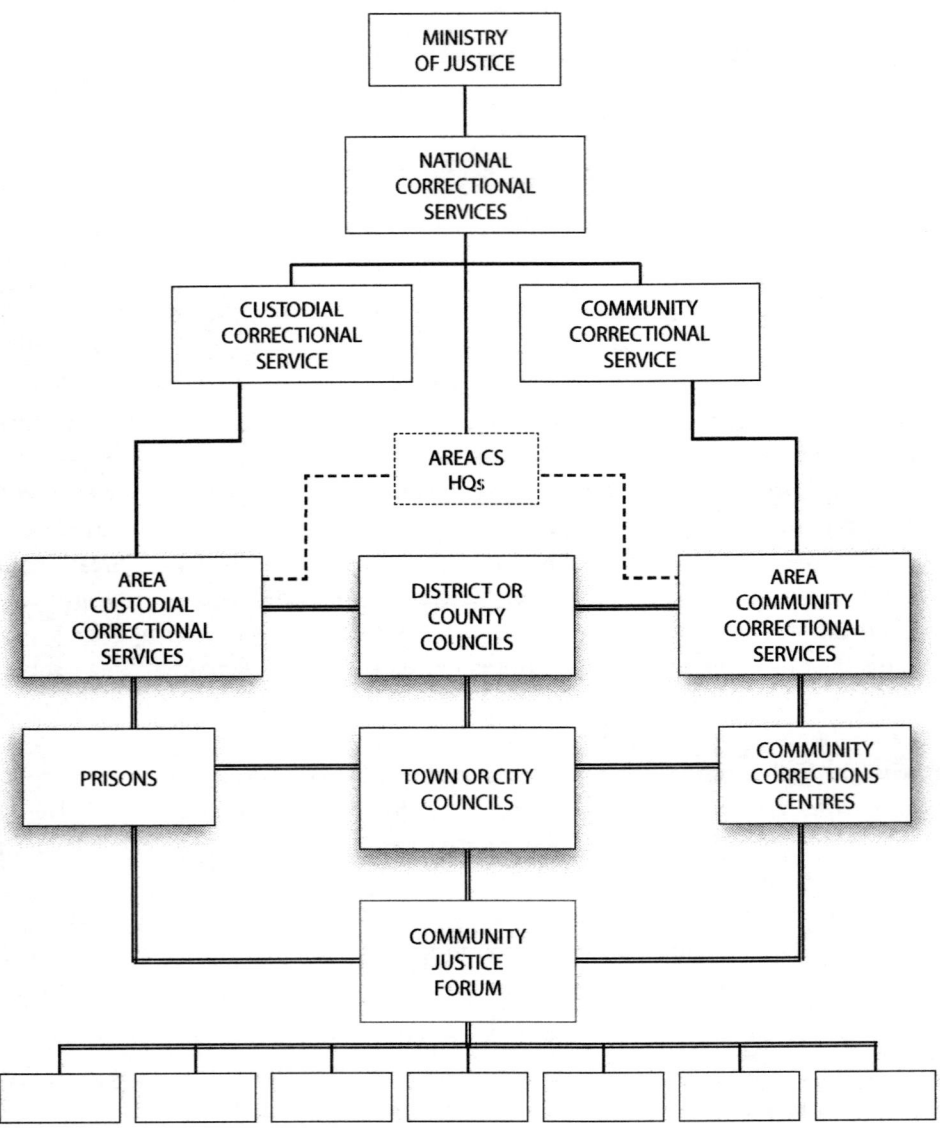

Figure 13:2: A Possible Structure for Delivery of Restorative and Reparative Correctional Services

cities more than one CCC might be required, located so that the different areas of the city had similar access to these resources. In principle, however, CCCs should be sited where consistent volumes of offenders sentenced to community penalties and ex-prisoners released on conditional licence to community project work would routinely require their coordination and services. The 'catchment' area for each CCC must, however, be of a size to sustain its own CJF and contain a sufficient availability of potential participant organisations.

Finally, for this part, CCCs as proposed here would be required to offer a range of facilities and services for offenders that would include at the least:

- daily supervision of offenders employed on community work projects in conjunction with employer organisations and agencies;
- provision for delivery of accredited offending behaviour and addiction programmes with individual and group counselling and support;
- dedicated supervision and support of individuals on community orders within manageable caseloads for correctional services counsellors[13];
- conferencing facilities and facilitation for offenders, victims and their families (or close others) at both the pre-trial mediation and post-sentence (or post-custody) phases of community sanctions;
- logistical and liaison support of participant organisations and agencies to ensure that offenders met personal performance targets and conformed to employment and behavioural conditions on a consistent basis; and,
- facilities and a venue for the regular meetings of the CJF to undertake project planning and review, co-ordination of employment vacancies for community service workers (CSWs), their progress assessment and future (post-sanction) employment training needs and prospects.

Community sanctions will only succeed if offenders perceive them to be of a positive, demanding, prospectively useful and well-organised nature, fairly enforced and supervised, and with an evident incentive to full participation. For these reasons it is proposed here that offenders undergoing community sanctions should be realistically paid for full participation from state funds on a weekly basis, and that the rate of pay should be marginally greater than the rate of benefits that they might receive if unemployed.[14] There also has to be an incentive towards satisfactory completion

---

13. These would be the professional core of former probation officers whose work in support of the courts would be entirely separate from that of community correctional service supervisory officers.
14. In this connection it will be remembered that in earlier chapters emphasis has been placed upon offenders working for realistic wages, a proportion of which is automatically deducted for the reparation of victims of crime. Offender pay rates must, therefore, reflect both the ability to make reparation and an incentive towards full participation in the conditions of the sanction.

of community sanctions, and it is further suggested that it might be appropriate to reward completion with a 'resettlement grant' of a sufficient sum to encourage full participation. Full participation and completion would be likely to increase the probability of subsequent employment, enhance public confidence, and reduce the risk of reoffending over the duration of the sanction period, and possibly subsequently. The potential cost-benefit outcomes would therefore seem to be considerable, including in terms of crime prevention.

The requirements of community sanctions outlined here call for a highly professional, well-organised and fully resourced Community Correctional Service, operating to national standards, and fully accountable to the state and to the public. In the chapter that follows we shall explore how this might be set in place most effectively, and to standards of performance and delivery in which public confidence in community corrections might become considerable and justifiable.

CHAPTER 14

Who Should Operate and Supervise Community Sanctions?

To the reader who has persevered thus far with the discussion within this work it will come as no surprise that what is suggested is – at least in Britain – a radical re-appraisal of the way in which both custodial and non-custodial criminal sanctions are designed and delivered. The important question that remains unanswered is that of how this might best be achieved in practice. In the previous chapter (at *Figure 13:2* and p.189 in particular) the proposal was made that correctional services would benefit from unification in a manner that, not unlike the ill-starred concept of the National Offender Management Service (NOMS) model, would provide for National Correctional Services comprising two distinctive elements: a Custodial Correctional Service and a Community Correctional Service.

On 30th January 2008 *The Times Online*[1] reported that only four years after its inception the NOMS 'is to be overhauled'. It is now more than two years (at the time of writing in May 2009) since NOMS was transferred from the Home Office to the then newly formed Ministry of Justice, and its implementation from 2003 onwards was a first step towards attempting the unification of the Prison and Probation Services of England and Wales. Why, then, has NOMS become in such need of 'overhaul', and what is the nature of the impending 'overhauling'?

The answer to this critically important question has been hinted at in earlier discussion (see *Chapter 12* at pp.166-169) as a 'marriage of extreme inconvenience' between two elements of the criminal justice system. Both have a professional ethos profoundly different to the other at the practitioner level, but the 'desirability' of whose union represents an indispensable 'managerialist' goal within the contemporary *realpolitik* of British criminal justice. The fact is, however, that the 'marriage', however much 'arranged', need not be incapable of compatibility: indeed it could become a thriving alliance if the partners could be persuaded to view it as an opportunity rather than as an imposition.

CREATING UNITY AND PRESERVING PROFESSIONAL IDENTITY

The image of a National Correctional Service identified in this work stems from a perceived need to make the processes of criminal justice delivery more logical, effective and capable of inspiring greater public confidence in the purposes and

---

1. In an editorial article bearing the title *Government 'Has No Strategy for Prisons'*, London: Times Online, http://www.timesonline.co.uk/tol/news/politics/article3273270.ece.

outcomes of corrections. This image recognises and acknowledges the very different roles hitherto performed by the Prison and Probation Services, but argues that these roles are, in fact, potentially more complementary and 'seamless' than either service might, at first sight, believe them to be. The fact that the roles reveal historical differences of approach towards offenders, the former in John DiIulio's aptly descriptive analogy termed the 'keeper philosophy' (DiIulio 1977 *op. cit.*: 167-187), and the latter more aligned towards a 'client advocacy and counselling philosophy' (Atkinson 2004:249), is no accident.

Both services, in their different perspectives, have a duty of care central to the manner in which they operate. The facts of institutional life, especially that of large institutions, inevitably call for order, control and regulation if chaos is to be avoided, but the duty to care is still present and cannot be abdicated. Where, on the other hand, there is no requirement to 'control' but rather to 'persuade and facilitate' change, a predominantly regulatory approach becomes inconsistent since it is the consent of the offender to seek change rather than the compulsion to do so that is of central importance. Care in such a context has an entirely different and more individualistic meaning.

One of the main problems confronting both services recently and in the future is the pressure on professionalism created by the 'managerialist' culture within government generally in Britain, and specifically within the criminal justice system. The pursuit of 'effectiveness' can place at some risk the nature of the relationships between practitioners and offenders, particularly when evidence-led practice is superseded or supplanted by initiatives to generate demonstrable 'results' that have not been subjected to sufficiently rigorous conceptual and user examination and analysis prior to implementation. The introduction of the Offender Assessment System (OASys) for offender risk and needs analysis within prisons and probation between 2001 and 2003 provides an excellent example of such developments (Mair *et al.*, 2006: 7-23). It also illustrates to some extent the frequent 'mismatch' between initiatives designed to improve effectiveness at the central level of government, and those conceived to improve delivery at the 'cutting edge' of professional practice.[2]

Another of the difficulties that has to be recognised in considering any form of unification between prison and probation services is, in addition to overcoming the 'keeper' and 'client-centred' philosophies, that of bridging the 'custody: community divide' in terms both of the professional perceptions and the realities of day to day

---

2. Such is not to suggest that the introduction of OASys was in any sense inappropriate, but rather that implementation occurred at precisely the same time as the Probation Service was being placed on a 'national' basis and pressures on practitioners were very considerable. This was also the same period (2002 onwards) in which the *naissance* of NOMS was becoming a reality, thus suggesting a further major reorganisation of probation practice within an immediate future. As Mair *et al.* note, there was comparatively little consultation with practitioners in relation to the potential advantages and disadvantages of OASys, or the implications that its introduction might have for caseload practice.

operation. Traditionally, and in a practical sense also, prison staff perceive their role as carried out in a manner that is predominantly '*ex civitas*', and thus not immediately subject to the scrutiny of the public or others beyond the walls. Those others, therefore, who enter prisons for professional purposes to undertake casework with offenders are, in such a view, a transient factor of daily life that has to be accepted and 'managed'. Probation officers and probation service staff, on the other hand, see themselves professionally as predominantly visible to the community, and to a much lesser extent as agents of a process that deprives offenders of their liberty.

Though it would be unrealistic to pretend that the 'custody: community divide' might be dismantled by edict, there is a very real sense in which both prison and probation services might be joined in common purpose, particularly if attention were to be given to the prescriptions for reparative custody described in this work. Reparative custody clearly envisages, from the stage of admission and induction within prisons onwards, a clearly identifiable crossover point from imprisonment to community sanction for each individual offender. This means that the onus for supervision shifts at that point *via* a shared responsibility for the transition period of conditional release[3], in which both services would have responsibilities for monitoring the behaviour of offenders.

Expanded use of community corrections through lesser use of imprisonment and the use of reparative custody would place an additional supervisory workload on the proposed Community Correctional Service identified in *Chapter 13* (see *Figure 13:2* and pp.188-192). Effective delivery of this workload is critical to the credibility of the new vision of corrections described in this work, and, as importantly, to the encouragement of public confidence in reduced use of custody and wider use of community sanctions. For these reasons it is proposed that the day to day supervision of offenders working within communities should be undertaken by *uniformed* correctional services officers (CSOs) specifically recruited and trained for that role within the Community Correctional Service. Such an arrangement would suggest many advantages, not the least of which might be:

- clearly evident supervision and support of offenders working on community projects in places to which the public have routine access;
- potential for liaison with the police in emergency, but relieving the police of the requirement to monitor additional numbers of offenders working in communities;

---

3. During which the ex-prisoner working in the community on a daily basis would return each evening to 'hostel-type' accommodation provided and supervised by the Prison Service. Conditional release implies that this period is one during which further offending or repeated failure to comply with the conditions of the conditional release licence would result in a return to custody. The period spent on conditional release is thus one during which both the prison and probation services share responsibility for the supervision of offenders in transition from custody to community sanction.

- increasing public confidence in the wider use of non-custodial sanctions;
- enabling probation officers to concentrate on the areas of their professional expertise in court liaison, counselling and probation supervision[4] without additional workload;
- ensuring that people undertaking unpaid work or community service in public areas are not subjected to abusive behaviour or treatment by members of the community;
- providing offenders with support and an incentive to engage fully in the work allocated to them;
- liaison with employing organisations to monitor offender attendance, punctuality, and work performance, and report on this in the event of disciplinary intervention;
- liaison with prison authorities in relation to the conduct of ex-prisoners released under conditional release and licence arrangements.
- liaison with supervising probation officers on the progress and engagement of offenders in assigned work, programmes, and compliance with licence requirements.

Such is not to suggest that CSOs should operate as 'gang-masters' on a full time basis, but rather that such officials should provide a consistent presence where offenders are deployed within communities to ensure that the conditions of community sanctions are met, offenders are supported, and that the public are safeguarded. Whether or not, like prison officers in Britain, CSOs should have some modified powers of police constables might be debatable, but that is a matter for others to decide upon.

The central point at issue here is to create a unified and effective Correctional Service within which each of the component elements feels professionally valued and the particular areas of expertise within either are used to maximum effect. The logical 'bridge' between the custodial and community corrections entities is the conversion of imprisonment to community sanction under the conditional release arrangements for reparative custody described here. In such a transitional arrangement public safeguards are set in place, and ex-prisoners have every incentive to cooperate with the requirements of community sanctions rather than remain in custody. In the event of default they have much to lose by being returned to prison

---

4. The term 'probation supervision' is used deliberately here. Although the probation order was renamed the community rehabilitation order in 2001 and the community service order was also renamed the community punishment order in the same year, it will be proposed later in this discussion that this situation should be reversed in the interests of clear public understanding of the new approach to community sanctions within this work. In renaming these two sanctions in 2001 the government resisted the temptation to rename the Probation Service as the Community Rehabilitation (or Punishment) Service for reasons that are possibly better left out of the equation here, even if these have profound significance for the discussion within this work. All previous community orders effectively 'dissappeared' within the generic community sentence in 2003 although most former orders have left significant practice-based traces.

within traditional regimes for the duration of their sentence periods.

MAKING COMMUNITY SANCTIONS VISIBLE

The suggestion has been made earlier that community sanctions involving offenders in working on projects to improve the quality of life and amenity within local areas (whether urban or rural) should be supervised by uniformed staff of the Community Correctional Service. Such a suggestion has to be balanced carefully between the possibility of attracting undue public attention towards these offenders and thus indulging in an unintended form of 'public shaming' on the one hand, and the reasonable need for public protection and reassurance on the other. It has to be acknowledged that to some practitioners within the pre-NOMS Probation Service the entire concept of working alongside uniformed colleagues might seem both incongruous and almost 'anathema', since it seems to run counter to the ethos of civil 'normalisation'[5] and officer: offender relationships that has been a hallmark of probation practice for decades past.[6]

This much admitted, expanded use of community sanctions would place increasing numbers of offenders within the community, some of whom might otherwise have been sentenced to imprisonment, and others released from reparative custody under conditional licence conditions. The potential difficulty that this causes lies deeply within the government's 'tough on crime' policy that has pervaded the criminal justice legislation of the past decade in Britain. As Julian Buchanan has appropriately noted:

> While a number of good initiatives have been implemented to help 'the poor', what limited progress there has been has to be set against the increasing privilege and wealth afforded to 'the rich'. The divide is growing not diminishing. It is a divide that goes beyond income and personal possessions – it is evident in widely different lifestyles, values and cultures, and understanding and communication between these polarized groups is poor.
>
> If government policy intends to be tough on these unacceptable causes of crime there is some contradiction in being tough on the individual who commits a crime partly as a result of inequality and disadvantage. It amounts to 'tough on the causes and tough on the victims of

---

5. By this term is meant the tradition of the British Probation Service for its practitioners to wear normal 'civilian' clothing when on duty, and deliberately to create a professional atmosphere in which relationships with offenders can be developed without unnecessary formality or feelings of superiority and inferiority. Traditionally this has underpinned the 'befriending' image of the Service that has to a marked extent enhanced its necessary supervisory role. Offenders have traditionally been referred to as 'clients' which implies a 'user of services' relationship between probation officers, staff, and the offenders whom they supervise and counsel.
6. Burnett and McNeill (2005) have described this situation very explicitly as the 'decline in the relationship basis for probation practice' that has taken place incrementally since the mid-1990s, in a most penetrating article entitled: 'The Place of the Officer – Offender Relationship in Assisting Offenders to Desist from Crime', *Probation Journal*, Vol. 52, no.3 (September), pp. 221-242.

those causes'. Clearly criminal action warrants sanctions, but the mantra to be 'tough on crime' is in danger of decontextualising crime, and imposing increasingly punitive (and arguably unfair) sentences... *The government's tough approach is mirrored by a growing toughness from the community towards people who have committed (a) crime, This leads to growing division, isolation, and makes reintegration more problematic.* (Buchanan, 2006: 107) (italic emphasis added).

If this analysis is correct, and it is supported entirely in this work, then the implications for community sanctions are profound indeed. The 'toughness on crime' mantra would tend to encourage a 'shaming' aspect of community corrections, and has actively done so through the 'punishment in the community' approach evident since 2001 and the re-naming of both the probation and community service orders noted earlier. Punitive public attitudes towards offenders within the context of this work are, however, of an entirely different concern. It seems bizarre by any standard of consideration to have to accept that contrary to popular belief it might be not so much the public that would be at risk from increasing use of community sanctions, but rather the offenders themselves from public disapprobation.

This possibility adds some credibility to the proposal that a uniformed presence in supervision of community service workers might also, in addition, have to monitor their safety and moderate public attitudes and behaviour towards them. In any event, once the operation of community sanctions as here envisaged had achieved credibility and lost some of its novelty, it would still seem prudent to have an identifiable presence in the supervisory role as a matter of public reassurance.

For all the same reasons it seems no more than reasonable that offenders themselves working publicly should wear some form of uniform clothing for ease of identification. This need not be of a 'high visibility' nature, but it should be sufficiently distinctive to enable supervision to be exercised whether remotely *via* CCTV or directly by corrections officials. And since in any case it is now the prevailing requirement for health and safety reasons for workers in many industries and construction trades to wear clearly identifiable outer clothing, there seems to be no case for offenders working in public places not to do so, as long as it is not specifically and primarily designed to identify them as such.

Making community sanctions visible suggests that there will be much merit in selecting project tasks that have evident community amenity, and which, once completed to high standards, will be valued by communities themselves. If, however, community sanction tasks are relegated to a menial level, are pointless and undemanding, and impart no skills, then the public estimation of their value will low and offenders thereby degraded. Projects such as the creation of adventure playgrounds for children, horticultural displays in civic areas, landscaping and transforming derelict or neglected sites into rest arbours in cities, and the like have immediately obvious community value: cleaning off graffiti, litter collection, and similar tasks, though useful, are less likely to be publicly appreciated.

It is also extremely important to publicise and acknowledge high quality work undertaken by offenders so that they feel valued for their contribution to civic life. Such acknowledgement also increases public awareness of constructive community project work and thus also of the preferable nature of these sanctions to that of imprisonment. Wherever possible the work done by offenders should impart marketable skills to enhance the likelihood of future employment, and lead to levels of recognised qualification to increase the competitiveness of ex-offenders in the employment market.

HOLISM AND REALISM IN COMMUNITY SANCTIONS

Many offenders will enter the world of community sanctions with few usable skills, low self-esteem, socially dysfunctional backgrounds and other personal deficits. Increasing numbers of offenders have a history of addiction, some an extent of mental impairment, unhealthy diet and poor general health and physical fitness. In addition to these disadvantages their offences often display behavioural characteristics that require correction through self-analysis, victim awareness, counselling, support and encouragement. For all of these reasons, the nature of community sanctions has to be structured in a way that will address these deficits in a holistic manner in addition to providing worthwhile work opportunities to enable reparation to be made to victims of crime.

The Community Corrections Centres proposed in *Chapter 13* (at pp.190-193) would need to be provided with a multi-purpose range of buildings and facilities that would enable all the various needs of offenders to be met in addition to being a focal point for daily assembly and deployment to work projects. This implies provision of offices, conferencing[7] and group-work rooms, training rooms, catering and ablution facilities, and communal areas for relaxation and limited recreation. In addition, secure garage, storage and workshop space would be necessary for servicing work projects, equipment and vehicles. An holistic approach to offender management in the community corrections context would envisage each participant working to a planned and regularly supervised individual programme that balanced the needs for assisted self-analysis, counselling and remedial programmes with work experience training, skills acquisition and community project work.

It is acknowledged that establishment of CCCs would represent no small capital investment and, in addition, require recurring expenditure, but this could be compensated for to a considerable extent by reductions in the prison population and the vast financial savings that would accrue from eventually having fewer

---

7. Provision of facilities for family group conferencing (FGC) would constitute an essential aspect of CCC design if pre-trial mediation, victim: offender counselling and inclusion and post-custodial sentence support are to be included in an holistic approach to offender management.

prisons in operation. The expansion of community corrections thus represents an investment in the future, in a more purposeful use of sanctions, in offenders, and ultimately in victims and communities. On balance also, the combination of these investments would be much more likely to reduce recidivism and increase public safety that the retributively punitive and incarcerative penology presently in place in Britain and elsewhere.

Adopting an holistic approach to offender management implies that all the needs and deficits of those undergoing community sanctions are viewed as a totality, and that immediate families and close others (including victims where this is appropriate) become involved, where possible, in the processes of pre-trial mediation and of social reintegration. This means that preoccupation with offences (either alleged or convicted) is not the only concern of the community corrections agenda, and that every effort is made to improve the ability of offenders to overcome the dysfunctional aspects of their lives and become crime-free. To enable such an approach there has to be a return to the situation in which the officer: offender relationship within probation work becomes the defining feature of that particular professionalism (see e.g. Burnett and McNeill, 2005 *op. cit.*: 221-231; Biestek, 1961; Goldberg *et al.*, 1985; Rex, 1999).

On the other hand, however, the need for realism in relation to what is 'achievable' within the mentoring approach to offender management has to be acknowledged. Indeed, the very term offender *'management'* might suggest an ability in professionals so to order the lives of offenders that crime is 'managed out' of their behaviours altogether. Supervising probation officers cannot absolutely or ultimately dictate where an offender resides, with whom he or she associates, what employment is undertaken, whether the offender accepts help to overcome addictions, or whether an attempt towards self-improvement is made in terms of educational or vocational training.[8] Encouragement towards making appropriate life choices can be extended in the creation and provision of opportunities to experience success through legitimate and constructive endeavour, but ultimately the offender has to perceive the relative advantages of a law-abiding lifestyle.

Realism involves the recognition that hitherto life-long influences over the conduct of some offenders are almost impossible to reverse in the short term. Inadequate parenting, peer group pressures and behaviours, educational truanting and under-achievement, periods spent in the care of local authorities or young offender institutions, addictions and substance abuse, can all take years to overcome and cannot be 'managed out' by fiat. Each individual offender needs the criminal

---

8. Though the range of provisions within the generic community sentence legislation in the Criminal Justice Act 2003 attempt to do just this and even more for the duration of the order. For while the regulatory powers within the Act amount to prohibitions on a short-term basis, the offender must ultimately opt to make such decisions appropriately when the power of the Act to dictate choices in these areas of conduct has expired.

justice system to respond *justly* to these deficits, and rather than punishing them, seek ways of enabling preferable alternatives to be adopted willingly by those who are sanctioned.

Realism also entails what Burnett and McNeill (2005 *op. cit.*) have so perceptively described as the recognition that case-management and casework with offenders are two entirely different propositions. If the Probation Service in England and Wales has failed offenders during the past two decades it is simply because the 'relationship' quality of casework has been relegated to a lesser status than the management and referral of offender cases to 'experts'. As they point out:

> It is difficult to pinpoint exactly when the relationship basis for probation practice fell from grace. It survived critiques of 'casework' and the period of correctional nihilism following the gloomy research message that 'nothing works'... This shift in focus from supportive to surveilling relationships seems indicative of how far the service has moved away from a paradigm that takes account of the 'client's perspective'...
>
> Similarly, other glimpses into current practice, gleaned from websites for probation areas and training consortia and from key documents, give little hint of the support, friendliness and warmth that once characterized the supervision of offenders. In description of the role of probation officers it is as if the relationship factor has been 'airbrushed' from the image portrayed. (Burnett and McNeill, 2005 *op. cit.*: 222-224)

There are signs that serious re-consideration is being given by senior managers within the Probation Service to a reversal of the 'managerialist' trend of recent years (National Probation Service, 2005), and that a return to a more casework-oriented approach will be centrally incorporated into core probation practice once NOMS finds its feet (Dowden and Andrews, 2005; Smith, 2004). Indeed, Christine Knott on her appointment as the National Offender Manager within NOMS, affirmed her view that "casework was a preferable label to case management, and that the former implies *hands on* involvement of the supervisor, who is not only the referrer and enforcer but also the motivator and the reinforcer, and the person who holds onto the longer-term aims of social reintegration and reducing reoffending." (Knott, 2004: 23 quoted in Burnett and McNeill, 2005 *op. cit.*:224).

This is a brave move in a realistic direction that could significantly re-empower probation officers in their traditional professional role and make community corrections a more coherent enterprise than that envisaged within the predominantly punitive and enforcement-centred product of the Criminal Justice Act 2003. It might also signal a return to wider use of the probation order (known as the community rehabilitation order from 2001 to 2003), and give the courts greater confidence that a reduction in recidivism might result from increased and more holistic casework intervention with offenders.

But this presupposes that at the political and policy-deliberative levels of criminal justice there might be a willingness to re-think the failures of past legislative approaches, and that the public might be better informed (by positive media intervention) about the value of a return to more traditional community supervision of offenders. In this particular respect there has been a curious silence of late, other than that as we have noted earlier[9] there has been some suggestion that NOMS is to be 'overhauled'. A resurgence of realism combined with telling the truth about crime might enable just the type of 'overhaul' suggested in this work.

CONCEIVING SIMPLICITY AND EFFECTIVENESS IN COMMUNITY JUSTICE DELIVERY

Up to this point the discussion within this chapter has made only passing reference to the central issue that runs through this work: that of how restorative justice might play a major part in the delivery of better justice within contemporary democratic societies. Within this and the preceding three chapters we have examined that sector of corrections that provides for community justice – particularly in the context of England and Wales – and have noted the spectrum of difficulties that presently stand in the way of making community sanctions effective in reducing offending and recidivism.

However, when all is said and done, reduction of offending is only part of the purpose of community sanctions, and our search for a more holistic approach opened up the possibility of meeting other equally desirable correctional outcomes such as the vindication of crime victims, creating a safer and more inclusive society, giving communities a role within corrections, and empowering offenders to become responsible citizens. Our present preoccupation with punishing offences and 'managing out' as many forms of social risk as possible tends to divert attention away from these outcomes, and focuses somewhat myopically upon punishing offenders instead.

With some justification it might be suggested that at present 'punishment in the community' actually addresses the wrong issues if our desired outcome is a more law-abiding society, and it does so in a complicated and prescriptive manner that has little practical relevance for offenders, victims and citizens who are the primary stakeholders in criminal justice. It addresses the wrong issues because it seeks to 'suppress' crime rather than change the behaviour of those who commit it, and it fails most significantly to recognise the person behind the crime and address funda-

---

9. At p.195 *supra*. This may also have some bearing on the fact that the most recently published British Crime Survey and Police Recorded Crime Statistics (2008) indicate that the risk of becoming a victim of crime have fallen to a 27 year low, and that the volume of recorded crime has shown an overall decrease of 9 *per cent* since 2006/7. Although drug-related offences have risen by 21 *per cent* – a fact attributed to increased use of police cautions for cannabis possession – violent offences and burglary show decreases of 8 *per cent*, and sexual offences a reduction of 9 *per cent* (Centre for Criminal Justice Studies, 2008; *The Times*, 25 January 2008: 31).

mental causes of offending. In many respects, and as matters presently stand, the outcome of criminal justice is quite predictable: *more criminal justice*.

Dissenters from such a view will undoubtedly protest that the development of cognitive behavioural interventions over recent years has represented a specific attempt to address causes of offending, but such a contention entirely misses the point that these programmes were designed primarily for assessment of social risk rather than for therapeutic intervention.[10] Indeed, one of the major criticisms of such programmes based on the Risks Needs Response (RNR) model is its 'one size fits all' approach that assumes all offenders to be of a similar nature (e.g. sexual, violent, etc.), and to a considerable extent ignores the social pathology and needs of the individual. There are, however, hopeful signs of a reappraisal of these approaches with the development of the Good Lives Model (GLM) that is considerably more oriented towards meeting individual needs and deficits based in positive psychology and humanistic traditions (Ward and Stewart, 2003 *op. cit.*; Ward and Gannon, 2008; Ward *et. al.*, *op. cit.*, 2007: 88-9).

What, then, is needed in effective community corrections? The answer to this bedrock question has to be unequivocal: clarity of vision and simplicity. We need to be clear about what the essential purposes of community sanctions are, and in what specific order of priority: we also need to devise a structure for meeting these priorities in a straightforward and appropriate manner that has 'stakeholder resonance'. The three preceding chapters and this one have provided a baseline for achieving these aims that can now be more clearly defined in an operational sense.

The structure proposed for National Correctional Services indicated at *Figure 13:2* (at p.192) clearly identifies an organisation of two distinctive elements: these were the Custodial Correctional Service and the Community Correctional Service respectively. Under the concept of reparative custody, the point of overlap between the two services is that at which offenders sentenced to this form of custody are, at an appropriate stage towards the expiry of their custodial sentences, released under conditional licence arrangements to work within local communities and return to prison custody each evening initially. This transition suggests that a joint working arrangement would be necessary between the two services for the supervision of released ex-prisoners by day (the Community CS), and by night (the Custodial CS) for those returning to prison custody each evening.

At *Figure 14:1* a comparison is provided of the different sentence structures between the 'traditional' model of imprisonment presently used in England and

---

10. Particularly in relation to sexual offending which has received the main focus of attention almost worldwide. Treatment programmes in North America, Britain, Australia and New Zealand have, in the main, concentrated on the Risks-Needs-Response (RNR) model that is primarily concerned with *risk management* rather than with individual change through therapeutic intervention. (Andrews and Bonta, 1998; Gendreau, 1996; Ward and Stewart, 2003 *op. cit.*).

Wales and the proposed reparative model of custody combined with a community service element. The illustrations show the different structures for sentences of 12 months and up to four years and those of over four years and of a determinate nature respectively. The following aspects of difference will be noted:

- both reparative custody models envisage a custody period of one third of the total sentence period combined with a community service period of similar (one third) length;
- the 'traditional' models involve mandatory imprisonment of one half of the sentence period, but combine automatic conditional release (ACR) and either extended imprisonment or discretionary conditional release (DCR /Parole) with ACR up to the two thirds point of sentence. Thereafter release is unconditional;
- the reparative custody model provides supervision in the community up to the three quarters stage in either sentence duration, but only the shorter (up to four years) sentence attracts unconditional release after this point;
- in both reparative custody sentence structures the period between one third and one half of the sentence spent on community service on conditional release requires offenders to return to prison-based custody at night;
- offenders sentenced to periods of over four years and selected for reparative custody remain subject to supervision in the community for the final (post-community service) third of their sentence periods, and do not attract unconditional release;
- parole (discretionary conditional release or DCR) would only apply to prisoners within the 'traditional' model of imprisonment serving sentences of four years or more, convicted of Criminal Justice and Immigration Act 2008 Schedule 15 (violent and sexual) offences, indeterminate or life sentences. DCR prisoners become eligible for parole consideration at or after the half-way point of their sentence, and remain on licence supervision (CR) to the date of sentence expiry (SLED): see Prison Service instruction 17/2008.
- the reparative custody model, while shortening the periods spent in prison custody, extends in both cases the periods spent under supervision in the community as compared with the 'traditional' model.

The impact of these arrangements on the size of the existing prison population is potentially considerable since sentences of less than twelve months (six months in custody) are abandoned. A sentence to two years reparative custody would reduce the time spent in prison from twelve to eight months, and one of four years from twenty-four to sixteen months in custody. These reductions are counter-balanced by the periods spent on community service under conditional release and supervision conditions which are of equal length. In terms of public protection the reparative

'TRADITIONAL' AND PROPOSED REPARATIVE CUSTODY SENTENCE STRUCTURES

'Traditional' model: ACR sentences of 12 months but less than 4 years imprisonment

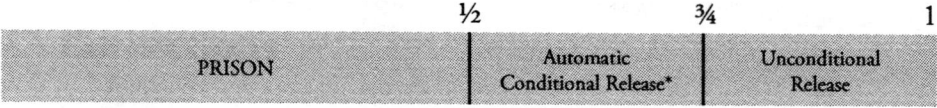

* On licence under supervision

Reparative Custody model: Sentences of 12 months and up to 4 years imprisonment

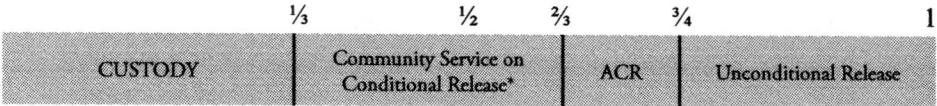

* From ⅓ to ½ point in night custody at prison

'Traditional' model: Fixed terms of 4 years or more subject to Criminal Justice and Immigration Act 2008 provisions post-9 June 2008*

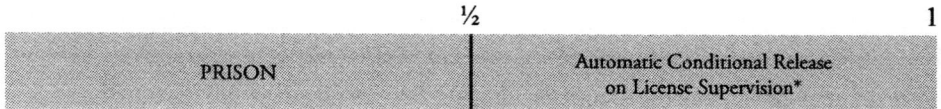

* Except those prisoners convicted of specified Schedule 15 (violent or sexual) offences who remain subject to the Criminal Justice Act 1991 DCR provisions for parole release at the half-way point of their sentences or later followed by supervision on licence to the supervision licence expiry date (SLED) (formerly the sentence expiry date (SED))

Reparative Custody model: Sentences of 4 years or more

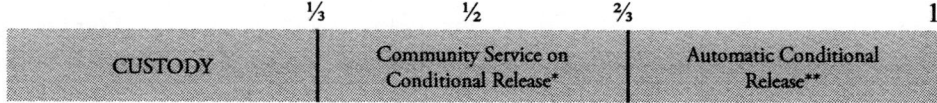

*From ⅓ to ½ point in night custody at prison. **On licence under supervision

Figure 14:1: 'Traditional' and Proposed Reparative Custody Sentence Structures

custody model provides for supervision in the community up to the two-thirds point of sentences between twelve months and four years, and for the entire sentence period for sentences of four years or longer, one quarter of which is presently spent on unconditional release within the 'traditional' model.

The suggestion has been made earlier in this chapter (at pp.197-8 *supra*) that the day to day supervision of offenders undertaking community service project work (whether as former prisoners on conditional release or those sentenced non-custodially to community service) should be exercised by uniformed members of the Community Correctional Service. The purpose of such a proposal is to create public confidence in community sanctions and also to ensure as far as possible that offenders would not subjected to abuse or opprobrium by the public while working in the community. It would also be appropriate for these officials to assume the responsibility for ensuring that former prisoners required to return to prison custody by night do so punctually, are in good order and properly accounted for, and are handed over officially to Custodial Correctional Service staff. The same officials would attend the prison on the following morning to accept responsibility for those offenders attending for community service project work that day.

Arrangements of the nature described here would, if implemented, enable community service project work to be visibly and accountably organised, and at the same time allow probation officers to concentrate on their primary role of counselling and supervising those offenders assigned to them on probation orders[11], and also take responsibility for the casework requirements of offenders undertaking community service in a similar manner.[12] In such a manner, the professional expertise of all correctional service staff would be used to maximum effect and enable viable career structures to be established for uniformed and non-uniformed grades of the Community Correctional Service alike.

Finally, under such conditions as have been described here, it is possible to envisage that only three or at the most four forms of non-custodial sanction would strictly be necessary in addition to the fine. These would be the probation order, the community service order, and possibly a modified version of the former attendance centre order that would require attendance at a Community Corrections Centre which would absorb the former role of attendance centres and be staffed by Community Correctional Service officials. Any of the remaining plethora of requirements[13] subsumed within the generic community order under the provisions of the

---

11. For which reason it is proposed that what became the community rehabilitation order and later part of a generic sentence should revert to its original form of the probation order, which is widely understood by the public and the courts, and has been so since 1907.
12. Such would include provision and delivery of accredited programmes, individual counselling and supervision, and, where appropriate, coordinating conferencing for offenders, victims and their families or close others.
13. These include the supervision, unpaid work, accredited programme, specified activity, prohibited activity, exclusion, residence, alcohol treatment, drug rehabilitation, mental health treatment, attendance centre

Criminal Justice Act 2003 might quite reasonably be made 'conditions' of either the probation or the community service order, or even of a combination order for both probation and community service.[14]

Arrangements of this nature would greatly simplify the entire operation of community corrections and make these sanctions much more easily understood by the public and offenders alike. More than this, perhaps, much needed public confidence in the entire concept of community corrections might be restored, and public attitudes, where such are punitive, might be amenable to modification. These are the issues that are drawn together in the final chapter of this work that follows.

---

and curfew. requirements Electronic monitoring can and in some cases must be added.
14. It would, however, make considerable sense to follow the Finnish model of sanctions by providing the courts with the ability to impose suspended sentences of imprisonment for periods up to two years in the form of community service or probation orders. These sanctions might be activated in the event of serious non-compliance with the latter sanctions in a custodial form, involving the offender in a return to either reparative or 'traditional' custody for the unexpired portion of the original sentence up to the two-thirds point, and thereafter on ACR and UR as indicated in *Figure 14.1*.

CHAPTER 15

Epilogue: The Case for Unified Restorative Corrections

Two of the recurring criticisms that have accompanied the rise to prominence of restorative justice within contemporary criminological discourse appear to be that it is too challenging in conceptual terms, and that it is entirely untested as a mainstream alternative to the traditional punitive justice model that has held sway for the past four decades at least. Neither of these objections is particularly remarkable except in the extent to which each reveals how evidently restorative justice has 'rattled the bars' of the traditionalist cage.

Within the present day penal system of England and Wales, as in many other countries that have become over-reliant on the use of imprisonment, the entire complex is in a state of gridlock that has created a sense of operational hopelessness and of conceptual paralysis. It is as though a new 'nothing works' era has percolated to the surface of criminal justice practice: all of the historically used punishment approaches have been tried (and have apparently proved ineffective), and increasing use of custody seems the only viable option for waging the 'war on crime'.

Restorative justice is, at least to politicians anxious to be seen to be 'tough on crime', and to their policy-makers, a very challenging proposition. It challenges many of the deeply entrenched belief systems about justice and retribution, the supposed effectiveness of deterrence, and the desirability of rehabilitation in a custodial penal context. Worse (or rather better perhaps), it starts by questioning and re-defining crime, guilt, and the nature of the harm done by crime to victims, communities and offenders themselves. And as much to the point, restorative justice speaks of punishing *less* and *differently* which places it immediately at odds with traditional culture of retributive justice.

This book, and the two that have preceded it in what has become a trilogy of commentaries on 'traditional' and restorative justice seeks to change that culture, not for the sake of change alone, but because there are sound and humane reasons for doing so. It does so because matters cannot remain as they are, because our contemporary retributive approach to justice causes more collateral damage than it repairs, and because, quite simply, there are ways of 'doing justice better', of doing it much less expensively, and of doing it with a greater potential to reduce offending and reoffending.

Within this final chapter there is no intention to rehearse in any considerable detail the discussion in those preceding it, but rather to suggest how the main issues that have been raised lead somewhat inevitably towards a different vision of how justice might be done better in a conceptual, structural and operational manner. This is now a matter of some compelling importance for politicians and those who make criminal justice policies, for academics and criminal justice practitioners, for victims of crime, for offenders and for communities.

CORRECTIONS IN CONTEXT

The term 'correction' has somewhat variable meaning in the different contexts in which it is encountered in modern usage. In relation to justice, however, there is a general consensus that it implies 'rebuking or punishing to set right': but to set what right? becomes a relevant question. Retributive justice insists that the 'right' is achieved by imposing reciprocal suffering on offenders in some or another proportion to a 'best guess' as to the harm that has been done (e.g. Wright, 2003:15-16 *op. cit.*). This is, at the least, a rather inexact way to behave, but it has traditionally attracted considerable support even though the 'deserved' extent of punishment is widely open to interpretation and evidently frequently exceeded.[1] Restorative justice, on the other hand, proposes that 'setting right' involves offenders in taking responsibility for wrongdoing and causing harm, and doing something substantial to make reparation to victims of crime.[2]

The difference between these two approaches precisely mirrors the nature of criminal justice within many modern democracies: retributive justice punishes without making any necessary demands upon offenders to respond or even accept guilt, but restorative justice perceives justice as unrequited unless or until guilt is acknowledged and reparation has been made. The former responds to the violation of the state and its law alone: the latter responds to victims primarily, and to providing the means by which offenders can, to some meaningful extent, make good the harm they have caused.

Correctional services within a restorative model of justice become facilitators of the 'setting right' process as opposed to being the agents of retrospective punishment, and do so from a number of different perspectives. First, these services provide the means by which reparation can be made and victims vindicated. Second, correctional services become enablers of offenders by identifying their social deficits and causes of offending, and by providing the counselling and support that can assist offenders to adopt law-abiding lifestyles. Third, these services can promote social cohesion within communities affected by crime by ensuring that the reparative actions of offenders are channelled towards improving the quality of community

---

1. Particularly in the form of 'extended sentences' and discretionary life sentences, the custodial terms of which are not specified at the time of conviction and imposition.
2. See here, for example the explanations of Schiff (1998), Marshall (1999:7) and Dignan (2002 *op. cit.*), each of whom describes the central purposes of restorative justice in almost identical terms.

life while at the same time making reparation to victims.

These simply made comparisons between retributive and restorative justice provide us with a number of indications as to why, in spite of its manifest potential advantages, restorative justice has been almost marginalized in Britain and in other countries that prefer to retain the 'traditional' approach to retributive justice. In the first place, restorative justice can be claimed to undermine the 'tough on crime' agenda simply because it urges less use of imprisonment and wider use of community sanctions. Second, restorative justice can be accused of being a 'soft option' for offenders against whom the 'war on crime' has to be waged with increasing intensity, no matter what the cost or the collateral damage in human terms. This is a matter as much of political expediency as much as one of political credibility. In the third place, public support for the 'war on crime' can only be maintained (apparently) by constant demonstration that citizens are made 'safer' because increasing numbers of criminals are 'neutralised' through incarceration in prisons where they can only harm each other. Restorative justice, it can be claimed, seeks to frustrate this apparently important social purpose.

The prevailing rhetoric of punishment – even punishment in the community – remains a powerful weapon in the political arsenal of social control. Reinforced by a visual and tabloid media that can be relied upon to 'demonise' criminal offenders, restorative justice can safely be marginalized because there is no evident need to test its claims and thus it seems to fail the 'evidence-led' litmus test of policy determination at the first hurdle. However, parts of the restorative penology that might attract some element of public approval (such as support for victims) can be 'cherry-picked' and used to demonstrate that criminal justice also has a 'caring face'. The cynical nature of this situation will not escape the reader of this work.

To make matters even worse from the viewpoint of proponents of restorative justice, any dilution of the term 'punishment' evokes strong reaction amounting to moral outrage in the political mind because it is an evident 'vote loser'. To confuse the public mind with an apparently semantic discussion of the merits of using the term 'correction' as opposed to 'punishment' can be dismissed as an exercise in obfuscation: the public mind has been conditioned to understand 'punishment' and applaud its use, and thus any other explanation amounts to the dilution of an essential social enterprise. This is the bleak side of the context within which an increasing worldwide interest in restorative corrections has to compete for space.

But is the 'public mind' actually made up and closed to further discussion, or is it rather a possibility that the passenger on the Clapham Omnibus is deliberately kept relatively uninformed about the potential advantages of adopting a restorative correctional agenda? How can it be the case that as short a time ago as 2003 the British government announced that it had a deliberate 'strategy' to 'maximise the use of restorative justice in the Criminal Justice System as it works well at both addressing the needs of the victim and in reducing reoffending'? (Home Office, 2003a:1 *op. cit.*). The reader will recall that this was also the year in which the same government published its Criminal Justice Act 2003 setting out the provisions for increased use of prison custody 'plus', 'minus', and 'intermittent'.

The counter-arguments in this context have been set out at some length in the preceding chapters of this book, and are at least as compelling as those of the punitive rhetoric are disingenuous. It suffices at this juncture to insist that a restorative penology represents no soft option for offenders: indeed, it demands more of them and does more for victims than any retributive agenda has ever even attempted. In insisting that less use can safely and usefully be made of prison custody the restorative penology can rely upon the practical (evidence-led) experience of countries such as Finland, Germany and elsewhere that have deliberately implemented such policies and found them successful. In advancing the case for greater use of non-custodial sanctions the restorative penology promotes the wider participation of citizens and communities within criminal justice, minimises the collateral damage to offenders and their close others, and maximises the social benefits to victims and communities.

REVIEWING THE STRUCTURE OF JUSTICE

Implementation of significant change in governmental structures is always resisted, resented and politically uncomfortable. These are the three major reasons why inertia and maintenance of the *status quo* remain preferable options for change avoidance however compelling the case for change may be. The entire criminal justice structure in Britain as elsewhere is to a marked extent protected from change by a massive reliance upon tradition, precedent, judicial independence, symbolism and dogma that are the 'sacred cows' to be unquestionably protected and even venerated. Indeed the pompous 'majesty' of the law is spoken of as an immutable entity, the 'dignity' of which must be upheld at almost any cost and upon every occasion. The law even expresses itself in its own linguistic *formulae* shrouded in historical anachronism to which deference must be paid.

A principal difficulty posed by restorative justice is that it openly questions the foundational basis upon which the law traditionally operates. It views crime as a violation of people and relationships rather than a violation of the law and state, and of violations as creating obligations as opposed to guilt (Zehr, 2002: 21 *op. cit*). In so doing, it places the importance of retributive punishment in a position secondary to that of involving citizens (victims, offenders, communities) in 'putting wrongs right'. This set of propositions, anathema to many lawyers, allows it to be marginalized, because it is uncomfortably contentious rather than because it is fundamentally erroneous.[3]

---

3. The reader will note that restorative justice does not deny that crime violates the law of the state, but proposes that this is ultimately of lesser importance than the violation that crime causes to victims and

The point made about axiomatic punishment in the preceding footnote (fn.3) is, I would venture to suggest, one of profound importance for this discussion. The reason for this contention is that 'axiomatic' punishment feeds the cause and effect relationship between offences and penalties that compels punishment, and that once there is a compulsion to punish there is a danger that punishment becomes 'instrumental'.[4] The compulsion to punish is nowadays sustained in a number of different ways: through the excessive use of discriminatory sentences of an extended and indeterminate nature for sexual and violent offences; discretionary release (parole) mechanisms which are heavily dependent on questionable predictions of dangerousness; and measures such as imprisonment for public protection that bear no distinct relationship either to desert or culpability.

Largely because of the virtual impossibility of making punishments proportionate to the harm caused by offences, and the danger that in the nature of sentencing processes (however apparently tightly controlled) the extent of punishment for like offences will inevitably be inconsistent, a number of writers on criminal punishment have argued strong cases for its total abolition as morally unjustifiable other than in a very few exceptionally serious cases demanding public protection. (e.g. Wright, 1999 and 2003 15-18 *op. cit.*; Fatić, 1995: 255; Hoyles, 1986:139). Most of these writers prefer the term 'sanction' to express social disapproval of criminal offending, and, like proponents of restorative justice, perceive reparation as preferable to retribution.

Whether or not the act of making reparation either voluntarily or as required by a court in response to an offence can be construed as 'punishment' becomes a moot point. The classical approach would insist that reparation could only be considered as punishment if it involved the infliction of 'pain' or unpleasantness (see e.g. Ewing, 1929; Hart, 1968 *op. cit.*: 4-5; Wasserstrom, 1977: 173; Galligan, 1981 *op. cit.*: 145). Reparation does, however, fulfil the criteria normally associated with sanctions, and brings with it the additional satisfaction of victim and community recompense in a neo-utilitarian sense. The rather more important point at issue here is that our traditionally inherited predisposition to regard punishment as an inevitable and necessary concomitant of guilt may have to be to some extent modified if the benefits of restorative and reparative justice are to be realised.

---

communities. Similarly, while crime does create guilt viewed in a traditional sense, the obligation of the offender to 'purge' this guilt is of greater social significance than the fact that the guilt exists and must, axiomatically, be punished.

4. My colleague John Blad has described 'instrumental punishment' most clearly as the use of sanctions as a means of achieving social policy objectives rather than within strict limits as a response to particular offences. He has termed this the 'seductiveness of punishment', particularly in relation to the use of imprisonment with its tendency to exacerbate rather than resolve the causal aspects of criminal offending. (Blad, 2006: 137-9 *op. cit.*).

This situation does not arise in relation to the concept of reparative custody proposed in this work since the element of deprivation of liberty during the custodial period of a reparative custody sentence is present and constitutes punishment in a strict and sufficient sense. Moreover, if we regard the 'traditional' non-custodial penalties of community service, probation and fines as sanctions, then dependence upon strict proportionality has not hitherto been perceived as a dominant issue.

Structural justice, it would seem, relies upon judicial processes being seen to be 'user conscious' and intelligible from the viewpoint not primarily of those who administer them, but possibly more importantly from the situation of the 'consumers' who are offenders, witnesses, victims and their advisers. To these 'consumers' fairness means rather more than strict impartiality; 'user consciousness' means more than merely being present (whether voluntarily or otherwise), and intelligibility means that one does not have to be an accredited legal professional to understand how the process is conducted and what is being said.

Restorative justice in practice suggests that for trial hearings to have meaning for all the legitimate stakeholders, it would be preferable for a more informal and inclusive process to be used than that of the 'traditional' courts. Such is not to suggest that the established rules of hearing procedure and evidence should be in any sense abandoned, but rather that the proceedings should at least be entirely intelligible to defendants, and that witnesses should not feel intimidated or over-awed by the *grandeur* of the court procedures and the behaviour of legal professionals.

Courts and court procedures deserve to be respected and important traditions need to be preserved, but it might be suggested as a *sine qua non* of real justice that all those tried within the courts should feel that the rules of natural justice have been fully applied in every case, that whatever their level of literacy and comprehension their account has been properly heard, and that the outcomes are indeed fairly arrived at. Internationally there is considerable debate as to whether adversarial[5] or inquisitorial[6] trial modes produce the greater fairness of outcomes (e.g. van Koppen and Penrod, 2003), but that particular discussion extends far beyond the scope of this analysis.

Structural justice implies that the law is enforced and justice is administered in a manner that is conscious of the outcomes for all the stakeholders legitimately concerned, and not merely as a self-serving process that must be undertaken in satisfaction of its own agendas. Thus to imprison offenders in conditions that cannot lead to their improvement or does not even seek to do so becomes a mechanistic

---

5. Adversarial justice systems are of the type used in Britain, the USA and in other countries such as those of the former British Commonwealth that inherited their judicial processes from the British model of jurisprudence.
6. Inquisitorial justice systems follow the original French model of post-revolutionary jurisprudence that has been widely adopted throughout the continent of Europe and in other countries worldwide that were former colonies of European nations.

and uncivilised endeavour that is, at least, morally questionable. To become morally acceptable, either the conditions have to be changed or other ways found of dealing with wrongdoing in a manner that strictly limits the social damage caused by the punitive process.

PROBLEMS OF ENHANCING OPERATIONAL JUSTICE

The central thread that has run through this work is that of making criminal justice operationally more 'useful' in a social sense, and of proposing the principles and practices of restorative justice as a means of doing so. When offenders are found guilty and punished (or sanctioned) it might be said that they have a reasonable expectation – if not a right – to believe that having endured the process of censure, a place within their communities and the wider society should be open to them contingent upon adoption of a law-abiding lifestyle. The duty of assisting them to do this is normally assigned within the mission statements or statements of purpose of national correctional services.

Within many modern democracies criminal offender populations display remarkably similar demographic characteristics, and are disproportionately represented by relatively young, socially disadvantaged, poorly educated, unemployed (or unemployable) persons many of whom also display symptoms of substance addiction or abuse, mental impairment, chronic ill-health, familial breakdown, and the like. In many penal populations also, people from ethnic minorities are over-represented within the population profile in addition to sharing the same socially dysfunctional backgrounds. In a number of respects these persons are already among life's casualties prior to their contacts with criminal justice systems.

When these already disadvantaged persons commit criminal offences they, like any others, must expect legal systems and processes to respond with measures that are consistent with the extent of the harm caused or seriousness of crimes committed, but the purpose of which is to promote desistance from offending in the future. Commitment to prison custody is now, in most democracies, the most severe response at the state's disposal for dealing with serious offenders and offences, and therefore should be used only when there is no reasonable alternative to doing so.

All of this stated, however, doing justice equitably[7] means that the causes of offending receive as much attention in a correctional sense as the nature of the offences committed and the harm these have caused to others – most notably the immediate victims of crimes. Criminal justice in Britain, as in many countries else-

---

7. Which in this context is taken to mean administering justice with the qualities of reasonableness, fairness and impartiality that should not necessarily be confused with the notion of 'uniformity'. It means dealing with offenders primarily in accordance with their needs and deficits rather than treating them as a homogeneous population supposedly displaying similar personal characteristics and behaviours.

where in the world over the past two or three decades, has demonstrated an abundant willingness to be 'tough on crime' and an equally abundant reluctance to demonstrate 'toughness on the causes of crime'. The results of such policies are evident in the over-use of prisons, a lack of 'corrective' regimes within them, and high rates of reoffending because offenders leave custody unchanged other than possibly for the worse as a result of their incarceration. As Andrew Scull has insisted:

> Not only does processing by such institutions inflict more visible, organised and ineradicable stigma than is commomly bestowed in informal inter-action, but it exposes the inmate to the powerful socialising impact of institutional existence. And contrary to a century and a half of rhetoric by institutional custodians, the effect of this socialisation is not to cure or rehabilitate, but to perpetuate and intensify the underlying pathology. (Scull, 1983: 151)

In the final analysis, to behave in such a manner represents, as Michael Tonry (2003:6 *op. cit.*), David Garland (2001 *op. cit.*) and others have indicated, the pursuit of policies of deliberate political choice. The outcomes are not accidental since other options are available, but these remain untried or unused because change-averse bureaucrats and politicians pathologically dislike risk-taking.

A reparative and restorative penology as sketched in this work does address these issues and responds in a very direct manner. It urges lesser use of imprisonment where this is avoidable, and when it is not avoidable it proposes using imprisonment for the shortest possible duration and linked to community sanctions. The same penology promotes increased use of community penalties *per se*, conscious of the fact that these can be both educative and of community benefit. More than this however, a reparative focus within both custodial and community sanctions places victims of crime at the forefront of considerations.

Both structurally and operationally, the unification of correctional services proposed here is, far from being an exercise in bureaucratic rationalisation, a deliberate attempt to use professional expertise appropriately and create a 'seamless' penal system that recognises the essential differences between custodial and community corrections but unifies them within a common ethos. We return to this particular innovation in some greater detail in the final part of this chapter, but it has a distinctive bearing upon the entire manner in which restorative practices could transform the way in which criminal justice is conceived in the future.

The ethos of a reparative and restorative penology is undoubtedly its defining strength and its ultimate morality. Its primary focus is upon repairing the harm and violation of relationships that crime causes between offenders, victims and communities. It is not insistent on inflicting retributive punishment for its own sake upon those who may already be disadvantaged or who might become so as a result of being so punished. Rather it seeks to enable and empower offenders to desist from further crime by treating them as rational actors and addressing, as far as possible, the dysfunctional aspects of their lives that encourage offending.

In exactly the same way that judicial processes should be intelligible to those dealt with in courts, the operational functioning of correctional services requires a coherence of purpose that is simple, visible, appropriate and reliable. In addition it should ideally *add* value and amenity to the lives of victims and communities, and restore the self-respect of those who are subject to its administration and supervision. Traditional criminal justice models heavily dependent on imprisonment consume resources voraciously without returning any value other than the supposition of social protection: at the same time the collateral damage that is created is immense, and extends to those persons close to offenders who may have committed no offences but who become social casualties by proxy.

The importance of effective operational management of correctional services cannot be over-stated. This starts with the necessity for absolute clarity about the aim[8] of criminal justice policy and its separation from the capricious behaviour of politicians who may use it instrumentally as a vehicle for electoral advantage or to further other social policy objectives. Criminal justice policy should exemplify the virtues of simplicity and pragmatism: if those who make this policy really want to know 'what works', then the best advice will invariably come from experienced practitioners who have to interpret policies into operational practice on a consistent daily basis. However, as David Garland (2001:151 *op. cit.*) has so clearly pointed out, the development of a managerial culture and the politicisation of crime over recent years have significantly reduced the influence of practitioners and professionals within the criminal justice policy arena, and with predictable results:

> Today, there is a new and urgent emphasis upon the need for security, the containment of danger, the identification and management of any kind of risk. Protecting the public has become the dominant theme of penal policy. (Garland, 2001:12 *op. cit.*)

And:

> The key problem facing governments is the need simultaneously to withdraw and reassert their authority as the provider of crime control and public safety. Garland argues that the state's efforts to adapt to or avoid this problem have resulted in a set of contradictory policies that in themselves represent a schizophrenic adherence to polarised criminological frameworks. (Matravers and Hughes, 2003:74 *op. cit.*)

Obsessive concentration upon public protection has successfully over-filled the

---

8. Here the singular form is of critical importance: multiple aims confuse and frequently conflict. If the central purpose of criminal justice is 'to reduce criminal offending' then there is much virtue in stating it thus and without further embellishment or qualification. Desired subsidiary outcomes such as 'providing support and reparation for crime victims', 'enabling offenders to desist from crime', 'enhancing public safety' and 'providing for the safe, secure and humane custody of prisoners' can be so expressed, but remain secondary considerations to the centrality of crime reduction.

prisons of England and Wales to record levels of occupation, and continues to do so in a current 'crisis of numbers' that shows no signs of abating. Many of those incarcerated are relatively low-risk offenders, and in particular, low-risk sexual offenders. Media pressure has, however, fuelled the obsession to 'manage out' the *presumed* risk posed by such offenders, and politicians have responded with criminal justice policies that reflect this obsession rather than making a rational assessment of the *actual* risk that these offenders present of further offending. Such behaviours make the operational management of criminal justice prone to crisis, confusion and failure.

For our purposes here, however, the question is whether adoption of a restorative penology would resolve the contemporary *impasse*, and if so, how this might be achieved. Much might depend upon the extent to which state governments decide, or can be persuaded to embrace restorative principles within criminal justice and implement these in operational practice. However, as Carolyn Boyes-Watson has so shrewdly observed:

> There is no denying the fundamental incompatibility between the state system of doing justice and the principles of restorative justice. The state operates through impersonal and rationalized procedures administered by disinterested professionals with specialized legal, administrative and penal expertise. The goal is to punish, manage or rehabilitate people who violate the law to maintain control over its jurisdiction. Restorative justice, by contrast, seeks to delegate decision-making and control to those individuals directly involved in the incident. The goal is to harness the power of relationships to heal that which has been harmed and to empower the community to engage in processes of repair, reconciliation and redemption in order to restore balance in the wake of harm...
>
> It is sensible to be skeptical about state involvement in restorative justice. One need only reflect on previous criminal justice reforms – the penitentiary, the reformatory, the juvenile court, probation, diversion programmes and community corrections – to see a dismal pattern of good intentions gone awry (Rothman, 1980). In each instance, the ideal vision of reformers was undermined by forces beyond their control and imagination. Likely pitfalls for state-sponsored restorative justice include: lip-service for victims (Reeves and Mulley, 2000); re-victimization of victims (Achilles and Zehr, 2001; Brown, 1994); the phenomenon of net-widening (Levant *et al.*, 1999; Polk, 1994); erosion of due process for offenders (Delgado, 2000, Warner, 1994); professionalization of the restorative process (Daly and Immarigeon, 1998), rationalization of the process (Umbreit, 1999) ... and deeper penetration of the state into the community (Cohen, 1985). (Boyes-Watson, 2004: 215-6)

Many of the prescriptions within this work have been made with a view to pre-empting the sort of pitfalls suggested by Boyes-Watson and others above[9], but there is already evidence that these are real in operational terms[10] and that it would be fanciful to overlook their potential to subvert the true purposes of a restorative penology.

---

9. And in particular Mark Umbreit *et al.* (2005b *op. cit.*) whose analysis follows a remarkably similar pattern.
10. As has been evidenced in Britain in the policies of the present government towards victims of crime as described in *Chapter 5* and elsewhere within this work.

UNIFICATION OR BUST?

The title of this book, *The Penal Crisis and the Clapham Omnibus: Questions and Answers in Restorative Justice*, though perhaps somewhat unusual, was deliberately chosen to reflect the critical nature of, and need for public engagement with, the search for a new criminal justice paradigm that might better meet the needs of modern societies intent on reducing criminal offending. It embraces the continuing need to retain the use of prisons, though on a much more modest scale and with somewhat different guiding purposes; the evident requirement to make more extensive and effective use of community sanctions; and the need to convince what might be anticipated to be a sceptical public that communities and citizens can have an active and vital involvement in criminal justice delivery.

In many respects the Clapham Omnibus and its passengers become both the vehicle and the facilitators of this restorative penology since without their acceptance that a new approach to criminal justice is necessary and a willingness within communities to become involved in its implementation, penal policies will, inevitably, remain much as they are and probably even worse. This is a situation far from unique to Britain, and it might be held to be reflected in many parts of the world in which prison custody is over-used, but it represents an almost wanton wastefulness of human lives, financial resources and social cohesion that few democracies can afford to contemplate and continue to prosper.

In terms of the British situation and specifically that of England and Wales, the present penal crisis must be regarded as the latest in a series of linked and recurring crises that have at intervals almost paralysed the Criminal Justice System over the past thirty or so years. The extraordinary feature of these crises is that they have proved to be predictable, avoidable, and display consistent similarities resulting from excessive use of imprisonment. Each successive crisis thus presents the same persistent dilemma: do we want fewer prisoners or more prisons? Historically in Britain, as indeed in the USA, The Netherlands, New Zealand and Australia, Canada and so many other nations, the selected option has been to 'build one's way out of trouble', lock up increasing numbers of citizens – and for longer periods – and absorb the vast cost which could better be invested in other forms of social provision which suffer as a result.

But lest it be still unclear, prisons do not change very many people for the better, have never done so, and probably never will. Moreover, there is as Doob and Webster (2003: 143) point out, 'little or no consistent evidence that harsher sentences reduce crime in Western populations.' Hence the lack of clarity of penal aims previously cited: is it to be 'social protection' which is illusory, or is it to be crime reduction – probably equally illusory through more and longer imprisonment- or is it time to accept the 'no win this way hypothesis'? Time perhaps at least to accept the adage that prisons are inherently an expensive way of making bad people worse. Does the averagely thoughtful taxpayer still want to continue to invest in failure indefinitely?

Within this book there have been glimpses of the ways by which criminal justice could be better delivered. As a starting point we could resolve to reduce the prison population, keep it stable, and eventually make better use of fewer prisons by introducing the concept of reparative custody.[11] At the same time we could resolve to increase and simplify the use of community corrections and make these work to the benefit of offenders, victims and communities themselves.[12] We could resolve to accept the marginal social risk of every reparative custody sentence including a community service element, and thereby create a visible 'bridge' between custodial and community corrections.[13] We could resolve to create and operate truly unified National Correctional Services with constituent Custodial and Community Correctional Service elements operated on an area basis.[14]

From the viewpoint of community involvement in criminal justice we could resolve to create area community justice forums[15] to identify community service projects and participate in the co-ordination of the work done by offenders to add amenity value to communities. We could also resolve to establish multi-purpose Community Corrections Centres[16] that would provide facilities for probation supervision, delivery of pre-trial and post-sentence conferencing, offending behaviour and addiction programmes, victim: offender counselling, and the co-ordination of community project work. All of these resolutions could be delivered if we were to resolve to decrease the use of imprisonment.

If, as seems to be probable, NOMS is to be 'overhauled' in the foreseeable future, then the combination of initiatives described here would seem to satisfy the needs of both the existing Prison and Probation Services for change that could enable both Services to deliver their roles more effectively. Indeed, such a re-structuring would be an essential starting point for such change to be implemented. But it has to be stressed that a reorganisation of this nature comes as a package of interdependent elements that rely for success on delivery of the whole, and that 'cherry-picking' them piecemeal would jeopardise the enterprise.

Ultimately, however, the 'war against crime' so often referred to by politicians as the dominant 'crusade' of the new millennium is the battle for the mind and acceptance of the passenger on the Clapham Omnibus. It has to be waged on terrain that has few of the familiar landmarks left that have been used for navigation in

---

11. See *Chapter 13* at pp.181-182
12. See *Chapter 14* at pp.204-209.
13. See *Chapter 14* at pp.205-208 and *Figure 14:1*.
14. See *Chapter 13* at pp. 189-194 and *Figure 13:2*.
15. See *Chapter 13* at pp.191.
16. See *Chapter 13* at pp. 189-194.

the past, and most probably under the heavy bombardment of the mass media and its artillery. It is, however, a battle that can be won by reason, determination, and a genuine desire to deliver better justice for the benefit of all the members of our communities.

Accepting change is undeniably difficult unless its outcomes are so evidently beneficial as to make the process desirable or inevitable. Change is individually and collectively challenging and unwelcome to those for whom the inertia of the *status quo* is comfortable, even if it is evidently ineffective. The outcomes of change are always uncertain to some extent, and require courage, commitment and energy to secure its advantages. Preserving tradition for its own sake is the last bastion of the anti-progressive and the ultimate refuge of the intransigent and the reluctant. The NOMS of England and Wales faces all of these uncertainties and resistances, but in the final analysis change is forced upon it and must be accepted if an even deeper crisis of 'numbers', professionalism and credibility is to be averted.

Many other jurisdictions face similar problems and the solutions to these difficulties cannot always be 'evidence-led', but they can stand the test of reason. Restorative justice has accumulated an impressive following of criminal justice practitioners, academics, legal professionals, and lay people who support its principles and practices as a means of creating more effective justice systems. These experienced and far-sighted proponents cannot all be deluded or misguided, and many of them have significant experience of 'what works'. The question is how long it will be before they are listened to seriously.

Both Prison and Probation Services in England and Wales are working under almost intolerable levels of organisational stress and overload in which professionals cannot deliver either the extent or the quality of service that society or the government expects of them. Exceptionally, Anne Owers, HM Chief Inspector of Prisons spoke publicly of the situation in February 2008 in these words:

> As you hit each new peak, the prison system is bumping against a new crisis. For the last six months we've been looking at a system that moves from panic stations to just about containing crisis...
>
> Prisoners are getting very frustrated; staff are struggling to survive the day. That's not a good recipe for running prisons. It's a very risky situation...
>
> You wouldn't start from here if you wanted to create a decent prison system.. This is a result of decisions taken – or not taken – a long time ago. (Anne Owers, HMCIP quoted in Doward, 2008:2)

At the same time as this statement was made, Harry Fletcher, the General Secretary of the National Association of Probation Officers was warning that the Service did not have the resources to handle a sudden influx of offenders diverted from prison to community sentences, and the Justice Secretary Jack Straw was urging on magistrates and judges a wider use of non-custodial sentences rather than expanding the use of early release schemes for prisoners introduced in 2007[17]. All in all, this describes a penal system verging on chaos.

Of course the answer is not to off-load offenders from one over-burdened sector of the penal system onto the other sector that is equally overstretched: the remedy, if there is one, is as suggested here, to have fewer prisoners in the first place and make wider use of community sanctions. In reality, and if present penal policies are to be retained, there is no solution other than to adopt a 'gulag' philosophy that will warehouse unlimited numbers of offenders, and accept high and increasing rates of recidivism. A restorative penology at least offers an alternative and more positive strategy. Unification or bust? Told the stark truth, one might suspect that the informed observer would opt for a unified correctional system and for a restorative penology.

This book has been written in the hope that common sense and reason rather than dogma and ideological blindness may one day prevail within the penal system of England and Wales in particular, and within other penal systems in, or approaching, similar crises. Until such a time is reached, neither offenders, victims, communities, nor the passengers on the Clapham Omnibus, will receive the criminal justice that they deserve. A restorative penology and a truly unified correctional services system would go a long way towards providing more effective justice.

---

17. Here, see Home Office, HM Prison Service (2007), *Prison Service Instruction27/2007 – End of Custody Licence (ECL)*, London: Home Office (June 19). This document sets out the arrangements and conditions for the release from custody up to 18 days prior to their scheduled discharge under AUR or ACR provisions of adult prisoners in certain categories serving sentences of between four weeks and up to four years in duration as a means of easing pressure on prison places. The provision specifically excludes sexual and violent offenders, those who have previously failed to comply with temporary release (ROTL) conditions, and those of no fixed abode on discharge.

Bibliography

Achilles, M. (2004), 'Can Restorative Justice Live Up To Its Promise to Victims?', in H. Zehr and B. Toews (eds), *Critical Issues in Restorative Justice*, Devon, UK: Willan Publishing and Monsey, NY: Criminal Justice Press, pp.65-73.

Achilles, M. and Zehr, H. (2001), 'Restorative Justice for Crime Victims: The Promise and the Challenge', in G. Bazemore and M. Schiff (eds), *Restorative Community Justice: Repairing Harm and Transforming Communities*, Cincinnati, OH: Anderson Publishing.

Acton, H.B. (ed) (1969), *The Philosophy of Punishment: A Collection of Papers*, London: Macmillan.

Adams, R. (1992), *Prison Riots in Britain and the USA*, Basingstoke: Macmillan.

Allen, F. A. (1959), 'Criminal Justice, Legal Values and the Rehabilitative Ideal', in *Journal of Criminal Law, Criminology and Police Science*, vol. 50 (3), pp.226-232.

Allen, F. A. (1972), 'The Rehabilitative Ideal', in R. J. Gerber and P. D. McAnany (eds), *Contemporary Punishment*, London and Notre Dame: University of Notre Dame Free Press, pp.209-218.

Allen, F. A. (1981), *The Decline of the Rehabilitative Ideal*, New Haven and London: Yale University Press.

American Friends Service Committee (1972), *Struggle for Justice*, New York: Hill & Wang.

Anderson, A. M. (2003), *Restorative Justice, the African Philosophy of Ubuntu, and the Diversion of Criminal Prosecution*, Pretoria, RSA: University of South Africa School of Law, pp.1-13 available at http://209.89.165.104/Search?q=cache:cw2mh_AIJ.www.isrcl.org/Papers/Anderson.pdf.

Andrews, D. A. and Bonta, J. (1998), *The Psychology of Criminal Conduct* (2nd Edition), Cincinnati, OH: Anderson Publishing.

Armstrong, K. G. (1961), 'The Retributivist Hits Back' in H. B. Acton (ed) (1969), *The Philosophy of Punishment: A Collection of Papers*, London: Macmillan, pp.138-158.

Ashworth, A. (1993a), 'Some Doubts About Restorative Justice', in *Criminal Law Forum*, vol.4, pp.277-299.

Ashworth, A. (1993b), 'Victim Impact Statements and Sentencing', in *Criminal Law Review*, (1993), pp.498-509.

Atkinson, D. (2004), 'The What Works Debate: Keeping a Human Perspective', in *Probation Journal*, vol.51 (3), pp.248-252.

Auden, W. H. and Kronenberger, L. (eds) (1962), *The Faber Book of Aphorisms*, London: Faber and Faber Limited.

Auld, Sir R. (LJ) (2001), *Review of the Criminal Courts of England and Wales – Report*, London: The Stationery Office.

Baier, K.E. (1955), 'Is Punishment Retributive?' in H. B. Acton (ed) (1969), *The Philosophy of Punishment: A Collection of Papers*, London: Macmillan, pp.130-137.

Barclay, G. C. and Tavares, C. (eds) (1999), *Information on the Criminal Justice System in England and Wales*, Digest 4, London: Home Office Research and Statistics Directorate.

Bazemore, G. (1999), 'After Shaming, Whither Reintegration: Restorative Justice and Relational Rehabilitation', in G. Bazemore (ed), *Restorative Juvenile Justice*, New York:

Criminal Justice Press.
Bazemore, G. and Umbreit, M. (1995), 'Re-Thinking the Sanctioning Function in Juvenile Courts: Retributive or Restorative Responses to Youth Crime', in *Journal of Crime and Delinquency*, vol.41, no.3, pp.296-316.
BBC News 24, *Numbers Pressure Causes Prison Suicides*, http//news.bbc.co.uk/i/hi/uk/3157873.stm (4 May 2004).
Bean, P. (1981), *Punishment: A Philosophical and Criminological Inquiry*, Oxford: Martin Robertson.
Beccaria, C. (1764), *On Crimes and Punishment*, (tr. H. Paolucci), Indianapolis: Bobbs -Merrill (1963).
Becker, H. S. (1963), *Outsiders: Studies in the Sociology of Deviance*, Glencoe, ILL: Free Press.
Bentham, J. (1830), 'Principles of Penal Law' (Part 2 – The Rationale of Punishment) in J. Bentham, *Collected Works*, (J. Bowring (ed) (1962)), London: Russell and Russell.
Bentham, J. (1948), *An Introduction to the Principles of Morals and Legislation*, London: Macmillan.
Bhui, H. S. (2005), 'Effective Probation Practice and NOMS' in *Probation Journal*, vol.52, no,3, pp.219-220.
Biestek, F.P. (1961), *The Casework Relationship*, London: Unwin University Books.
Blad, J. R. (2003), 'Against Penal Instrumentalism: Building a Global Alliance for Restorative Justice Processes and Family Empowerment', *Proceedings of the 4th International Conference on Conferencing, Circles and Other Restorative Practices*, pp.130-141.
Blad, J. R. (2006a), 'The Seductiveness of Punishment and the Case for Restorative Justice: The Netherlands', in D. J. Cornwell, *Criminal Punishment and Restorative Justice*, Hook, UK: Waterside Press, pp.135-148.
Blad, J. R. (2006b), 'Institutionalising Restorative Justice: Transforming Criminal Justice', in I. Aertsen, T. Daems and L. Roberts (eds), *Institutionalising Restorative Justice*, Devon, UK: Willan Publishing, pp.93-117.
Blom-Cooper, L. and Drewry, G. (eds) (1976), *Law and Morality: A Reader*, London: Duckworth.
Bottomley, A. K. (1979), *Criminology in Focus*, London: Martin Robertson.
Bottoms, Sir A.E. (1977), 'Reflections on the Renaissance of Dangerousness' in *Howard Journal of Criminal Justice*, vol. XVI, no.2, pp.70-96.
Bottoms, Sir A.E. (1995), 'The Politics of Sentencing Reform', in C. Clarkson and R. Morgan (eds), *The Philosophy and Politics of Punishment and Sentencing*, Oxford: Oxford University Press, pp.17-49.
Bottoms, Sir A. E. and Stevenson, S. (1992), 'What Went Wrong? Criminal Justice Policy in England and Wales 1945-1970', in D. Downes (ed), *Unravelling Criminal Justice*, Basingstoke: Macmillan, pp. 1-45.
Bottoms, Sir A. E., Rex, S. and Robinson, G. (eds) (2004), *Alternatives to Prison: Options for an Insecure Society*, Devon, UK: Willan Publishing.
Box, S. (1971), *Deterrence, Reality and Society*, London: Holt Reinhart & Winston (and see 2nd Edition, 1981).
Boyes-Watson, C. (2004), 'What Are the Implications of the Growing State Involvement in Restorative Justice?' in H. Zehr and B. Toews (eds), *Critical Issues in Restorative Justice*,

New York: Criminal Justice Press and Devon, UK: Willan Publishing, pp.215-226.
Braithwaite, J. (1989), *Crime, Shame and Reintegration*, Cambridge: Cambridge University Press.
Braithwaite, J. and Strang, H. (2001), 'Introduction: Restorative Justice and Civil Society' in H. Strang and J. Braithwaite (eds), *Restorative Justice and Civil Society*, Cambridge: Cambridge University Press.
Brown, J. (1994), 'The Use of Mediation to Resolve Criminal Cases: A Procedural Critique' in *Emory Law Journal*, vol.43, pp.1247-1309.
Brunk, C. (2001), 'Restorative Justice and Philosophical Theories of Criminal Punishment' in M. L. Hadley (ed), *The Spiritual Roots of Restorative Justice*, Albany, NY: University of New York Free Press, pp.31-56.
Buchanan, J. (2006), 'The Paradox of Penal Policy' in *Probation Journal*, vol.53(2), pp.107-108.
Burnett, R. and McNeill, F. (2005), 'The Place of Officer-Offender Relationship in Assisting Offenders to Desist from Crime' in *Probation Journal*, vol. 52(3), pp.221-242.
Carlen, P. (1994), 'Crime, Inequality and Sentencing', in A. Duff and D. Garland (eds), *A Reader on Punishment*, Oxford: Oxford University Press.
Carlson, P. M. and Garrett, J.S. (2005), *Prison and Jail Administration: Practice and Theory*, Sudbury, Massachusetts: Jones and Bartlett Publishers.
Cavadino, M. and Dignan, J. (1997), *The Penal System: An Introduction* (2nd edition), London: SAGE Publications.
Cavadino, M., Crow, I. And Dignan, J. (1999), *Criminal Justice 2000: Strategies for a New Century*, Hook, UK: Waterside Press.
Cid, J. (2005), 'Suspended Sentences in Spain: Decarceration and Recidivism' in *Probation Journal*, vol. 52(2), pp.169-179.
Centre for Criminal Justice Studies (2008), 'Risk of Becoming a Victim of Crime at 27-year Low', *Daily News Summary*, London: King's College, (25 January), p.1.
Clemmer, D. (1940), *The Prison Community*, New York: Rinehart and Co.
Cloward, R. (ed) (1960), *Theoretical Studies in the Social Organisation of the Prison*, New York SSRC: Occasional Paper 15.
Coates, R.B., Umbreit, M.S. and Vos, B. (2000), *Restorative Justice Circles in South Saint Paul, Minnesota*, at: http://2ssw.che.umn.edu/rjp/Resources/Documents/Circles.Final.Revised.pdf.
Cohen, S. (1985), *Visions of Social Crime, Punishment and Classification*, New York: Polity Press.
Cohen, S. and Taylor, L. (1972), *Psychological Survival: The Experience of Long-Term Imprisonment*, Harmondsworth: Penguin Books.
Cohen, S. and Taylor, L. (1978), *Prison Secrets*, London: NCCL/RAP.
Cole, G. F. and Smith, C. E. (2004), *Criminal Justice in America* (4th Edition), Belmont, California: Thomson Wadsworth.
Conrad, J. P. (1973), 'Corrections and Simple Justice', in *Journal of Criminal Law and Criminology*, vol.64, pp.208-217.
Cormier, R. B. (2006), 'Where There's a Will, There's a Way: A Canadian Perspective on Restorative Justice', in D. J. Cornwell, *Criminal Punishment and Restorative Justice*, Hook, UK: Waterside Press, pp.149-162.

Cornwell, D.J. (1989), *Criminal Dangerousness and Its Punishment: Beyond the Phenomenological Illusion*, D. Phil. Thesis, University of York, pp.210-222.

Cornwell, D. J. (2006), *Criminal Punishment and Restorative Justice: Past, Present and Future Perspectives*, Hook, UK: Waterside Press.

Cornwell, D. J. (2007), *Doing Justice Better: The Politics of Restorative Justice*, Hook, UK: Waterside Press.

Cornwell, D. J. and Boag, D. (1991), 'The Multi-Perpetrator Dimension in Prison Siege Negotiation: Psycho-Strategic Considerations', *Proceedings of the Prison Service Psychology Conference*, London: Home Office, HM Prison Service (October), pp.104-125.

Coyle, A. (2001), 'Restorative Justice in Prisons', Paper to the *International Prison Chaplain's Association (Europe)*, (May), at www.icps.net

Crime Info Factsheet. (2008), *Community Sentences in England and Wales*, www.crimeinfo.org.uk/servelet/factsheetservelet/command=printable Factsheet, pp.1-7.

Cross, Sir A. R. N. (1971), *Punishment, Prison and the Public: An Assessment of Penal Reform in Twentieth Century England by an Armchair Penologist*, London: Stevens and Sons.

Cullen, F. T. and Gilbert, K. E. (1982), *Reaffirming Rehabilitation*, Cincinnati: Anderson Publishing.

Cullen, F. T., Fisher, B.S. and Applegate, B.K. (2000), 'Public Opinion About Punishment and Corrections' in M. Tonry (ed), *Crime and Justice: A Review of Research*, Chicago, Illinois: University of Chicago Press.

Cullen, F. T., Pealer, J. A., Fisher, B. S., Applegate, B. K. and Santana, S. (2002), 'Public Support for Correctional Rehabilitation in America: Change or Consistency?' in J. Roberts and M. Hough (eds), *Changing Attitudes to Punishment: Public Opinion, Crime and Justice*, Devon, UK: Willan Publishing, pp.128-147.

Cunliffe, J. and Shepherd, A. (2007), *'Reoffending of Adults: Results From the 2004 Cohort*, London: Home Office Research, Development and Statistics Directorate.

Daly, K. and Immarigeon, R. (1998), 'The Past, Present and Future of Restorative Justice: Some Critical Reflections' in *Contemporary Justice Review*, vol.1, no.1, pp.21-45.

Da Silva, A., Cowell, P., Chow, T. and Worthington, P. (2006), *Prison Population Projections 2006-2013, England and Wales*, London: Home Office Research, Development and Statistics Directorate.

Davies, A. Y. (2003), *Are Prisons Obsolete?* New York: Seven Stories Press.

Delgardo, R. (2000), 'Goodbye to Hammurabi: Analysing the Atavistic Appeal of Restorative Justice', in *Stanford Law Review*, vol.52, pp.751-775.

Denning, Sir A. (1949), *Freedom Under the Law* (The Hamlyn Lectures, First Series), London: Stevens and Sons Limited.

Devlin, P. (1965), *The Enforcement of Morals*, London: Oxford University Press.

Dickey, W. J. and Smith, M. E. (1998), *Dangerous Opportunity - Five Futures for Community Corrections: The Report From the Focus Group*, Washington, DC: Department of Justice.

Dignan, J. (2002), 'Reparation Orders' in B. Williams (ed), *Reparation and Victim- Focused Social Work: Research Highlights in Social Work*, 42, London: Jessica Kingsley.

Dignan, J. (2004), 'Restorative Justice and the Law: The Case for an Integrated, Systemic Approach', in L. Walgrave (ed), *Restorative Justice and the Law*, Devon, UK: Willan Publishing, pp.169-190.

DiIulio, J. J. Jnr. (1987), *Governing Prisons: A Comparative Study of Correctional Management*, New York: The Free Press, and London: Collier Macmillan.
Ditchfield, J. (1990), *Control in Prisons: A Review of the Literature*, Home Office Research Study No. 118, London: HMSO.
Dodgson, C. L. (1872), (aka Lewis Carroll), *Through the Looking Glass, and What Alice Found There*, London: Macmillan and Co. Ch.7 (The Lion and the Unicorn).
Doob, A. N. and Webster, C. M. (2003), 'Sentence Severity and Crime: Accepting the Null Hypothesis' in *Crime and Justice: A Review of Research*, 30, pp.143-195.
Doward, J. (2008), 'Overcrowded Jails At Breaking Point, *The Observer*, London, (24 February), p.2.
Dowden, C. and Andrews, D. (2004), 'The Importance of Staff Practice in Delivering Effective Correctional Treatment: A Meta-Analysis' in *International Journal of Offender Therapy and Comparative Criminology*, 48, pp.203-214.
Downes, D. and Morgan, R. (2002), 'The British General Election 2001: The Centre Right Consensus' in *Punishment and Society*, 4:1, pp.81-96.
Doyal, L. and Gough, I. (1991), *A Theory of Human Needs*, Basingstoke, UK: Macmillan Publishing.
Duff, R. A. (1999), 'Penal Communities', in *Punishment and Society*, vol.1, no.1, pp.27-43.
Eaton, J. and McElrea, F. W. M. (J) (2003), *Sentencing: The New Dimensions*, New Zealand Law Society Seminar, (March).
Ellis, D. (1984), 'Crowding and Prison Violence', in *Journal of Criminal Justice and Behaviour*, vol.11, no.3, pp.277-307.
Ervin, L. and Schneider, A. (1990), 'Explaining the Effects of Rehabilitation on Offenders: Results of a National Experiment in Juvenile Courts', in B. Galway and J. Hudson (eds), *Criminal Justice, Restitution and Reconciliation*, Monsey, NY: Criminal Justice Press.
Esmée Fairbairn Foundation (EFF) (2004), *Crime, Courts and Confidence: Report of an Independent Inquiry Into Alternatives to Prison*, (The Coulsfield Report), London: The Stationery Office.
European Commission (2007), *European System of Social Indicators*, Mannheim, Germany: ZUMA Social Indicator Department.
Ewing, A.C. (1929), *The Morality of Punishment*, London: Kegan Paul, Trench and Trubner.
Farrow, K. (2004), 'Still Committed After All These Years? Morale in the Modern-Day Probation Service', in *Probation Journal*, vol.51, no.3, pp.206-220.
Fatić, A. (1995), *Punishment and Restorative Crime-Handling: A Social Theory of Trust*, Aldershot, UK: Avebury Press.
Findlay, M. (2004), *Prisons as Progressive Punishment? The State of Corrective Services*, Sydney, Australia: University of New South Wales (The Evatt Foundation), available at http://evatt.labor.net.au/publications/books/145.html.
Fitzgerald, M. and Sim, J. (1979), *British Prisons*, (1st Edition), Oxford: Basil Blackwell.
Fitzgerald, M. and Sim, J. (1980), 'Legitimating the Prison Crisis: A Critical Review of the May Report', in *Howard Journal of Criminal Justice*, vol.19, pp.73-84.
Fitzgerald, M. and Sim, J. (1982), *British Prisons*, (2nd Edition), Oxford: Basil Blackwell.
Flanaghan, T.J. (1996), 'Public Opinion On Crime and Justice: History, Development and Trends', in T. J. Flanaghan and D.R. Longmire (eds), *Americans View Crime and Justice:*

A National Public Opinion Survey, Thousand Oaks, CA: SAGE Publications, pp.1-15.
Fleisher, M.S. (1989), *Warehousing Violence*, London and Newbury Park, CA: SAGE Publications.
Ford, R. (2007), 'Big Rise in Dangerous Prisoners Reoffending While On Parole', *The Times*, London, (October 23), p.4.
Fry, M. (1951), *Arms of the Law*, London: Gollancz.
Fryers, T., Brugha, T. and Grounds, A. (1998), 'Severe Mental Illness in Prisoners', in *British Medical Journal*, vol.317, pp.1025-6 (October).
Galligan, D.J. (1981), 'The Return to Retribution in Penal Theory', in C.H.F. Tapper (ed), *Crime, Proof and Punishment*, (Essays in Honour of Sir Rupert Cross), London: Butterworth, pp.144-171.
Garland, D. (2001), *The Culture of Control: Crime and Social Order in Contemporary Society*, Oxford: Oxford University Press.
Garland, D. and Young, P. (1983), *The Power to Punish*, London: Heinemann.
Garrielides, T. (2003), *Restorative Justice Theory and Practice: Mind The Gap!*, available at http://www.euforum.org/readingroom/Newsletter/Vol04Issue03.PDF.
Gendreau, P. (1996), 'Offender Rehabilitation: What We Know and What Needs to be Done', in *Journal of Criminal Justice and Behaviour*, vol.23, pp.144-161.
Gibbs, F. (2007), 'Is This an Unseemly Rush to Change? *The Times*, London, (May 1), Law Supplement, p.1.
Gibbs, F. and Ford, R. (2007), 'Criminals Must Have Terms Cut in Full Jails', *The Times*, London, (November 5), pp.1-2.
Glaser, D. (1964), *The Effectiveness of a Prison and Parole System*, New York: Bobbs-Merrill.
Glaser, D, and Stratton, J. (1961), 'Measuring Inmate Change in Prison', in D.R. Cressey (ed), *The Prison: Studies in Institutional Organisation and Change*, New York: Holt, Reinhart and Winston.
Goldberg, E.M., Stanley, S.J. and Kenrick, J. (1985), *Task-Centred Casework in a Probation Setting*, London: George Allen and Unwin.
Grimshaw, R. (2004), *Whose Justice? Principal Drivers of Criminal Justice Policy, Their Implications for Stakeholders, and Some Foundations for Critical Policy Departures*, London: Centre for Crime and Justice Studies, School of Law, King's College, (July).
Gross, H. (1979), *A Theory of Criminal Justice*, Oxford: Oxford University Press.
Grubin, D. (1998), *Sex Offending Against Children: Understanding the Risk*, Police Research Series Paper 99, London: Home Office Research, Development and Statistics Directorate.
Hakiaha, M. (2007), 'Ubuntu and Whakawhanaungatanga: The Maori Equivalent in Restorative Justice Practices', in correspondence with the author, 24 June 2007.
Harris, J. and Grace, S. (1999), *A Question of Evidence? Investigating and Prosecuting Rape in the 1990s*, Home Office Research Study No. 196, London: Home Office.
Hart, H.L.A. (1968), *Punishment and Responsibility*, Oxford: Oxford University Press.
Hawkins, G. (1976), *The Prison: Policy and Practice*, Chicago and London: The University of Chicago Press.
Hewitt, T. (2002), 'A Question of Justice', in *Peace Review*, vol.14, no.4 (December), pp.447-453.
Hobbes, T. (1973), *Leviathan*, London: Everyman Edition.

Home Office (1975), *Report of the Parole Board in England and Wales*, London: HMSO.
Home Office (1979), *Committee of Inquiry Into the United Kingdom Prison Services*, (The May Report), Cmnd. 7673, London: HMSO.
Home Office (1991), *Custody, Care and Justice: The Way Ahead for the Prison Service in England and Wales*, Cm. 1647, London: HMSO.
Home Office (2000), *Setting the Boundaries*, London: Home Office.
Home Office (2001a), *Criminal Justice: The Way Ahead*, CM 5074, London: The Stationery Office.
Home Office (2001b), *Making Punishments Work*, (The Halliday Report), London: Home Office.
Home Office (2001c), *Victim Personal Statements*, (Circular 35/2001), London: Home Office.
Home Office (2002a), *World Prison Population List*, (R. Walmsley (ed)), London: Home Office Research, Development and Statistics Directorate.
Home Office (2002b), *Protecting the Public*, CM 5568, London: Home Office.
Home Office (2002c), *Justice for All*, CM 5563, London: Home Office.
Home Office (2003a), *Restorative Justice: The Government's Strategy*, (Consultation Document), London: Home Office Communications Directorate.
Home Office (2003b), *A New Deal for Victims and Witnesses: National Strategy to Deliver Improved Services*, London: Home Office. (Also at: http://www.cjsonline.gov.uk/home/html).
Home Office (2005a), *Victims' Rights*, London: Home Office, and also available in summary format at: http://www.homeoffice.gov.uk/crime-victims/victims/victims-rights/?version=1.
Home Office (2005b), *The Code of Practice for Victims of Crime*, London: HMSO (October).
Home Office (2005c), *Re-building Lives – Supporting Victims of Crime*, CM 6705, London: HMSO (December).
Home Office (2005d), *Government Proposes New Compensation Arrangements and Better Support for Victims of Crime*, at: http://cjsonline.gov.uk/the_cjs/whats_news_3258.html of 7 December.
Home Office (2007a), *Sentencing Statistics 2007*, London: Home Office, and also available at: http://www.press.homeoffice.gov.uk/pressreleases/sentencestatistics/2005/?version=1.
Home Office (2007b), *Crime in England and Wales 2006/7*, (4th Edition), S, Nicholas, C. Kershaw and A. Walker (eds), London: Office for National Statistics.
Home Office (2008), *Crime in England and Wales 2006/7 Report*, S. Nicholas, C. Kershaw and A. Walker (eds), London: Home Office Research, Development and Statistics Directorate.
Home Office, HM Prison Service (2007), *Prison Service Instruction 27/2007 – End of Custody Licence (ECL)*, London: Home Office, (19 June).
Home Office, Ministry of Justice, Cabinet Office and Department for Children, Schools and Families (2008), *Youth Crime Action Plan*, London: Home Office/Youth Justice Board.
Houchin, R. (2003), 'Significant Change is Likely in Our Prisons: The Question Is, Change In What Direction?' in *Probation Journal*, vol.50, no.2, pp.142-148.

Hough, M. and Roberts, J. (eds) (1998a), *Attitudes to Crime and Punishment: Findings from the 1996 British Crime Survey*, Home Office Research Findings 64, London: Home Office, pp.1-4.

Hough, M. and Roberts, J. (eds), (1998b), *Attitudes to Crime and Punishment: Findings from the 1996 British Crime Survey*, Home Office Research Studies 179, London: HMSO, pp.1-79.

Hough, M. and Roberts, J. (2004a), *Confidence in Justice: An International Review*, Home Office Research Findings 243, London: Home Office.

Hough, M. and Roberts, J. (2004b), *Confidence in Justice: An International Review*, London: Institute for Criminal Policy Research, School of Law, King's College London, available at: http://www.kcl.ac.uk/depsta/law/research/icpr/publications/confidence%20 in%justice.pdf.

Hough, M. and Park, A. (2002), 'How Malleable Are Attitudes to Crime and Punishment? Findings From a British Deliberative Poll', in J. Roberts and M. Hough (eds), *Changing Attitudes to Punishment: Public Opinion, Crime and Justice*, Devon, UK: Willan Publishing, pp.163-183.

Hoyles, J.A. (1986), *Punishment in the Bible*, London: Epworth Press.

Hudson, B. (1987), *Justice Through Punishment: A Critique of the Justice Model of Corrections*, Basingstoke, UK: Macmillan Education Limited.

Hudson, B. (2003), *Understanding Justice*, (2nd Edition), Buckingham, UK: Open University Press.

Indermaur, D. and Hough, M. (2002), 'Strategies for Changing Public Attitudes to Punishment', in J. Roberts and M. Hough (eds), *Changing Attitudes to Punishment: Public Opinion, Crime and Justice*, Devon, UK: Willan Publishing, pp.198-214.

International Centre for Prison Studies (ICPS) (2006a), *World Prison Population List*, R. Walmsley (ed), London: King's College.

International Centre for Prison Studies (ICPS) (2006b), *World Prison Population Statistics*, available at: http://news.bbc.co.uk/1/shared/spl/hi/uk/06 prisons/html/nn2.stm.

Irwin, J. and Cressey, D.R. (1962), 'Thieves, Convicts and the Inmate Culture', in *Social Problems 10*, pp.142-155.

Johnstone, G. (2004), 'How, and in What Terms Should Restorative Justice be Conceived? in H. Zehr and B. Toews (eds), *Critical Issues in Restorative Justice*, Monsey, New York: Criminal Justice Press, and Devon, UK: Willan Publishing.

Joutsen, M., Rahti, R. and Pölönen, P. (2001), *Criminal Justice Systems in Europe and North America – Finland*, Helsinki: Academic Bookstore.

Judge, N., Mutter, R., Gillett, T., Hennessy, J. and Mauger, J. (2002), 'Restorative Processes and Outcomes for Victims', *Restorative Justice Project: Family Group Conference Project-Research Outlines and Lessons Learned*, Braintree, UK: Essex County Council.

Killias, M., Aebi, M. and Ribaud, D. (2000), 'Does Community Service Rehabilitate Better Than Short-Term Imprisonment? Results of a Controlled Experiment', in *Howard Journal of Criminal Justice*, vol.39, no.1, pp.40-57.

King, R.D. and Morgan, R. (1976), *A Taste of Prison: Custodial Conditions for Trial and Remand Prisoners*, London: Routledge and Kegan Paul.

Knott, C. (2004), 'Evidence-Based Practice in the National Probation Service', in R. Burnett and C. Roberts (eds), *What Works in Probation and Youth Justice: Developing Evidence-*

Based Practice, Devon, UK: Willan Publishing.
Krasnov, P. (1998), *Correctional Facility Design and Detailing*, New York: McGraw-Hill.
Kreuger, C., Raeke, R. and Nguyen, D-P. (2004), 'The Problem With Probation', *St. Petersburg Times*, Florida, (June 13) at: http://www.sptimes.com/2004/06/13/Stare/ The_Problem_with_prob.shtml.
Kyvsgaard, B. (2001), 'Penal Sanctions and the Use of Imprisonment in Denmark', in M. Tonry (ed), *Penal Reform in Overcrowded Times*, New York: Oxford University Press.
Lappi-Seppälä, T. (2001), 'Sentencing and Punishment in Finland: The Decline of the Repressive Ideal', in M. Tonry and R.S. Frase (eds), *Sentencing and Sanctions in Western Countries*, New York: Oxford University Press.
Larsson, P. (2001), 'Norway Prison Use Up Slightly: Community Penalty Lots', in M. Tonry (ed), *Penal Reform in Overcrowded Times*, New York: Oxford University Press.
Lemert, E.M. (1967), *Human Deviance, Social Problems and Social Control*, Englewood Cliffs, NJ: Prentice Hall.
Levant, S., Cullen, F.T., Fulton, B. and Wozniak, J.F. (1999), 'Reconsidering Restorative Justice: The Corruption of Benevolence Revisited?' in *Journal of Crime and Delinquency*, vol.45, pp.3-27.
Lewis, D. (1997), *Hidden Agendas: Politics, Law and Disorder*, London: Hamish Hamilton.
Lewis, S. (2005), 'Rehabilitation: Headline or Footnote in the New Penal Policy?' in *Probation Journal*, vol.52(2), pp.119-135.
Liebling, A. and Arnold, H. (2004), *Prisons and Their Moral Performance*, Oxford: Oxford University Press.
Lipton, D., Martinson, R. and Wilks, J. (1975), *Effectiveness of Treatment Evaluation Studies*, New York: Praeger Publications.
Lloyd, C., Mair, G. and Hough, M. (1995), *Explaining Reconviction Rates: A Critical Analysis*, Home Office Research Study 136, London: Home Office.
Maden, A., Taylor, C.J.A., Brooke, D. and Ginn, D. (1996), *Mental Disorder in Remand Prisoners*, London: Home Office Research, Development and Statistics Directorate.
Mair, G., Burke, L. and Taylor, S. (2006), 'The Worst Tax Form You've Ever Seen? Probation Officers' Views About OASys', in *Probation Journal*, vol.53(1), pp.7-23.
Marshall, T. and Merry, S. (1990), *Crime and Accountability*, London: HMSO.
Marshall, T.F. (1999), *Restorative Justice: An Overview*, London: Home Office Research, Development and Statistics Directorate.
Martinson, R. (1974), 'What Works? – Questions and Answers About Prison Reform', in *The Public Interest*, vol.35, pp.22-54.
Maruna, S. (2001), *Making Good: How Ex-Convicts Reform and Rebuild Their Lives*, Washington DC: American Psychological Association.
Maruna, S. and King, A. (2004), 'Public Opinion and Community Penalties', in Sir A.E. Bottoms, S. Rex and G. Robinson (eds), *Alternatives to Prison: Options for an Insecure Society*, Devon, UK: Willan Publishing.
Matravers, A. and Hughes, G.V. (2003), 'Unprincipled Sentencing? The Policy Approach to Dangerous Sex Offenders', in M. Tonry (ed). *Confronting Crime: Crime Control Policy Under New Labour*, Devon, UK: Willan Publishing, pp.51-79.
Matravers, A. and Tonry, M. (2003), ''Is Sentencing in England and Wales Institutionally Racist? In M. Tonry (ed), *Confronting Crime: Crime Control Policy Under New Labour*,

Devon, UK: Willan Publishing, pp.156-181.
Matza, D.M. (1964), *Delinquency and Drift*, New York: John Wiley.
Matza, D.M. (1969), *Becoming Deviant*, Englewood Cliffs, NJ: Prentice-Hall.
Mawby, R. (1987), *Crime Victims: Needs, Services and the Voluntary Sector*, London: Tavistock Publications.
May, C. (1999), *Explaining Reconviction Following Community Sentences: The Role of Social Factors*, Home Office Research Study 192, London: Home Office.
Mayhew, P. and van Kesteren, J. (2002), 'Cross-National Attitudes to Punishment', in J. Roberts and M. Hough (eds), *Changing Attitudes to Punishment: Public Opinion, Crime and Justice*, Devon, UK: Willan Publishing, pp.63-92.
McCold, P. (2004), 'What is the Role of Community in Restorative Justice Theory and Practice?' in H. Zehr and B. Toews (eds), *Critical Issues in Restorative Justice*, Monsey, NY: Criminal Justice Press, and Devon, UK: Willan Publishing.
McElrea, F.W.M. (J) (2002a), 'Restorative Justice Issues and Trends: Where is Restorative Justice Going? In *Proceedings of the 4th Annual Conference of the International Corrections and Prisons Association* (ICPA), Ottawa: ICPA, pp.64-74.
McElrea, F.W.M. (J) (2002b), 'Restorative Justice: A New Zealand Perspective'. Paper to the Conference *Modernising Criminal Justice: New World Challenges*, London (June).
McElrea, F.W.M. (J) (2005), 'The New Zealand Experience of Restorative Justice Legislation'. Paper to the *11th Annual Restorative Justice Conference*, Fresno Pacific University, California (September).
McElrea, F.W.M. (J) (2006), 'Restorative Justice: A New Zealand Perspective', in D.J. Cornwell, *Criminal Punishment and Restorative Justice*, Winchester, UK: Waterside Press, pp.119-134.
McIvor, G. (1992), *Sentenced to Serve: The Operation and Impact of Community Service by Offenders*, Aldershot, UK: Avebury Press.
McIvor, G. (1998), 'Pro-Social Modelling and Legitimacy: Lessons From a Study of Community Service', in *Pro-Social Modelling and Legitimacy: The Clarke Hall Day Conference*, Cambridge: Cambridge University Institute of Criminology, pp.55-6.
McIvor, G. (2004), 'Reparative and Restorative Approaches', in Sir A.E. Bottoms. S. Rex and G. Robinson (eds), *Alternatives to Prison: Options for an Insecure Society*, Devon, UK: Willan Publishing, pp.162-194.
McWilliams, W. and Pease, K. (1990), 'Probation Practice and an End to Punishment', in *Howard Journal of Criminal Justice*, vol.29, no.1, pp.14-24.
Miers, D., Maguire, M., Goldie, S., Sharpe, K., Hale, C., Netten, A., Uglow, S., Doolin, K., Hallam, A., Enterkin, J. and Newburn, T. (2001), *An Exploratory Evaluation of Restorative Justice Schemes*, Crime Reduction Research Series Paper 9, London: Home Office.
Mill, J.S. (1859), 'On Liberty', (Extract) in 'Mill – A Nineteenth Century View of Liberty Under the Law', reprinted in L. Blom-Cooper and G. Drewry (eds) (1996), *Law and Morality: A Reader*, London: Duckworth, pp.9-12.
Mill, J.S. (1951), 'On Liberty', in *Utilitarianism, Liberty and Representative Government*, New York: Dalton Press.
Ministry of Justice (2007a), *Population In Custody Monthly Tables, May 2007, England and Wales*, London: National Offender Monitoring Service (NOMS), Table 1.

Ministry of Justice (2007b), *Prison Population (England and Wales)*, available and extracted from: http://www.justice.gov.uk/docs/population-in-custody-may07.pdf.

Ministry of Justice (2009), Prison Poluation in Custody, London: NOMS (February).

Moore, D. and O'Connell, T. (1994), 'Family Conferencing in Wagga-Wagga: A Communitarian Model of Justice', in C. Alder and J. Wundersitz (eds), *Family Conferencing in Juvenile Justice: The Way Forward or Misplaced Optimism?* Canberra: Australian Institute of Criminology.

Moxon, D., Sutton, M. and Hedderman, C. (1990), *Unit Fines: Experiments in Four Courts*, Research and Planning Paper 59, London: HMSO.

Mundle, C.W.K. (1954), 'Punishment and Desert', in H.B. Acton (ed) (1969), *The Philosophy of Punishment: A Collection of Papers*, London: Macmillan.

National Probation Service (2005), *The NOMS Management Model, Version 1*, at: http://www.probation.homeoffice.gov.uk/files/pdf/NOMS%20Offenders%Management%Model.pdf. (Consulted February 2005).

National Offender Management Service (2005), *Prison Population (England and Wales)*, available at: http://www.reform.co.uk/filestore/pdf/population%20%custody%20%20September%2005%pdf.

Nellis, M. and Chui, W. (2003), 'The End of Probation?' in W. Chui and M. Nellis (eds), *Moving Probation Forward: Evidence, Arguments and Practice*, London: Pearson Education.

O'Connor, A. (2007), 'Jail Where It's Always Pay-back Time', London: *The Times*, (October 26), p.46.

Office for National Statistics (2006), *Social Trends*, London: HMSO/Palgrave Macmillan.

O'Hear, M.M. (2005), 'Is Restorative Justice Compatible With Sentencing Uniformity?' in *Marquette Law Review*, vol.89, no.2, pp.305-326, (Winter).

Ostapiuk, E. (1982), 'Strategies for Community Intervention in Offender Rehabilitation: An Overview', in P. Feldman (ed), *Developments in the Study of Human Behaviour*, (Volume 1: The Prevention and Control of Offending), New York: John Wiley, pp.135-166.

Pakes, F. (2004), *Comparative Criminal Justice*, (Chapter 5), Devon, UK: Willan Publishing.

Parker, T. (1970, *The Frying Pan: A Prison and Its Prisoners*, London: Hutchinson.

Parliamentary All-Party Penal Affairs Group (PA-PPAG) (1980), *Too Many Prisoners: An Examination of Ways of Reducing the Prison Population*, Chichester and London: Barry Rose Publishers, (June).

Parrish, D. (2005), *Commission on Safety and Abuse in America's Prisons*, Full text and Summary at: http://www.prisoncommission.org/statement/parrish_david.pdf+direct+supervision+in+prisons+USA&hl-endct-al-nx&al=128gl=uk.

Polk, K. (2001), 'Family Conferencing: Theoretical and Evaluative Questions', in C. Alder and J. Wundersitz (eds), *Family Conferencing and Juvenile Justice: The Way Forward or Misplaced Optimism?* Canberra: Australian Studies in Law, Crime and Justice, Australian Institute of Criminology.

Pratt, J. (2002a), *Punishment and Civilisation: The Acceptability of Prisons in Modern Society*, London: SAGE Publications.

Pratt, J. (2002b), 'Emotive and Ostentatious Punishment: Its Decline and Resurgence in Modern Society', in *Punishment and Society*, vol.2, no.4, pp.417-439.

Prison Reform Trust (2004), *Prison Reform Trust Factfile*, London: PRT, (December).
Prison Reform Trust (2007a), *Life Sentence Prisoners*, (Briefing Paper), available at: http://www.prisonreformtrust.org.uk/subsectionaspd?id=345.
Prison Reform Trust (2007b), *Prison Factfile*, (Selective Menu of 75 Facts About Prisons) available at: http://www.prisonreformtrust.org.uk/subsection.asp/id=10708fact=75.
Prison Reform Trust (2008), *Prison Factfile January 2008*, (Selective Menu of Prison System Facts) at: http://www.prisonreformtrust.org.uk/section.asp?id+188fact.
Rawls, J. (1955), 'Two Concepts of Rules', in *The Philosophical Review*, vol.64, pp.3-32. Also in H.B. Acton (ed) (1969), *The Philosophy of Punishment: A Collection of Papers*, London: Macmillan, pp.105-114.
Rawls, J. (1958), 'Justice as Fairness', in *The Philosophical Review*, vol.LXVII, pp.164-194.
Reeves, H. and Mulley, K. (2000), 'The New Status of Victims in the UK: Threats and Opportunities', in A. Crawford and J. Goodey (eds), *Integrating a Victim Perspective Within Criminal Justice Debates*, Aldershot, UK: Ashgate Press.
Reimer, H. (1937), 'Socialisation in the Prison Community', in *Proceedings of the Sixty-Seventh Annual Congress of the American Prison Association*, pp.151-155.
Rex, S. (1999), 'Desistance from Offending: Experiences of Probation', in *Howard Journal of Criminal Justice*, vol.38, no.4, pp.366-383.
Rex, S. and Gelsthorpe, L. (2002), 'The Role of Community Service in Reducing Offending: Evaluating Pathfinder Projects in the UK', in *Howard Journal of Criminal Justice*, vol.41, no.4, pp.311-325.
Roberts, J.V. (1992), 'Public Opinion, Crime and Criminal Justice', in M.Tonry (ed), *Crime and Justice: A Review of Research*, Chicago, ILL: University of Chicago Press, pp.99-180.
Roberts, J.V. (2002), 'Public Opinion and the Nature of Community Penalties', in J.V. Roberts and M. Hough (eds), *Changing Attitudes to Punishment: Public Opinion, Crime and Justice*, Devon, UK: Willan Publishing, pp.1-14.
Roberts, J.V. and Stalans, L. (eds) (1997), *Public Opinion, Crime and Criminal Justice*, Boulder, COL: Westview Press.
Roberts, J.V., Stalans, L., Indermaur, D. and Hough, M. (eds) (2003), *Penal Populism and Public Opinion: Lessons From Five Countries*, Oxford and New York: Oxford University Press.
Roberts, J.V. and Gabor, T. (2004), 'Living in the Shadow of Prison: Lessons from the Canadian Experience of Decarceration', in *British Journal of Criminology*, vol.44, no.1, pp.92-112.
Roberts, J. and Smith, M.E. (2003), 'Custody Plus: Custody Minus', in M. Tonry (ed), *Confronting Crime: Crime Control Policy Under New Labour*, Devon, UK: Willan Publishing, pp.182-210.
Rothman, D.J. (1973), 'Decarcerating Prisoners and Patients', in *Civil Liberties Review*, 1, p.8.
Rothman, D.J. (1980), *Conscience and Convenience: The Asylum and its Alternatives in Progressive America*, Boston, MA: Little Brown.
Rotman, E. (1986), 'Do Criminal Offenders Have a Constitutional Right to Rehabilitation?' in *Journal of Criminal Law and Criminology*, vol.77, no.4, pp.1023-1068.

Rubin, S. (1979), 'New Sentencing Proposals and Laws in the 1970s', in *Federal Probation*, vol.43, no.2, pp.3-8.

Rutherford, A. (1986), *Prisons and the Process of Justice*, Oxford: Oxford University Press.

Rutherford, A. (1993), *Criminal Justice and the Pursuit of Decency*, Oxford: Oxford University Press.

Scheingold, S. (1995), 'The Politics of Street Crime in Criminal Justice', in L. Joseph (ed), *Crime, Communities and Public Policy*, Centre for Urban Research and Policy Studies, University of Chicago, Chicago, ILL: University of Illinois Press.

Schiff, M. (1998), 'Restorative Justice Interventions for Juvenile Offenders: A Research Agenda for the Next Decade', in *Western Criminology Review*, 1(1), at: www.wcr.Sonoma.edu/vin1/schiff.html.

Scull, A.T. (1977), *Decarceration, Community Treatment and the Deviant: A Radical Review*, New Jersey: Englewood Cliffs.

Scull, A.T. (1983), 'Community Corrections: Panacea, Progress or Pretence?' in D. Garland and P. Young (eds), *The Power to Punish: Contemporary Penality and Social Analysis*, London: Heinemann Educational Books, pp.146-165.

Shapland, J., Willmore, J. and Duff, P. (1985), *Victims in the Criminal Justice System*, (Cambridge Studies in Criminology), Aldershot, UK: Gower Publications.

Sharpe, S. (1998), *Restorative Justice: A Vision for Healing and Change*, Edmonton, Alberta: Offender Mediation Society.

Sharpe, S. (2004), 'How Large Should the Restorative Justice "Tent" Be?' in H. Zehr and B. Toews (eds), *Critical Issues in Restorative Justice*, Monsey, NY: Criminal Justice Press, and Devon, UK: Willan Publishing, pp.17-31.

Sherman, L.W. and Strang, H. (1997), *Restorative Justice and Deterring Crime*, (RISE Working Paper Number 4), at: www.aic.gov.au/rjustice/rise/working.html.

Sherman, L.W. and Strang, H. (2007), *Restorative Justice: The Evidence*, London: The Smith Institute in collaboration with The Esmée Fairbairn Foundation.

Shohan, S. (1972), 'Moral Dilemmas in Rehabilitation', in R.J.Gerber and P.D.McAnany (eds), *Contemporary Punishment*, London and Notre Dame: University of Notre Dame Free Press, pp.200-208.

Singleton, N., Meltzer, H., Gatward, R., Coid, J. and Deasy, D. (1998), *Psychiatric Morbidity Among Prisoners*, London: HMSO.

Smith, D. (2004), 'The Uses and Abuses of Positivism', in G. Mair (ed), *What Matters in Probation*, Devon, UK: Willan Publishing.

Stalans, L. (2002), 'Measuring Attitudes to Sentencing', in J. Roberts and M. Hough (eds), *Changing Attitudes to Punishment: Public Opinion, Crime and Justice*, Devon, UK: Willan Publishing, pp.15-32.

Stead, M., McFadyen, L. and Hastings, G. (2002), *What Do The Public Really Feel About Non-Custodial Penalties?* London: Esmeé Fairbairn Foundation.

Strang, H. (2002), *Repair or Revenge: Victims and Restorative Justice*, Oxford: Clarendon Press.

Strang, H. (2004), 'Is Restorative Justice Imposing Its Agenda on Victims?' in H. Zehr and B. Toews (eds), *Critical Issues in Restorative Justice*, Monsey, NY: Criminal Justice Press, and Devon, UK: Willan Publishing.

Sutherland, E.H. and Cressey, D.R. (1970), *Criminology*, (5th Edition), Philadelphia: J.B.

Lippincott.

Sykes, G.M. (1958), *The Society of Captives: A Study in a Maximun Security Prison*, Princeton, NJ: Princeton University Press.

Sykes, G.M. and Messinger, S.L. (1960), 'The Inmate Social System', in R.A. Cloward, D.R. Cressey, G. Grosser, R. McCleery, S. Messinger and L. Ohlin (eds), *Theoretical Perspectives in the Social Organisation of the Prison*, New York: SSRC.

Tak, P. (2001), 'Sentencing and Punishment in The Netherlands', in M. Tonry and R.S. Frase (eds), *Sentencing and Sanctions in Western Countries*, New York: Oxford University Press.

Thomas, J.E. (1972), *The English Prison Officer Since 1850: A Study in Conflict*, London and Boston: Routledge and Kegan Paul.

Thomas, J.E. and Pooley, R. (1980), *The Exploding Prison*, London: Junction Books.

Tonry, M. (ed) (2003), *Confronting Crime: Crime Control Policy Under New Labour*, Devon, UK: Willan Publishing.

Tonry, M. (2004), *Punishment and Politics: Evidence and Emulation in the Making of Crime Control Policy*, Devon, UK: Willan Publishing.

Tutu, D.M. (Abp) (1999), *No Future Without Forgiveness*, London: Rider Publishing and New York: Doubleday.

Umbreit, M.S. (1996), 'Restorative Justice Through Victim: Offender Mediation: The Impact of Programmes in Four Canadian Provinces', in B. Galway and J. Hudson (eds), *Restorative Justice: International Paradigms*, Monsey, NY: Criminal Justice Press.

Umbreit, M.S. (1999), 'Avoiding the Marginalization and McDonaldization of Victim Offender Mediation: A Case Study in Moving to the Mainstream', in G. Bazemore and L. Wakgrave (eds), *Restorative Juvenile Justice: Repairing the Harm of Youth Crime*, Monsey, NY: Criminal Justice Press.

Umbreit, M.S., Coates, R.B. and Vos, B. (2002), 'Impact of Victim- Offender Mediation: Two Decades of Research', in *Federal Probation*, vol.65, no.3, pp.29-35.

Umbreit, M.S., Vos, B., Coates, R.B. and Lightfoot, E. (2005a), 'Restorative Justice in the Twenty-First Century: A Social Movement Full of Opportunities and Pitfalls', in *Marquette Law Review*, vol.89, no.2, pp.254-263.

Umbreit, M.S., Vos, B. and Coates, R.B. (2005b), *Opportunities and Pitfalls Facing the Restorative Justice Movement*, University of Minnesota Center for Restorative Justice and Peacemaking.

Umbreit, M.S., Vos, B. and Coates, R.B. (2006), *Restorative Justice Dialogue: Evidence-Based Practice*, University of Minnesota Center for Restorative Justice and Peacemaking.

United Nations (1955), *Standard Minimum Rules for the Treatment of Prisoners*, New York: United Nations.

United Nations (2001), *Adoption of UN Basic Principles on the Use of Restorative Justice Programmes in Criminal Matters*, at: http://www.un.org/esc/coordination/ecosoc/doc2002htm.

United Nations (2002), *Resolutions and Decisions Adopted by the Economic and Social Council at its Substantive Session of 2002*, (E/2002/INF/2/Add.2), New York: United Nations.

Van den Haag, E. (1975), *Punishing Criminals: Concerning a Very Old and Painful Question*. New York: Basic Books Inc..

Van Koppen, P.J. and Penrod, S.D. (eds) (2003), 'Adversarial Versus Inquisitorial Justice', in

Perspectives in Law and Psychology, vol.17, Heidelberg: Springer Publications, and New York: Humana Press.
Van Ness, D.W. (2005), 'Restorative Justice in Prisons', *Paper to Session 204 of the Symposium on Restorative Justice and Peace*, Columbia, California: PFI Centre for Justice and Reconciliation, Prison Fellowship International, (February 9-12).
Van Ruller, S. (1986), 'Honderd Jaar Vrijheidsbenehmung in Cijfers', in D.H. Jong (ed), *De Vrijheidsstraf*, Arnhem: Gouda Quint.
Von Hirsch, A. (1976), *Doing Justice: The Choice of Punishments*, New York: Hill and Wang.
Von Hirsch, A. (1993), *Censure and Sanctions*, Oxford: Oxford University Press.
Vorenberg, J. (1972), 'The War on Crime: The First Five Years', in *Atlantic Monthly*, (May), pp.63-69.
Waller, I. (1989), 'The Needs of Crime Victims', in E. Fattah (ed), *The Plight of Victims of Crime in Modern Society*, Basingstoke, UK: Macmillan.
Walker, N., Hough, M. and Lewis, H. (1988), 'Tolerance of Leniency and Severity in England and Wales', in N. Walker and M. Hough (eds), *Public Attitudes to Sentencing: Surveys From Five Countries*, Aldershot, UK: Gower Publications, pp.178-202.
Walsh, D. and Poole, A. (eds) (1983), *A Dictionary of Criminology*, London: Routledge and Kegan Paul.
Ward, T. and Stewart, C.A. (2003), 'The Treatment of Sex Offenders: Risk Management and Good Lives', in *Journal of Professional Psychology: Research and Practice*, vol.34, no.4, pp.353-360.
Ward, T., Mann, R.E. and Gannon, T.A. (2007), 'The Good Lives Model of Offender Rehabilitation: Clinical Implications', in *Journal of Aggression and Violent Behaviour*, 12, pp.87-107.
Ward, T. and Gannon, T.A. (2008), 'Goods and Risks: Misconceptions About the Good Lives Model', in *The Correctional Psychologist*, vol.40, no.1, pp.1-7.
Wargent, M. (2008), 'Release Me From This Paperwork', *The Times*, London, (August 5th), p.5.
Warner, K. (1994), 'The Rights of the Offender in Family Group Conferences', in C. Alder and J. Wundersitz (eds), *Family Conferencing and Juvenile Justice: The Way Forward or Misplaced Optimism?* Canberra: Australian Studies in Law, Crime and Justice, Australian Institute of Criminology.
Warr, M. (1995), 'Public Opinion on Crime and Punishment', in *Public Opinion Quarterly*, vol.59, pp.296-310.
Wasserstrom, R. (1972), 'Some Problems With Theories of Punishment', in J.B. Cederblom and W.L. Blizeck (eds), *Justice and Punishment*, Cambridge, Massachusetts: Ballinger Publishing Company (J.P. Lippincott).
Wener, R. (2006), 'Effectiveness of the Direct Supervision System of Correctional Design and Management: A Review', in *Journal of Criminal Justice and Behaviour*, vol.33, no.3, pp.392-410.
White, P. (1998), *The Prison Population in 1997: A Statistical Review*, Home Office Findings No.76, London: Home Office Research, Development and Statistics Directorate.
Wiegend, T. (2001), 'Sentencing and Punishment in Germany', in M. Tonry and R.S. Frase (eds), *Sentencing and Sanctions in Western Countries*, New York: Oxford University

Press.

Wiles, P. (1976), *The Sociology of Crime and Deviance in Britain*, London: Martin Robertson.

Winkle, B.J. (1991), 'Harnessing the Power to Bet: Wagering With the Governor as a Mechanism for Social and Individual Change', in D.B. Wexler and B.J. White (eds), *Essays in Therapeutic Jurisprudence*, Durban, NC: Carolina Academic Press.

Woolf, H. (LCJ) and Tumim, S. (J) (1991), *Prison Disturbances April 1990*, Cm 1456, London, HMSO.

Worrall, A. and Hoy, C. (2005), *Punishment in the Community: Managing Offenders, Making Choices*, (2nd Edition), Devon, UK: Willan Publishing.

Wright, M. (1999), *Restoring Respect For Justice*, Winchester, UK: Waterside Press.

Wright, M. (2003), 'Is It Time to Question the Concept of Punishment?' in L. Walgrave (ed), *Repositioning Restorative Justice*, Devon, UK: Willan Publishing, pp.3-23.

Wright, R. (2002), 'Counting the Cost of Sentencing in North Carolina', in M. Tonry (ed), *Crime and Justice: A Review of the Literature*, vol.29, Chicago: University of Chicago Press.

Wundersitz, J. and Hetzel, S. (1996), 'Family Conferencing for Young Offenders: The South Australian Perspective', in J. Hudson, A. Morris, G. Maxwell and B. Galway (eds), *Family Group Conferences: Perspectives on Policy and Practice*, Sydney, Australia: Federation Press and Criminal Justice Press.

Youth Justice Board (2006), *Developing Restorative Justice: An Action Plan*, London: YJB, available at: http://www.yjb.gov.uk/rdonlyres/F475830A.

Zehr, H. (1990 and 1995), *Changing Lenses: A New Focus for Crime and Justice*, Scottdale, PA: Herald Press.

Zehr, H. (2002), *The Little Book of Restorative Justice*, Intercourse, PA: Good Books.

Zehr, H. and Mika, H. (1998), 'Fundamental Principles of Restorative Justice, in *Contemporary Justice Review,* vol.1, no.1, pp.47-55.

Zetterbaum, M. (1967), *Toqueville and the Problem of Democracy*, Stanford: Stanford University Press.

Zimring, F.E., Hawkins, G. and Kamin, S. (2001), *Punishment and Democracy: Three Strikes and You're Out in California*, New York: Oxford University Press.

Glossary of Some Key Terms Used in this Book

Due to the complexity of post-Second World War criminal justice legislation in England and Wales relating to sentences and their implementation, this *Glossary* indicates various commonly recurring acronyms and abbreviations encountered within the text with their legislative origins and a brief explanation. CJA = Criminal Justice Act.

Abbreviation or Acronym	In full	Origins	Explanatory notes
ACR	Automatic conditional release	CJA 1991	Automatic release on licence at the mid point of a sentence of 12 months but less than four years.
AUR	Automatic unconditional release	CJA 1991	Automatic release without licence supervision at the mid-point of a sentence of up to 12 months.
ALS	Automatic life sentence	Crime (Sentences) Act 1997	Imposed on offenders aged over 18 found guilty of a second serious violent or sexual offence – but see the replacement effect of the IPP sentence (q.v.) for such offences committed on or after 4 April 2005.
APO	Action plan order	Crime and Disorder Act 1998	A means of monitoring the progress of a juvenile offender through supervision of an action plan by a youth offending team (YOT).
ASBO	Anti-social behaviour order	Crime and Disorder Act 1998 (and subsequent statutes)	See also CRASBO (the criminal anti-social behaviour counterpart of an ASBO) made following conviction.
CO	(1) Combination order	CJA 1991	(1) An order combining probation with community service.
	(2) Curfew order	CJA 1991	(2) One restricting absence from a place of residence between stated hours.
	(3) Community order	CJA 2003	(3) A generic order including former probation, community service and other non-custodial sanctions – but see CRO and CPO.
	(4) Compensation order	CJA 1972	(4) A 'financial order' requiring an offender to pay compensation. Compare the reparation order below.
CO (+ EM)	Curfew order (plus electronic monitoring)	Crime (Sentences) Act 1997 (and later provisions)	Curfew order (enforced with electronic monitoring aka 'tagging').
CPO	Community punishment order	Criminal Justice and Court Services Act 2000	Re-naming of the former CSO (q.v.) to reflect 'punishment in the community'.

Glossary of Some Key Terms Used in this Book

CRD	Custodial release date	Criminal Justice and Immigration Act 2008	Date of automatic release at the mid-point of the 'custodial period' of an extended sentence (q.v.), followed by supervision on licence to the supervision licence expiry date (SLED) (q.v.).
CRO	Community rehabilitation order	Criminal Justice and Court Services Act 2000	Re-naming of the former probation order (PO) (q.v.) as with CPO above.
CP&RO	Community punishment and rehabilitation order	Criminal Justice and Court Services Act 2000	An order combining elements of a CPO and CSO (see above) - and a successor to the combination order.
CS	(1) Community supervision (2) This abbreviation may also be used (a) generally to describe any 'community sentence'; or (b) as shorthand for a CSO below.	(1) Criminal Justice and Court Services Act 2000	(1) Generic term used to describe a combination of measures such as supervision under a generic community order, a curfew, electronic monitoring, and exclusion or other prohibitive measures including by surveillance or monitoring within the community.
CSO	Community service order	CJA 1972	Court order requiring offenders to perform community tasks for a stated number of hours under supervision – but see CPO above. This has become a 'requirement of unpaid work' within a generic community order.
CM	Custody 'minus'	CJA 2003	A shorthand term used by some people (but not universally) to describe a sentence of imprisonment which has been suspended for a specified period, but which is liable to enforcement if it or its conditions are breached.
CP	Custody 'plus'	CJA 2003	This theoretically replaced all former CJA 1991 sentences of less than 12 months with a combination of custody and community supervision on licence. Due originally to begin in 2006, the provisions have not been implemented.
DCR	Discretionary conditional release	CJA 1991	Applied to sentences of imprisonment of four years or more, permitting parole release between the ½ and 2/3 points of a sentence followed by ACR (q.v.) to the ¾ point and by AUR (q.v.) to the SED (q.v.).

DLS	Discretionary life sentence	CJA 1991	The maximum sentence for persons over 21 years convicted of serious offences such as manslaughter, rape, arson or armed robbery etc. The equivalent for those aged ten but under 18 at the time the offence is detention for life; and for those aged 18 but under 21 custody for life.
DTTO	Drug treatment and testing Order	Crime and Disorder Act 1998 Criminal Justice and Court Services Act 2000	Non-custodial disposal requiring an offender to undergo treatment for drug addiction reinforced by testing for compliance. Now, in effect, part of a generic community order.
DTO	Detention and training order	Crime and Disorder Act 1998	Sentence for young (15-21 year-old) offenders effectively replacing youth custody which had been introduced in the CJA 1982.
ECL	End of custody licence	Prison Service Instruction (PSI) 42/2007 Probation Circular 34/2007	By executive action, this permits prisoners serving sentences between four weeks and up to four years to be released up to 18 days early (in practice) on temporary licence before ACR or DCR (both q.v.).
EDR	Earliest date of release	CJA 1991	Applies to determinate AUR/ACR and DCR sentences at the mid-point. See also LDR which occurs at the 2/3 point of a sentence.
EM	Electronic monitoring (aka 'tagging')	CJA 1991 Criminal Justice and Court Services Act 2000	Electronic surveillance of an offender under a curfew requirement and/or home detention curfew (HDC) (q.v.). EM thus reinforces community sanctions or a temporary release licence.
ES	Extended sentence (aka latterly an extended sentence for public protection or ESPP)	Criminal Justice Act 1967 Powers of the Criminal Courts Act 1973 Crime and Disorder Act 1998 Powers of the Criminal Courts (Sentencing) Act 2000 CJA 2003 Criminal Justice and Immigration Act 2008	The use of extended sentences fell largely into disuse following the two earliest Acts cited, but has been revived in the latter three Acts to make provision for confining those violent and sexual offenders considered a public risk beyond the period deserved by a standard determinate sentence (SDS) (q.v.). The period of extension follows the relative 'SDS term', so that an ES comprises both 'custodial' and extension periods. Those sentenced after 14 July 2008 must be automatically released at the mid-point of the aggregated SDS and ES 'custodial' term on licence to the expiry of the total sentence period.

Glossary of Some Key Terms Used in this Book 243

HDC	Home detention curfew	Crime and Disorder Act 1998	Provisions for the early release of offenders serving less than four years imprisonment after the mid-point of their sentence, and on licence under monitored home curfew conditions within the community.
HMP	Detention at Her Majesty's pleasure	Children and Young Persons Act 1933	This must be imposed on a child or young person under the age of 18 years found guilty of murder. Release is at the 'discretion' of the Justice Secretary on the (largely 'binding') advice of the Parole Board.
IC	Intermittent custody	CJA 2003	A provision for prison sentences to be served at weekends or during the week interspersed with periods on licence supervision in the community. The arrangements have been piloted but not been implemented.
IPP	Imprisonment for Public Protection (sometimes latterly called an Indeterminate Sentence for Public Protection or ISPP)	CJA 2003	For offenders aged 18 years or over, convicted of a serious violent or sexual offence committed on or after 4 April 2005 for which the maximum penalty is ten years or more, and who are assessed as posing a significant public risk.
PED	Parole eligibility date	CJA 1991	This occurs at the mid-point of a DCR sentence of four years or more, and on expiry of the 'tariff period' of a mandatory or discretionary life sentence or IPP (above).
PO	Probation order	Probation of Offenders Act 1907 CJA 1991 Criminal Justice and Court Services Act 2000	Originally not a sentence of the court, but made into a sentence on conviction in the CJA 1991. Superseded by the CRO (and CP&RO) in the 2000 Act and now by a requirement, especially supervision of a generic community order.

RO	(1) Reparation order (2) Referral order	(1) Crime and Disorder Act 1998 (2) Youth Justice and Criminal Evidence Act 1999	(1) An order available to youth courts to require juveniles committing less serious ('entry level') offences to make reparation. (2) This is for juveniles appearing before a youth court for the first time who plead guilty to an offence. They are referred to a youth offending panel (YOP) to agree a 'compact' to address offending behaviour and 'make amends'. Note significant changes to youth court powers generally late in 2009: see yjb.gov.uk for contemporaneous information
SLED	Supervision licence expiry date	CJA 1991	The date upon which an offender serving an ACR or DCR sentence completes the mandatory period of licence supervision followed by an AUR period in the community. Also the end of the AUR period on a sentence of less than 12 months.
SDS	Standard determinate sentence	CJA 2003	A sentence of 12 months or more from which prisoners are discharged on supervision licence at the mid-point until their SED (q.v.).
SLED	Supervision licence expiry date	Criminal Justice and Immigration Act 2008	Applicable to DCR sentenced prisoners and those serving extended sentences (ES) whose release from custody at the sentence mid-point is followed by a period of licence supervision until what would formerly have been their SED with a period of AUR.
UF	Unit fine	CJA 1991	A variant of the standard fine determined on monthly or weekly income less allowable expenses expressed in *per diem* rates multiplied by the number of days imposed. Abolished by CJA 1993.
UR	Unconditional release	CJA 1991	Release from a custodial sentence of less than 12 months at the mid-point without any liability to licence supervision – see AUR (q.v.). The same applies to the final ¼ of an ACR and DCR sentence following a period of licence supervision on ACR (q.v.).

Index

A

accepted wisdom xi
accountability 43, 73, 178
acculturation 141
accusation 171
Achilles, Mary 85
'acting out' 68
addiction therapy 49
'adjustment' 113
adversarial system 79, 80, 171, 215
alarm 33
Albany Prison 88
alienation 44
Allen, Francis 112
allocution 80, 82
All-Party Penal Affairs Group (PA-PPAG) 99
alternative 101
    alternative to custody 165
amends 76, 100, 105
amenity 89
    amenity value to communities 150, 183
    social amenity 186
A New Deal for Victims and Witnesses, etc. 42, 77
anger
    public anger 39
'Anglo-Saxon attitudes' xi
anti-social behaviour 66, 76
apology xii, 78, 80, 83, 125, 131, 155
area community justice forum 221
Argentina 114
assault 64
'assist and befriend' 160
'assisted transition' 161
asylum 118
attendance centre order 164
attitude
    'attitudinal' components xvii
    changing xii
    'evidential attitudinal change' 96
    public attitudes 38
Auld Report 77
Australia ix, xviii, 42, 116, 122, 175, 220
Austria xviii

B

battle terminology 52
'befriending' 199
behaviour
    changing xii
Belgium xviii
'beneficiaries' 48
Bentham, Jeremy 56
bifurcation xxiii, 58, 117, 150, 181, 182
Blad, John 51, 56, 61
Blair, Tony MP xix
Boyes-Watson, Carolyn 219
breach 165
'bridge' 221
    between custody and community aspects 198
British Crime Survey 39, 64
British penological psyche 167
Buchanan, Julian 199
burglary 38, 64
'buying public protection' 29

C

Canada xviii, 151, 156, 176, 220
capital punishment 108
car theft 39
causes of crime xi, 50, 52, 61, 81, 108, 199
CCTV 200
censure 155
'centre-ground' 48
certainty xiii
Changing Lenses: A New Focus for Crime and Justice 43
'cherry-picking' tendency 187, 221
circles 85, 175
citizen 204
Clapham Omnibus xx, xxiv, 68, 94, 163, 178, 212, 220, 223
Clemmer, Donald 119
'client advocacy and counselling philosophy' 196
closure viii
'collateral damage' 187
combination order (former) 164
commensurability 103
Commissioner of Correctional Services 158

community 43
  as a benificiary of corrections 186, 217
  community corrections 36, 149
  'community friendly' prison 136
  community involvement 48
  community justice 164, 169
  Community Justice Forum 190
  community needs 83
  community order 188
    'essential operational attributes', etc. 178
  community project 107
  community rehabilitation order (former) 203
  community sanctions 85, 173
    credibility 150
  community sentence
    breach 156
  community service (former) 133
  community service order (CSO) (former) 164
  community value 200
  empowering communities 155
  need to strengthen community sanctions 72
Community Correctional Service 195, 197, 199, 205, 208
Community Corrections Centre 190, 201, 208, 221
commutation of sentence 103
'compact' 127, 128
compensation 80
competencies 185
'conditional imprisonment' 156
conferencing 81, 83, 85, 193, 201
confidence 39, 66, 157, 195, 198
  public confidence xvii
consistency xiii
'consumers' 215
containment 29, 159
  'containment of the wicked' 97
'contamination' 111
conviction
  RJ after ix
coping 141, 144
correctional services officer (CSO) 197
correctional staff
  'belonging' 144
corrections x, 141
  community corrections xii
  'correctional imprisonment' 96

cost 72, 99, 104, 107
  cost-benefit ix
counselling 49, 129, 130, 151, 193, 201
Coyle, Andrew 136
credibility xiii, 36
  electoral credibility xiii, 40
  political credibility xix
crime
  crime as 'officially defined' 52
  crime control xvii, 63
  crime rate 151
  sensationalism of crime 63
crime reduction viii, xi, 49, 54, 83, 87, 148, 186, 203
criminal damage 64
Criminal Injuries Compensation Scheme 176
criminal justice
  costs of 31
Criminal Justice Act 1967 117, 164
Criminal Justice Act 1972 164
Criminal Justice Act 1991 103
Criminal Justice Act 2003 55, 71, 77, 101, 117, 156, 164, 166, 169, 176, 202, 209, 213
Criminal Justice and Court Services Act 2000 133
Criminal Justice: The Way Ahead 34
'crisis of control' 167
'crisis of legitimacy' 115, 166, 167
'crisis of numbers' 115, 166, 167, 219
Cross, Rupert 143
culture 173, 179
  traditional culture 143
'cure' 122
curfew 156
Custodial Correctional Service 195, 205
'custodial vision' 90, 97, 125
Custody, Care and Justice 37

D

damaging effects of prison custody 157
dangerousness 51, 68
  dangerous people 33
  'decreased dangerousness' 96
Davis, Angela 164
decarceration 69
demonisation 33, 212
Denmark xviii, 94, 104
denunciation 149
dependence 161

depersonalisation 119
deprivation xvii, 50
desert 30, 55, 96, 103, 106, 211
    just deserts 30
desistence 87
deterrence xi, 54, 96, 108
    general detterence 73
de Tocqueville, Alexis 167
DiIulio, John 89, 91, 143, 196
Diploma in Probation Studies (DipPS) 160
Direct Supervision 90, 126
discrimination 33, 144
disorder 66
disruption 153
disruptiveness 36
diversion ix, 81, 164
    court processes from 106
    custody from 72
'doing justice better' 210
drug 64, 74, 122, 138, 188
    drug trafficking 38
    drug treatment and testing order (former) 165
dysfunction 51
    dysfunctional backgrounds 201
    dysfunctional influences 161

E

economy 99
education 161, 202
effectiveness viii, 39, 40, 99, 179, 185, 204
    in the public mind 183
effects of crime 50
emotional aspects viii, 78
    emotional maturity ix
empathy 167
employment 83
    employability 186
empowerment of offenders 113
engagement of offenders 198
England and Wales xviii
equality 175
ethical aspects 108
ethnicity 175, 179, 216
Europe 42, 116, 179
    Council of Europe 42, 76
    European Commission 64
evidence
    'evidence-led' litmus test 212

'evidence-led' solutions 222
    need for viii
exclusion order 164
exclusivity 45, 85, 136
exemplary sentence 54
extended sentence 33, 68, 117

F

face-to-face meetings
    victims and offenders ix
failure
    setting offenders up to fail 156
fairness 40, 50, 57, 186, 215
    fair treatment of victims 80
family group conferencing 49
fear
    fear of crime xii, xix, 33, 83, 178
    fear of repeated victimisation 78
fine 164, 208
    'day fine' (Finland) 183
Finland xviii, 64, 72, 85, 94, 134, 138, 156, 183, 213
Fletcher, Harry 222
forgiveness 83
France xviii, 169
    inquisitorial method 215
freedom 175
Fresh Start 145
'front line' correctional officials 144
frugality 56
Fry, Margery 96

G

Garland, David xv, 68, 217, 218
Gartree Prison 88
Germany xviii, 44, 94, 114, 156, 169, 213
Good Lives Model (GLM) 122, 130, 132, 205
graffiti 185, 200
group-work 201
guilt xxi, 44

H

Halliday Report 70, 101, 156
harm xxi, 43, 53, 59, 105, 125, 185
    repairing harm viii, ix, 61
    'setting right' xxiv
Havel, Vaclav 136
healing 83, 175

HM Chief Inspector of Prisons 222
Holland 72
Home Office 195
'hostel-type' accommodation 142, 151
Houchin, Roger 125
Howard, Michael 37
Hudson, Barbara 114
Hull Prison 88
humane aspects xii, xv
humanity 162

I

ideology 93
imprisonment 56
incapacitation 37, 98
incarceration 38, 212
inclusive approach 45, 85
Independent Monitoring Board 49
indeterminate sentence 33, 55, 117
    indeterminate life sentence 68
induction unit 129
'inevitability' 55
infatuation with incarceration 40
influences xv
inquisitorial method 215
institutionalisation 118
intermediate treatment unit (ITU) 129
intimidation 114
intuition viii, xv
isolation 30
Italy 114

J

Jerry Lee Program ix
Johnstone, Gerry 52
joint working 159
judiciary xvii
just deserts 116
justice xi, 103, 115, 140, 148
    better justice 41
    community justice xxiii, 187
    criminal justice
        collateral damage xxv
    justice delivery 81
    justice model xxi, 31, 88, 115, 120, 165
    operational justice 216
    retributive justice 211
    structural justice 215

    traditional justice 45
Justice for All 34, 70, 77, 101, 156
juvenile 151, 172
    juvenile justice 49
    juvenile offending 106

K

'keeper philosophy' 143, 146, 196
Kilroy-Silk, Robert 99
Klare, Hugh 108
Knott, Christine 203

L

landscaping 200
'law and order' lobby 30, 134, 159
'leaks' xix
legitimacy 46
lesser eligibility 50, 109
Lewis, Derek 145
liaison 198
life-changing aspects viii
life skills 83
literacy 142
litter picking 200
Little Book of Restorative Justice, The 43

M

Mactaggart, Fiona 82
mainstream system, RJ in viii, xx
'making good' 185
Making Punishments Work 156
management
    indifferent management of prisons 89
managerialism xxiv, 159, 165, 168, 203
mandatory minimum sentences 68
marginalising 50, 173
marital relationships 49
mass media x, xii, xix, 36, 63, 97, 180
    focus on shortcomings 183
McCold, Paul 49
McIvor, Gill 74, 124, 132, 173
mediation 201
mens rea 55
mental impairment 35, 37, 118, 144
Ministry of Justice 157, 195
moral aspects 59, 61, 96, 108, 110, 167
    moral high ground 62
    'moral mission' 168

moral panic 32, 33
moral philosophical 'direction' 169
moral status of the law 55
myth xxv, 67

N

National Correctional Service xxiv, xxv, 195, 205
  unified 221
National Offender Management Service (NOMS) xx, 147, 157, 195
National Probation Service 147
Netherlands (The Netherlands) xviii, 64, 94, 104, 151, 156, 169, 220
New Labour 166
New South Wales 176
New Zealand xviii, 42, 122, 172, 176, 220
'normalisation' 199
North America 176
North Carolina 94
Norway 94, 104
'nothing works' xxi, xxiv, 29, 41
numeracy 142

O

obligation 46
offence
  offence analysis 129
  offence recognition 151
offender viii, 40
  antipathy towards 149
  motivation 115, 124
  Offender Assessment System (OASys) 196
  offender management 202
  'offender manager' 161
  victim: offender mediation 81
Office for Criminal Justice Reform 82
O'Hear, Michael 106
'one size fits all' 58
order 89
Ostapiuk, Eugene 134
over-criminalisation 51
overcrowding 33, 35, 159
over-penalisation 51
Owers, Anne 222
ownership viii

P

'paedophiles' 67
pain 54, 141, 164, 214
Parkhurst Prison 88
parole 33, 117, 123, 206
  Parole Board 55, 117
parsimony 56
participation 127
partnership 191
  'Partnership for Crime Reduction' 191
Pathfinder projects 133
pathway out of crime ix
paying back 54
peacemaking 175
penal
  'penal bite' xxiv, 182
  penal crisis xxi, 29, 41
  'penal instrumentalism' 57
  penal policy xi
  penal vacuum 48
penological pragmatism 94
penology
  incarcerative penology 202
  need for a contemporary penology xiii
  penological vacuum 112
  reparative penology xiii
  restorative penology x, xiii, 99, 106
persistent offending xvii
personal
  personal deficits 201
  personal officer 128, 129
personality disorder 144
pisoner
  prisoner population 181
plea-bargain 106
police officer ix
policy
  criminal justice policy-making xv
political aspects xiii, 125
  political expediency 94
  political ideology xvii
  'political panic' 33
  'populist political decision-making' 68
politicians 69
'populist punitiveness' 180
Portugal xviii
poverty xvii, 161, 199
principle xxi
prison x, 88

artificial environment 118
'build your way out of trouble' xi
community friendly prison xxiii, 148
community prison 37
conditional release xxiii
'correctional imprisonment' 96
daily 'events' 91
diet, etc. 92
disturbances 88
dysfunctional aspects of prison life 119
'facts of prison life' 119
ineffectiveness 95, 100
'mechanistic imprisonment' 96
overcrowding 88, 93, 98, 99
over-use xi
poor security 35
prison building 99, 220
'prison: community' 142
'prison: community divide' 136
prison discipline 33
prisoner population (capping) 103
prison management xxii
prison officer ix
'prison works' 37, 159
re-branding 141
riots 35, 36, 88
security 36
staff unrest 35
'taste of prison' 71
understaffing 35
'universal factors' 120
prisoner
   Direct Supervision 90
   population 100
   predatory prisoners 33
   'Robin Hood-like' status 36
   'trusted' population 143
'prisonization' 119, 141
Prison Officers' Association (POA) 90, 145, 168
Prison Reform Trust 108
Prison Rules 127
probation x, 156
   probation officer ix, 147
   probation order 164
   Probation Service 37, 180
process 43
professional identity 195
programme 183
   accredited programme 208

proportionality xxiv, 55, 60
propriety 178
prosecution
   RJ before ix
protection
   public protection 38, 51, 103, 218
   social protection 37
public
   'mood and temper' 63
   public attitudes 67, 179
   'public opinion' 63, 67
   public protection 59
punishment xi, 30, 44, 45, 105, 212
   'expressive punitivism' 81
   'instrumental' ue of 51
   'justifications' of 53
   public punitiveness 149
   'punishment by proxy' 57
   punishment in the community 157
   punitive attitude 38
   'punitive bite' 150
   punitive justice 51
   punitive responses 53
   'punitive time warp' 31
   retributive punishment 50
purposeful activity 35, 89, 107
'putting wrongs right' 104, 131, 213

Q

'qualitative factors' 183
'quick fix' xi

R

rape 67, 105
realism 202
Rebuilding Lives - Supporting Victims of Crime 82, 176
'rebuking or punishing to set right' 211
recall 103
recidivism 87, 116, 124, 138, 150, 155, 189
reciprocity 60, 74
recompense 186
reconciliation 106, 187
reconviction rate 74, 189
reductionist measures 104
reductivism 150
reform
   reform of offenders viii, 113

rehabilitation 29, 45, 49, 97, 112, 161, 177
   'rehabilitation by stealth' 59
   'state-obligated rehabilitation' 114, 162
reintegration x, xii, 43, 49, 58, 69, 106, 132, 134, 137, 161, 202, 203
   social reintegration 83
relapse
   relapse prevention 122, 130
relationships xii, xvii, 44, 49, 74, 81, 104, 199, 203, 219
   staff 144
   staff: prisoner relationship 144
release 70, 161
   conditional release 101, 153
   discretionary conditional release 102
   preparation for to begin on day one 142
   pre-release assessment 129
   pre-release planning 129
reliability 178, 185
religious aspects 179
remand in custody 71
remorse 83, 153, 155, 182
reoffending 57, 74, 101, 102, 137, 156, 186
   reducing reoffending 148
reparation xii, 49, 58, 61, 69, 80, 83, 90, 131, 148, 182
   reparative custody xxiv, 151, 182, 206
resettlement grant 194
re-socialisation 120, 121
resources 85, 218
respect 127, 151
responsibility 76, 80, 98, 105, 127, 148, 155, 186
   'responsibility model' 126
restoration xxv
restorative corrections 210
restorative justice 41, 85, 220
   'practitioner-led' 41
   restorative justice facilitator 83
   restorative justice movement 41
Restorative Justice: The Government's Strategy 42, 76, 157
retribution xi, xxv, 30, 45, 52, 69, 106, 149, 164, 187
   retributive justice 211
riot 66, 88
risk 89, 102, 182, 219
   balancing risk 137
   low risk approach 187
   perception of risk 65

public risk 63, 69, 73, 75, 99, 110, 138, 168
   'reduced public risk' 96
risk-aversion 59, 134
Risk-Need Model 130
risk-obsession 134
risk reduction 122
Risks-Needs-Response (RNR) 205
social risk 204
to the public 38
robbery 64
Rutherford, Andrew 88, 159, 167

S

'sacred cows' 213
safety 89, 212
   feeling safe 155
   public safety x, 185
Samaritans 49
scapegoating 185
Scotland xviii
Scull, Andrew 217
security 83, 89, 137, 146
self-confidence 125
self-esteem 74, 125, 201
self-worth 131
sensationalism 97, 179
sentence
   RJ before ix
sentencing 103
   discretion 103
   fairness 121
serious offence 34, 38, 40, 106, 137, 150
   RJ in relation to ix
service 89
severity 140
sex offender 130
sexual offence 51, 56, 63, 67, 122
shaming 185
   Reintegrative Shaming Experiments (Canberra) ix
Sharpe, Susan 42, 124
Shoham, Shlomo 113
'silver bullet' viii
simplicity 178, 183, 204
skills 185
social cohesion 83
social control 156
social damage (imprisonment) 179
social deficit 152, 155, 162

social inequality 109
social risk xvii
'soft option' 152, 179, 183
South Africa xviii, 90
Spain xviii, 114, 151, 156
special hospital 35
stakeholders 46, 54, 81, 83, 104, 105, 148, 186, 204, 215
    community stakeholders 146
stake in society 108
standards 144, 145
Strangeways Prison 88
    Strangeways riot 36
Strang, Heather viii, 78, 86
Straw, Jack 222
'structural' components xvii
substance abuse 161
suffering 141
suicide 36
superstition 62
support 83
'suppression' of crime 204
surveillance society 38
suspended sentence 151, 156, 164, 189
Sweden xviii, 169

T

theft 64
therapy 113, 122
thinking differently 45
Tihar Jail 111, 130
'time out of cell' 126
Tonry, Michael 217
Too Many Prisoners 99
'tough on crime' xxv, 30, 40, 52, 93, 115, 116, 138, 149, 159, 210
trade unionism 145
traditional criminal justice 104, 171, 218
traditional model of imprisonment 205
training 29
transforming derelict or neglected sites 200
transparency 98
treatment 29, 57, 116, 122
    treatment model 112
trivial offending x
truth 67
'turnkeys' 145
twin-track prison system (advocated) 107

U

uniformity of outcomes 185
United Nations 76
    United Nations Congress on Crime Prevention 42
    United Nations Minimum Rules for the Treatment of Prisoners 114
USA 64, 220
'user consciousness' 215
utilitarianism 53, 162

V

value 178, 186
    community value 200
    value for money 92
vandalism 39, 185
van den Haag, Ernest 114, 116
Van Ness, Daniel 136
vehicle crime 38, 64
victim viii, 40, 59, 61, 76, 98, 147, 152, 177, 204
    attitude ix
    Code of Practice for Victims of Crime 79, 82
    empowering victims 155
    needs 43, 83, 213
    post-traumatic stress ix
    re-victimization 219
    secondary victim 46, 173
    trauma 78, 80, 82, 105
    Victim and Confidence Unit 82
    victim awareness 201
    victim care unit 176
    Victim Fund (Tihar Jail) 111
    victim: offender mediation (VOM) 41, 42, 81, 83, 105
    Victims' Charter 176
    victims' rights 176
    Victim Support 176
    vindication xii
Victorian penitentiaries 136
vilification of offenders 97
vindication 81, 83, 86, 104, 132, 152, 155, 186
violence 33, 38, 56, 63, 64, 105, 122
visibility 178, 185, 200
vocational training 202
voluntarism 126

W

'war on crime' 210, 221
warehousing xii, 29, 94, 100
waste 72
'Whakawhanaungatanga' 170
what works xi, xv, 41
Whitelaw, William 99
witness 81
women's imprisonment 188
Woolf Report 36, 166
work ethic 186
Wormwood Scrubs Prison 88

Y

'yob culture' 66
young adult 172
youthful offenders 151
Youth Justice Board 42

Z

Zehr, Howard 43, 44, 59, 176

Putting justice into words

A selection of books on Restorative Justice

Restorative Justice in Prisons:
A Guide to Making it Happen
by **Tim Newell** and **Kimmett Edgar**

'Successfully translates theory into practice and provides a model for organisational and cultural change in prisons':
International Review of Victimology

'A book of international importance . . . An authoritative guide': Michael L. Hadley, University of Victoria, Canada

2006 | P/back | ISBN 978-1-904380-25-2

Restoring Respect for Justice:
A Symposium
by **Martin Wright** Foreword **Howard Zehr**

'There is a wealth of data including research references in [this] volume. I thought I was familiar with RJ literature. [This] volume taught me much about RJ that I had not known':
International Criminal Justice Review

2nd Ed. | 2008 | P/back | 978-1-904380-38-2

Also by **Martin Wright:**

Making Good: Prisons, Punishment and Beyond
by **Martin Wright** Foreword **Vivien Stern**
Classic and original - one of the works that paved the way for the development of the Restorative Justice movement.
2nd Ed. | 2008 | P/back | ISBN 978-1-904380-41-2

Free previews at **WatersidePress.co.uk**

≋ WATERSIDE PRESS

Putting justice into words

The Pocket A-Z
of Criminal Justice

by Bryan Gibson

A quickly absorbed jargon-busting introduction to the language of criminal justice and its unique and fascinating usages.

- **Get up to speed with the language of criminal justice**
- **Touchstones aid understanding and memory**
- **Handy reference guide for students and practitioners**

The Pocket A-Z draws together words and phrases commonly encountered by practitioners and researchers - connecting key terms, concepts, processes, laws, people and events. The 2,000 plus entries and cross-references provide insight and perspective, making it invaluable to anyone involved in criminal justice work or study.

Also includes extensive sections on:
Touchstones and Curiosities,
commonly encountered **Acronyms and Abbreviations**
and a **Timeline**.

May 2009 | P/back | ISBN 978-1-904380-50-4

View sample entries and order at **WatersidePress.co.uk**

☵ WATERSIDE PRESS